HANS KELSEN

ESSAYS IN LEGAL AND MORAL PHILOSOPHY

SYNTHESE LIBRARY

MONOGRAPHS ON EPISTEMOLOGY,

LOGIC, METHODOLOGY, PHILOSOPHY OF SCIENCE,

SOCIOLOGY OF SCIENCE AND OF KNOWLEDGE,

AND ON THE MATHEMATICAL METHODS OF

SOCIAL AND BEHAVIORAL SCIENCES

HANS KELSEN
(1881–1973)

HANS KELSEN

ESSAYS IN LEGAL AND MORAL PHILOSOPHY

Selected and Introduced by

OTA WEINBERGER

Translated by

PETER HEATH

D. REIDEL PUBLISHING COMPANY

DORDRECHT-HOLLAND / BOSTON-U.S.A.

First printing: December 1973

Library of Congress Catalog Card Number 73–86090

ISBN-13: 978-94-010-2655-0 e-ISBN-13: 978-94-010-2653-6
DOI: 10.1007/978-94-010-2653-6

Published by D. Reidel Publishing Company,
P.O. Box 17, Dordrecht, Holland

Sold and distributed in the U.S.A., Canada and Mexico
by D. Reidel Publishing Company, Inc.
306 Dartmouth Street, Boston,
Mass. 02116, U.S.A.

CONTENTS

PREFACE

In his choice of texts, the Editor has been faced with the difficult task of selecting, from among the author's more than 600 publications, those of the greatest philosophical interest. It is chiefly the topics of value-relativism and the logic of norms that have been kept in view. The selection has also been guided by the endeavour to reprint, so far as possible, texts which have not hitherto appeared in English. At times, however, this aim has had to be discarded, in order to include works of key importance and also the latest expressions of Kelsen's view.

In addition to the two topics already mentioned, the Editor has considered Kelsen's discussions of the causal principle to be so far worthy of philosophical attention, that some writings on causality and accountability have been included in this collection of philosophical studies.

OTA WEINBERGER

Hans Kelsen died on April 19th, 1973. Only his work now lives, for the inspiration of future generations of jurists and philosophers.

Graz, 25th April, 1973 OTA WEINBERGER

TRANSLATOR'S NOTE

I am obliged to the Editor for his careful scrutiny of the translation, which has led to a number of corrections and improvements in the text. I am also indebted to Mrs. Eusebia Shifflett and Mrs. Judy Catto for their accuracy and diligence in typing the manuscript.

INTRODUCTION: HANS KELSEN AS PHILOSOPHER

The jurist of our century, as Hans Kelsen has been called, has now celebrated his ninetieth birthday – he was born in Prague on 11th October 1881. Despite all the vicissitudes of a richly productive and contentious life, he is one of the few men in the intellectual history of mankind to whom it has been granted to take an active part for six decades – and always in the forefront – in the scientific fray. He has not yet laid down his pen, and is working with a great thinker's sure touch for the actuality of the problems, on questions concerning the logic of norms and the relation between law and logic. In this foreword to a selection of his philosophic writings, I am therefore by no means intent on making a final assessment of the achievement of this great man; I shall merely endeavour to bring home to the English-speaking reader the philosophical relevance of his ideas. An exhaustive account and evaluation of his work in the philosophy of law and his contribution to the clarification of juristic method is needless, for as a master teacher of legal methodology he is so well-known that there is scarcely a single philosopher of law who has not had to come to grips with his views.

In the Foreword to *Hauptprobleme der Staatsrechtslehre, entwickelt aus der Lehre vom Rechtssatze*, an epoch-making work, in which Kelsen first took the road towards the founding of the Pure Theory of Law, we find a passage which gives clear expression alike to his scientific position and his ethos as a thinker:

> The blending of mutually exclusive approaches necessarily leads to *fiction*, the claim to actuality in conscious defiance of the real state of affairs. And nothing is so typical of the state of contemporary legal science than that its theory is riddled with fictions. The struggle against fiction, that contemptible white lie of science, is one of the aims of my book.[1]

In addition to the moral attitude of unconditional integrity, characteristic of the thinker striving for knowledge and clarity, three fundamental features at least of Kelsen's outlook find expression in this declaration of his programme:

(1) The conviction that the mode of approach determines the knowl-

edge and structure of the scientific system, and that for the intellectual unity and correctness of science it is therefore necessary to isolate the different approaches from one another, and to build up each science as a methodologically unitary system;

(2) The endeavour, by exact analysis of concepts, to sift out the essentials in formal generality, and to set them forth explicitly;

(3) The connection with reality, one aspect of which it is the business of every science to present objectively, as an answer to a particular way of asking questions.

The philosophical foundations on which the Pure Theory of Law is constructed are conceptions of general philosophic interest. In accordance with the aims of this survey, I should like to discuss the philosophical character and significance of Kelsen's main ideas and beliefs, together with their overall consequences, while omitting consideration of the implications of the Pure Theory of Law for questions of juristic detail.

In speaking of the philosophical and scientific views of a thinker whose work embraces so large a span of time, there will inevitably arise questions also about the development of his doctrine, and the changes of opinion that have occurred over the years. In Kelsen's work we find, from this standpoint, a most uncommon stability in his basic views. According to Métall's valuable bibliography, dating from 1969, Kelsen's *oeuvre* comprises 604 items, in which he expounds his position, discusses a series of interesting related problems, and at times also engages in polemics against other views and in rejoinders to critics.[2] Kelsen's work strikes me as so much of a piece, that I would even venture to claim that already in the *Hauptprobleme* all his essential attitudes are present at least in embryo; the firm outlines of his thought, no less than the elaboration of its details, appear to me as a rational unfolding of the basic position, and an answer to the academic developments of the period, fashioned by a lucid and unremittingly active mind.

I should now like to set forth under a few headings what seem to me the key conceptions underlying the fabric of Kelsen's thought.

1. Kelsen's Conception of Legal Science: The Struggle Against Syncretism of Methods

Kelsen, like Max Weber, champions the notion of a value-free science, a science which seizes and sets forth what is actual, without evaluating what it finds. This also applies even when the object of knowledge consists of facts which are themselves by no means value-neutral, which contain – as law does – an 'ought' and valuations which man certainly does not approach with any lack of concern or evaluative interest. It is precisely here that it is important to view the law as it actually exists, and to distinguish the purely cognitive tasks of science from any evaluation of the law. In juristic methodology this leads to a sharp separation of considerations *de lege lata* from those *de lege ferenda* – of which only the first are in Kelsen's opinion juristic – even where questions of interpretation or discretion are concerned.

In addition to its value-free character, Kelsen's general conception of science and his delimitation of legal science are responsible for the idea that every science must constitute a methodologically unitary whole, and hence – in his neo-Kantian phraseology – that the subject-matter of science is first determined by its method, its mode of observing and apprehending. This must be taken to mean that science does not depict entities as they may happen to be in and for themselves, but rather that the objects of the scientific system are constituted by the perspective, which is itself defined by the statement of the problem and the mode of approach. Science is an ordered whole, a system of cognitions answering to the setting of a problem.

The two ideas thus introduced, the value-free character of science, and its systematic unity, constituted by method, are the source of Kelsen's postulate of the purity of legal theory: Legal theory must be a general theory of positive law, employing the specifically juristic method of apprehension, while excluding all admixture of considerations drawn from psychology, sociology, politics or ethics. The Pure Theory of Law ignores, though it does not deny, the law's connection with the facts of psychology, sociology, morals and politics, but it insists emphatically on purity in the avoidance of any syncretism of methods, "which obscures the essential character of legal science and erases the boundaries set for it by the nature of its subject-matter".[3]

The issue of syncretism, with all the intellectual background and consequences of the postulate of purity, are naturally matters of general philosophical interest, inasmuch as the question is decisive in determining the essential nature of legal science.

According to modern views – although even today it is mostly not stated in Kelsen's idiom – science is regarded as a system which depicts one aspect of a sphere defined by the questions put. From this point of view, Kelsen's conception of science and his clear-cut delimitation of legal science appear justified; and all the more so in that the juristic method as a way of looking at law, as a normative determination of accountability, which can be represented by the general schema of a normative linking of conditions and consequences of right- or wrong-doing, guarantees a unitary view of the subject. Nevertheless, it is precisely one of the main points on which Kelsen's theory has been exposed to critical attack. For it has often been doubted whether it is possible to effect a strict isolation of the purely normative conception of positive law, without reference to sociological considerations; and also whether it is not in fact precisely the jurist's task to study the immensely complex fabric of the law from every side, in all the wealth of its relations to psychology, sociology and the theory of value. As to this it must be said that, having started from an initially somewhat dismissive attitude to the sociology of law, Kelsen began increasingly to recognise and become interested in it. Himself the author of so important and essentially sociological a work as *Society and Nature*, he insisted nonetheless upon confining juristic and legal science to nothing other than the normological apprehension of the meaning of positive law.

It might be thought a purely terminological or external question, whether to adopt Kelsen's view of legal science as merely the study of positive law, and to assign all other questions concerning the law to other sciences, notably legal sociology and political science. But then there is the problem, that without sociological arguments the positive nature of the norm-system could scarcely be vindicated, and that all the elements which carry weight here – namely those of legal operativeness – are sociological facts. Moreover, in my view, there are complex questions calling for a consideration and confrontation of the observation of the legal phenomenon from many angles, and such as must interest the jurist, since they are needed to explain this very complex phenomenon of law. Can the jurist disregard the question of whether and how law is made real, or whether it remains 'on paper'? He will certainly have to take into consideration, and rightly so, the genetic relations of law, its specific institution in regard to social conditions, and the social effects of setting up norms. Although, therefore, I do not care to accept Kelsen's anti-sociological pure jurisprudence as a pointer to the exclusion of such important considerations from legal science, I think that his battle against syncretism of methods is justified, and has elevated legal science to a new level. Syncretism of methods is to be fundamentally avoided, i.e., the description and explanation to be given by science must be framed in pure fashion – according to the problem in hand; it would be an error, for example, to answer such a legal question as whether this or that legal duty exists under a particular system of law, by considerations drawn from sociology or value-theory, rather than by an enquiry into norms. This perfectly justified postulate of Kelsen's does not, in my view, exclude even complex enquiries such as that concerning the genetic relation between social facts and the shaping of the content of the law – so long as we pay proper attention in our investigations to the different elements of the problem.

I believe, therefore, that the methodological separation of the normological consideration of law – which represents the aim of the Pure Theory of Law – from other legal enquiries, especially from the sociological and evaluative angle, is well-founded. But it seems to me inexpedient to exclude from legal theory, as metajuristic, all questions not of a purely normological kind. Legal theory cannot renounce such enquiries, if it wishes to arrive at a full understanding of law as an actual phenomenon, and is concerned to offer scientific guidance to the lawyer in his work.

Kelsen's demand for a purely cognitive science of law is connected with the exclusion from jurisprudence of any considerations *de lege ferenda*, and of the theory of the reasons for law. Much as I concur with Kelsen in postulating a separation of the *de lege lata* and *de lege ferenda* viewpoints, it seems to me nonetheless possible and necessary to make a scientific study also of the grounds for law, the reasons *de lege ferenda*. Here too it is the task of science to analyse the 'how' of such argumentation; though it may not be called upon to take a stand on the subject, it can discuss the pros and cons of the normative regulations which are under enquiry. Indeed, I regard this as a task for jurisprudence.

Kelsen's endeavour to create a general theory of law, its essential concepts, and the structural connections within the legal system, is in every way valuable and justified. Here he stands in the line of those authors who – like Bentham, Austin, Hohfeld, Hart and many others – have put forward a so-called analytical theory of law. I believe it is here that Kelsen's greatest merits must be acknowledged. When he seeks to depict the universal characteristics of law, this must be understood in terms of structural generality, and not of inductively-based empirical generalisation. In opposition to these analytical enquiries into structure, and especially in criticism of the Pure Theory of Law, we often encounter the quite unwarranted objection that Kelsen leaves the content of law out of account and wishes to see legal theory and legal science concerned only with the form of law. Such objections testify to a fundamental misunderstanding of all structural analysis and an incomprehension of the relation between form and content. Positive law is content; and legal cognition, for Kelsen, is a knowledge of the content of positive orders. The structural theory merely provides instruments for a clear depiction of content. To criticise Kelsen because he allegedly turns away from the study of legal content, is a sign of utter failure to comprehend the basic ideas of his theory.

As a matter of intellectual history it should not be overlooked that the direction of attention to the structural relations in law was an important incentive to the development of the logic of norms, and that the Pure Theory of Law has disclosed essential principles of the logic of norm-systems.

2. The contrasting of 'is' and 'ought'

The clear separation of judgement and norm, of 'is' and 'ought', undoubtedly derives from the philosophy of Kant. But while for Kant it is above all the problem of causality and freewill ("Causality through freedom") which occupies the centre of discussion in this problem, for Kelsen it is causality and accounting (or imputation) which are contrasted as characteristic modes of conjunction in the fields of the 'is' and the 'ought'.[4] This contrasting of realms of experience – nature and human behaviour – with their correspondingly different ways of conjoining and explaining, is typical of Kelsen's basic philosophical attitude.

> Nature, according to one of the many definitions of it, is a determinate order of things, or a system of elements, related to one another as cause and effect, i.e., according to a principle we refer to as causality. The natural laws by which science describes this subject-matter, e.g., that metals expand when heated, are applications of this principle. The relation between heat and expansion is that of cause and effect.[5]

If, nonetheless, we analyse our statements about human behaviour, it appears that we connect acts of human behaviour with one another, and with other facts, not only according to the principle of causality (i.e., as cause and effect), but also according to another principle quite distinct from that of causality....[6]

Only if society is understood as a normative order of mutual human behaviour, can it be conceived of as an object different from the causal order of nature; only then can social science be opposed to natural science [...]. The ordering principle, different from causality, that we apply when describing a normative order of mutual human behaviour, may be called *imputation* [or accounting].[7]

"The principle of causality says that if *A* is, then *B* is (or will be). The accounting-principle says that if *A* is, *B* is to be".[8] Causality is independent of human intervention, whereas accounting is set up through norms posited by men; it is set forth in moral or legal laws. Causal chains are endless and overlapping. Accounting has a terminal point.

... man alone is held to account, because and insofar as moral and legal orders command only human behaviour; and they do so because it is assumed that only in man does the idea of their norms occasion acts of will, which in turn cause the behaviour commanded.[9]

The normative mode of apprehension, rooted in the concept of accounting, leads to Kelsen's answer to the problem of freewill.

Man is not held to account because he is free; he is free because he is held to account. Accounting and freedom are indeed essentially connected with each other. But this 'freedom' cannot exclude causality; and nor, in fact, does it do so in the least. If the claim that, as moral or legal personality, man is free, is to have any possible meaning, then this moral or legal freedom must be compatible with the determinacy of his behaviour under the causal law. Man is free because and insofar as reward, atonement or punishment are accounted as consequences to a particular piece of human behaviour as condition: not because this behaviour is causally undetermined, but although it is causally determined, and indeed, because it is so. Man is free because this behaviour of his is a terminal point in the accounting-series.[10]

For Kelsen the distinction of 'is' and 'ought', the cognitive and the normative, has epistemological and logical significance. Following Simmel, he associates the conceptual distinction of 'is' and 'ought' with the question of how being and obligation are grounded. "The question of why anything ought to be can invariably lead back only to an ought, just as the question why anything is, invariably finds an answer only in the being of something else."[11] In Kelsen's view (which I believe to cover the facts) the distinction of 'is' and 'ought' is to be understood as a conceptual differentiating of thought-contents, as a semantic distinction between different types of sentences which cannot be translated into one another. The logical relevance of the distinction lies in the fact which finds brief expression in the slogan: You cannot derive an 'ought' from an 'is', or an 'is' from an 'ought'.

> The difference between *is* and *ought* cannot be further explained. It is immediately apparent to us. Nobody can deny that the statement: 'Something is' – i.e., a statement describing a matter of fact – is essentially different from the statement that 'something ought to be' – i.e., a statement describing a norm; or that, from the fact that something is, it cannot follow that anything ought to be, or *vice versa*.[12]

It was Henri Poincaré who alerted logicians to the fact that, in what we nowadays call the logic of descriptive language, there are no rules whereby commands (norms, ought-sentences) can be derived from statements (cognitions); he thereby gave a significant impetus to the building-up of a logic of norms.[13] Kelsen's postulate, that no 'ought' can be derived from an 'is' (and *vice versa*), is imbued with the same spirit as the thesis of Poincaré. Yet there is a not unimportant difference. The norm-logicians inspired by Poincaré say that among the arguments justifying an ought-sentence at least one normative sentence must always appear, which means, in effect, that an 'ought' cannot be founded on an 'is' alone. In those inferences which have normative and indicative premises,[14] they see both premises equally as arguments for the conclusion. 'Ought', therefore, is never founded on 'is' alone, but is often derived from 'ought' and 'is' together. Kelsen emphasises that 'ought' depends on 'ought'. He is naturally aware that there are inferences with normative and assertive premises, but interprets the ties of validity in legal dynamics in such a way as to see the ground of validity only in the higher norm, not in the facts as well (*cf.* for example, *Reine Rechtslehre*, 2nd edn., p. 196; *Pure Theory of Law*, pp. 193f.). The legal dynamic thereby appears self-enclosed, but its connection with the facts is pushed into the background.

Obligation is a product of the human will, not something that exists outside the sphere of human willing and society. The will of the state is expressed in legal enactments, being nothing else but a system of norms; at all events, it is something distinct from the will of the persons who create law.

The conceptual relation of norm and law to the will is in my opinion an essential feature of Kelsen's theory. Not only is it connected with the postulates of the unity and exclusiveness of the norm-system, and the principle of legal positivism; Kelsen's firm conviction that law must be expressed in the form of a norm-sentence prescribing a sanction is also to be understood on this basis (cf. pp. XVIII–XXIV).

The postulates of the unity and exclusiveness of the norm-system have found their way into the logic of norms. The unity of the norm-system finds expression there in the demand that the system should be free from logical contradiction; the exclusiveness of the norm-system states that every normative consideration or judgement must proceed strictly from one system. In jurisprudence these postulates lead to the monistic constructions of international law; and they are also the justifiable foundation of Kelsen's arguments against the possibility of a natural law having validity over and above that of positive law.

As types of 'ought' Kelsen distinguishes commanding, permitting and authorising.

'Ought' usually expresses the idea of being commanded, not that of being authorised or permitted. The legal 'ought', i.e., the copula connecting condition with consequence in the statement of law, embraces all three meanings: that of being commanded, that of being authorised and that of being (positively) permitted the consequence; the 'ought', that is, which is set forth in the statement of law, designates all three normative functions. This 'ought' merely expresses the specific sense in which the two sets of facts are connected together by – which means in – a legal norm.[15]

Later he also introduces derogation, as a specific form of 'ought'.[16] The norm-logicians should take note of these observations and test the relation between Kelsen's distinctions and the customary deontic modalities.

3. The Validity of the Norm

Kelsen sees validity as the specific mode in which norms exist. We are then confronted with the question of how the validity of a norm is grounded. Kelsen's answer is connected with his distinction of static and dynamic norm-systems, and also with his theories concerning the hierarchical structure of law and the basic norm of the legal system. In static systems the norm's validity is based on relations of content; in dynamic ones it rests on the creation of norms through particular instances, which are determined by other norms and depend in the last resort upon an authorisation by the basic norm. There can be no doubt that the theory of validity in dynamic systems has been worked out with much greater thoroughness by Kelsen than in the case of static systems, whose discussion leaves something to be desired in the way of precision.[17]

The theory of legal dynamics and the hierarchical structure of law – Kelsen's fellow-traveller Adolf Merkl has done particularly important work here[18] – represents an integral constituent of the Pure Theory of Law. The whole of legal life, legislation, legal transactions, the judicial or administrative decision, official action and execution, are similarly explained and defined as the creation and fulfilment of norms. Every legal norm of this many-tiered system, held together logically by ties of delegation, receives its justification by reference back to already existing (well-founded) norms of the system; the final norm which underlies the creation of law – Kelsen's basic norm – gives authorisation for setting up the constitution and hence, through the chain of delegatory relations, for the framing of the entire legal system.

One may dispute about the nature of the basic norm, debating its semantic character – as a norm or an assertion – and also about whether it involves merely an expedient doctrinal assumption or a postulate in need of sociological justification; but at all events, this theory is an imposing conception, making it possible to present a unified, logically ordered picture of law, to furnish a consistent scientific explanation of what happens in law, and to create a unitary concept of legal validity, in a way that has not been done with similar clarity by any other theory with which I am acquainted.

Kelsen's theory of legal validity is distinguished by a sharp opposition to all justifications based on content; the validity of a legal norm is founded solely on the fact of a legitimate norm-creating act, and not on teleological considerations. The expediency or inexpediency of a norm is irrelevant to its validity in the hierarchical system of law. It is not disputed that the legal norm has purposes in view, but the juristic viewpoint is contrasted with the teleological one[19], accounting is non-teleological in character[20], and the teleological assessment of a norm plays no part in determining the validity or invalidity of legal norms.

4. Kelsen's conception of legal norm and legal duty; philosophical problems of the sanction theory of the legal norm

Kelsen's conception of the legal norm is a theory which, although it has often been criticised, has exerted a very great influence on legal science, and possesses features of interest to philosophy and the logic of norms.

Law is not only a dynamic system of norms, but also a coercive order. It is inseparably bound up with the normatively regulated activity of a state apparatus of coercion. The coercive character of law – wherein it chiefly differs from morality and custom[21] – and the endeavour to make a sharp conceptual and even structural separation between legal and other types of norms, leads Kelsen to the sanction theory of the legal norm. On two points, indeed, Kelsen's theory of the legal norm has changed in the course of developing the Pure Theory of Law; namely, in his attitude to the imperative theory, and on the question of the judgemental character of the legal norm, which has now been clarified by the distinction between legal norm and statement of law. But the basic structure of the sanction theory remains unaltered. A piece of behaviour is legally commanded, when and only when, and only because, a legal norm posits the opposite course of conduct as the condition of an ordained sanction. The legal order commands a course of conduct

> by prescribing a sanction as obligatory in case of the opposite behaviour.... The obligatoriness of the sanction incorporates the forbiddenness of the behaviour which is its specific condition, and the commandedness of its opposite. It should be noted here that by the 'commandedness' or 'forbiddenness' of a particular course of conduct we mean, not the obligatoriness of this behaviour or its opposite, but the obligatoriness of the consequence of this behaviour, namely the sanction. The behaviour commanded is not that which is made obligatory; it is the sanction which is made obligatory. The commandedness of a course of conduct signifies that the opposite of this behaviour is the condition for the obligatoriness of the sanction.[22]

Kelsen frequently describes the execution of the sanction as a legal duty (here he uses the term in such a way that only the state or its organs could have legal duties); but mostly he understands by legal duty the commanded behaviour of those who have duties, which arise out of, and are based on the fact, that a sanction is imposed on the opposite course of conduct. Legal duty in this sense is a consequence of legal duty in the first sense. This perhaps rather odd construction, in which the norm determining the behaviour of those having duties (citizens) is relegated to a secondary position, goes back to Kelsen's conception of the will and his view of the relation between will and norm. In his *Hauptprobleme* we read:

> In order that we may speak of a willing in the true sense, and not merely of a wishing, the idea of a future occurrence or situation calculated to satisfy a need or urge must be coupled in consciousness *with some activity of his own* on the part of the willer.[23]

The state, as the supporter of the legal will, can therefore will only its own behaviour; what it wills, finds expression in the legal norm. Legal norms express the self-obligation of the state (cf. *op. cit.*, pp. 190f.).

The sanction which the rule of law must contain, precisely for its purpose of instigating the legal subjects (other than the state itself) to a particular course of conduct, and which customarily consists in punishment or distraint, represents an activity of the state (*ibid.*, p. 205).

The conditioned will of the state to punish or distrain, as the legal order may disclose it – in other words, the rule of law – is the ground of cognition for the legal duty of the subject (*ibid.*, p. 207).

In the *Hauptprobleme*, this view of willing, and the thesis that the legal norm determines the state's own behaviour, were associated with a campaign against the imperative theory of the legal norm.

The will directed merely to the behaviour of another finds expression in a command. On the prevailing theory, the rule of law appears to order or prohibit; and this view of objective law is commonly described as the imperative theory.[24]

The imperative form attributed by the prevailing theory to legal norms is taken over from the norms of morality, which pursue a similar purpose (namely a particular course of conduct on the part of individuals), and are generally and rightly acknowledged to be *imperatives*. But to maintain of legal rules what is valid for the norms of morality can only be done by overlooking the fundamental difference which exists between the two kinds of norms on this very point.[25]

The imperative is a willing directed to the behaviour of another, but the will of the state must always be directed towards its own behaviour.

The starting-point of the imperative theory, which assumes the content of the state's will, expressed in the rule of law, to be correct behaviour on the part of the subject, is the element of purpose. The goal pursued by means of the state legal order, namely a condition of orderliness of law-abiding action and abstention on the part of the legal subjects, becomes the standard for formulating those norms whose essential content constitutes the legal order.[26]

... an imperative formulation of the legal rule, in which there appears as content of the state's will, not its own behaviour, but the corresponding action and abstention of other legal subjects, is impossible.[27]

The citizen cannot be motivated by the will of another, but only by his own interest. (pp. 202f.).

The more appropriate, therefore, the imperative form may be for the norms of an autonomous morality, the more inadequate it appears for the heteronomous rule of law.[28]

The sanction which the rule of law must contain, precisely in view of its purpose of instigating those subject to it (apart from the state itself) to a certain course of conduct, and which customarily consists in punishment and distraint, represents an activity of the state. It is this behaviour of its own that the state 'wills' in the rule of law aimed at bringing about the corresponding behaviour on the part of its subjects[a], and not this behaviour of those subjects, which is alien to the state and is to be inferred only indirectly from the rule of law, as an aim of the latter. This behaviour is presented as the negative of that state of affairs to which punishment or execution is attached in the rule of law.[29]

Against the imperative theory Kelsen argues:

The psychological characteristic of the imperative – unlike the judgement – is that it is the *immediate* expression of a *will* directed to the behaviour of another, whereas the judgement represents a function of the *intellect*.[30]

It is not only the rule of law in the narrower sense, decreeing the state's will to punish or distrain under certain conditions, that is a *hypothetical* judgement; this is also true of law in the wider sense, since the will of any state can only appear in the legal order as a conditioned will.[31]

Every legal norm is thus a judgement, and the only peculiarity of this judgement is that the synthesis of concepts in it is valid simply *because the legislator wills it*.[32]

In the *Hauptprobleme* Kelsen still ascribes truth to this judgement expressing the will of the state (cf. *ibid.*, p. 260).

Kelsen – in the view of some of his interpreters – has perhaps somewhat modified his attitude to the imperative theory. He accepts, indeed, the thesis of Dubislav, that there can be "no imperative without an *imperator*", and also relates it to law.[33] In the *Reine Rechtslehre*, 2nd edn., he explains obligation as the meaning of certain human acts of will, intentionally directed to the behaviour of others, but the legal norm is still primarily concerned merely with the behaviour of the state, i.e., its sanctional structure is retained, and the teleological view of the norm rejected as metajuristic. The *imperator*, the willer of the legal norm, is spoken of only as the agent who lays down positive norms. For the clarification of his position concerning the judgemental character of the norm, see Section 5.

It seems needful for us, on the one hand, to emphasise the motivating role in the generation of the sanction theory played by the idea that willing, and therefore the norm, is directed to the willer's own behaviour; and on the other, to subject the thesis itself to critical examination. There is warrant for characterising the peculiar nature of the 'ought' (the norm) by depicting it as a product of human willing. But I think that willing should then be regarded, not merely as a psychological activity directed to one's own behaviour, but in more general terms, as a decision governed by the setting of goals, and a goal-directed activity determining behaviour. If we designate morality, custom and law as volitional 'ought'-

systems, the willing here cannot signify the psychological activity directed to the actions and bodily movements of the person willing. The content of the will that posits norms – if we choose to employ these terms – cannot possibly, in that case, be the willer's own behaviour. The state, as the conceptual willer of law, is utterly incapable of so acting as to realise the content of its willing, in the way that the individual man is able to do this by bodily movement. The willing of the state cannot therefore be directed to its own material movement. If we view the state as the agent or conceptual willer of law, this agency always commands action on the part of others, who either act in terms of their own objectives, and by their own will and choice, or operate in the name of the state, as its organs. The acts of an organ are certainly imputed to the state, but there is no question here of any such realisation of willing as occurs in the execution of Jones' intention to get up from his seat, when Jones gets up in accordance with his will. We must therefore abandon the idea that the content of obligation, and particularly legal obligation – the legal norm – can be only the state's own behaviour and not that of its subjects. If we speak of the will of a collective, such as society, or of the state's will as the basis of law, we cannot then insist that the object of this willing can only be its own behaviour.

Even with the individual, it is wrong to suppose that there is only wishing and not willing, when one's own action is not implied in the realising of one's will. Where the subject himself acts as he wills, it is certainly implied that it is a matter of willing and not just of a wavering or fanciful wishing, but there can also be definitive willing where the realisation of it does not consist in action of one's own; at all events, the object of willing – that which is willed – does not have to be identical with what the willing subject does, i.e., the content of willing is not always the willer's own behaviour.

When a father orders his son to do *A*, he wills that the son should behave in manner *A*. The content of his willing is the son's behaving in manner *A*. Coercive measures in case of disobedience – or the will to reward if the son obeys – certainly do not have to be willed along with this. To command is itself an action, not a mere fanciful wishing, since the imperative is an instrument for determining behaviour, even in the absence of punishment or reward – for man is accustomed to his role in society and is generally willing to play it.

The psychological and sociological question of fact, as to how man is motivated, must be examined with care. A person can obviously be motivated, not merely by punishment and execution, but also by the offer of inducements and by reward. We also have to reckon with the possibility that the content of the norm coincides with the will of the subject himself, and with his willingness to adopt a role, to accept normative coordination and guidance, even where certain wishes tell against this. If I want to play football, I shall submit to the rule that the ball may not be stopped with the hand, even when no referee is present to blow the whistle on this infraction, and even when observance of the rule in a concrete situation is to my disadvantage. Sociologically and psychologically it is simply not true that man only fulfils his role when he is given an interest in law-abiding behaviour by the threat of sanctions to follow; for he is above all interested in taking part in the life of society – in playing the game, as we might say.

The theoretical motivation of the sanction theory of legal norms appears, therefore, to be dubious. In my opinion other arguments also tell against this theory:

(a) It lays excessive stress on the element of coercion, underestimating the organising role of law and pushing this role out of sight.

(b) Even within the framework of a coercive system, it seems to me that so-called *leges imperfectae* are by no means meaningless. They appear chiefly as norms imposing duties on the paramount organs, or as defining duties with vague consequences for wrong-doing, where the possible disadvantages are not legally specified.[34]

(c) From the form of the sanction-norm "If *A*, then *B* (the sanction) is to be", i.e., a hypothetical 'ought'-sentence, the forbiddenness of *A* can be logically inferred when and only when it is known that *B* is posited as a *sanction*. This is the case when and only when the behaviour posited as condition of the obligatoriness of the sanction is assumed to be forbidden. In other words, the concept of a sanction contains an implicit reference to a behavioural norm, whose violation is the condition of the sanction. The behavioural norm must therefore be presupposed in any case, and it will not do to regard law, in Kelsen's fashion, as a mere system of sanction-norms.[35]

(d) As Kelsen himself has recognised, the legal system as a whole cannot in any case be viewed as a set of sanctioned norms, since the basic norm, which terminates the chain of justification of the legal system, can only authorise – it cannot coerce by means of sanctions.

(e) Kelsen has shown with strict logical consistency that although "*A* is to be" and "*A* is not to be" exclude one another, the same conduct could be simultaneously enjoined and forbidden in a normative order consisting solely of norms in the form of sanction-norms, without any logical contradiction arising; for the sanction-norms corresponding to injunction and prohibition, "If not *A*, a sanction is to follow" and "If *A*, a sanction is to follow", do not contradict one another.[36] Thus if law is expressed solely in the form of sanction-norms, the enjoining and prohibition of the same conduct does not appear as a logical contradiction or logical defect of the system. Kelsen is content with this; but we see it as a serious argument against the sanction theory of the legal norm.

5. Legal norm and statement of law

In the *Hauptprobleme* Kelsen characterises the statement of law, representing the general structure of law, as the judgement that under certain conditions a consequence of wrong-doing is to be realised. Even in the First Edition of the *Reine Rechtslehre* we find a similar formulation: the legal norm is defined here as a hypothetical judgement expressing the specific linkage of a conditioning circumstance with a conditioned consequence.[37] In the Second "completely revised and enlarged" Edition of the *Reine Rechtslehre*, legal norms and statements of law are sharply distinguished and the semantic and ontological difference strongly emphasised. Legal norms are created by acts of human behaviour; they constitute the normative relation between conditioning and conditioned circumstances. But

> *statements* of law are hypothetical judgements asserting that, according to some – national or international – legal order of which we have legal cognisance, certain conditions defined by this legal order being given, certain consequences defined by this order are to follow. Legal *norms* are not judgements, i.e., statements about an object given to cognition.[38]
>
> Since a legal order in the sense just specified is a coercive order, it can be described in sentences stating that under defined conditions (defined, that is, by the legal order) defined acts of coercion (also defined by that order) are to be performed. All the material given in the legal norms of a legal order fits into this schema of the statement of law formulated by legal science – which statement is to be distinguished from the legal norm posited by the legal authority.[39]

Here, therefore, a general schema of legal description is being enunciated, in which law can be correctly and completely described.

In contrasting legal norm and statement of law, Kelsen is formulating an important philosophical and logical problem. In what way is this distinction logically relevant? How are we to conceive the justificatory relation between legal norm and statement of law, or more generally, between the verbally formulated norm and the statement affirming the normative relation? What should the logic of norms be fastening upon – the norms (the sentences expressing them) or the declarative statements about norms, or about the relations constituted by norms? Kelsen's statements of the problem are uncommonly stimulating, even if, in my opinion, they provide no final solution.

6. Kelsen's Legal Positivism and Value-Relativism – The Ideological and Democratic Consequences

Kelsen may be considered the most important champion of legal positivism. The latter is, as it were, a self-evident consequence of the value-free, purely cognitive science which he has in view. The assumption of a natural law, standing behind positive law and functioning as the ground and/or standard of the latter, is an absurdity. There is no absolute obligation, no 'ought' independent of human positing; it would be in contradiction with the separation of 'is' and 'ought' if there were an immanent 'ought' existing in independence of the will. A duality of positive law and natural law, in which the latter was the ground or standard of the former, also contradicts the principle of the exclusive character of every sovereign order of norms. Quite apart from the historical fact of the variety that has existed among legal obligations, there is no possibility of cognising or justifying natural law as a set of obligations having *a priori* correctness, since 'ought' is not derivable from 'is' alone, and is determined only through willing and positing.

Kelsen's value-relativism naturally implies no denial of values or making light of value-attitudes: it is simply a matter of regarding them as decisions, as something that cannot be demonstrated in purely cognitive fashion.

Kelsen's pure positivism and his relativist theory of value are not unrealistic and neutral in their pragmatic consequences; they lead, rather, to a critique of ideology, to an understanding of value-pluralism, to the postulate of tolerance, to a pluralistic democracy based on the free play of ideas in the self-correcting dialectic of clashing opinions within the field of legal development. They do this, however, without the fiction that in the process we shall simply apprehend "correct" law that has somehow been previously given.

Kelsen's attitude and his work – precisely because of his resolute struggle for pure knowledge, criticism and clarification – seem to me imbued, therefore, with a high moral tone, in keeping with the modern spirit, which is sustained equally by the idea of democratic freedoms and by creative responsibility and the will to betterment.

On the occasion of his 90th birthday, we must not only congratulate Hans Kelsen on a well-spent life, but also thank him for his contribution to the science and wisdom of our age.

It should be mentioned that a full-length biography of our author, by R. A. Métall, appeared in 1969 under the title *Hans Kelsen, Leben und Werk*. It is supplemented by an extensive bibliography of Kelsen, and by a catalogue of writings on his work and on the Pure Theory of Law.[40]

NOTES

[1] Kelsen, H., *Hauptprobleme der Staatsrechtslehre, entwickelt aus der Lehre vom Rechtssatze*, Tübingen 1911, p. VIII.

[2] Métall, R. A., *Hans Kelsen, Leben und Werk*, Vienna 1969.

[3] Kelsen, H., *Reine Rechtslehre*, 2nd edn., Vienna 1960, p. 1. Cf. *Pure Theory of Law*, Transl. by Max Knight, Berkeley, Los Angeles, London, 1970, p. 1. [Although page references are given to this translation, it is neither adequate nor complete and has not been relied on in rendering quotations from the original – Transl.].

[4] Kelsen, H., *Hauptprobleme*, p. 8. Cf. also the essay 'Causality and Accounting' in this volume, pp. 154–164.

[5] Kelsen, H., *Reine Rechtslehre*, 2nd edn., p. 78. Cf. p. 154 below, and *Pure Theory of Law* (*PTL*), p. 75.

[6] Kelsen, H., *op. cit.*, p. 79. Cf. p. 154 below, and *PTL*, p. 76.

[7] *Ibid.*, p. 79. *PTL*, p. 76.

[8] *Ibid.*, p. 93, Cf. p. 161 below, and *PTL*, pp. 89–90.

[9] *Ibid.*, p. 100. *PTL*, pp. 96–97.

[10] *Ibid.*, p. 102. Cf. pp. 163 below, and *PTL*, p. 98.

[11] Kelsen, H., *Hauptprobleme*, p. 8. Cf. also Simmel, G., *Einleitung in die Moralwissenschaft*, Berlin 1892.

[12] Kelsen, H., *Reine Rechtslehre*, 2nd edn., p. 5. Cf. *PTL*, pp. 5–6.

[13] Poincaré, H., *Dernières pensées*, Paris 1913; on this subject, cf. Weinberger, O., 'Die Sollsatzproblematik in der modernen Logik', *Rozpravy ČSAV*, 1958, p. 8.

[14] For example, in inferences of the following form:

If *A*, then B is to be
A
B is to be

both premises are equally arguments, but only together do they justify the inferred norm.
[15] Kelsen, H., *Reine Rechtslehre*, 2nd edn., p. 81. *PTL*, p. 77.
[16] Cf. the essay on 'Derogation' below, pp. 261–275.
[17] See Kelsen, H., *Reine Rechtslehre*, 2nd edn., pp. 198f. *PTL*, pp. 195f.
[18] See Merkl, A., 'Prolegomena einer Theorie des rechtlichen Stufenbaues', in *Gesellschaft, Staat und Recht* (Kelsen Festschrift), Vienna 1931, pp. 252–294.
[19] Kelsen, H., *Hauptprobleme*, pp. 69ff.
[20] *Ibid.*, pp. 75ff.
[21] In a sense, indeed, custom is certainly not without sanctions, but breaches of custom are mostly not defined in advance, or exposed to sanctions to be carried out by an organised official machinery.
[22] Kelsen, H., *Reine Rechtslehre*, 2nd edn. p. 26. [*PTL*, p. 25, omits a part of this passage – Transl.].
[23] Kelsen, H., *Hauptprobleme*, p. 110.
[24] *Ibid.*, p. 190.
[25] *Ibid.*, p. 203.
[26] *Ibid.*, p. 201.
[27] *Ibid.*, p. 202.
[28] *Ibid.*, p. 204.
[29] *Ibid.*, p. 205. (*a*) "The word 'subjects' is used here simply as a very practical collective term for *all legal subjects other than the state*" (Kelsen's note).
[30] Kelsen, H., *Hauptprobleme*, p. 210.
[31] *Ibid.*, p. 254.
[32] *Ibid.*, p. 256.
[33] Kelsen, H., 'Recht und Logik', *Forum* XII/143 (1965), p. 496: No norm without an act of will, of which this norm is the meaning"; in the footnote to this, Dubislav's "No imperative without an *imperator*" is referred to. Cf. p. 237f. of this volume.
[34] Even if no sanction is *expressly* laid down in law, there are often actual consequences of wrong-doing. Thus a legal time-limit, for example, by which an official has to settle some matter, is not therefore meaningless because no sanction is expressly envisaged in advance. It has a motivating effect, and the official can have a real interest in complying even with a "sanctionless" legal norm. The reputation of being continually in arrears might impair, for example, his chances of promotion.
[35] Law is a coercive system, but it does not follow from this, in my view, that it can contain only norms expressly furnished with sanctions. This by no means implies, however, that the behavioural norms whose observance is to be enforced become superfluous.
[36] Kelsen, H., *Reine Rechtslehre*, 2nd edn., p. 27. *PTL*, p. 25.
[37] Kelsen, H., *Reine Rechtslehre*, 1st edn., Leipzig-Vienna 1934, p. 22.
[38] Kelsen, H., *Reine Rechtslehre*, 2nd edn., p. 73. *PTL*, p. 71. [The term "Rechtssatz" is commonly rendered by Kelsen translators as "rule of law". Although there is some warrant for this in his earlier writings, it is clearly inappropriate once the distinction has been made – as it is here – between norms (of which rules are a species) and statements *about* norms, made, e.g., by jurists. For the sake of uniformity, "Rechtssatz" has here been translated virtually throughout (except in quotations from the early *Hauptprobleme*) as "statement of law".

But it should be borne in mind that in the earlier essays, at least, no clear contrast between a statement, proposition or judgement and a norm, law or rule was apparently envisaged by the author himself. I am indebted to my colleague Professor A. D. Woozley for clarification on this troublesome point – Transl.]

[39] *Ibid.*, p. 59. *PTL*, p. 58.

[40] See note 2 above.

CHAPTER I

WHAT IS JUSTICE?*

When Jesus of Nazareth, in the hearing before the Roman prefect, confessed to being a king, he said: "I was born and am come into this world to bear witness to the truth". At which Pilate asked "What is truth?" The sceptical Roman obviously expected no answer to this question, nor did Our Lord give any. For to be witness to the truth was not the essence of his mission as a Messianic king. He was born to bear witness to justice, that justice which he wished to realise in the Kingdom of God. And for this justice he died on the cross.

So behind Pilate's question: What is truth? there rises from the blood of the crucified another and still weightier question, the eternal question of mankind: What is justice?

No other question has been so passionately debated; for no other has so much precious blood, so many bitter tears been shed; on no other have the noblest minds – from Plato to Kant – brooded so deeply. And yet today this question remains as unanswered as ever. Perhaps because it is one of those questions of which a resigned wisdom would tell us, that man can never discover a final answer to it, but can only attempt to ask it better.

I

1. Justice is primarily a possible but not necessary property of a social order. Only secondarily is it a human virtue. For a man is just when his conduct conforms to an order which ranks as just. But what does it mean to say that an order is just? That this order regulates the conduct of men in such a way that all are satisfied, so that all find their happiness under it. The longing for justice is man's eternal longing for happiness. Since he cannot find this happiness as an isolated individual, he seeks it in society. Justice is social happiness, the happiness guaranteed by a social order. In this sense Plato identifies justice with happiness, when he maintains that only the just man is happy, while the unjust man is not.

In claiming that justice is happiness, the question is obviously not yet answered, but only postponed. For now the question arises: What is happiness?

2. It is clear that there cannot be a just order, i.e., one which guarantees happiness to all, if by happiness we mean – as the original sense of the word would imply – a subjective feeling, namely that which each understands by it in his own case. For it is then unavoidable that the happiness of one should conflict with the happiness of another. To give an example: love is the most potent source of happiness, as it also is of unhappiness. Suppose that two men love one and the same woman, and that each believes – rightly or wrongly – that he cannot be happy without having just this woman for himself alone. But according to law, and perhaps also in accordance with their own feelings, the woman can only belong to one of them. The happiness of the one cannot help but be the unhappiness of the other. No social order can resolve this problem justly, i.e., in such a way that both men are made happy. Not even the famous judgement of the wise King Solomon. He, it will be remembered, proposed that a child, for whom two women were disputing possession, should be divided in half, but was going to award it to whichever of them should withdraw her claim in order to spare the child's life. For this – so the king assumed – would show that she really loved the child. If Solomon's judgement is just at all, it is so only on the condition that just one of the two women loves the child. If both do so – which is possible and even probable, since both wish to have it – and if both therefore withdraw their claims, the quarrel remains undecided; and if the child is then eventually awarded to one of the two parties, the judgement is certainly not just, for it makes the other unhappy. Our happiness very frequently depends on a satisfaction of needs which no social order is able to guarantee.

Another example: the commander of an army is to be named. Two men are in contention; but only one can be chosen. It seems self-evident that the fitter for the post should be selected. But what if both are equally fit? A just solution is then ruled out. Let us suppose that one is held to be the fitter because he has a fine appearance and a handsome face, and so creates the impression of being a strong personality, whereas the other is small and insignificant-looking. If the first gets the job, the other will by no means feel the decision to be just; he will say, why am

I not so good-looking as he is, why has nature fashioned my body so much less attractively? And in fact, if we assess nature from the standpoint of justice, we have to confess that nature is not just: she makes one man healthy and another diseased, one clever and another a fool. No social order can wholly compensate for the injustice of nature.

3. If justice is happiness, a just social order is impossible so long as justice means the same as individual happiness. But a just social order is impossible even on the presumption that it aims to secure, not the individual happiness of everyone, but the greatest happiness of the greatest number. Such is the celebrated definition of justice formulated by the English philosopher and jurist Jeremy Bentham. But Bentham's formula is likewise inapplicable, if by happiness be meant a subjective value. For different individuals have exceedingly different ideas as to what their happiness consists in. The happiness that a social order is able to guarantee cannot be happiness in a subjective and individual sense, but only in an objective and collective one. By happiness, that is, one should understand only the satisfaction of certain needs which are recognised by the social authority, the legislator, to be such as are worthy of satisfaction, for instance the needs for food, clothing, shelter and the like. There can be no doubt that the satisfaction of socially recognised needs is something altogether different from the original sense of the word. For in its inmost essence this sense is a supremely subjective one. The wish for justice is so elemental, so deeply rooted in the heart of man, because it is merely the expression of his indestructible wish for his own subjective happiness.

4. In order to become a social category, the happiness of justice, the idea of happiness must undergo a radical change of meaning. The metamorphosis, in which individual and subjective happiness becomes the satisfaction of socially recognised needs, is similar to that which the idea of freedom must undergo in order to become a social principle; and the idea of freedom is frequently identified with that of justice, in the sense, that is, that a social order is reckoned just if it guarantees individual freedom. Since true freedom, i.e., freedom from all compulsion, from every sort of governance, is incompatible with any kind of social order, the idea of freedom cannot retain the negative meaning

of being free from governance. The concept of freedom must take on the meaning of a special form of governance. Freedom must mean rule by the majority, if needed, rather than the minority of ruled subjects. The freedom of anarchy is thus transformed into the self-determination of democracy. The idea of justice is similarly transformed from a principle guaranteeing the individual happiness of all into a social order which protects particular interests, namely the interests acknowledged to be worth such protection by the majority of those subjected to this order.

5. But what human interests have this worth, and in what order are we to rank such values? This is the question which arises when there are conflicts of interest. And only where such conflicts exist does justice become a problem. Where there are none, there is no need for justice. But a conflict of interest occurs when an interest can only be satisfied at another's expense, or, what amounts to the same thing, when two values are at variance, and it is not possible to realise both of them at once; when one can be realised only inasmuch as the other is neglected, when there is no option but to prefer the realising of one to that of the other, when it has to be decided which of the two values is the higher and more important, and which, ultimately, is the highest value. The problem of values is first and foremost the problem of value-conflicts. And this problem cannot be settled by methods of rational cognition. The answer to the questions which arise at this point is always a judgement governed in the last resort by emotional factors, and thus highly subjective in character. Which is to say that it only holds good for the judging subject, and is in this sense relative.

II

6. A few examples may serve to illustrate what has just been said. According to one particular moral conviction, human life, the life of each single individual, is the highest value. It is therefore absolutely forbidden, on this view, to kill a human being, even in war or in execution of the death penalty. This is notoriously the view of the conscientious objector and of those who are radical opponents of capital punishment. But there is an equally moral conviction running counter to this, according to which the interest and honour of the nation is the highest value.

Thus everyone is morally obliged to sacrifice his own life, and to kill others in war as the nation's enemies, if the interest and honour of the nation demand it; and it seems justifiable to impose the death penalty on those guilty of serious crime. It is absolutely impossible to decide in any rational or scientific way between the two value-judgements underlying these conflicting views. It is, when all is said, our feelings, our will, not our understanding, the emotional rather than the rational element of our consciousness, which resolves the conflict.

7. Another example: a slave or prisoner in a concentration camp, where escape is impossible, is faced with the question whether suicide is morally admissible. This question is continually debated, and played a large part especially in the ethics of the ancient world. The answer depends on deciding which of the two values is the higher: life or freedom. If life is the higher, suicide is not justified; but if freedom is the higher, if a life without freedom is valueless, then suicide is not only permitted but enjoined. It is a question of the ranking of the values of life and freedom. Only a subjective answer can be given to this question, an answer which is valid only for the judging subject; there can be no conclusion valid for everyone, like the judgment, say, that metals expand with heat. But the latter is a judgement of fact, not a value-judgment.

8. Let us suppose – without actually maintaining it – that it be possible to prove that the condition of a people can be so radically improved by a so-called planned economy, that economic security would be equally guaranteed to everyone, but that such an organisation is possible only if all individual freedom is abolished or seriously abridged. The answer to the question whether a planned economy is preferable to a free one, will then depend on our choice between the respective values of individual freedom and economic security. A man of strong self-assurance will prefer individual freedom, while one who labours under an inferiority-complex will opt for economic security. This means, however, that the question whether individual freedom is a higher value than economic security, or *vice versa*, is capable only of a subjective answer, and not of an objective judgement, like the statement, say, that iron is heavier than water and water heavier than wood. The latter, though, are judgements about matters of fact which can be verified through

experiment – not judgements of value, which do not admit of such verification.

9. After careful examination of a patient, a doctor diagnoses an incurable disease, which must shortly lead to death. Should the doctor tell the victim the truth, or may he, perhaps should he even, lie and tell him that his disease is curable and that there is no immediate danger? The decision rests upon the priorities we accept in the relation of the two values: veracity and humanity. Telling the patient the truth means exposing him to the torments of mortal fear; lying to him means sparing him these torments. If the ideal of truthfulness takes precedence over that of humanity, the doctor must tell the truth; but if the ideal of humanity takes precedence over that of veracity, he must lie. Yet the question, which of these two values is the higher, cannot be answered on the basis of rational or scientific considerations.

10. As noted earlier, Plato took the view that the just man – meaning the man who behaves justly – and only the just man, is happy, while the unjust – meaning he who behaves unjustly – is unhappy. Plato says that "the justest life is the happiest". Though he concedes that perhaps in one case or another a just man might be unhappy and an unjust one happy. Yet it is absolutely necessary, so the philosopher adds, that the citizens subject to the rule of justice should believe in the truth of the claim that only the just man is happy, even if this claim be untrue; otherwise nobody would obey the law. Hence the rulers, so Plato argues, have the right to use all means of propaganda in disseminating the doctrine that the just man is happy and the unjust unhappy, even if this is a lie. If it is a lie, then it is a supremely useful lie, for it guarantees obedience to the law.

> Could a legislator ... supposing him to have ventured on any fiction ... have devised a more useful fiction than this, or one more potent to induce us all to practise all justice freely, and without compulsion?
>
> Were I a legislator, I would do my best to constrain my poets and all my citizens to proclaim ... that the justest life is happiest [1]

According to Plato, the rulers are fully entitled to make use of lies which they consider beneficial. He ranks justice, and that means here what the rulers consider to be justice, namely obedience to law, above truth.

But there is no sufficient reason which would forbid us to rank truth above obedience to law, and to reject as immoral an official propaganda that rests upon lies; even if these lies serve a good purpose.

11. The answer to the question about the ranking of values – such as life and liberty, freedom and equality, freedom and security, truth and justice, veracity and humanity, individual and nation – is bound to turn out differently according to whether the question is addressed to a believing Christian, who considers his spiritual welfare, i.e., his fate after death, to be more important than earthly goods, or to a materialist who has no belief in the immortality of the soul; and the answer cannot be the same if it is given on the assumption that freedom is the supreme value, i.e., from the standpoint of liberalism, as it is on the supposition that economic security is the ultimate goal of a social order, i.e., from the standpoint of socialism. And the answer will always have the character of a subjective, and therefore purely relative, judgement of value.

III

12. The fact that genuine value-judgements are subjective, and hence that very different and contradictory value-judgements are possible, by no means implies that every individual has his own system of values. In practice, many individuals concur in their value-judgements. A positive value-system is not the arbitrary creation of an isolated individual, but always a product of the mutual influence which individuals exert on each other within a given group – such as family, tribe, clan, caste or calling – and under particular economic conditions. Every value-system, especially a moral order, with its central idea of justice, is a social phenomenon, and therefore differs according to the nature of the society in which it comes about. The fact that certain values are generally acknowledged within a particular society is perfectly consistent with the subjective and relative character of the judgements in which these values are upheld. That many individuals concur in a value-judgement is in no sense a proof that this judgement is correct, i.e., valid in an objective sense. Just as the fact that most men believe, or have believed, that the sun goes round the earth, neither is nor was a proof that this belief is founded on truth. The criterion of justice, like

that of truth, is certainly not to be found in the number of factual or value-judgements expressed. Very often in the history of human civilisation, quite generally acknowledged value-judgements have been displaced by others more or less opposed to them, and no less generally acknowledged on that account. Thus in primitive society, collective responsibility, e.g. in the case of a vendetta, was regarded as a perfectly just principle, while in modern society the opposite principle, of individual responsibility, accords with our sense of justice; notwithstanding that in certain areas, e.g., that of international relations, the principle of collective responsibility, and in the field of religious belief, that of inherited responsibility, as original sin – which is also a sort of collective responsibility – would be compatible with the moral feelings of many people even today. Nor is it by any means impossible that in time to come – should socialism come to prevail – a collective responsibility divorced from any religious considerations might again be quite generally regarded as moral within the field of inter-personal relations.

13. Although the question of what is actually the highest value cannot be rationally answered, the subjective and relative judgement by which it is answered in practice is commonly put forward as postulating an objective value or – what comes to the same thing – an absolutely valid norm. It is a peculiar feature of man that he has a deep need to justify his conduct, that he possesses a conscience. The need to justify or rationalise is perhaps one of the differences between man and animal. The outward behaviour of men is not very different from that of animals: big fish eat little fish in the animal kingdom, as in the world of man. But if a human fish, impelled by instinct, acts in this way, he still seeks to justify his behaviour, to himself and to society, and to ease his conscience with the notion that he behaves well by his fellow-men.

14. Since man is a more or less rational being, he attempts to justify his behaviour, governed as it is by fear and desire, on rational grounds, i.e. by a function of his understanding. But such rational justification is possible only to a limited degree, to the extent, that is, that his fear or desire is related to a particular means whereby a particular end is to be attained. The relation of means and end coincides with that of cause and effect, and can thus be determined on the basis of experience, and

hence in a scientific and rational way. Admittedly, even this is not always possible, if the means for realising a particular end are specifically social measures. For such is the present state of social science that we have no clear insight into the causal nexus of social phenomena, and therefore lack sufficient experience to enable us to determine precisely what the aptest means may be for realising particular social ends. This is the case, for example, when a legislator is confronted with the question whether to impose capital punishment or mere imprisonment in order to discourage a certain crime. This question can also be formulated by asking whether capital punishment or imprisonment is the just penalty. In order to decide it, the legislator would have to know the effect which the imposition of the different penalties would have upon those inclined to commit the crime which the legislator is trying to prevent. But unfortunately we have no exact knowledge of this effect, nor are we in a position to obtain such knowledge, for this could only be done, if at all, by instituting experiments; in the field of social life, however, experiment can be employed only to a very limited extent. Hence, even if it is restricted purely to the question whether a social measure is an appropriate means for attaining some specified end, the problem of justice is not always rationally soluble. But even in those cases where this question can be exactly answered, the answer cannot provide full justification for our conduct, the justification that our conscience demands. Exceedingly appropriate means may be used to attain exceedingly questionable ends. We have only to think of the atomic bomb. The end justifies or – as we also say – sanctifies the means. But the means does not justify the end. And it is precisely the justification of the end, that end which is no longer a means to some higher end, the last or highest end, which alone provides ultimate justification for what we do.

15. If anything, especially a human act, is justified only as a means to some particular end, the inevitable question arises, whether the end too can be justified. And to ask it must eventually lead to the acceptance of a last, highest end, which is the true problem of morality in general and of justice in particular. If a human act is justified only as an appropriate means to some proposed end, it is justified only conditionally; on condition, that is, that the proposed end is also justified. Such a conditioned, and in this sense relative, justification does not exclude the

possibility of the opposite; for if the final end cannot be justified, nor can the means towards it. Democracy is a just form of government because it secures individual freedom. This means, however, that democracy is a just form of government only on the assumption that the preservation of individual freedom is the highest end. If economic security is taken to be the highest end, in place of individual freedom, and if it can be shown to be unobtainable under a democratic regime, then it is no longer democracy but some other form of government that will have to be regarded as just. Other ends call for other means. So democracy can be justified only as a relatively, not an absolutely, good form of government.

16. Our conscience may not rest content with such a conditional justification. It may demand an unconditional and absolute one. Our conscience is not at ease if we are able to justify our conduct only as an appropriate means to an end whose own justification itself remains in doubt. It then requires that we justify our conduct as a final end, or, which is the same thing, that it should conform to an absolute value. Yet such justification is not possible on rational lines. All rational justification is essentially justification as an appropriate means; and a final end is by that very fact no longer a means to some further end. If our conscience demands absolute justification for our conduct, and thereby postulates absolute value, our reason is not in a position to satisfy this demand. The absolute in general, and absolute values in particular, are beyond human reason, for which only a conditioned and in that sense relative solution is possible to the problem of justice, as the problem of justifying human behaviour.

17. But the need for absolute justification seems to be stronger than all rational considerations. So man turns to religion and metaphysics, that there he may find this justification, i.e. absolute justice. This means, however, that justice is translated from this world into another and transcendent one. It becomes the essential property, and its realisation the essential function, of a superhuman authority, a divinity whose properties and functions are by nature inaccessible to human knowledge. Man must believe in the existence of God, and this means in the existence of an absolute justice, but he is incapable of conceiving this, or defining

it in conceptual form. Those who cannot accept such a metaphysical solution of the problem of justice, but yet still uphold the idea of absolute values, in the hope of being able to define them in rational or scientific terms, cheat themselves with the illusory possibility of finding certain principles in human reason which shall be constitutive of these absolute values – though the latter are actually constituted by the emotional elements of their consciousness. The determination of absolute values in general, and the definition of justice in particular, turn out, when attempted in this fashion, to be utterly empty formulae, by which any social order whatever can be vindicated as just.

It is therefore not surprising that the numerous theories of justice put forward from the earliest times to the present day can be easily reduced to two basic types: one metaphysico-religious, and the other rationalistic, or more accurately speaking, pseudo-rationalistic.

IV

18. The classic representative of the metaphysical type is Plato.[2] Justice is the central problem of his entire philosophy. And to solve this problem he evolves his celebrated theory of Ideas. The Ideas are transcendent entities existing in another world, an intelligible sphere inaccessible to men, who are in the toils of sensibility. They are essentially representative of values, and absolute values at that, which should indeed be realised in the world of sense, but never can be wholly so realised. The supreme Idea, to which all others are subordinate and from which they all obtain their validity, is the Idea of the absolutely Good; and in Plato's philosophy this Idea plays exactly the same part as the idea of God in the theology of any religion. The Idea of the Good includes that of justice; the justice of which knowledge is sought in virtually all Plato's dialogues. The question: "What is justice?" is therefore bound up with the question: "What is good, or what is the Good?" In his dialogues, Plato makes numerous attempts to answer this question on rational lines. But none of these attempts leads to any final conclusion. Whenever some definition appears to have been reached, Plato at once declares, through the mouth of Socrates, that a great many further enquiries are needed. Plato repeatedly alludes to a specific method of abstract thinking, divorced from all sensuous imagery, the

so-called dialectic, which – so he claims – enables those who master it to apprehend the Ideas. But he does not himself employ this method in his own dialogues, nor does he impart to us the findings of this dialectic. Of the Idea of the absolutely Good he even says expressly that it lies beyond all rational knowledge, and therefore all thought. In one of his letters, the VIIth, where he gives an account of the innermost motives and ultimate aims of his philosophy, he declares that there can be no conceptual knowledge whatever of the absolutely Good, but only a sort of vision, and that this vision occurs in the course of a mystical experience to which few indeed are privileged, and then only by divine grace; it is, however, impossible to describe the object of this mystical vision, and hence the absolutely Good, in terms of human speech. As a result – and this is the final conclusion of Plato's wisdom – there can be no answer to the problem of justice. For justice is a secret which God – if he discloses it at all – has entrusted only to a chosen few, and it must remain their secret, since they cannot convey it to others.

19. It is remarkable how close the philosophy of Plato stands in this respect to the preaching of Jesus, whose primary concern was likewise with justice. After firmly rejecting the rationalistic formula of the Old Testament, "an eye for an eye; a tooth for a tooth" – the principle of retaliation – he proclaims as the new and true justice the principle of love: Not to return evil with evil, but with good; not to resist evil but to love the evil-doer, and even your enemy.[3] This justice lies beyond any order of things possible in a social reality; and the love which constitutes this justice cannot be the human feeling we call love. Not only because it is against human nature to love one's enemy, but also because Jesus most emphatically rejects that human love which unites husband and wife, and parents with their children. He who would follow Jesus and attain to the Kingdom of God must forsake house and parents and brethren and wife and children.[4] Anyone, indeed, who does not hate his father, and mother, and wife, and children, and brethren and sisters, and his own life also, cannot be Jesus' disciple.[5] The love which Jesus teaches is not the love of man. It is the love whereby a man is to become perfect, as is his Father in heaven, who makes his sun to rise on the evil and on the good, and the rain to fall on the just and on the unjust.[6] It is the love of God. The strangest thing about this love,

however, is that it must be accepted as consistent with the terrible and everlasting punishment to be visited upon sins at the Last Judgement, and hence also with the deepest fear of which a man is capable, the fear of God. Jesus made no attempt to explain this contradiction. And nor, indeed, is any such explanation possible. For it is a contradiction only to the limited human reason, not to the absolute reason of God, which is beyond man's comprehension. Whence Paul, the first theologian of the Christian religion, tells us that the wisdom of this world is foolishness with God,[7] that philosophy, i.e., rational and logical knowledge, offers no road to the divine justice which lies in the hidden wisdom of God,[8] that God imparts this justice to a man only through faith,[9] the faith which works by love.[10] Paul insists upon Jesus' doctrine of the new justice, the love of God.[11] But he admits that the love which Jesus teaches passes knowledge.[12] It is a mystery, one of the many mysteries of faith.

V

20. The rationalistic type, which seeks to give an answer to the problem of justice by methods of human reason, to provide a definition of the concept, has appeared in the folk-wisdom of many nations, and also in some celebrated systems of philosophy. One of the seven sages of Greece is credited with the well-known saying that justice is giving to everyone his own. This formula has been accepted by many eminent thinkers and especially by philosophers of law. It is easy to show that it is utterly empty. For the crucial question, what it actually is that everyone may regard as "his own", remains unanswered. Hence the principle "to everyone his own" is applicable only on the assumption that this question has already been settled beforehand. And it can be decided only by a social order set up as a positive moral or legal order by way of custom or legislation. Thus the formula "To everyone his own" can be used to justify any desired order of society, whether it be capitalist or socialist, democratic or autocratic. According to all these orders, everyone will be given "his own", only in each order "his own" is different. This possibility, of defending any given social order as just – because it accords with the formula "To everyone his own" – explains its general acceptance; but it also shows at the same time that it is utterly worthless as a definition of justice, insofar as it is supposed to determine an absolute

value which cannot be identical with the purely relative values guaranteed by a positive moral or legal order.

21. The same applies to that principle which has probably been most often put forward as the essence of justice: good for good and evil for evil; this is the principle of retaliation. It is meaningless so long as an answer to the question: what is good, what is evil? is not presupposed as self-evident. But this answer is not self-evident at all, since opinions about what is good and evil have differed greatly at different times and among different peoples. The principle of retaliation expresses only the specific technique of positive law, which adjoins to the evil of wrong-doing the evil of a penalty. But that is a principle underlying all positive legal norms, and thus every legal order can be justified as a realisation of the retaliation-principle. But the question of justice is ultimately the question of whether a legal order is just in its employment of the retaliation-principle, i.e., of whether the fact to which the law responds, as to a wrong, by the evil of a penalty, is really an evil for society, and whether the evil which the law ordains as a penalty should be regarded as appropriate. That is the true question, the question of whether the law is just. And the principle of retaliation is not an answer to it.

22. Insofar as retaliation amounts to returning like with like, it is one of the many forms taken by the principle of equality, which has likewise been insisted on as the essence of justice. Starting from the assumption that all men, "everything that wears a human face", is by nature alike, it culminates in the demand that all men should be treated alike. But the assumption is plainly false, since men are in fact very different, and no two of them are really alike, and hence the only possible meaning of this demand is, that in protecting rights and imposing duties the social order should have no regard to certain differences. Only certain differences, not all, by any means! To treat children like grown-ups, or madmen like those of sound mind, would be absurd. But what are the differences to be attended to, and what are those that should not? That is the crucial question, and the principle of equality fails to give it an answer. In practice, actual legal orders vary widely in the way they decide this question. They all conform to the principle of neglecting certain differences among men. But as to the differences they do not ignore, and which they take

into account in protecting rights and imposing duties, there are hardly two legal systems in agreement. Some accord political rights to men only, and not to women; others treat both sexes alike in this respect, but require only men to engage in military service; others, however, make no distinction between men and women even in this respect. But what is just? A person himself indifferent to religion will be inclined to regard religious differences as of no account. But a believer will see the difference between those who share his faith – which as a believer he must take to be the only true one – and all others, the unbelievers, as more important than any other difference. He will feel it entirely just to grant rights to the one which are denied to others. He will interpret the principle of equality quite properly as saying that only equals are to be treated alike. This to aliens, to members of a given race or religion only, not to members of by the so-called equality-principle. Any desired difference can thus be ranked as essential in the treatment of its subjects by an actual legal order, and hence be the basis of differential treatment, without the régime thereby coming into conflict with the principle of equality. This principle is too empty to be able to determine the content of a legal system.

23. And now what of the special principle of so-called equality before the law? All it means is that the machinery of the law should make no distinctions which are not already made by the law to be applied. If the law grants political rights to men only, not women, to citizens only, not aliens, to members of a given race or religion only, not to members of other religions or races, then the principle of equality before the law is fully upheld if in concrete cases the judicial authorities decide that a woman, an alien, or the member of some particular religion or race, has no political rights. This principle has scarcely anything to do with equality any longer. It merely states that the law should be applied as it is meant to be applied. It is the principle of legality or legitimacy which is by nature inherent in every legal order, regardless of whether this order is just or unjust.

24. The application of the equality-principle to the relation between doing work and the product of working leads to the demand, that an equal amount of work done should receive an equal share in the product. This, according to Karl Marx,[13] is the justice underlying the capitalist

order of society, the alleged "equal right" of this economic system. In fact it is an unequal right, since it takes no account of the differences between men in respect of their capacity for work; and is thus not a just right, but an unjust one. For the same amounts of work, done by a strong and skilled man, and a weak and unskilled one, are only apparently equal; and if both receive the same proportion of the product for their labour, they get an equal return for what is unequal. True equality, and thus true and not merely apparent justice, would be realisable only in a communist economy, where the principle would be: From each according to his capacity, to each according to his need.

If this principle were to be applied within an economy whose production is planned, and thus ultimately regulated by a central authority, there would at once arise the question: what are a person's individual capacities, for what sort of work is he fitted, and what is the amount of work to be expected of him in terms of his natural aptitudes? This question will obviously have to be decided, not by each individual himself according to his own estimation, but by an appointed organ of the community according to general norms laid down by the social authority. And then comes the further question: what needs can be satisfied? Only those, obviously, which the planned production-process, managed, of course, by a central authority, operates to satisfy. And even if, as Marx tells us, "the forces of production are destined to grow" and "all the wellsprings of social wealth to flow more freely" in the communist society of the future, neither the selection of needs which the social production-process must plan to cater for, nor the measure of their satisfaction, can be left entirely to the whims of individuals. This question, too, will have to be settled by the social authority according to general principles. Thus even the communist principle of justice – just like the formula of "to each his own" – presupposes that the questions to be decided in applying it will be answered by a positive social régime. Nor is this – as with the formula "to each his own" – a matter of any social order you please, but of a quite specific one. Yet nobody can foresee how such a social order, to be realised only in the distant future, is going to function, or how it will answer the questions which need deciding if the communist principle of justice is to be applied.

If these facts are taken into account, the communist principle of justice – so far as it claims to be any such thing – will amount to the rule: From each according to his capacity, as recognised by the communist social order, to each according to his need, as determined by that order. That such a régime will recognise the capacities of each in full accord with his own inclinations, and will guarantee the satisfaction of all his needs, so that within the community it creates there will be a harmony of all collective and individual interests, and thus unlimited individual freedom, is a utopian illusion; the typical Utopia of a Golden Age set in the future, a paradisal condition in which not only, as Marx prophesies, will "the narrow horizon of bourgeois legality" be surpassed – since there will be no further conflicts of interest – but also the much broader horizon of justice itself.[14]

25. Yet another application of the equality-principle is the maxim known as the Golden Rule, which runs: Do not unto others as you would not have them do unto you; or in positive terms: Do unto others as you would have them do unto you. What everyone wishes that others should not do to him, is to cause him pain; and what everyone wishes that they should do to him, is to cause him pleasure. Hence the Golden Rule amounts to the injunction: Inflict no pain on another, but give him pleasure. However, it all too frequently happens, that it gives a man pleasure to inflict pain on others. If that is a violation of the Golden Rule, the question arises: how should one behave towards such a violator of the rule? And that is just the question of justice. For if nobody were to give pain to another, and everybody were only to give him pleasure, there would simply be no problem of justice. But if one tries to apply the Golden Rule to the case of its own violation, it is at once apparent that this leads to absurd consequences. Nobody wishes to be punished, even when he has committed a crime. According to the Golden Rule, therefore, criminals should not be punished. A person may have nothing at all against others telling him lies, since – rightly or wrongly – he thinks himself clever enough to find out the truth and so protect himself against liars. But if so, then by the Golden Rule, he is permitted to lie. If this rule is taken literally, it must lead to the abolition of all morality and law. Now that is certainly not its intention; quite the reverse. Morality and law are supposed to be upheld by it. But if the Golden Rule is to be interpreted in terms of its intention, then it cannot establish, as it professes to do, a subjective criterion for right conduct, and a man cannot be

enjoined to act towards others as he would have them act towards himself. Such a subjective criterion is incompatible with any social order. The Golden Rule must be understood to establish an objective criterion. Its meaning must be: act towards others, as they ought to act towards you; and ought indeed to act according to an objective order. But then how ought they to act? That is the question of justice. And the answer to this question is not given by the Golden Rule, but is presupposed by it. And it can only be presupposed, because it is the order of positive morality and positive law which is presupposed in doing so.

VI

26. If the subjective criterion overtly contained in the Golden Rule is replaced in course of interpretation by an objective criterion, the rule will frame the injunction: Act in accordance with the general norms of the social order. Although this is a tautological formula, since every social order consists of general norms, and it is already implicit in the concept of a general norm that one should act in accordance with it, the Golden Rule, so interpreted, in fact inspired Immanuel Kant to that celebrated formulation of the categorical imperative which is the cardinal result of his moral philosophy, and the solution he offers to the problem of justice. It runs: Act only on that maxim of which you can at the same time will that it should be a universal law.[15] In other words, human conduct is good or just when it is determined by norms, of which the agent can or should will that they be binding on all men. But what are these norms of which we can or should will that they be universally binding? That is the crucial question of justice; and to this question the categorical imperative – like its prototype, the Golden Rule – gives no answer.

27. If one examines the concrete examples with which Kant attempts to illustrate the application of his categorical imperative, one is bound to conclude that they are in every case precepts of the traditional morality and positive law of his day. They are in no sense derived from the categorical imperative, as the theory makes out, for nothing can be derived from such an empty formula. They prove to be merely consistent with the categorical imperative. But every precept of any given social order is consistent with this principle, for it says no more than that a man should

act in accordance with general norms. Hence the categorical imperative, like the principle of "to each his own", or the Golden Rule, can serve as a justification for any given social order in general, and for any given general precept in particular, and has also been employed in this way. This possibility explains why these formulae, in spite of – indeed precisely because of – their utter emptiness, continue to be accepted as satisfying answers to the problem of justice, and will doubtless also be so accepted in the future.

VII

28. Another very characteristic example of the vain attempt to define the concept of an absolute justice by means of a rational, scientific, or at least quasi-scientific, method, is the ethics of Aristotle. It is an ethics of virtue, i.e., it aims at a system of virtues, among which justice is the chief or perfect virtue.[16] Aristotle claims to have found a scientific, viz. mathematico-geometrical method for defining virtues, that is, for answering the question of what is morally good. The moral philosopher – so Aristotle maintains – can discover the particular virtue whose nature he seeks to determine in a manner identical, or at least very similar, to that whereby a geometer can find the point equidistant between the two end-points of a line and dividing it into two equal halves. For virtue is a mean between two extremes, i.e., between two vices, one too little and one too much.[17] Thus the virtue of bravery, for example, is a mean between the vice of cowardice (a deficiency of courage) and the vice of rashness (excess of courage). This is the celebrated doctrine of the *Mesotes*, or mean. In order to assess it, we have to remember that a geometer can divide a line into two equal halves only on the assumption that both end-points are already given in advance. But if these are given, then the mid-point is given along with them, i.e., already determined in advance. If we know what vices are, we already know also what virtues are; for a virtue is the opposite of a vice. If mendacity is a vice, truthfulness is a virtue. But Aristotle presupposes the existence of vices as self-evident; and the vices he presupposes are those stigmatised as such by the traditional morality of his day. This means, however, that the ethics of the mean-doctrine only pretends to solve its problem; the problem, what is bad or a vice, and consequently, what is good or a virtue? For the question of what is good is answered along with the question of what is bad;

and the answering of the latter question abandons the Aristotelian ethic to the positive morality and law of the existing order of society. It is the authority of this social order – and not the formula of the mean – which decides what is too much and too little, which fixes the two extremes, i.e. the two vices, and hence the virtue lying between them. In assuming the validity of the existing social order, this ethic thereby justifies it. That is the true function of the tautological formula of the mean, which amounts to saying that good is what the existing social order considers good. It is a thoroughly conservative function: the maintenance of the existing order of society.

29. The tautological character of the mean-formula is particularly clearly evident in its application to the virtue of justice. Aristotle tells us that just conduct is the mean between doing injustice and suffering it. For the former is to have too much, the latter too little.[18] In this instance, the formula that virtue is the mean between two vices does not even make sense as a metaphor; for the injustice done, and the injustice suffered, are by no means two vices or evils; they are one and the same injustice, which one man does to another, and the other therefore suffers from the one. And justice is simply the opposite of this injustice. The crucial question, of what is injustice, is not answered by the formula of the mean. The answer is presupposed, and Aristotle quite self-evidently assumes injustice to be that which positive morality and law consider to be unjust. The true achievement of the mean-formula is not to define the nature of justice, but to reinforce the validity of the existing social order established in positive morality and law. The great political importance of this achievement preserves the Aristotelian ethic from such critical analysis as would demonstrate its scientific worthlessness.[19]

VIII

30. Both the metaphysical and the rationalistic types of legal philosophy make their appearance in the school of natural law, which dominated the scene during the seventeenth and eighteenth centuries, was almost entirely abandoned during the nineteenth, and yet is again acquiring influence in our own day. The doctrine of natural law maintains that there is a perfectly just ordering of human relations, which comes from nature,

either nature in general, or the nature of man as a being endowed with reason. Nature is depicted as a normative authority, as a sort of legislator. In the course of a careful analysis of nature, we can discover the norms immanent within her which prescribe what is right, and so just, for men to do. If nature is assumed to be God's creation, then the norms inherent in her – namely natural law – are an expression of the will of God. In that case, the theory of natural law has a metaphysical character. But if it is the nature of man as a being endowed with reason from which natural law is to be derived – without regard to any divine origin for this reason – if it is assumed that the principle of justice can be found in human reason – without recourse to a divine will – then the theory of natural law appears in a rationalistic guise. From the standpoint of a rational science of law, the religious and metaphysical version of the natural law theory does not come into the matter at all. But the rationalistic version is manifestly untenable. Nature, as a system of facts conjoined with one another according to the causal principle, has no will, and thus can prescribe no specific course of human conduct. From facts, i.e. from that which is or actually happens, no conclusion can be drawn as to that which ought to be or to happen. So far as the rationalistic theory of natural law attempts to derive norms for human conduct from nature, it rests on a fallacy. The same applies to the attempt to deduce such norms from human reason. Norms prescribing human conduct can only proceed from a will; and this will can only be a human one, if metaphysical speculation is ruled out. The claim that man should behave in a particular fashion – when perhaps he does not in fact so behave – can be established by human reason only on the assumption that, by an act of human will, a norm is set up prescribing this behaviour. Human reason can understand and describe, it cannot prescribe. To find norms for human behaviour in reason is the same illusion as that of extracting such norms from nature.

31. It is no wonder, therefore, that the various adherents of the natural law theory have deduced utterly incompatible principles of justice from divine nature, or found them in human nature.[20] According to one leading figure of this school, Robert Filmer, autocracy, absolute monarchy, is the only natural, and so just, form of government. But another equally outstanding natural law theorist, John Locke, shows by the same

method that absolute monarchy ought not to be regarded as a form of government at all, and that only democracy can be reckoned as such, since it alone accords with nature, and is therefore alone just. Most of the natural law theorists maintained that private property, the foundation of the feudal and capitalist orders of society, was a natural and therefore sacred and inalienable right, which nature or reason had granted to man; and hence that collective ownership or communal property, i.e., communism, is against nature and reason and therefore unjust. But the eighteenth century movement aiming at the abolition of private property and the establishment of a communist social order, which played a certain part during the French Revolution, also appealed to natural law; and its arguments have the same efficacy as those used to defend the private property of the existing order of society, namely none. For by the fallaciously grounded methods of the natural law theory one can in fact prove anything, and therefore nothing.

IX

32. If the history of human knowledge can teach us anything at all, it is the futility of attempting to discover by rational means an absolutely valid norm of just conduct, i.e., one that excludes the possibility of also regarding the opposite conduct as just. If we can learn anything at all from the intellectual experience of the past, it is that human reason can grasp only relative values, and hence that the judgement in which something is declared just can never advance any claim to exclude the possibility of an opposite value-judgement. Absolute justice is an irrational ideal. From the point of view of rational knowledge, there are only human interests, and thus conflicts of interest. To solve them, there are only two methods available: either to satisfy one interest at the expense of the other, or to engineer a compromise between the two. It is not possible to prove that one solution alone, and not the other, is just. If social peace is assumed to be the highest value, the compromise solution may appear to be just. But even the justness of peace is only a relative, not an absolute, form of justice.

33. But what is the morality of this relativistic philosophy of justice? Has it any morality at all? Is relativism not amoral, or even immoral, as

many suppose?[21] I do not share this view. The moral principle underlying a relativistic theory of value, or deducible from it, is the principle of tolerance, the demand, that is, that the religious or political outlook of others should be understood in a spirit of goodwill, even if one does not share it, and indeed precisely because one does not; and hence that peaceful expression of such views should not be prevented. It will be self-evident that a relativistic world-outlook engenders no right to absolute tolerance; it enjoins tolerance only within the framework of a positive legal order, which guarantees peace among its subjects, in that it forbids them any use of force, but does not restrict the peaceful expression of their opinions. Tolerance means freedom of thought. The highest of moral ideals have been compromised through the intolerance of those who have championed them. The bodies of heretics were not all that was burnt at the stakes kindled by the Spanish Inquisition in defence of the Christian religion, for one of Christ's principal teachings was also sacrificed: Judge not, that ye be not judged. During the frightful religious wars of the seventeenth century, in which the persecuted church was at one with the persecutor only in its will to destroy the other, Pierre Bayle, one of the great liberators of the human mind, was already arguing against those who believed an existing religious or political order could best be defended by intolerance towards the dissentients: "All disorder arises, not from toleration, but from intolerance". One of the most admirable pages in Austrian history is the edict of toleration of the Emperor Joseph II. If democracy is a just form of government, it is so only because it means freedom; and freedom means tolerance. But can democracy remain tolerant, if it is obliged to defend itself against anti-democratic intrigues? Yes, it can. To the extent that it does not repress peaceful expressions of anti-democratic views. It is precisely such tolerance which distinguishes democracy from autocracy. We are entitled to repudiate autocracy, and to be proud of our democratic form of government, only so long as we preserve this distinction. Democracy cannot defend itself by abandoning its own nature. But every régime, including a democratic one, has the right to put down by force, and to prevent by suitable means, attempts to overthrow it by force. The exercise of this right is in conflict neither with the principle of democracy, nor with that of tolerance. It may be hard in the process to draw a clear dividing-line between the dissemination of certain ideas and the preparation of a revolutionary coup. But the possibility of preserving democracy depends on the possibility of finding such a dividing-line. It may also be true that such line-drawing itself contains a certain danger. But it is the nature and pride of democracy to take this danger upon itself; and if it cannot endure such danger, it is not worthy of defence.

34. Since the heart of democracy is freedom, and freedom means tolerance, there is no other form of government so favourable to science and learning as democracy. For these can only flourish if they are free; and they are so, not only when they are free from without, i.e., are independent of political influences, but when they also are free inwardly, i.e., when complete freedom prevails in the play of argument and counter-argument. No doctrine can be suppressed in the name of science; for the soul of science is tolerance.

I began this essay with the question: What is justice? Now, at the end of it, I am well aware that I have not answered this question. My excuse is, that in this respect I am in the best of company. It would be more than presumptuous to lead my readers to believe that I could have succeeded where the greatest thinkers have failed. And in fact I do not know and cannot say what justice is, justice in the absolute, that beautiful dream of mankind. I must be content with a relative justice, and can only say what justice is for me. Since science is my calling, and thus the most important thing in my life, it is that justice under whose protection science, and with science, truth and sincerity, are able to flourish. It is the justice of freedom, the justice of peace, the justice of democracy, the justice of tolerance.

NOTES

* Vienna 1953. [Also published in English in *What is Justice?*, Berkeley 1957, pp. 1–27; a different translation Transl.]

1 Plato, *Laws* 663b, 662a, b (Transl. by A. E. Taylor).

2 Cf. my essay: 'Die Platonische Gerechtigkeit', *Kant-Studien* **38** (1933) 91ff.

3 *Matthew* V, 38, 44.

4 *Luke* XVIII, 29, 30.

5 *Luke* XIV, 26.

6 *Matthew* V, 45, 48.

7 *I Corinthians* III, 19.

8 *I Corinthians* II, 1ff.

9 *Philippians* III, 9.

[10] *Galatians* V, 6.
[11] *Romans* XIII 8 ff., *1 Corinthians* XIII, 1 ff.
[12] *Ephesians* III, 19.
[13] 'Zur Kritik des sozialdemokratischen Parteiprogramms', Aus dem Nachlass von Karl Marx. *Neue Zeit*, IX, **1** (1890–91) 361 ff.
[14] Cf. my *Sozialismus und Staat*, 2nd edn., 1923, pp. 90 ff.
[15] Immanuel Kant, *Fundamental Principles of the Metaphysics of Morals*, Section 2.
[16] Aristotle, *Nicomachean Ethics* 1129b.
[17] *Ibid.*, 1107a, 1106a, 1905b.
[18] *Ibid.*, 1133b.
[19] Cf. my essay: 'The Metamorphoses of the Idea of Justice', in *Interpretations of Modern Legal Philosophies, Essays in Honor of Roscoe Pound*, Oxford University Press, New York, 1947, pp. 399 ff.
[20] Cf. my essay: 'The Natural-Law Doctrine before the Tribunal of Science', *The Western Political Quarterly* **2** (1949) 481ff.
[21] Thus the view that justice is something relative, an opinion necessarily linked to legal positivism, and hence legal positivism itself, which recognises no absolute justice, have lately been held responsible for the totalitarian state. A very typical example in this respect is an anti-relativist work by the protestant theologian Emil Brunner: *Gerechtigkeit. Eine Lehre von den Grundgesetzen der Gesellschaftsordnung*, Zürich 1943 (English transl. by M. Hottinger, *Justice and the Social Order*, London 1945). Brunner maintains (p. 16) that the totalitarian state is "the ineluctable consequence of... a positivism void of faith and inimical to metaphysics and religion". This claim is obviously at variance with the undeniable fact that Plato's ideal State, the archetype of a totalitarian State, springs from his theory of Ideas, which is directed against relativism, aims at absolute values, and culminates in assuming the existence of an absolute good, incorporating an absolute justice. (Cf. my previously cited essay 'Die Platonische Gerechtigkeit', p. 116, and K. R. Popper, *The Open Society*, London 1945, vol. I *passim* and pp. 89 f.) If there is a connection between value-philosophy and politics, political absolutism, the autocracy of the totalitarian State, is associated with the belief in absolute values, while democracy with its characteristic demand for tolerance, is aligned with value-relativism. I pointed to this connection in my book *Vom Wesen und Wert der Demokratie*, 2nd. edn., Tübingen 1929.

Brunner, moreover, is not very consistent, for he feels himself obliged to admit that "the Church, which today protests, and rightly so, against the oppression it suffers at the hands of the totalitarian state, would do well to remember who first set the State the bad example of religious intolerance by using the secular arm to safeguard by force what can only spring from a free act of will. The Church should always bethink itself with shame that it was the first teacher of the totalitarian State at nearly every point" (p. 57). This is true enough; but it is true not because the Church teaches a positivism and relativism void of faith and inimical to religion and metaphysics, but rather because of – or in spite of – the fact that it teaches the very opposite, a belief in absolute justice.

Brunner's book is more a vindication than a refutation of relativism. In propounding his theory of "what is recognised as just by Christian faith" (p. 8), he sets out from the premise that either there is an absolute divine justice, or there is no justice whatever. "Either there is a valid criterion, a justice which stands above us all, a challenge presented *to* us, not *by* us, a standard rule of justice binding on every State and every system of law, or there is no justice, but only power organized in one fashion or another and setting itself up as law" (p. 16). The divine law of absolute justice is to be found, he thinks, in a "divine order of creation", which is presented as the Christian – rather than the rationalistic – version of natural law (pp. 78 f.). But having declared the belief in an absolute divine justice, the acceptance of the Christian law of nature – as an order distinct from positive law and capable of opposing it – to be inescapable, if a halt is to be called to the erosion of the idea of justice by relativistic positivism, he then admits – and this is the outcome of his doctrine of the absolute justice of Christian natural law – that all positive law can only be relatively just (p. 17). This means that in addition to absolute justice he also acknowledges a relative justice, although this embodies a contradiction. For an order which does not coincide with absolute justice is unjust, and so cannot, even relatively speaking, be just. There can no more be a relative alongside an absolute justice, than there can be an absolute alongside a relative. Brunner endorses this at bottom himself, when he is obliged to concede that belief in natural law should not be coupled with the notion "that a law of the State must not be obeyed if it conflicts with the law of nature, and hence is unjust" (p. 87). No State law can tolerate "competition ... by a second legal system. The laws of the State actually obtaining must possess a monopoly of binding legal force; the law of nature must claim no binding legal force for itself if the legal security of the State is to remain unshaken" (p. 87). A law of nature having no binding legal force cannot be the "valid criterion" which Brunner, on p. 16, declares absolute justice to be. A non-binding law of nature is no normative order at all, for the existence of such an order lies only in its power to bind. In this astonishing switch to relativistic legal positivism, Brunner professes to be following the theory of justice held by the Reformers, who "in their profound respect for the authority of the State and positive law" (p. 88), "took their stand clearly on the side of positive law, only granting to the law of nature the function of a criterion". (p. 87).

Now relativistic legal positivism itself maintains no more than that it is relatively just positive law which alone has legal binding force, not an absolutely just law of nature. If positivism declines to accept the latter even as a normative criterion, it does so because such an assumption harbours the possibility of justifying positive law, and as a science, relativistic legal positivism rejects the right to such a justification.

But of this possibility the Brunnerian theory of justice makes abundant use. For that which it proclaims to be the content of an absolutely just law of nature: State, family, individual freedom and private property, is essentially the foundation of the positive non-communist legal orders prevailing at the present day, which are thus legitimised in principle as conforming to absolute divine justice. Only communism, on this theory, is in conflict with the absolute justice of God. But even the communist State, which as a totalitarian State is initially damned as "a monster of injustice" (p. 17), as the "acme of injustice" (p. 137), is eventually acknowledged once more as a State, and hence as "God's ordinance" (p. 71), for "even the unjust State is still a State" (p. 174), and its legal order is granted a certain degree of justice, i.e., a relative justice, as an "order of peace" (p. 176). But in this the totalitarian communist State does not differ essentially from the capitalist States, whose legal orders are also acknowledged to be only relatively just.

A theory of absolute justice which deals in such palpable contradictions can make no claim, in its polemic against relativistic legal positivism, to be considered in any way scientific; even if it were not itself prepared to declare in advance – as Brunner does in the preface to his book – that its purpose "is not primarily theoretical, but practical, as all theological work should be" (p. 8).

CHAPTER II

THE IDEA OF NATURAL LAW*

1. Ever since men have thought about their mutual relationships, ever since "society" has been a problem at all – and this problem is older than any other topic of knowledge, even than that which we call 'nature' – the question of a *just order* of human relations has never ceased to be a burning one. And although this question has penetrated to the roots of our thinking and feeling and willing as scarcely any other has done, although the best minds, the most passionate hearts, the most iron hands have wrestled with it, although the whole of history, the whole unhappy history of mankind, can be seen as but a single constantly renewed attempt to answer this question, at a most frightful and infinitely costly sacrifice of blood, it is no more solved for us today than at the moment when this fearsome mystery of justice first flashed into a man's mind, into the mind of the *first man*.

This is certainly strange and disturbing, and must strike us as stranger and more disturbing still, if we compare the immense advances in the far more youthful field of *science* with this outcome, this lack of an outcome, in the *theory of society*. The long and short of which remains – despite all the attempts of modern sociology to align itself with natural science, to resolve society into nature and social theory into natural science – the problem of a just order of human conduct. This whole trend in social theory, away from the normative towards a causal statement of the problem, means nothing more nor less than a denaturing of the object of knowledge. It cannot be wholly explained by saying that the great success of natural science during the 19th and 20th centuries has commended its specific method – that of establishing causal laws – as an example to be followed, and indeed as scientific method *per se*; whereby social theory, which as ethics, politics, theology and natural law, had hitherto possessed a purely normative orientation, was forced in a manner to dissolve itself. The transformation, already now largely accomplished, of the theory of human relations, from a doctrine of justice, and thus a theory of value, into a sociology offering causal explanations of the reality of actual behaviour, and consequently free of value, is at bottom a turning-away of knowledge from a subject which it has lost the hope of mastering; it is the – involuntary – admission by an age-old discipline that, perhaps only for the time being, it is abandoning its most characteristic problem as insoluble.

There is an essential contrast existing between the idea of "nature" and the idea of "justice"; between the conception of everything real which actually occurs in a manner directly or indirectly perceivable to the senses and must take place according to the *causal law*, and the notion of that which – even if it does not actually happen – *ought* nevertheless to occur according to another law, a *norm*, and should at least come about within the field of human conduct. In the light of this contrast, which our thinking must preserve if the idea of value, and especially that of justice, are not to be lost beyond recall, it must be seen as a paradox of such thinking, that the notion of a "just" order of human conduct has always appeared as that of a "natural" order, not only among the French and Germans, but also among the Greeks, the master teachers of social theory. "φύσει δίκαιον", "lex naturalis", "l'ordre naturel", "das Naturrecht", "natural law" – they all seek merely to express what is "just". In this strange play of words, which for the notion of the highest *value* makes use of precisely the same term which also signifies the very opposite, namely the highest *reality*, one might be led to discern a deeper meaning. Is it perhaps the shadow of resignation which language casts ahead upon thought when the latter has so far struggled in vain to solve a problem whose insolubility the former seems to point to in advance; since it already abolishes the presupposition of the posing of the problem, namely the *contrast* between value and reality, ought and is, society, i.e., *justice*, and *nature*, and makes the just the natural, and the natural the just?

2. The word "nature", especially in its adjectival form "natural", is able to take on many meanings, whereby its sense may undergo a protean transformation into its exact opposite. In the present context, where "natural" means the same as "just", "right" or "appropriate", the meaning chiefly in view is that which arises from the contrast with "artificial". By a "natural" order we mean one which does not rest on a human and therefore inadequate will, an order which is not created

"arbitrarily", but comes about "on its own", so to speak, from a basic fact somehow *objectively* given, and thus existing independently of man's subjective willing, though it can somehow be grasped and recognised by him; from a basic principle not originally produced by human understanding or will, yet capable of being reproduced thereby. This objective fact or basic principle is "nature", or, in its religious personification, "God". For the *doctrine of justice*, which is how we apprehend the *theory of natural law*, it makes no essential difference whether it seeks to derive the desired "just" or "natural" order from "nature" or from "God"; save only that – having been systematically evolved for the purpose by theology – the concept of God more evidently claims to embody not only the idea of supreme causality, but also that of the highest justice. It is of greater importance, however, whether the source of natural law is conceived to be nature as a whole, the nature of things and relations – from which one has only to read it off, as it were, as a norm or rule lying immanent therein; or whether it is the physical and mental nature of man which is held to furnish such a source. For this implies a turning-away from the originally objective principle to a more or less subjective one, a deviation or falling-off from the tendency to objectivity which is inherent in the idea of justice; and hence a diversion from the pure idea of natural law to that of positive law. The equivalence we postulate here between the ideas of God and nature in regard to the doctrine of natural law, is apparent, however, in this, that the same turn from a more objective to a more subjective principle also recurs within a theory relying on God as the source of natural law (i.e., the just order), and hence within a theological scheme. As can be shown by a critical analysis of natural law methods, it is by no means indifferent whether the natural order of human life is deduced from God's wisdom, i.e., from the divine *reason*, or merely from God's *will*. To base it on the divine will, which is elevated above the lawfulness of divine reason, and thus – as omnipotence – is exalted into divine arbitrariness, is entirely parallel to the more subjectivist deduction from the nature of man, the divine personality which finds expression precisely in the *will*, representing merely an anthropomorphic extension to infinity. The natural law to be derived from the nature of *man* already approximates closely to the positive law flowing from the human *will*. The contrast between a theory of natural law founded on *reason*, which essentially finds expression in *laws*, and one which relies on the *omnipotence* of God, divorced from any subjection to law, already sets forth clearly the relative opposition between natural and positive law within a higher sphere.

Hence the difference which obtains between a theory of natural law proceeding from "nature" or "God", and one which seeks to create the just order from "reason", is also not relevant; but only so long as we are dealing with an *objective* reason, in which the purpose of nature, the wisdom of God, are easily recognised, and in contrast to which human reason is merely an inadequate reproduction. It is a different matter, however, when there is no thought at all of such a natural or divine objective reason, and recourse is had wholly and solely to human reason, such as it may be, as a final authority. For here we again encounter that selfsame subjectivist turn, with the consequences referred to above, namely that the whole contrast from which the idea of natural law acquires its specific meaning, the contrast between the objective or natural – independent of man – and the subjective or artificial – arbitrarily created by him – is done away with or deprived of force.

3. It is only from the opposition between natural and positive law that the essential nature of either of them can be understood. Positive law, too, is an order of human conduct; but it differs from the "natural" order in that it is merely an "artificial" one, i.e., a human creation, and as such presents itself purely as the work of man. Insofar as it proceeds from the inadequate human will, it always appears more or less "arbitrary" in comparison with the "natural" order. And hence, in contrast to the latter, it is not necessarily just, but may also perhaps be unjust. The "artificial" or positive order finds in the "natural" order its standard of merit or demerit. From the standpoint of *natural law*, positive law is always good or bad, just or unjust, according to its degree of coincidence or conflict with natural law.

But positive law, in its own intrinsic sense, is "law", i.e., a valid, binding order, independently of this relation to natural law; and is so, therefore, even when by virtue of its contradiction of the latter it must be reckoned unjust. This possibility even of an "unjust positive law" is of the greatest importance for a proper definition of the difference between the two systems of norms: for the difference in their respective *sources* – in the one case nature (God or reason), in the other the human will – marks the difference between two essentially distinct *grounds of validity*. For the "source" of a norm is nothing else but its specific ground of validity. For natural law this is an objective, or at least relatively objective principle, while for positive law it is a subjective, or at least relatively subjective one. The norm of natural law holds good by virtue of its inner content, because it is "good", "right" or "just"; the norm of positive law, because it has been created only in a particular way, specially; because it has been laid down by a particular man, who for that very reason is counted an "authority". It is precisely in this indeed, that we find the "positivity" of a law – vis-à-vis natural law – that it has been "posited" through human willing; a ground of validity which for this reason is quite essentially alien to natural law, in that the latter, *qua* "natural" order, is not created by man, and ranks indeed as *intrinsically* incapable of creation by human agency. It is the contrast between a *material* and a *formal principle of validity*. The "formalism" of positive law – repeatedly stressed and often most misguidedly complained of – has its chief source in this formal principle of validity. It is an inveterate prejudice of the natural lawyer which, in total misapprehension of the special nature of positivism, repeatedly sounds the reproach of "formalism" against the scientific treatment of positive law.

4. It accords with the idea of natural law as a "natural" order that its norms, since they proceed directly from nature, God or reason, are just as self-evident as the laws of logic; and that it therefore requires no *coercion* in order to realise them. This is the second point on which natural law differs essentially from positive law. The latter is in essence an *order of coercion*, and must be so – in direct contrast to natural law – because its norms derive from the decision of a human authority, and if only because this source so radically distinguishes them from natural law, they cannot have the property of immediate self-evidence. The content of the norms of positive law is in no way possessed of that inner "necessity" which – owing to their origin – is typical of the norms of natural law; they do not regulate a way of life in such a fashion that it could not also be otherwise regulated by norms of positive law; and hence it cannot be presumed among those whose conduct is determined by these norms that in coming under them they simultaneously perceive them to be right or just. One has to reckon with the possibility that men may behave

otherwise than as the norms of positive law prescribe. It is precisely this factor which makes coercion an indispensable constituent of positive law. The theory which holds *coercion to be an essential feature of law* is a positivistic theory; it relates only to positive law. And all efforts to dismiss the element of coercion from law as inessential are ultimately intended *to wipe out the difference between positive and natural law*; whether consciously or otherwise, they largely result from the endeavour to make positive law itself rank in some way as natural law. They are attempts which – predominantly from political motives – are aimed at conferring on positive law a justification foreign to its nature.

If positive law is described as an order of coercion, and its norm as a coercive one, this implies that it is a norm *ordaining* coercion. Nor is it so-called mental coercion which is intended here. The latter also attaches to the norm of natural law – and attaches to it, *ideally*, in a very much higher degree than to the norm of positive law. For the consciousness, the idea, of a natural law norm is supposed to carry with it the feeling of that "inner necessity" which renders superfluous, and even meaningless, the notion of any "coercion", i.e., the coercive ordinance peculiar to positive law. The latter is an "external" constraint, an act of coercion which one man has to impose on another under quite specific circumstances. And this is also the *basic form of the statement of positive law* [Rechtssatz: see p. XXVI f. above]: that under specific conditions a specific act of coercion is to be imposed. If – pursuing matters beyond the formally closed character of positive law – we ask for its purpose, it can be stated that the threat of coercive action is supposed to secure coercion-avoiding behaviour (by the agent threatened with coercion), as the social situation which is somehow desired. As an order threatening coercion, positive law is a specific social and technical means towards ends whose determination lies beyond the cognisance of positive law. Its form, i.e., the *basic form of the legal statement*, is sufficiently characterised as a hypothetical judgement, whose "ought" conjoins a particular circumstance as condition to a particular act of coercion as consequence. The consequence laid down as obligatory in the positive legal statement does not, however, decree the behaviour of *one* man only, but must at least refer to *two* of them. One is the man *against* whom the ordained act of coercion is directed, and who by the ordainment of the coercive act so directed is obligated in positive law (I ought, or am obligated, not to steal, or I ought, or am obligated, to repay a loan received, means in *positive* law *nothing else* but that if I steal, I ought to be punished, if I fail to repay a loan received, there should be execution against me). The other man is he who must inflict the coercive act upon the first. This is what is characteristic of positive law, the "organ" exercising coercion which – itself "obligated" in a specific manner to its coercion-realising behaviour – *confronts* him who was initially obligated. The development of positive law inevitably brings it about that realisation of the coercive act is entrusted, not – as is still the case under primitive law – to the injured party, but to a functionally specialised "organ" in the narrower sense, the "judge" or "official". If we first see in the formation of such functionally specialised organs an "organisation", in the narrower technical sense of the word, then positive law – owing to its nature as an arbitrary human institution whose norms, failing self-evidence of their correctness, must be norms of coercion, and owing to the associated need for an organ to exercise that coercion – has an innate tendency to evolve from a coercive order into a specific coercive "organisation". This coercive order, more especially if it is a coercive organisation, is the *state*. And hence we may also say that *the state is the perfected form of positive law*.

5. Now at this point arises a further difference from natural law. The basic form of *its* norms is also, to be sure, that a particular circumstance as condition is conjoined by the "ought" to a particular consequence. Even the norm of natural law is expressed by a hypothetical judgement of what ought to be. But – as already emerges from the foregoing – the consequence is not an act of coercion. It is then and there, rather, the right or just conduct of the man obligated by the norm, the conduct to which, under given conditions, he is in each case obliged. It is this consequence which on natural law principles must be given with complete selfevidence here, once the condition has made its appearance. It is therefore at times envisaged as being itself, so to speak, contained in the conditioning circumstances, in the life-situation, in the "facts of the case". For this very reason there is no need here for the act of coercion characteristic of positive law. The natural law norm is realised as it were, "by itself". Everyone to whom it applies himself posits the consequence which is immediately evident to him once the condition has

come about. In the natural law statement, therefore, the consequence contains the conduct of only *one* man, namely the person obligated; and his obligation is grounded, not by the threat of a coercive act, but simply by the fact that his conduct is laid down as obligatory. And hence in the consequence decreed by the natural law statement there is an absence of that dualistic pattern characteristic of the statement of positive law; the person obligated is not confronted by any "organ" entrusted with the act of coercion against him. And along with the "organ" there lapses here the possibility and necessity for an "organisation": *the form of natural law is not the state*; neither the "state" in the broader sense of a coercive order, nor in any sense the "state" in its narrower acceptation of a functionally specialised coercive "organisation". If by "anarchy" we mean, not absolute lack of order, but only the idea of a non-coercive order in which the state is absent, then natural law can be described as an "anarchic" order. Every *anarchistic* theory, in fact, is nothing else but a *doctrine of natural law*. The presuppositions of anarchism are the specific conditions of the idea of natural law. In contrast to this stands the essential conjunction of positive law with the state, and indeed the identity of the two from the standpoint of the coercive order. All attempts to divorce law from the state, to apprehend law and the state as two distinct entities, the whole *dualism of law and state* in all the many forms it takes, are at deepest bottom and in ultimate aim *derivative from natural law*.

6. Just as natural and positive law govern the same subject-matter, and relate, therefore, to the same norm-*object*, namely the mutual relationships of men (whose order, so constituted, is "society"), so both also have in common the universal form of this governance, namely *obligation* [Sollen]. This merely gives expression to the fact that both natural and positive law are *norms*, or more accurately, norm-*systems*. One may deny that the two concepts – as is suggested in advance by the delusive appearances of language – are species under the common genus of "law", if, by starting from the standpoint of positive law, one conceives of "law" solely as an order of coercion. But then we still have as a common category, embracing both natural and positive law, the concept of "norm", which is in fact a mere expression of *obligation*. In that case, however, the relation of so-called natural to positive law

will be no different from that of *morality*, which – in spite of all attempts that have been made in this direction – will turn out difficult to distinguish from natural law. To confine the one to the external, the other to the internal behaviour of man – the only attempt worth serious consideration – proves futile as soon as we recognise the indissoluble ties connecting "outer" and "inner" behaviour, perceive how natural law also relates to inner, and morality also necessarily to outer behaviour, and more especially when we notice the thoroughly *social* character even of those norms that are described as "moral".

If "ought" is described as the common form, or – to put it otherwise – as the element of lawfulness in both natural and positive law, this means that in either case, in the natural law statement as in that of positive law (i.e., the legal enactment), the specific conjunction of condition with consequence – which is the basic form of a "*law*" – is effected by means of the "ought"; whereas in the system of nature, in the law of nature or causal law, the condition is conjoined with the consequence, as cause and effect, in terms of "must". It is precisely in this difference in the terms of conjunction that we find the crucial distinction between norm and natural (causal) law, upon which the whole opposition between society and nature is built. Yet natural law theory is actually at times inclined to abolish this distinction. It is led to do so by the notion that in the natural law statement the consequence follows from the condition with such immediate self-evidence, that any "external" coercion is superfluous, that here the consequence is realised by itself, as it were, and with "inner necessity". This "necessity" (which is really just another word for "lawfulness", and serves equally to signify both causal and normative lawfulness) it then misinterprets as causal, and thus as natural necessity, and connects the consequence with the condition in the natural law statement as if it was a causal connection, in the manner, therefore, of a "must" and not an "ought". The law as a legal rule is transformed into a law of nature. The earlier theory of natural law actually referred to the supreme principle of justice as *lex naturalis*, the law of nature, without becoming clearly aware of its difference from the causal law; which is indeed connected with the fact that the concept of law as such originally made its appearance in the field of the normative, and still retains its primary normative meaning, now that it has been taken over – at first without clear distinction – by scientific thought. Yet this still reacts, up to a point, on the meaning of the natural lawyer's *lex naturalis*, which has its consequences in the *naturalistic tendency* within natural law theory, to which reference has just been made. The "natural" order sought in "natural law" is discerned in the scientific, i.e., causally determined reality of actual events. The result of this shift in the object of cognition is the doctrine of "might is right", which is merely an affirmation of the actual in a normative terminology. The problem of natural law has thereby laid aside its specifically evaluative character, has thus descended from the normative plane, and in this way has forfeited, in terms of method, any possibility of a relationship with positive law. It is essentially the same shift which makes itself felt in more recent jurisprudence as the demand for a "*sociological theory of law*". It has an intrinsic connection with the tendency in contemporary legal theory to deny the *coercive character* of positive law and its *identity with the state*. For the ultimate motive to which we must trace the naturalistic and sociological movement in legal theory is the endeavour to vindicate positive law as the "real" law, as the order given necessarily, that is, with "*natural* necessity", and hence as the "natural" order; to represent positive law as natural law, and hence to make it legitimate. We are also involved here with the tendency to abolish the boundary between natural and positive law, in that the normative lawfulness typical of natural and positive law alike is replaced by the causal lawfulness of the "must", which is essentially alien to them both.

7. This lawfulness of the '*ought*' – if it is to rank as the form not only of natural but of positive law – can be understood only in an entirely *relative* and *formal* sense. It is first necessary to recognize as *relative* the contrast between *is* and *ought*. For positive law appears *in relation to natural law* as an artificial thing, i.e., as something "posited" through an empirical act of man's will taking place in the realm of *being*, in the sphere of actual happenings, and hence as a *being*, a reality, to which natural law stands contrasted as a *value*; which gives rise, indeed, to the possibility of a positive law having value or disvalue. As a norm, on the other hand, positive law, from its own immanent standpoint, is an ought, and thus a value, and as such confronts the reality of man's actual behaviour, evaluating it as legal or illegal. The problem of the *positivity* of law consists precisely in this, that it figures simultaneously

as both 'ought' and 'is', although these two categories logically exclude one another.

But then we must especially beware of the error – only too often committed – of identifying the category of what ought to be with the idea of the "good", "right" or "just" in a *material* sense, insofar as we seek to apprehend natural and positive law as normative, and yet wish to distinguish them. Only in the norm which appears as natural law does the "ought" carry with it that sense of the *absolute*, which we are accustomed to associate with the notion of the "just" as such. If positive law also gives expression to an "ought" – which is unavoidable if, according to its intrinsic meaning, it is apprehended as a norm – this can then have only a *relative* sense. To be sure, even if something is declared to be law only in the positive sense, what is meant to be expressed by this is that it is somehow "right", somehow "just". But yet if the possibility must remain open, that something which is merely positive law is from any particular standpoint wrong or unjust, the "rightness" or "justice" intended along with the idea of positive law can only be a *relative* one. "*Relative*" means that an act ordained by a statement of positive law is reckoned "obligatory" and hence as "right" or "just", only upon a *presupposition* whose "rightness" or "justice" is not, however, itself guaranteed. The "ought" of positive law can never be other than a *hypothetical* one. And this necessarily follows from the nature of the *ground of validity* which distinguishes positive from natural law. The norms of positive law are "valid" (or, what comes to the same, they "oblige") not because, like those of natural law, they derive from nature, God or reason, and thus from a principle of the *absolutely good*, right or just, from an *absolutely supreme value*, but because they are created in a certain way, are posited by a particular man. As to the value of this method of creation, of this man who functions as a positive legal authority, nothing categorical is thereby stated at all; this value is – *hypothetically* – presupposed. *On the presupposition* that one ought to obey the commands of a particular absolute monarch, or conduct oneself according to the decrees of a particular popular assembly or particular parliament, the commands of this monarch, the decrees of this assembly or parliament, are lawful, the norms thereby brought into existence are "valid", the content of these enactments "ought" to take place. Just as there corresponds to the idea of natural law the *absolute* validity of its norms, so to that of positive law there corresponds a purely *hypothetical and relative* normative validity; which is to say, that its norms are valid only if we presuppose or assume a *basic norm* instituting the supreme legal authority, whose own validity neither is nor can be grounded within the sphere of positive law. It is precisely in this – for many reasons difficult – renunciation of an absolute, material justification, in this self-denying restriction of itself to a purely hypothetical, formal grounding by way of the basic norm, that we find the essential characteristic of positivism vis-à-vis the theory of natural law. Positivism and (epistemological) relativism belong together, just as natural law theory and (metaphysical) absolutism do. Every attempt to shatter the purely relative and hypothetical basis of positive law, to get beyond it somehow, whether covertly or openly, to an absolute justification – and for obvious political reasons, this attempt must repeatedly be made – signifies an abolition of the distinction between positive and natural law, an incursion of natural law theory into the scientific treatment of positive law, and – if an analogy with the sciences is permitted – an intrusion of metaphysics into the field of experience.

That in virtue of its provenance from an absolute value, natural law lays claim to *absolute* validity, is equivalent to saying that – in accordance with its pure idea – it makes its appearance as an *eternal, unalterable* norm. Positive law, by contrast, in its purely hypothetical and relative validity, is inherently an order capable throughout *of change*, to meet spatially or temporally changing circumstances. If natural law theory, as the analysis of its specific methods demonstrates, is constantly inclined – directly or indirectly – to abandon or weaken the postulate of unalterability; if in place of, or along with, the absolute, it upholds a purely hypothetico-relative natural law and declares it to be changeable and adapted to particular circumstances; if it thereby seeks to erect a communicating bridge from pure natural law to positive law; – this erasure of the boundary between the two norm-systems is also undertaken in the conscious or unconscious intention of vindicating the hypothetico-relatively valid system of positive law, with its essentially changeable content and constant subjection to change, as natural law, or at least as a kind of natural law.

8. The comparison of natural with positive law, which illuminates the

nature of the one in relation to that of the other, eventually leads to a point at which there appears no difference of principle between the two, but rather a fundamental nature common to both; yet here, precisely, we encounter the whole *problem of natural law*. It is the necessity that exists – a necessity given with every normative order, a natural law system no less than a positive legal order – for an *individualising* (or rendering concrete) of the *general* (abstract) norms. Here, where it is a matter of *actualising* natural law, where its norms must be brought directly, exactly as with those of positive law, to the real facts of social life which it governs, because they have to be *applied* to those facts, the question arises whether natural law can maintain its existence above and beyond all "positivity", whether – as its idea requires – it is possible as a system of norms distinct and independent from positive law, *whether natural law as such is therefore possible at all.*

In the following enquiry, the existence of an objective order of natural law is to be presupposed. The question, from what cognitive sources and by what cognitive means the norms of this order are obtained, is to be taken as answerable, and as somehow answered. Once the material content of natural law is assumed to be assured, it remains only to establish the form in which this content presents itself. Like any normative order, the order of natural law must necessarily be thought of first of all in a general, abstract form. In so doing it makes no difference whether, as is commonly done, one assumes a *single* supreme principle, a highest rule of justice, from which, in some manner appropriate to the diversity of the objects to be regulated, the various rules of law are obtained, albeit still in a general form requiring further individualisation; or whether the establishment of the general norms which constitute natural law is conceived in some other fashion. The primary form of natural law is in any case, like that of positive law, a general or abstract one, even if it be thought possible, as likewise sometimes happens, to make a direct application of the supreme principle of justice, the basic norm of natural law, to the concrete facts of the case. Such a possibility is not in fact ruled out even in the system of positive law, if the latter confines itself to empowering an authority to decide or enact as he thinks fit in each particular case. The smaller the diversity of content in the primary manifestation of the legal order, the more abstract and general it must be kept. The belief that a social order could consist entirely of individual concrete norms governing only the particular case, rests on a delusion. In positive law it overlooks the basic norm which initially institutes the norm-giving authority and enjoins obedience to all his commands; in natural law, the supreme and yet material principle of justice which is essential to it. Only in this *general* form does the "legal" character of the order find expression, does the "order" first secure itself as such at all, does it raise itself from a state of pure "arbitrariness" and naked anarchy. In this connection, the relativity of the contrast between order (legality) and arbitrariness deserves to be noted. (Positive law presents itself, indeed, as relative arbitrariness in relation to the "natural" order). And by "anarchy" here we mean a complete absence of order. Nor, on the other hand, should we go so far as is sometimes done in identifying the element of "generality" directly with "reason", and so perceiving the "rational" already in every general order; a tendency which stems from the ambition to portray and so legitimise positive law under all circumstances as rational, and hence as natural law.

The general (abstract) norm is only *one*, however, and not *the* manifestation of the normative order as such. At all costs we must avoid the fatal, but alas, now traditional error, that law exists only in the general form, that all law is comprised in general norms, and that "statute" is the general norm with which law is identical. The *hierarchical theory of legal structure* has exposed this error in all its consequences, and – one hopes – has finally put an end to it. If the theory of positive law has clung so long to the prejudice of law as comprised in statute (the general norm), this is certainly to be attributed to specific political motives. This error, as will soon appear, has its ultimate root in *natural law thinking*.

The general norm cannot be the sole manifestation of law, because in order to achieve its appointed goal it must be applied to the concrete case, and because this application is throughout an act of *generating* or *creating* law, whose product must equally be regarded as "law", because and insofar as it is a norm, a legal norm, albeit an individual one, valid only for the concrete situation, the particular case. In spite of the logical priority which the general norm has over the individual one, it should not be overlooked that law in the general norm is still in an unfinished state; and then one must perceive that it is precisely in the individual norm that the idea of law finds its true fulfilment. Every normative order – the natural law order no less than that of positive law – evolves, therefore, basically in two stages, if we merely have regard to the two main phases in which law transforms itself from its general to its individual, from its abstract to its concrete shape. We shall see later on why, in the system of pure natural law, the second stage, which even at this point can and must be distinguished from the first, is more easily overlooked, why the theory of natural law has paid no attention to the hierarchical arrangement of the legal order, and hence believes itself driven to apprehend law simply as a general norm. But this is just the question at issue here, namely whether and to what extent the idea of natural law can be sustained, precisely in view of the individualising of the general norm which is also unavoidable in the system of natural law (and in which process we may perceive the "realising" of natural law).

9. The process of individualising (or rendering concrete), i.e., the process wherein a general norm, whether of positive or natural law, is "applied" to an individual situation, a concrete "case", proceeds *in two directions*, corresponding to the basic structure of the legal statement. The general statement of this type unites two circumstances together by means of the "ought": a specific condition and a specific consequence. In the system of natural law, for example, if two persons have come to an agreement together, then each of them ought to act in accordance with the agreement (*pacta sunt servanda*); or, to take a proposition of positive law, if anyone has committed theft, he ought to be punished by the magistrate with loss of liberty. The *first* act of individualising (or rendering concrete) the general norm consists in establishing the actual existence (in "reality") of a circumstance laid down in the general norm as the condition of a consequence. For example, that two particular men actually did, at a specific time and place, give concordant expression to a decision of perfectly definite import, or that a particular man, at a specific time and place, took away from another a determinate thing belonging to that other, against the latter's will. The act of individualising which relates to the conditioning circumstance is also somewhat inaccurately described as "subsumption of the circumstance under the norm". More is comprised in this, as we shall

shortly see, than the purely *logical* function of subsuming an instance under a universal. Nor is it just "the" circumstance, to which this act of individualising relates, for it is only one of the pair of circumstances coupled together in the general norm. And lastly, subsumption occurs, not under "the norm", but only under the *general* norm. It is not, as the traditional account would have it, that we have on the one side the norm under which the real circumstance is subsumed, and on the other side the circumstance embedded in natural reality. For between the general norm and the real circumstance there is interposed the individual concrete norm created in the act of concretion, which in its function relating to the conditioning circumstance, of establishing that a circumstance designated in the general norm is present, creates in a *constitutive* way the precondition for the realising of a concrete consequence. This so-called "subsumption" of the circumstance under the general norm is thus an act of *creating* law, an essential constituent of the process in which the law is "posited", whereby, in fact, it is a "positive" law.

The *second* act of the individualising process consists in the laying-down of a consequence determined according to content, time and place. It must first be established *which* consequence as such is assigned in the general norm to any such previously established circumstance; and since the *general* definition of the consequence in the general norm is not sufficient, all further determinations must be adduced which are needed for a concrete consequence to be realised. The statement of natural law that we mentioned earlier, for example, contains only a blanket definition in regard to the consequence as such; since the consequence here consists in acting according to the agreement, the establishment of the conditioning circumstance coincides with the establishment of the consequence. Only through the establishment of the conditioning circumstance can it be determined what each of the contracting parties has to do, namely that which was actually agreed upon. But even this agreement will by no means provide a *complete* definition of what they are obliged to. Supposing it was a loan agreement, the bargain actually struck may have left it open *when* or *where* the loan is to be repaid, and whether or what interest is to be charged. But even if all this had been foreseen, there would still remain over a wealth of determinations, which of necessity intervene between a norm and its realisation. In the case of the positive law statement, matters are much the same. It imposes on theft, say, a penalty of imprisonment extending from one to five years, and leaves it to the judgement of the magistrate to determine the concrete amount according to the particular circumstances of the actual crime. But even if no such discretion is granted in the general norm, the determination, for example, of the date the sentence is to run from, the place of punishment and so on, can only come about through an act of judgement which individualises the statute. The most perfect possible definition of the consequence is eventually approximated by its carrying-out, i.e., the positing of the appropriate circumstance in the real world.

10. At this point we must draw attention to an important and crucial distinction which obtains between an ethico-juridical, i.e., *normative* system and a system of *scientific laws*. This distinction results from the different type of lawfulness prevailing in the two systems, and needs stressing all the more in that natural law theory, as already noted earlier, tends on occasion to obliterate it, insofar as it is inclined to interpret the legal precept as a sort of law of nature. Yet if they are actually compared together, a very characteristic difference emerges precisely in regard to the *conditioning circumstance*. In mathematics and geometry, this condition is virtually *presupposed*, and hence there is no concern whatever about establishing its concrete fulfilment (thus if it is required to prove the Pythagorean theorem, that in a right-angled triangle the square on the hypotenuse is equal to the sum of the squares on the other two sides, the question *whether* a right-angled triangle is present, i.e., whether the one drawn on the blackboard is actually right-angled or not, does not arise, since this is *presupposed*). Where this is not the case, the question as to the individual presence of the circumstance given generally in the natural law as condition (cause) of a consequence (effect), receives in physics a virtually automatic answer *from the effect*. For if the effect expected according to the law, on the assumption that a circumstance foreseen therein as cause is present, does *not* take place, this means that the assumption of such a circumstance was *erroneous*, and that some other circumstance than that supposed was present. Thus if one dips a thermometer into a chemical compound which, according to a law of chemistry, has the property of generating heat, and the mercury fails to rise, one is driven to conclude that no such compound was present,

i.e., that the conditioning circumstance designated by the natural law to be applied was not actually in force.

In the ethico-juridical, or normative system, and especially also in that of natural law, the case is essentially different. Here the consequence is not so related to the condition, that from the appearance of the one it is possible to infer the existence of the other. For here there is no *naturally necessary* connection between the two; it is the *ought* in this case, not the *must* of causal law, which conjoins the two circumstances together. In spite of the appearance of the condition, the realisation of the consequence may not take place; and even though the circumstance specified in the law as condition of the consequence is *not* in fact present, the consequence may still come about. *Whether* the circumstance laid down in the law as condition of a specific consequence is actually present, is therefore, in the normative system, a critical question which must be answered first of all, because here the consequence does not, as in the system of nature, become actual "on its own", i.e., bound to occur with *natural necessity* (and *bound* so to occur, even if the law of nature relates to human behaviour), but is required, rather, to be posited by the *act of a man's will*; and so *may* also *not* be posited even though the condition is present; and because the man only ought to posit this consequence here if it is decided, i.e., again established *merely by a human act*, that the condition has come about.

11. This situation is of the greatest importance for an assessment of the *possibility* of natural law. For even if we assume forthwith the existence of an objective natural law, i.e., of a "natural" order uncreated by man and independent of any human choice, we still have to admit that the individualising of its at first only generally given norms is possible *only through a human act*, that human thinking, feeling and willing are indispensable for the realisation of natural law. Only in its general form as an abstract principle of justice, as a general norm, can natural law be envisaged in the sphere ideally assigned to it, transcending the empirical world of man. As soon as it has to be applied to the concrete case or individual circumstance – and that is obviously the final goal appropriate to the inherent purpose of both natural and positive law – it has to make use of human acts. The second stage of natural law must be the work of man; at this level its order can no longer be "natural"

in any strict sense, and must be an "artificial" one. But this means nothing more nor less than that natural law, at the stage of the individual norm, must become a "positive" law, i.e., a law posited by the act of man. The *process of individualising*, to which natural law is no less subject than positive law, is (if it is natural law, however presupposed, whose general norms are being applied) *at once and necessarily a process of positivisation*, at least in a *formal* sense; so far, that is, as it can still be assumed that universal natural law finds full expression in the individual norms so produced. True as this is of the establishing of the conditioning circumstance, if is truer still, as we shall see later on, of the laying down of the consequence.

Here, however, there exists a certain quantitative, if not qualitative, difference between natural law, as *ideally* constituted, and positive law. In the system of natural law, the act of individualising which relates to the conditioning circumstance is the concern of the very person directly obligated by the general norm to a realisation of the consequence, and not, as in the system of positive law, the business of an objective "organ" distinct from the person obligated. The same is true of the second act of individualising, that of laying-down and ultimately realising the consequence. This is indeed the reason why, in natural law theory, the whole process of individualising as such is not so clearly brought to mind as it can be in the system of positive law, where a whole conspicuous machinery of state courts and administrative authority is specially entrusted with this function. Hence natural law theory is constantly preoccupied with law in its *general* form merely, pays no attention at all to the problem of individualisation, and identifies law with statute.

12. The ideal of natural law according to which the application of its norms, especially also in regard to the establishing of the conditioning circumstance, is carried out, not through a functionally specialised organ, but directly *by the person obligated himself* – this renunciation of a "judge" – rests on a presupposition which on closer examination must stand revealed as an *utterly utopian* one. Insofar as the natural law, whose objective existence is presupposed, has to be applied to the concrete case, insofar as in process of its individualisation it has to be brought into touch with the reality of what actually occurred, insofar as it has

to be *applied* by an empirically real man, the possibility of its realisation becomes dependent upon the capacities and properties of these same *empirically given* men. But whether these men have the qualities, either at all, or to the necessary degree which the ideal of natural law must presuppose, if it is to be able to dispense with a "judge", is thus *a question of experience*. Capacities of understanding are no less involved here than capacities of will. So let us begin by considering only the first act of the individualising process, the establishment of the conditioning circumstance. To keep on with our already adopted example of the natural law proposition "*pacta sunt servanda*", let us suppose that two men have concluded an agreement with each other. When it comes to fulfilling it, one of them denies that the agreement was ever finally arrived at; there were merely non-binding preliminary discussions; or a difference of opinion arises about the substance of the agreement or over when its performance is due. Such differences can arise through faulty recollection, or inadequate knowledge (supposing performance is made to depend on the occurrence of some event), or through the bad faith of one or other of those obliged or entitled by the pact. But the pure idea of natural law obviously presupposes that any such difference of opinion, which is to say, any *dispute* between the party obliged and the party entitled, is ruled out; and this presupposition is governed by the assumption that the parties possess the required properties of understanding and will, that they are wise and good, and are all these things alike, i.e., in the same manner and the same degree – in short, that they are perfect. Included more especially in this presupposition is the proviso that the interests of the participants do not obscure their judgement of facts, and that they are capable of recognising the whole "truth". *In just such an assumption, and in nothing else whatever, lies the essence of all utopias!*

If this assumption be dropped, as being manifestly contrary to all experience, it at once proves necessary to hand over the individualising, in regard to the conditioning circumstance, of the general norms of a natural law which is still taken to be objectively existent, to a functionally specialised organ, which will establish the facts "objectively", i.e., with minimum subjection to private interest, and which is specially equipped by training for this task. This is the situation of positive law, insofar as it has become "judicial law". But this type of individualising, or more precisely, its presupposition, namely an abandonment of the Utopia of wise and good men, represents a further step into positivity.

13. If the assumption of perfection is inapplicable to men in general, it can equally little be upheld in regard to the organs whose function is to apply the law (although attempts of this kind are customarily made in natural law theory). The institution of such organs is assuredly successful, because they are *more objective* and *more experienced* than the parties interested in the decision, because although not perfect, they are anyway more perfect, at least in regard to deciding the concrete case, than the obligated or entitled are. However, the key point is, that in the organ's business of establishing the facts, it is not so much a matter of eliciting the absolute "truth", as of *putting an end to the dispute*. If the search for the "real" facts, the pursuit of the "truth", were to have no ending – and how could it have an end, since absolute truth remains humanly unattainable – then in process of its application the justest law, even natural law, would be defeated. Hence positive law endeavours above all else to be an *order of peace*. And it achieves this purpose not so much on its general, but rather on its individual plane, through the principle of *legal validity*, which here has its primary, though not its only, abode. For the act of individualising which relates to the conditioning circumstance, its meaning is that the consequence shall follow, not if the condition laid down in the general statement of law has "actually" occurred, but if the designated organ affirms the existence of the conditioning circumstance, *regardless of whether this accords with the truth or not*. Whether the law, be it positive or natural, is realised, depends not only on whether the "correct" consequence laid down in the legal statement comes about in the concrete case, but primarily on whether this consequence is annexed to the "correct" circumstance prescribed in the legal statement, and not with any other; hence even in the individualising establishment of the conditioning circumstance, there is an act of *creating* law, and no mere logical "subsumption". The progression of legal procedure from the general to the individual norm signifies that the circumstance prescribed in the former is replaced by the circumstance established by the latter. In the possibility, sanctioned by the principle of validity, of an unbridgeable discrepancy between the two, the law-creating power of so-called legal application is operative

in the highest degree, in that it not only has the function of amplifying the general norm, but also that of *replacing or even supplanting* it. And this also shows to what a large extent the *positivity of law* makes itself felt precisely in the individualising of the general norm. If somebody is validly convicted of a theft which in fact he never committed, the *general* norm of positive law, that "whoever steals shall be punished" is certainly not realised, but yet "law" has been made. If an undoubted precept of natural law, such as our oft-used example of "*pacta sunt servanda*", is to come to application, and the law-applying organ has validly decided the question of fact in a manner contrary to "truth" or "reality", having established, for example, that an agreement was concluded, although only non-binding prior discussions had taken place, then natural law has remained unrealised. Yet law has been made, though it is *positive law*. This has taken the place of natural law, and has supplanted it, whereas in the previous example it was only one positive law which replaced the other, the individual positive law which supplanted the general but equally positive law. The positivisation of natural law here is no longer purely formal, it is also *material* in character.

This possibility, fateful alike to the realisation of both positive and natural law, of a conflict between individual and general levels of the legal order, has its ineradicable ground in the inadequacy of man, who is liable to both error and wickedness. But yet the necessary process of individualising natural no less than positive law has to go through this man. Another reason, perhaps, why natural law theory has taken no account of this process of individualising, why it has stopped short at the general form of law and failed altogether to think out to the end the problem of realising natural law, is that at this end stands that inadequate creature, man, who threatens to bring the whole idea of natural law to grief.

14. Continuing to presuppose the existence of natural law as a general order, let us now examine how, according to its idea, the individualising of this law must take shape in regard to the circumstance designated in the legal statement as the *consequence*. We thereupon light on the same presupposition that emerged in applying natural law with regard to the establishment of the circumstance designated as condition. Not only does the occurrence of the condition have to be established by the

obligated and entitled parties themselves; they also have to determine directly which consequence has to occur in accordance with the norm to be applied in the concrete case. And if they are thus obliged to realise this consequence themselves, and without the intervention of any organ, then the consequence linked by the relevant natural law statement to a specific circumstance must be immediately *evident* to these men whose behaviour is regulated by the order of natural law; they will have to know how they are to behave "rightly" or "justly" in the given case. And not only must they *know* which is the "right" or "just" consequence, i.e., how they are to behave according to natural law in the given case; they must also be imbued with the *willingness* so to behave. It should be noted that this assumption of men's perfect knowledge and will in regard to the consequence is, if anything, even more essential for the idea of natural law than the corresponding assumption in regard to the conditioning circumstance. The former is directly, the latter only indirectly necessary in applying the norms of natural law to the concrete case. Perhaps, indeed, it might still be supposed at first, that in regard to knowledge of the conditioning circumstance, the objective order of natural law requires for its realisation no special, or at any rate no other human qualities than are demanded by the application of positive law. At first sight the only thing that seems ineluctably necessary is the immediate self-evidence of the consequence. That justice may descend from heaven to earth and be able to set up its kingdom here, it appears sufficient that men should have the capacity to be *just*; they do not have to be *cleverer*, better informed, i.e., *wiser*, than they are under the domain of positive law. Only on closer examination does it appear that even defective knowledge of the conditioning circumstance defeats the realisation of natural law, and that establishment of that condition also requires no less of a good will, and hence of the quality of "goodness" or "justness", than does the establishing and realising of the consequence.

The process of individualising, to which a natural law order is just as much subject as positive law, leads to a *positivisation*, no less in the case of the consequence annexed to the circumstance in the legal statement, than in that of the conditioning circumstance itself. The individual norm, in which the appearance of the concrete condition is constitutively established, and the latter then conjoined with a concrete consequence, can be nothing else but a norm set forth in "positive" fashion, i.e., by a *human act*. In the very process of decreeing it, and the subsequent realising of the consequence, this leads to quite peculiar results.

15. We have already pointed out in an earlier connection, that the idea of natural law is at times pushed so far, that its realisation in the individual agent is pictured as well-nigh automatic. According to this view, men are driven by a sort of "inner necessity" to do the "right" or "just" thing in any given case. But this illusion is only created by the misconceived interpretation of the legal ordinance as a law of nature. Only so is it possible to assume that the consequence, annexed in the legal statement to a particular condition, realises itself "on its own", as the effect of a cause. This view, however, would eliminate the necessity of a positivising of natural law at its lower level. For the realising of the consequence upon occurrence of the condition in a virtually automatic fashion, i.e., with natural necessity, has initially the negative meaning that the consequence annexed to the condition in the natural law statement, and thus natural law as such, are *not* realised through "free" human action; but this means nothing else than that they are *not realised through a human act of will*, which has no sort of causal connection with the conditioning circumstance, and can thus be absent despite the presence of the condition.[1] This view, however, not only removes the *individualising* of natural law from the realm of the *positive* norm; as already explained earlier, it banishes *natural law* as such, even in its general form, from the sphere of the *normative*. If thought out logically to the end, it turns out that the "consequence" – here become the "effect" of a cause – is no longer "right" or "just" conduct, but behaviour necessitated by the laws of nature. Which is also why this naturalistic theory of natural law devotes its primary enquiries to how man behaves, in accordance with his "drive", his "instinct", or whatever other name may be given to the personification of the cause of his behaviour. Natural *law* can be spoken of as a *norm* only so long as the consequence has to be conjoined with the condition in its statement of law by means of an *ought*, and not by the *must* of causal law; so long, that is, as the individualising of the general statement of law, and hence the realising of the consequence, requires a human act of will that is *not causally determined* by the condition posited in the norm. In dealing with the problem of individualising a natural law order, it cannot therefore be a question of whether the consequence annexed to

the condition in the statement of law is realised by natural necessity or by free human agency; it can only be a question of how we are to envisage this human act. And here, as in the establishment of the conditioning circumstance, only two possibilities come into account: the determining of which concrete consequence is to come about according to the condition assumed given, and hence the realising of this consequence, is left to the parties obligated or entitled by the legal norm themselves; or else this task is handed over to a functionally specialised "organ" distinct from them both.

Here we may refer to what was said about the individualising of the conditioning circumstance. If it be assumed that, on the occurrence of the conditioning circumstance, the consequence annexed to such a particular condition by the natural law norm is immediately evident to the men whose behaviour is prescribed as consequence, and that these men are not lacking in willingness to behave according to natural law, then it obviously requires no mediation by third parties in order to realise the consequence; "organs" are entirely superfluous. And then it is evident that the act of realising the consequence will seem to be not, properly speaking, a human *act*, i.e., not a *volitional* act, not an act of *free* will, but simply an act of *cognition*, a mere logical "subsumption"; more especially if the immediate self-evidence of the consequence is not indeed exactly identified with an internal necessity of positing it, i.e., of acting rightly, but is at least confusedly associated with some such idea; as all are accustomed to do who believe, with *Socrates*, that virtue can be taught. But on grounds of experience it will have to be accepted, that insight into the "right" or "just" consequence, i.e., the one prescribed by the order of natural law, and that knowledge of the "right" or "just" conduct is *lacking* in men, or at least in the majority of men. – And the utopian nature of a *contrary* assumption will no doubt be more easy to guard against if "right" or "just" conduct is in question, than if it is merely a matter of the knowledge needed to establish the conditioning circumstance; for even among those professionally concerned with it, the problem of "justice" still ranks today, despite centuries of effort, as without a solution, and we may surely be allowed to disregard the fact that here or there a professor may be claiming, doubtless under the ironic smiles of his colleagues, that he knows what is just. But then there remains only the second of the possibilities mentioned above. We must rule out the idea of completely eliminating any third party functioning as an organ and just leaving the application of natural law, even as regards the consequence, to those of whom it must be assumed that they are simply unacquainted with it; either because they lack any such insight into the consequences annexed by the natural law order to particular conditions; or because they are without the willingness to actualise these consequences, even if the latter were immediately self-evident to them – the willingness, that is, to behave in accordance with the norm of natural law. If, indeed, it is still to be possible to presuppose intelligibly the existence of a natural law order as a general order at all, then here one will no doubt have still to assume *for the time being* that to one person or some persons at least, there is granted this insight and the willingness required. To these, then, the application of the natural law order to the concrete case will have to be handed over, especially in regard to the establishing and realising of the concrete consequence.

16. But this, however, is linked with a quite radical *alteration of legal technique*. So far as the great mass of men are lacking in the necessary insight, or willingness, or both, to behave according to natural law, they must plainly be *compelled* to do so. If the natural law order, ideally speaking, is not a coercive order like positive law, it is so only on the presupposition that it, and more especially the consequence annexed in its norm to a specific condition, namely "right" or "just" conduct, is immediately self-evident in like fashion to all men whose conduct is ruled by this order, and that these men all have an equal willingness to live according to their insight. *In default of this presupposition, which is in the truest sense of the word a utopian one, a coercive order is inescapable.* Its gist would have to be: anyone who does not behave according to natural law is to be visited with a coercive act, established and inflicted by functionally specialised organs, the same as those entrusted with establishing the conditioning circumstance, and of whom it is assumed – whether rightly or wrongly may be left undecided here – that they are somehow possessed of the necessary insight and willingness required for the realisation of the order of natural law. *But this coercive order can only be a positive order.*

This is not only because the element of coercion is incompatible with the idea of a natural order, but also because this coercive order must be *posited* by those very organs – or one of them – which are commissioned to apply the order of natural law. If the problem of an application of the natural law order is regarded from this viewpoint, it then emerges that the realising of such an order not only makes necessary a positive declaration of law at the last stage of individualisation, but that between this and the pure order of natural law a layer of positively ordained, general norms of law must also be inserted, which lay down specific acts of coercion for the various circumstances of behaviour contrary to natural law. This positive order must incorporate natural law as content, albeit with a negative sign prefixed, as it were. At the general level it represents *a complete positivisation of natural law*. Yet it is by no means merely the *form* in which an essentially natural law content is presented. For quite apart from the fact that this content is denatured by the element of coercion, which must signify more than a mere "form" in relation to the character of natural law, which is foreign to all coercion, this coercive order, with all its content, and in spite of the same, can rank for the men to whom it is alone directed, and for whom it is alone determined, *only as a positive legal order*. For these men, as has already been presupposed, are lacking in insight into natural law, and are deficient, precisely, in immediate knowledge of what is just. From their standpoint, indeed – *and it is the standpoint of scientific positivism* – it is wholly indifferent, because completely untestable, whether the behaviour threatened with coercion by the positive legal order is really contrary to natural law, i.e., is absolutely "wrong" or "unjust", and for that very reason associated with the coercive act. From this standpoint, the legal order, which is essentially a coercive order, consists in nothing else save the conjunction of a particular circumstance with a coercive act. As we have already emphasised in another connection, within this system of positive law, the fact that anyone is legally *obligated* to a particular course of conduct means nothing whatever except that the contradictory opposite of this conduct stands under the sanction of a coercive act. The common view has it that there are two legal duties, or norms, specifically connected with each other: (1) You are to behave in a certain way; (2) If you behave otherwise, i.e., if you violate the duty or norm designated in (1), a coercive act is to be directed against you. But this will not do, for it does not correspond to the structure of positive law, which essentially presents itself as an order of coercion. This whole distinction between a primary norm and a secondary statement of law, which in case of violation of the first-mentioned norm decrees an act of coercion, is not only superfluous but misleading. For the function of obligating to an appropriate, i.e., coercion-avoiding course of conduct is perfectly and completely carried out by the coercion-ordaining statement of law introduced under (2), and, in the system of positive law, *qua* essentially coercive order, by this *alone*. If the norm introduced under (1) is omitted, nothing in the actual legal situation is altered; but if it is retained, *and in first place at that*, it creates an appearance as if, in the positive legal system, there could be a legal obligation even without a coercive act. Moreover, this whole dualism of a first norm and a second, which threatens violation of the first with an act of coercion, is manifestly derived *from natural law thinking*. It takes over into the positive law system, which is nothing but a system of norms ordaining coercion, the natural law imperative, which is here entirely out of place and superfluous. If the first norm be conceived capable of constituting a legal obligation without itself being a coercive norm – and this is what is expressed in its formulation as an independent norm – this can only come about on the tacit assumption that this norm has a "just" content, that it obliges, not by virtue of a coercive order contained in it, but by virtue of its "just" content. Thus in truth it can enter into the system of positive law only as a *natural law* norm; which is in itself a contradiction since it then actually makes the second, coercion-ordaining, norm superfluous, and indeed impossible. If one allows the positive law statement ordaining coercion to be preceded, as a primary legal norm, by a norm prescribing the conduct which avoids coercion, and permits a legal obligation to be constituted by this primary norm alone, so that the statement ordaining coercion takes on a secondary character, functioning merely as a sort of protection and guarantee for the primary norm – a construction connected, at its inmost point, with the dualism of law and state – this implies an attempt to vindicate the coercion decreed by positive law as "just", which is, in fact, to legitimise the positive law order by means of natural law. It is *natural law ideology*, when the conjunction of a particular circumstance with a coercive order is founded on the claim that this circumstance represents the violation of a norm that is binding without any threat of coercion, and is thus obviously "just". So far as the question about the ground of the coercive order can be posed at all, from positivist standpoint – it actually has no place in a theory of positive law, being in fact a problem of legal politics – it is sufficiently answered if we take it that a particular form of behaviour is considered undesirable or harmful by the powers who impose the positive legal order, and that motives for abstaining from it are therefore provided by means of coercive threats against any case of such behaviour.

17. If we drop the presupposition that the content of the "natural" order is evident to all whom it applies to, and confine ourselves to the assumption that insight into the requirements of justice is granted only to a few, then we have to take account of yet a further factor which essentially diminishes the chance of realisation of natural law. For if it is not so immediately apparent to everyone how he should behave in the concrete case in order to conform with the norms of natural law, as it is that twice two are four, then we shall doubtless have to assume that even among the few to whom it is possible at all, insight into what is just does not come about *immediately*, and without further ado. The knowledge of natural law norms in general, and especially of those which have to be applied to the concrete case, will be attended with certain *difficulties*. And in fact even the teachers of natural law find themselves constantly compelled to draw attention to these difficulties; it may be a question of the problems which arise in deducing the diversified content of natural law norms from the supreme principle of justice (in fact there is a virtually insuperable difficulty here, namely an *impossibility*, so that artfully concealed subterfuges have to do duty for logical inferences); it may be that in the administration of a particular legal institution, or the decision of a concrete case, different natural law norms are in competition with each other, and so forth. These difficulties present themselves when it is a matter of giving a content in accordance with natural law to the coercive order which, for reasons above-mentioned, is now unavoidably positive; of shaping positive law "justly", even in its general form. They are thus difficulties of the positive *legislator*. But they also present themselves either in direct application to the concrete case of the general norms of natural law themselves, or in similarly applying the general coercive norms of positive law which correspond to natural law. These are the difficulties of the *"judge"*. And these numerous difficulties represent so many possibilites of *error*, which seriously threaten the realisation of natural law. One might allow oneself initially to disregard the necessity

of first transforming pure natural law into a system of positive general coercive norms, and the very significant sources of error inherent in this. One might consider only those sources of error that arise at the lowest level of individualising, and in laying down the concrete consequence, e.g., whether, in a given case of murder from legitimate jealousy, and in terms of the appropriate general norms of natural law, as such, it would be "just" to inflict punishment, either of death or imprisonment, and if the latter, what the term of imprisonment should be. Or again, in the concrete case of an error having crept into a contract of sale, one might ask whether, according to the determinations of the relevant general statement of natural law, it would be "just" to pay the purchase price, or deliver the goods, or to claim execution in case of non-payment or non-delivery. But then in cases such as these, no less than in the establishing of the conditioning circumstance, the principle of "legal validity" has to come into play, precisely with reference to the possibility of error about which consequence is the "right" one. If the legal order is to discharge the function of an order of peace – and this function must be ascribed to it, as soon as the men whose behaviour it governs are no longer supposed perfect – an end must be made of the search for the "right" law, and hence of *dispute* about the matter. What comes into play is not the norm of *pure* natural law: "If a particular circumstance is given, a particular consequence, and this alone, is to ensue", but rather the norm of *applied* natural law: "If a particular circumstance is authentically established by the organ appointed for the purpose, then the consequence determined by this organ is to ensue". Nevertheless, for reasons whose strength we shall not here consider, it is believed that just as this organ determines the conditioning circumstance only in accordance with "truth", so it decrees the consequence only in conformity with "justice". Yet the individual norm so posited is *legally valid*, even if it deviates alike from either truth or justice. And in the latter case, as we have already pointed out over the individualising of the conditioning circumstance, *positive law takes the place of natural law*, not only in a formal, but also in a material sense.

18. A similar consideration emerges if we start from the necessity which we here began by neglecting, of first transforming pure natural law into a system of general positive coercive norms, in order to render it applicable by and to imperfect men. Even if we do not rely on the highly questionable

assumption that the positive law-giver *alone* has the capacity to know and will the just – an assumption by no means infrequently made, as it happens, by exponents of natural law – we shall still have to interpose against every doubt about the justice of some positive law norm he lays down, every assertion contrary to such a statement of law, the principle that, in the interests of "peace and security", it must remain out of the question that any random individual should be allowed to put his own subjective opinion about what is just in place of the norm laid down by the "appointed authority". Even in the legislative process, the search for right law must somewhere be brought to an end, if law is to be an *order of peace*. If pure natural law has to be *positivised* into a general order of coercion, so that the judge can then apply it to the individual case, this *positive legal order* is bound also to *gain in legal validity over natural law*, regardless of whether and how far it accords with the latter, or the latter is supplanted by it. With the principle of legal validity, the ideal of *justice* is replaced by that of *peace*. And this *ideal of peace*, whereby any given positive law can be defended against any given natural law, *is directly opposed to the ideal of justice*. This relationship has not hitherto been sufficiently scrutinised, since for obvious political reasons it has been carefully concealed; but it finds expression in the typical argument, no less brutal than resigned: It is not so much a question of whether a particular good shall be taken from one person and allotted to another, and indeed to just the one and only person "entitled" to it, whether the natural law of *"suum cuique"* is to be realised in the relationship between them; what matters, rather, is that their dispute shall be brought to an end. Hence arises the necessity of *instituting* both general and individual law, i.e., the necessity of positive law. In this relative sense then, which is all that man without access to the absolute can attain to, the "just" is what corresponds to the norm *laid down*, and the unjust, what contradicts it. And this relativising of the "just" is accomplished, not only in passing from natural to positive law, i.e., from the absolute ideal of justice to the relative ideal of peace, but also within positive law, in the process leading from its general to its individual stage.

And it is possible to gauge by this last fact how great is the chance that natural law, whose objective existence we continue to presuppose here, will in course of its application be supplanted by positive law. It need only be noticed to what an extent within *positive law* the lower stage diverges from the higher, though it is supposed to be merely an amplification (completion) of the latter, to what an extent the one can set itself virtually in contradiction with the other, a discrepancy that is only formally evened out by the positive law establishment of the principle of legal validity. It should be noted in this connection that the matter is one of applying consciously framed written law, of individualising duly published statutes, whose content is by and large unambiguously determined. If the *positive* law embodied in general norms can already get lost in course of application, and in large measure actually does get lost, if here already the painful fact of a "dual standard" in the law can not be avoided, how much the more extensively must this be the case when natural law, so problematic in its content, embarks on the process of individualisation, and more especially when it is not applied directly to the concrete case, but must first be rendered positive in a general coercive order. In which context it should be observed that in the case of individualising a positive general order it is merely one *positive* law which is replaced by another, whereas in case of an individualising of natural law, it is just this *natural law* which is replaced by *positive* law.

19. Our account hitherto has adhered to the assumption that a "natural" order is objectively given as a system of general norms, and has merely examined the presuppositions governing an application of this order and enquired into the consequences resulting from such application. In so doing the imperfection of men as they are met with in experience, the men through whose act alone the application of natural law can be accomplished, has emerged as the decisive factor. To this it might be objected that it makes no sense to suppose the existence of a natural law if this does not enter entire into the knowing and willing of the men whose conduct it regulates, and thus if one does not also presuppose men to be perfect and "just". For the human ability to be just, the want of which leads to the necessity of replacing natural by positive law, is itself only the subjective version of an objective principle of justice, and is not, properly speaking, an empirically verifiable, mental quality; from the psychological standpoint the contrast between just and unjust has no existence whatever. In the value judgement implicit in the claim that a man is just, that he has the capacity or property of being just, there lies concealed behind a psychological mask the just order itself. Only so far as it cor-

responds to this objective order is a piece of behaviour just. And the finding that men are incapable, or insufficiently capable, of such behaviour, that they lack this quality of "justice", means only that there exists no objective order in which the principle of justice achieves espression. This objection certainly has point. But this it has from an *empirical* standpoint, such as that adopted by positivism (and which must especially be adopted in regard to the problem of *realising* a normative order); not, however, from the immanent standpoint of pure natural law itself which, since it in no way claims to be the work of man, can maintain its existence independently of whether men accept it into their knowing and willing or not; and not from the standpoint of a natural law theory, which accordingly takes no notice at all of the problem of application, i.e., of realising natural law. If the present enquiry proceeds from the intrinsic standpoint of pure natural law, it is to show by way of an immanent critique that natural law – in contradiction to its own idea – must still ultimately become the work of man, that the unavoidable application of natural law to the concrete case, its individualisation, is necessarily a *positivising*, which is to say, however, that the *process of realising natural law destroys the idea of it*, so that if it is possible at all, it is so only in a sphere transcending the empirically human one.

But this, however, is to reject that special assumption which, in common with many natural law theorists, we began by making here, namely that although the natural law order may be inaccessible to the great majority of men, it is recognisable at least to a few and is also willed by them. They are those who, according to the natural law theory governed by this assumption, are assigned the function of applying natural law, either directly, or mediately by way of a positive coercive order of general norms, into which pure natural law must first be transformed. That the positive law, whether of general or individual form, created in this process of application, gives a presentation in its content of natural law, depends wholly and solely on the claim – *unproven and for those who are subject to the norm, unprovable* – that the authority dispensing positive law is somehow in possession of natural law and of justice. It can easily be shown that here it is simply a matter of attempting to legitimise positive by means of natural law, to justify any given content of positive law by invoking natural law to empower the norm-giving authority, and thus to lend stability to an autocratic or aristocratic form of government; and hence that it is not *natural* but rather *positive* law, because it is a particular form of the *state*, that is to be given a foundation thereby.

NOTES

* *Zeitschrift für öffentliches Recht* 7 (1928) 221–250.

[1] The problem of freewill involves a contradiction between the necessity, on the one hand, that all events, including human action therefore, shall be causally determined, and on the other, the necessity that within any ethico-juristic and hence normative system, this action shall be free. One might find a solution of this in the fact that obligatory action is certainly not causally determined by the condition to which the norm attaches this action, and that it appears as "free" precisely because, and only because, it can be absent even when the condition is present. But yet that, if it comes about, this action, seen not from the standpoint of the norm, but from that of a law of nature, turns out in another way to be causally determined.

CHAPTER III

GOD AND THE STATE*

1. The religious problem and the social problem exhibit a remarkable parallelism, and do so, in the first place, from the *psychological* point of view. For if one analyses the mode and manner in which God and society, the religious and the social, are experienced by the individual, it appears that in broad outline his state of mind is in both cases the same.

The *social* experience proclaims itself in individual consciousness to be bound up with other beings, who because they too are presupposed as united and bound together, in virtue of the same conjunction in which they stand with the person having the social experience, are felt by him to be similar in kind, to be comrades. But this is only the first stage. In knowing oneself to be united with others, and so bound to them in many different ways, one feels entangled and trapped in this network of ties, enlaced in this structure of relationships, as the dependent part of a whole, within which one's own little member-function is first completed through the functioning of the other members; a whole whose significance is precisely this uniting into harmonious completeness, and which is therefore felt to stand over oneself, the mere part, as something higher, by which one's own existence as a member is conditioned and made possible, and towards which a feeling of dependence must therefore ensue. And this idea of one's own subordination and dependence is necessarily matched by the complementary idea of an authority creating the social nexus, the obligation or social bond, in which form society – or to put it concretely and not abstractly – the social group, takes root in individual consciousness.[1] This is the second stage.

The *religious* experience is crystallised around the belief in an authority standing over the individual, conditioning his existence and determining his behaviour, by whom and on whom he feels himself alike both obliged and totally dependent. If we compare the wholly normative authority wherewith the deity takes possession of the soul of the individual, to that claim to unconditioned obedience with which society enters into his consciousness, to extend itself ever more widely there, we shall be able to discern no essential difference, nor even one of degree. For it should not be overlooked that the absoluteness of God's authority is acknowledged only in dogmatic theology; empirical psychology, however, knows of no psychical phenomenon having absolute power, efficacy or intensity. Even in the heart of the most faithful of all believers, the notion of a divine command will at times grow faint and lose its motivating effect on the behaviour of the otherwise obedient servant of God. In contrast, however, we can repeatedly observe with astonishment the mighty power with which the social authority compels men against their deepest instincts, even into renouncing the will to live, the urge to self-preservation, and into sacrificing themselves with the utmost cheerfulness.

The consciousness of a supraindividual authoritarian being is by no means exhaustive of the religious experience. Its characteristic content includes the feeling of the person experiencing the divine that he is caught up in a universal interconnection, is merged into an inclusive totality which also takes in others besides himself, and is mediated through the deity. In the creation of this community embracing the individual on every side, of the cosmos as an intimate communion between himself and all other beings imbued with the spirit and will of God, in this sense of all things as children of God, and by means of this, brothers in God, the thought of the divine first achieves its ultimate meaning and the religious experience is perfected. The more it is deepened, the more even the idea of a supraindividual deity, distinct from the individual and conjoining him with other beings into a cosmic community, is merged therein pantheistically with the idea of this divine community gathering the individual with all other beings into a single being. And hence it is merely an illusion created by the arbitrariness of presentation, if one gets the impression that the sequence of stages in the dynamic of the religious experience is the reverse of that in the social, because the latter first progresses from community to authority, whereas the former advances only by way of authority to community. For to the social feeling also, *authority* and *community* are not two distinct objects, but merely different stages in the mind's progress, which are not successive in only one way.

The cosmic community which forms the content of the religious experience seems, however, to differ rather importantly from the social in this, that the latter is confined to men, and is merely a human association, whereas the former embraces all objects whatsoever, organic and inorganic alike. *Nature* and *society* aim to confront one another.

This objection threatens to call in question once more, or at least to limit severely, the parallel we began by asserting between the religious and the social problem; but it can be met. The perfected concept of God fulfils two functions which are very different from each other. God is the expression both of the highest purpose, the supreme value, the absolutely good, and also of the ultimate cause. He serves equally to justify all that ought to be and to explain all that is; His will is at once both the ethical norm and the law of nature. Yet this content, which theology has evolved in its perfected concept of God, and by which it has shattered the notion logically, owing to the irreconcilable dualism implanted therein, is still alien to the original conception of deity. The primitive makes all the less distinction in his deity between an ethico-normative and a natural cause aspect, inasmuch as his needs for justification and explanation are the same. To his still utterly anthropomorphic understanding, the behaviour of a thing is explained if he can think of it as the execution of a command; and his divinity, whether it be one or many, tells the sun to rise in the morning, and the trees to blossom in springtime, in just the same way as it tells a man not to kill his brother. Since, according to the primitive's notion, all things and not just man alone are subject to norms, and are recipients of normative commands, any essential dividing-line between man and the rest of nature disappears. It is precisely in this that we find, of course, the anthropomorphic world-view of myth, whereby the behaviour of everything is construed in the manner of human behaviour, as a sort of human behaviour, with all things viewed as similar to men, i.e., as animate beings. Nature, on the mythological world-view, is in fact a – society, i.e., a union, a nexus or compact among men and other beings regarded as men; it is a universal system of norms which have as their content the behaviour of all things and hence make all things into "men", i.e., into men in the ethico-normative sense of "persons" or recipients of norms. As this mythological world-view is gradually driven into retreat, the field is occupied by the modern scientific view of nature, which no longer asks in regard to the behaviour of things why they should so behave, or be obliged so to do, but conceives this behaviour as the effect of a cause; – and has trouble enough in purifying the common conception of a cause from the idea of a command directed to, or aiming at, the effect.

But in systematically extending this type of apprehension to men as well, society, so far as it is regarded as an aggregate of actual, causally determined modes of behaviour among men, becomes transformed into – nature, into a branch of nature not essentially to be distinguished from other parts of the universal causal order of things. And only insofar as consideration directed to the social maintains itself as an ethically (or juristically) normative viewpoint, can society be constituted as an object distinct from nature.

If we disregard the later function imposed by the advance of the scientific attitude on the concept of God, namely that of supplying an ultimate causal explanation – a function which destroys the concept – and if we cling instead to the original ethico-normative meaning which has always been most deeply typical of this idea, we are then assured of an unclouded insight into the intimate relation between the religious and the social pattern. For the community mediated by the idea of God is society, and in the society which confronts the individual as a supra-individually binding and normatively obligating authority, it is easy to recognise the bidding and forbidding God. The essence of the religious experience involves a social element, the essence of the social experience a religious one. It is therefore intelligible that every religion has its social form of manifestation, that it only emerges historically at all as a specific social order, and that the primitive social group is at the same time a religious community. It is not, as is commonly supposed, that the primitive distinguishes two different orders, the social and the religious, and construes the latter on the pattern of the former, making God rule over nature just as he sees the king or chief rule over himself and his fellows. The two orders in fact coincide, since for the primitive his king is identical with God, or ranks at least as the representative, the son, servant or instrument of God, and his command as God's will.

When Durkheim [2] concludes, from his researches into totemism, that God is simply an expression for society, it needs only to be added that society is also an expression for God, i.e., for the religio-authoritarian experience of the men who compose that society. In this reduction of the religious to the social, or raising of the social to the religious, the point at issue is this: that from the standpoint of psychological enquiry into the facts – and not that of theological or metaphysical speculation – the religious experience is exhaustively describable as the social, and that in the element of authority and community which is equally essential to religious and social experience alike, no difference of content is discernible in either case.

It was already recognised by Feuerbach that there is no special religious feeling, no special religious sense, and consequently no special religious object either, to which the religious experience is wholly and solely related, or religious veneration directed.[3] Between the worship of God and the worship of idols – from the psychological standpoint at least, for the theological is still not in question here – there is no essential difference. More especially is the reverence for heroes and princes (in its state of mind, as in its outward manifestations) of exactly the same kind as the adoration of the deity. The decisive feature is not that the reverence for heroes and princes, once it has reached a certain level, takes on religious forms and deifies its object also in verbal and ceremonial expression; it is that both the religious and the social attitudes of man are derived from the same spiritual root.

The psychological similarity of the religious and social attitudes is in Freud's[4] view to be explained not least by the fact that both ties go back to one and the same elementary psychical experience, which is similarly operative in the relation to both religious and social authority. It is the child's relationship to his father, who intrudes into the child's mind as a giant, an overwhelming force, and becomes for the child authority as such. Every authority thereafter is then also experienced as father; the worshipped god, the admired hero, the prince beloved with respectful awe, appear as father-substitutes, and only as representatives of the father can these authorities release for themselves all those psychical affects which make men into children without wills or opinions of their own. Goethe himself, in his profound 'Pandora', has Epimeleia, the daughter of Epimetheus, utter the words: "O father thou! Yet is a father at all times a God!" From this point of view, certainly, we can explain the by no means self-evident fact that the deity of all religions, and not only the most primitive, is revered under the name of father, and that princes also have at all times laid claim to the same name and the same attitude on the part of their subjects, and, guided no doubt by the surest of instincts, have thereby supported their rule upon the deepest and strongest foundation in the soul of man.[5]

It is precisely from this relationship to the beloved father that one can learn to understand how the subjection which can only be undergone with injury to self-consciousness may yet be pleasurable, how there can be virtually a drive to such subjection under an authority experienced – consciously or otherwise – as father. Yet it would certainly be a very poor and incomplete conclusion, if we were to rest content with recognising the common root of man's religious and social attitude in his original drive to subjection; and were not also prepared – thanks to Freud's psychoanalytical researches – to take into account the ambivalence, the equivocal character, the Janus-headed facing-both-ways of this drive, as of every other. Just as love is at the same time hatred, so every passion for self-subjection which in some way aims at pleasure is at the same time the wish to subject others to oneself; humility, though it is not logically, is yet somehow psychologically identical with the will to power. If we take religion in its historical manifestation, there was never yet a believer contented to be alone with his god; people have always subjected themselves to a god so that they could subject others to that god. And the deeper one's own subordination, the more fanatical the religious renunciation of oneself, then all the more powerfully is the deity exalted, the more passionate the fight for this deity, the more boundless the drive to dominate others in his name, and the more triumphant his victory, because it is merely a victory of the warrior of faith who identifies himself with his god. This is by no means, however, the special psychology of the religious man, for in fact it is simply the psychology of social man: self-subjection under the authority of the group, so that others may also be equally subjected to it; precisely those others whom I will not have over me, whom at most I allow beside me and wish to have *equal* to me, and whom, since I cannot master them directly, I master indirectly, in that I see them, subdued in fact to my own chosen authority, bow themselves before my banner; – and "my" authority is not merely, nor even so much, the authority I bow to because I acknowledge it, but also and much more the authority which I thereby become. And this banner, though outwardly the mere symbol of the group, is inwardly an all the more exhaustive expression of the repressed self, the more unconditionally this self identifies itself with the boundlessly exalted group, thereby balancing its self-subjection by also exalting itself. Just as the primitive at certain times, when he dons the mask of the totem animal which is the idol of his tribe, may commit all the transgressions which are otherwise forbidden by strict norms, so the civilised man, behind the mask of his God, his nation or his state, may live out all those instincts which, as a simple group-member, he must carefully repress within the group. Whereas anyone who praises himself is despised as a boaster, he may still unashamedly praise his God, his nation or his state, although in doing so he merely indulges his own conceit; and whereas the individual as such is in no way thought entitled to coerce others, to dominate or even to kill them, it is nevertheless his supreme right to do all this in the name of God, the nation or the state, which for that very reason he loves, and lovingly identifies with, as "his" God, "his" nation and "his" state.

If we take the actors who play out the religious or social drama on the political stage, and strip the masks from their faces, then we no longer have God rewarding and punishing, or the state condemning and making war, but men putting coercion on other men, whether it be Mr. X triumphant over Mr. Y, or a wild animal slaking its reawakened thirst for blood. Once the masks have fallen, the play loses its proper meaning; once we discount the masks, we renounce just that specific interpretation in which a thing like religion or society alone consists! Contained in this picture there is a final methodological insight: this discounting of the masks, this looking through them to the naked, naturally necessary, causally determined motions of souls and bodies, is the viewpoint adopted by a scientifically oriented psychology and biology. From it one sees neither religion, nor the nation, nor the state. For these are simply the "masks", the specific ideologies which arise upon the foundation of the real facts; ideal systems of value-relations or norms which the human mind creates for itself, and into whose own immanent schemes of law one must enter and install oneself, in order to be vouchsafed any of those objects that are referred to as religion, the nation, the state, etc. A person who sees only physical and mental acts, and asks for their causes and effects, will see only nature and nothing else. That an expression of will on the part of one organism should become a cause of the behaviour of another, is in itself no more a social fact than that the bird flees the snake, or that bodies expand on heating. Only from the standpoint of the ideology governed by its own laws, which operate quite differently from those of the scientific standpoint, is it possible to make that interpretation which yields the specifically social meaning.

If society is to be understood as a mere ideology, then religion is simply a particular social ideology. It is originally identical with that social ideology which may be described, in the broadest sense, as the state; at this stage of development the ideas of God and the state entirely coincide; the national God is simply the deified nation in a personified form. It is the situation already mentioned in another connection, in which the religious and the legal organisation, church and state, are identical. Gradually, and more especially in the development of Christianity, there occurs a separation of the concept of God from the national community. This formation of a supranational God goes hand in hand, and in fact is basically identical, with the creation of a consciousness of mankind, the idea of a society above the state, a community of all men which bursts the bounds of the individual state. The cosmopolitan God of Christianity, who as a God of "love" is already an eminently social God, can assuredly be wholly understood only as the personification of this idea of mankind. That in spite of this Christian God of mankind, who transcends the state, and in addition to this one-and-only God, there are still a multitude of other Gods, namely as many as there are nation states, can remain hidden solely to one who declares to be God only that which so names itself. As Feuerbach said, so long as there are many peoples, there will also be many Gods, for the God of a people, at least its real God, who is certainly to be distinguished from the God of its dogmatists and philosophers of religion, is nothing else but its national feeling,[6] or more correctly still, is the people itself.

In view of this state of affairs, it is no wonder that the theory of the state, this most perfect of all social structures and most developed of all ideologies, should display very striking parallels to theology, the doctrine of God. Nor is this true merely of that theory of the state which, following Hegel's example, aims consciously even in the ethical sense at an absolutising and thus deification of the state, to which it attributes all those essential features which theology is accustomed to affirm of God. It is true to an unexpectedly large extent of the whole ancient and modern theory of the state as such. If its problems and their solutions run parallel, to a quite staggering extent, with those of theology, then, quite apart from the essentially psychological viewpoint from which the relationship of the religious to the social has thus far been regarded, this has its basis in an epistemological situation which will be elucidated in what follows.

2. From the standpoint of a critique of knowledge,[7] the concept of God presents itself as a personification of the world-order. In seeking to apprehend the world, we presuppose it as a meaningful whole, which is to say, as a unitary order of all events. In this connection it makes no difference whether this order is conceived as a system of norms, or of causal laws, or as both. The only thing that matters is the fact that the abstract idea of the unity of this order seeks an intuitive expression for itself in the anthropomorphic mental aid of personification. In a confusion typical of primitive thought, between a means and an object of cognition, the personification is hypostatised, i.e., what was merely a tool for grasping the object is taken for a real object; but in this way the object of knowledge is duplicated, and hence is created the pseudo-problem of the relationship of the two entities, where at bottom only the unity of one and the same object should come to be expressed. The relation between God and the world is the proper object of theology.

The state also is essentially conceived as a person, and as such is merely the personification of an order: the legal order. The concept of the legal order enables us to apprehend as a unity the multitude of legal relations between individuals. But the abstract unity of the legal order is rendered palpable in the idea of a person, whose will signifies the content of this legal order, just as the will of God finds expression in the world-order – whether as a moral order or an order of causal law. If law is the will of the state, then the state is the person, which is to say, the personification, of law. This insight loses much of its initially paradoxical appearance if we remember that the state must be apprehended as an *order*, as a specific order of human behaviour, as τάξις or σύντάξις, to quote the descriptions already given to it by Plato and Aristotle [8]. But what order other than precisely the *legal* order could the state well be, if it has to be conceded from the start that the state stands in some sort of essential relation to law, and if it cannot be seriously supposed that two orders, a state order and a legal order distinct from it, should stand in competition alongside one another? The detailed proof advanced in another connection, that the state in every respect can only be the legal order, is uncalled for here, since it is sufficient to recognise that, so far as it is an object of legal science – and even on the prevailing doctrine the theory of the state is predominantly the theory of the *law* of the state – the state can only be the law. For the object of legal cognition is only the law and nothing but the law, and to conceive the state legally – which is the purpose of constitutional law theory (*Staatsrechtslehre*) – can only mean to conceive the state as law. To be sure, the word "state" has many meanings, and not every one of the numerous usages, whereby the state now rules, now is ruled, now designates a people, now a territory, now a constitution, and is identified now with a larger, now with a smaller, though never a sharply delimitable group of somehow qualified persons, can be covered by the concept of the state as we have here defined it. But that state which appears as the creator or at least as the "bearer" of the legal order; the state to which – as the prevailing doctrine assumes – every statement of law must relate in its content, at least insofar as every such statement – no matter how its origin may be thought of – terminates eventually in the institution of a coercive act, whose character as an act of state has never yet been doubted by anyone; the state whose universal relation to law is so far presupposed that the theory of the legal state can concede no part of the state to stand outside the law, and the theory of positive law no part of the law to stand outside the state; – this state of general state-theory is identical as an order with law, and as a person is merely the personification, the anthropomorphic expression, of the unity of law. If the person, created by legal cognition to symbolise the unity of the legal system, and called "the state", is hypostatised in the usual way and set up as a special entity over against the law – of whose unity this personified state is a mere expression – we then have exactly the same problem – or pseudo-problem – situation as in theology. The latter can exist as a discipline distinct from moral or natural science only insofar as it clings to God's transcendence over the world – this fundamental dogma of all theology – to the existence of a supernatural God above and beyond the universe; just as a theory of the state distinct from legal theory is likewise possible only so long as we believe in the transcendence of the state vis-à-vis the law, in the existence, or more exactly the pseudo-existence, of a metalegal, supralegal state.

In that the state, as an entity transcending the law, continues nevertheless to be characterised at bottom only in relation to law, the attempt to define the properties of the state leads to the establishment of purely negative qualities. The *sovereignty*, which is commonly regarded as the most essential feature of the state, means fundamentally nothing else but that the state is the supreme power, which cannot be defined except in a negative fashion, namely that it has no higher power over it, and is a power neither derived from, nor limited by, any higher power. So too does the emphasis on God's transcendence lead in theology to the depicting of His nature in negative predicates. The state-jurist's concept of sovereignty must have permitted of a ready application to the purposes of theology, for it gives expression merely to the absolutising of the object. Without having even the least awareness of the connection with theology, jurisprudence has recognised that the state, so far as it is declared to be sovereign, i.e., absolutised, presupposed as the absolutely supreme legal entity, must be the *only* legal entity, because, if the concept of sovereignty is thought out to its logical conclusion, the sovereignty of one state excludes that of every other, and so rules out every other state as a sovereign commonwealth. That this insight has been employed as an argument against the ascription of sovereignty to the individual state, is of no significance here, where it is merely a matter of showing that even the dogmas enunciated with such powerful emotion concerning the uniqueness of the theological God confirm this concept's total conformity in logical structure with that of the jurist's concept of a sovereign state. If the sovereignty of the state is interpreted as power, so power it is likewise which every theology declares to be the essence of its God, and which, exalted to absolute omnipotence, is also proclaimed of the state; at first, to be sure, in a normative sense only, in that the state's omnipotence is intended only to express that, in its specific sphere of law, the state can do anything it wishes, that the legal order can incorporate any desired content. Yet there is not infrequently talk of the state's omnipotence also in a natural sense. The state-jurist's view is all too liable to slide out of the sphere of legal into that of natural reality, and to confuse the power of the state, which as a legal power is a potentiality of *validity*, with a natural source of *efficacy*, a psycho-physical force. Not as if such a psycho-physical force did not actually exist! The psychological act of entertaining the norms which compose the political order is a fact existing in the world of natural reality, and has – as a cause – its effects. Now greater, now less, the motivating force of these ideas is certainly a "power" in the natural sense; it is only that this fact should not be confounded with the ideal normative order which alone comes into consideration as a state or legal order. Yet there is an evident tendency to identify the state with this fact of a real power operating as a cause of effects, and to contrast it precisely in this sense with the law as a purely ideal system of norms. However, one can equally well claim the ideal order to be the *state* order, and call its *realisation* the law, conceiving law as the power of the law, as a real power commanding the minds of men and determining their doings in a causal manner. Just as it is at times assumed in theology that God is merely the world in thought, and the world merely God in actuality, the actual God.[9] There is no accommodating law and the state to the *opposition* between thought and reality, if it is thought possible to apprehend *both* of them under the two points of view. In actual fact the identity of state order and legal order (which presents itself solely to a view directed upon the ideal), and the concrete fact of entertaining and willing such an order (given only to a view directed upon natural reality), must be kept clearly separated from each other as two different things. And yet, just as the state-jurist's view identifies the ideal state-order in its specifically normative role with the state as a power really operating in the world, so at times the juristic omnipotence of the state is misconstrued as a natural, absolutely irresistible force. Not without the conscious or unconscious afterthought of crucially intensifying a natural force that is doubtless present already – the motivating force of normative ideas – by creating a *belief* in their irresistibility. Do we not see preserved in this very direction the analogy between the state and God, who has been wittily said to exist only at such times and to such an extent as people believe in Him?

Through the emphasis it lays – especially against pantheism – on God's transcendence vis-a-vis the world, theology runs into the same difficulty as that of the state-jurist's theory in regard to its claim about the metalegal nature of the state. Epistemologically speaking, the difficulty, indeed the impossibility of the situation in both cases, consists in the fact that two mutually distinct and independent systems, God and the world, the state and law, make their appearance within one and the same sphere of knowledge, whereas the inherent tendency of all knowledge is directed towards systematic unity. This difficulty is not, however, expressed, either in theology or in political and legal theory, in a purely epistemological manner. In theology the case is somewhat as follows: a world independent of God cannot be reconciled with the divine attributes. To exist at all, the world must somehow come from

God. God is the world-cause; he has created the world and continues to sustain it. And conversely, men, as part of the world, could form no idea of God or grasp the notion of God at all, if He was not also in some way of the same nature as the world and man. The two mutually exclusive principles of God's elevation above the world, and his positive relation to it, must therefore somehow be rendered compatible with each other, for though God is by His nature unconfounded with the world, it is nonetheless impossible to conceive Him without the world, or the world without Him. The same assault upon logic is evinced in the theory of the state-jurist, which maintains a precisely analogous set of claims: the state is an entity distinct and independent from the law, it is ultimately of a metalegal nature, but yet it is impossible to conceive of the state without law, or of law without the state. The state is the creator or sustainer of law, and is therefore above the law; but on the other hand is again of the same nature as the law, is subject to law, is a legal entity, a legal person.

And just as the problem in theology and state-theory is the same, namely the common pseudo-problem of the relationship between a system and its hypostatisation (a relationship being conceivable only *within* the system), so we also find in both disciplines the same solution, if indeed we can allow as a solution to a logically insoluble problem anything else but a radical dissolution of the problem, i.e., its unmasking as a pseudo-problem. The world-transcending God transforms Himself into the world, or into its representative, man, in that the divine essentiality splits into two persons, God-the-Father and God-the-Son, the God-Man or God-World. In the person of the God-Man, God subjects Himself to the world-order, ethical as well as natural, posited by Himself, and the initially limitless power of the divine will sets limits to itself. As God-Man, God renounces His omnipotence, the course of the world does not conform to His will, but on the contrary, rather, as God-the-Son He disposes Himself in dutiful obedience to God-the Father. This theory of God's incarnation in the world is put forward in theology under the aspect of the self-limitation and self-obligation of God. It is matched to a hair's breadth by the well-known doctrine which forms the heart of the state-jurist's theory, concerning the *self-obligation of the state.* The state, which differs essentially from the law, which must be conceived as power, which is almighty and hence by nature unlimited, "sovereign" and bound by no norm, must yet eventually become law, must transform itself into a legal entity, a juridical person; a person which, because it has the legal order *over* it, and derives its "power" from that order, can no longer be "sovereign", if indeed the concept of sovereignty is still to have any meaning. For somehow, after all, regard must be paid to unity of system, and here, understandably, the standpoint of *legal* cognition must prevail. But now how does it come about, this metamorphosis of the state as power into the state as law, which critics of the self-obligation dogma constantly allude to as a mystery? Very simple, says the state-theory: the state sets up a legal order, which is in fact an essential thing for it to do, and once it has done so, it freely submits itself to this, "its own" legal order. All the doubts which have repeatedly been voiced by the jurists against this theory of self-obligation – and since these doubts have never been able to subside, the self-obligation theory and hence the foundation of the state-jurist's theory have constantly remained problematic – all these doubts have been expressed almost word for word in theology against the theological dogma of God's incarnation as man. How can God be almighty, by nature unbound and unconstricted, and yet at the same time, *qua* man, be set under nature's laws, be born, live, suffer, die, and be subject to the moral law? Such has been the utterance of religious doubters in all ages. And the critical jurists have asked: How can the state, whose essence, we were taught, is – unlike the law – that of power, be in any way legally bound, were it even by its "own" law itself? If the state – as is presupposed from its essence – can by nature do everything it has power to do, how can it then be maintained from any standpoint, that it can only do that to which it is entitled or obliged by the legal order? The God of the theologians was described by certain heretics as a "minotaur", half man and half superman; while the critics have rejected as a "fabulous monster" a state which, according to the prevailing theory of the state-jurists, was supposed to be half a legal person, and half a power existing in nature.

The striving towards unity of system which springs from the deepest essence of knowledge often comes to the surface – without the subject of cognition being aware of it – in strange and circuitous ways. Once theory has split asunder state and law as two different things, it seeks again to unite them. In so doing it reinterprets the unity of state and law –

a logical postulate, since it merely gets rid of a pseudo-dualism – into a political postulate, and teaches that state and law do not necessarily coincide, but may merely contingently do so. Whereas in earlier days, especially under absolute monarchy, state and law were in hostile opposition, historical development tends towards the unification of both. Only in the modern constitutional state does the state order become a legal order; only there is the demand for a unity of state and law fulfilled as a historical fact. From the standpoint of a positive, rather than a natural law type of legal theory, which in fact is the standpoint of the modern juridical theory of the state, the unity of state and law must be recognised as a conceptual reality, independent of all historical development; the union of state and law can be no historical fact, and every state, even the absolute police state, must be a legal order. It is not just a matter of recognising the democratically created legal order as "law" in the true sense, because only that legal order, and *every* such order, must rank as *positive* law, which has the state "behind it", as – duplicating the picture – we are accustomed to say; which means, however, that legal order which is the order of the state. It is in this identity of the legal order with the state order that the essence of the law's positivity actually lies. In opposition to orthodox theology, which sees in the incarnation of God, in the union of the transcendent God with the extra-divine world, a uniquely occurring historical fact, which came to pass at a particular time and a particular place, the doctrines of certain mystical and pantheistic sects wish to see in Christ only an eternal symbol, and to conceive God's incarnation, not as a once-and-for-all historical event, but as an experience grounded in the nature of man: the incarnation of God takes place in every man; God *is* man, man God, for God is in His nature identical with the world.

The dualism of state and law betokens not only a contradiction in the logically systematic sense; it is also more particularly the source of a politico-legal abuse. Under the guise of an argument in legal and political *theory*, it provides a way of enabling purely *political* postulates to break in upon positive law. The dualism of state and law becomes a dualism of two different and mutually contradictory norm-systems, of which one, under the names of "state", reason or interest of state (also public welfare, public "law"), is then repeatedly brought to bear whenever the other, namely "positive" law, leads to a consequence unwelcome to the rulers, who are in truth identical with this "state". In order to see into a connection all-too-thoroughly darkened by the doctrines of the schools, it is necessary only to realise that the question about the nature of the state boils down to this: under what conditions is a human action (and only the acts of individuals are initially there to be explained) to be attributed, not to the agent himself, but to an entity, the state, conceived to be "behind" him; under what conditions are human acts to be interpreted as acts of state? The problem of the state appears as a problem of ascription, the state as a locus of ascription, a specific point of reference, and the crucial question relates to the criterion for ascription. That God, too, must be conceived as such a locus of ascription – lying in the infinite – is no longer our concern here. We simply wish to establish that the criterion for ascription to the state can only be a legal one. A human action can be accounted an act of state only when and insofar as it is qualified in a specific manner by a legal norm, is decreed in the system of the legal order. In ascribing a state of affairs to the state, there is basically nothing else expressed but the relation of this content to the unity of the system, in which this content is combined with others into a specific order. The state, as a terminus of ascription, is simply an expression for the unity of this order, the legal order. To apprehend an act legally, especially an act of state, is to apprehend it as a determinately qualified content of the legal order. To the organs who execute it, however, especially the supreme organs, this legal order is at times a limitation running counter to their interests. Even under an absolute monarchy, the legal order is not fashioned exclusively in the interests of the monarch and his retinue, for opposing interests must also somehow be attended to. The legal order always has more or less the character of a compromise. It should also be noted that even in an autocracy, where the elaboration of the law is basically effected through the will of the monarch, and precisely there indeed, a large part of the law is created by way of custom, and hence democratically; it is under autocracy, precisely, that the importance of customary law increases, just as, for obvious reasons, it declines within a democracy. But now if, in a constitutional monarchy, the monarch, or the executive organs who represent him, perform acts which are not covered by the legal order, the doctrine (sprung up on the soil of constitutional monarchy) then recognises these acts nonetheless as acts of state, in that it justifies them by the nature of the state, the interest of the state, and so forth. These acts, which from the standpoint of the positive legal order are utterly inconceivable and not to be construed as legal acts, are ascribed by this doctrine to the state, on the basis of an order different from the positive legal one; and since this order must indeed be somehow conceived as a *legal* order, and these acts of state as *legal* acts, such an order – which is largely deduced, natural law fashion, from the nature of an imaginary state – is designated "public law", so as thereby to bring off the conjuring trick of construing law out of non-law, and a legal act out of a naked act of power. Here lies the root of that logically impossible dualism, in which public law has been set up against so-called private law.[10] But this public law, so far as it is deduced from the nature of this imaginary state, this whole state established contrary to positive law, is merely the expression of particular postulates unrecognised in the legal order, of a political, and hence natural law kind; and is intended only to facilitate the satisfaction of political desires, of interests which the positive legal order does not countenance, and which stand in contradiction thereto. It is in this meaning, of an autocratic order directed against a law essentially customary and thus grown democratic, set aside in the interest of the prince and his following, that the word 'state' – the *ragione di stato* of Machiavelli's *Principe* – has found entry into the language of the law. And although the conflict between the new autocratic and the old democratic order only found expression in the conflict between the old and the new state-*law* – for the new order indeed became a legal order which supplanted the old – the concept of the state has nonetheless retained its anti-legal significance, has often remained a cloak for political postulates directed against positive law, and has preserved in the contrast between state and law the dualism of two systems, with which the theory operates simultaneously, employing now the one and now the other, as political occasion serves.

Theology finds itself in a precisely analogous situation. On the one hand it must grant the world to be nature, i.e., a systematic unity of natural laws, and all the more because God Himself has founded nature's laws along with nature, and only as expressions of the divine will can they rank as natural laws; but on the other hand it is impossible for theology to suppose that God is bound by the laws of nature. God's freedom in regard to natural laws is expressed in the concept of *miracle*.

The latter is a happening which cannot be brought under natural laws, and for whose determination it is necessary to have recourse to the supernatural system of the divine will. But the concept of God as a being distinct from the world stands or falls with the concept of miracle. Both are made possible solely through the unrelated juxtaposition of two systems independent of each other. It is precisely in this excursion beyond nature, in this assumption of a supernatural order of the divine will distinct and independent from the order of nature, that the characteristic motive of theology lies; this is what constitutes the *theological method.* It is the method of the state-theory, which, with its supralegal system of a meta- or superlegal state distinct from the system of law, endeavours to render the legally unintelligible intellible nonetheless – in a legal manner and to secure belief in a legal miracle, exactly as theology does with a natural one. And just as the other-than-legal state – whose will is positive law, and which yet can operate above this law and outside this legal order, and thus work legal miracles – was recognised to be merely the expression of certain political postulates extending beyond the positive legal order, so Feuerbach recognised God – the supernatural God distinct from the world, who is not bound by the restraint of natural laws, though they are merely what he wills – as an expression of human desires extending beyond the bounds of what is actual and necessary, as a product of wish-fulfilling fantasy.[11] And just as he declared the concept of a God who ruled in adherence to the laws of nature, and only according to those laws, to be wholly superfluous, so a concept of the state whose acts are possible only as legal acts, likewise proves to be superfluous; unless it be that we are willing to let it exist as an expression for the unity of the legal order.

Just as the state-jurist's theory ascribes certain acts to the state as *legal* acts, though it finds no justification for them in the positive legal order, so, on the basis of that order, it believes it can ascribe certain doings to the state as *illegal*, though it gives out the legal order to be the will of the state. The unitary person of the state is thus supposed to will simultaneously both law and its negation, an impossible contradiction! With the assumption of *state illegality* the theory falls into the same difficulties which confront theology in the problem of *theodicy*: How can God, whose will is goodness, will sin and evil? And yet evil, too, must be ascribed to Him, for nothing is possible without His will. It is no longer of any moment here that theology and jurisprudence, in total independence of each other, have struck out the same path to release themselves from this conflict. Yet it is perhaps not redundant to point out the parallels between a theological and a juristic institution which both have to do with the problem of illegality in the system of law, of evil in the system of good, of error in the system of truth. According to the content of a statement of law, a coercive act is to be imposed under specific conditions, and *only* under these conditions; and yet in a concrete case in which the coercive act, e.g., punishment, was imposed, it may be doubtful whether the condition foreseen in the statement of law, e.g., crime, was actually present, whether an innocent person has not been wrongly convicted by the state. The legal order provides for a series of checks on the judgement by superior courts, yet it understandably sets a limit to this series. The final judgement terminates in *legal validity*, and can no longer be altered. And hence, properly speaking, the statement of law should not be held to run: If anyone steals, murders, etc., he is to be punished – for how is the *absolute* truth about whether anyone has done a thing to be established? It should be: If, under a specific procedure, it is presumed in the last resort of any one that he has stolen, murdered, etc., then he is to be punished. And in regard to this statement of law, there is no judicial error, no illegality on the part of the state. Merkl [12] has lately pointed out that the theological dogma of the *infallibility* of the papal office is really nothing else but an application to theology of the institution of legal validity. Just as in the one case, possible illegality is made legal, so in the other, possible error is made truth.

Theological and juristic speculation are in closest analogy, finally, over the relationship between *God and man*, or *state and individual*. Just as man, made in the image of God, a spiritual being, appears within the system of theology not really as a physical, i.e., animal organism, but as a soul, so jurisprudence must stress emphatically that man enters its consideration, not as a biologico-psychological unit, but as a 'person', a legal subject, a specifically legal entity; and hence it creates its man likewise after the image of the state, the legal person κατ' εξοχην. The essential similarity of the state to the individuals composing it is the (more or less conscious) guiding thought which leads to the so-called organic theory of the state: a theory which, when it seeks to construe the state as a magnified man, only goes astray because it looks for the state in the sphere of existence of the natural man, in the world of *nature* instead of in that of the *spirit*. Hence it is a mistake to include among these organic theorists the name of Plato, who, in his *Republic*, in order to discover *justice* in the individual, and thus the nature, merely, of the ethico-juristic person on his own, first enquires into the nature of the just state, as the ethico-juristic person collectively understood.

The theological *doctrine of the soul* and the juristic theory of the *person*, the legal soul, are related in many ways. Sufficient to point out here that the central problem of politics, the relationship between individual and state, and all its possible or attempted solutions, are in part a verbatim repetition of those speculations which theology and religious mysticism have set going concerning the relationship of God and the individual soul. It is the aim of religious and political thinking alike to restore unity between the two opposite poles, and to portray their duality as really a unity. And even the paths which lead to this goal are the same: either we start from the isolated individual in order to have him absorb the universe, or we start from the universe so that it may swallow up the individual. Individualism and universalism are the two primary schemata for religious and political theory alike.

From this aspect we should also consider the parallel which obviously exists between *atheism* and *anarchism*. Yet it should not be overlooked in doing so, that the question concerning God or the state, to which atheist and anarchist return a similarly negative answer, is not, however, posed in quite the same way. The atheist asks whether a God exists – as a being distinct from the world; the anarchist, whether a state *ought* to exist, whose "existence" he presupposes in the very act of answering "no" to the question. To be sure, the existence of God – not in the sense in which the atheist denies it, but in one which even he must admit – is the same as that "existence" of the state which the anarchist contends against: it lies in the motivating force of certain normative ideas. In this sense, God and state exist only if and insofar as they are believed in, and all their enormous power, which fills the history of the world, collapses if the human soul is able to rid itself of this belief. But atheism, in addition to its significance as a critique of knowledge, also takes on an ethico-political meaning and becomes an anarchism directed against *this* version of divine existence, when it answers "no" to the question whether a God, a divine existence in this sense of a belief in God, *ought* to exist. And in like fashion ethico-political anarchism can also take on significance as a critique of knowledge, in first asking what the state *is*, and then answering this question negatively, in the sense of denying the state to be an entity distinct from the legal order. This is what Stirner was doing, for example, in his repeated assurances that the state is merely a spectre, merely a creation of fantasy, merely a fiction. Yet between this epistemic anarchism and a political anarchism, which denies altogether the validity of binding coercive norms, there is no more a necessary connection than there is between ethico-political atheism and the epistemic variety, which, even if it denies the existence of God, can still presuppose a moral order of the world.

And yet even a purely epistemic anarchism – if so one may describe a reduction of the concept of the state to the concept of law – is not without at least a negative ethico-political effect. For it disposes of the idea that the state is an absolute reality, looming fatefully over the individual as a sheer given, independent of him. In teaching him to apprehend the state as simply the legal order, it makes the individual aware that this state is a human artefact, made by men for men, and hence that nothing can be deduced *against* man from the nature of the state. If it has always been the rulers under the prevailing state order, who have met every attempt at changing this order with arguments drawn from the nature of the state, who have declared the contingent historically given content of the state order to be absolute, because it suited their interests, then the doctrine which declares the state to be the legal order prevailing at any time, whose content is changeable and can always be changed, and thus concedes to the state no other criterion beyond the formal character of a supreme coercive order, is a doctrine which disposes of one of the most politically effective obstacles which at all times has been laid in the path of *reforming* the state in the interests of the ruled. But by this indeed the doctrine preserves its character as a *pure* theory of law, for it only destroys the political misuse of a spurious theory of the state.

This *purely legal theory* of the state, which gets rid of the idea of a state distinct from law, is a *stateless theory of the state*. And however paradoxical it may sound, it is only by means of it that legal and political theory first push forward from the level of theology into the ranks of modern science. The concept of the state evolved by the older political and legal theory stands epistemologically – like the concept of God – on a par with the concept of the soul in the old psychology, or the concept of force in the old physics. The state as a person could equally well be called the soul of the law or the force of the law. Like God, soul and force, it is a substance-concept.[13] Since modern science seeks everywhere to dissolve substance into function, and has long since thrown the concept of the soul overboard, along with that of force, modern psychology has become a soulless theory of the soul, and modern physics a forceless theory of force. And if the absorption of the concept of a supernatural God by the concept of nature was the presupposition, first created by pantheism, for a genuine natural science devoid of all metaphysics, so likewise is the reduction of the supralegal concept of the state to the concept of law the indispensable precondition for the development of a genuine science of law, as a *science of positive law* purified of all natural law. That is the aim of the pure theory of law, which is simultaneously the pure theory of the state, because a theory of the state is possible only as a theory of state-law, while all law is state-law, because every state is a legal state.

NOTES

* *Logos* **11** (1922/23) 261–284.

[1] Cf. Menzel, A., *Zur Psychologie des Staates*, 1915.

[2] Durkheim, E., *Les formes élémentaires de la vie religieuse*, Paris 1912, p. 322. Cf. also pp. 295 and 597.

[3] Feuerbach, L., *Wesen der Religion*, Sämtliche Werke, Stuttgart, vol. 8, pp. 281–283.

[4] Freud, S., *Totem and Taboo*, 2nd edn. 1920.

[5] Cf. also Kirchmann, J. von, *Die Grundbegriffe des Rechts und der Moral*, 2nd edn., 1873, p. 72.

[6] *Op. cit.*, p. 49.

[7] Cf. Kelsen, H., *Der soziologische und der juristische Staatsbegriff*, Tübingen 1922.

[8] Cf. Pitamic, L., 'Plato, Aristoteles und die reine Rechtslehre', in *Zeitschrift für öffentliches Recht* (ed. by Hans Kelsen), **2**, 683 ff.

[9] Feuerbach, L., *op. cit.*, p. 143.

[10] Cf. Weyr, F., 'Zum Problem eines einheitlichen Rechtssystems', *Archiv des öffentlichen Rechts* **23** (1908) 529ff.

[11] *Op. cit.*, pp. 306 and 410.

[12] Merkl, A., 'Die Lehre von der Rechtskraft, entwickelt aus dem Rechtsbegriff', *Wiener staatswissenschaftliche Studien* (ed. by Hans Kelsen) **15** (1923) No. 2, Leipzig-Vienna.

[13] Sander, F., 'Das Faktum der Revolution und die Kontinuität der Rechtsordnung', *Zeitschrift für öffentliches Recht* (ed. by Hans Kelsen) **1** (1919/20) 132–164. Also his 'Die transzendentale Methode der Rechtsphilosophie und der Begriff des Rechtsverfahrens', *ibid* pp. 468–507.

CHAPTER IV

LAW AND MORALITY*

1. Moral norms as social norms

In defining law as norm, so far as it is the subject-matter of a specific legal science, it is marked off from nature, and legal science from natural science. But in addition to legal norms there are also others which regulate the mutual behaviour of men, namely social norms, and legal science is therefore not the only discipline concerned with the study and description of social norms. These other social norms can be collectively given the name of morality, and the discipline concerned with their study and description may be called ethics.[1] In so far as justice is a demand of morality, the relation between justice and law is included in the relation between morality and law. It should be noted here that in ordinary usage, just as law is confused with legal science, so morality is very often confounded with ethics, and things are said of the latter which apply only to the former: that it governs human behaviour, that it imposes duties and rights, i.e., that it lays down authoritative norms, whereas it can only study and describe the moral norms laid down by a moral authority or arisen out of custom. Now not only is the methodological purity of legal science endangered by failure to observe the boundary separating it from natural science; it is still further endangered by the fact that it is not divided, or not clearly enough divided, from ethics – that no sharp distinction is made between law and morality.

The social character of morality is sometimes questioned by pointing out that, in addition to moral norms regulating a man's behaviour towards other men, there are also those which prescribe his behaviour towards himself, such as the norm forbidding suicide, or those enjoining courage or chastity. But even these norms only enter the consciousness of man living in society. The behaviour they define for a man is indeed directly related only to himself; but indirectly it is related to the other members of the community. For only in virtue of the effects which this behaviour has on the community does it become a moral norm in the minds of the community-members. Even the so-called duties of a man towards himself are social duties. For an individual living in isolation they would be meaningless.

2. Morality as the Regulation of Internal Behaviour

A distinction between morality and law cannot relate to the behaviour which the norms of the two social orders oblige men to. Suicide can be forbidden, not only by morality, but also by law; courage and chastity can be not only moral duties, but also legal ones. Even the frequently maintained view that law prescribes external, morality, internal behaviour, will not do. The norms of both orders define both kinds of behaviour. The moral virtue of courage consists not only in a mental state of fearlessness, but also in an outward behaviour conditioned by this state. And if a legal order forbids murder, it not only forbids the causing of a man's death through the outward behaviour of another; it also forbids an inward piece of behaviour, namely the intention of producing such a result. The "inner" behaviour which – in the opinion of many moral philosophers – is demanded by morality, as opposed to law, is said to consist in this, that for a piece of behaviour to be moral, it must take place contrary to inclination,[2] or – which is the same thing – contrary to egoistic interests. So far as this says no more than that the duty to a particular line of conduct laid down by a moral norm exists, i.e., that this norm holds good, even if inclination or egoistic interest run counter to the conduct ordained, the same applies equally to the duties laid down by legal norms. That a social order should prescribe conduct which may possibly run counter to some inclination or egoistic interest of the individuals whose behaviour is regulated by the order, is not to be avoided. Yet to prescribe conduct in accordance with all the inclinations or egoistic interests of those subject to such norms would be superfluous, since men follow their inclinations, or seek to realise their egoistic interests, without being obligated to do so. A social order, i.e., a set of norms prescribing a particular course of human behaviour, only makes sense, if another state of affairs ought to exist than that which results from everyone following the inclination, or seeking to realise the one egoistic interest, which would be present without the validity and efficacy of a social order; that is, if men ought to behave also against their inclinations or egoistic interests. It should be noted here, that if the individuals subject to the social order do actually behave in accordance with the norms of this order, this too occurs only because such behaviour accords with their inclination or egoistic interest – a motivation evoked by the social order, and possibly but not necessarily opposed to those other motives which would be present only if the social order did not intervene. A man can have mutually incompatible inclinations or interests. His actual behaviour depends upon which inclination is the more intense, which interest the stronger. No social order can do away with men's inclinations or egoistic interests as motives for their acts and omissions. If it is to be effective, it can only create the inclination or interest to behave in accordance with the social order, and to repudiate the inclinations or egoistic interests which would operate if it were absent.

The above-mentioned ethical doctrine is at times, however, understood to mean that only conduct directed against inclination or egoistic interest is of any moral value.[3] Since "to have moral value" means nothing else but to accord with a moral norm, one must be maintaining by this doctrine that morality simply prescribes that in one's conduct one should repress one's inclinations, and not realise one's egoistic interests, but act from other motives. This means that the moral norm relates only to the motive of behaviour. Quite apart from the psychological impossibility of complying with the requirement to act from motives other than inclination or egoistic interest, a morality whose norm relates only to the motive of behaviour presupposes another social order, prescribing an external course of conduct. The norm of a morality relating only to the motive for outward behaviour is incomplete; it can hold good only in conjunction with those norms which prescribe the outward behaviour, and these too must be moral norms. It is not any conduct you please that can be moral, so long as it is carried out contrary to inclination or egoistic interest. If somebody obeys another's order to commit a murder, his act can have no moral value, even though performed against his inclination or egoistic interest, so long as murder is forbidden, i.e., deemed of negative value, by the social order assumed to prevail. Conduct can have moral value only if, not only its motive, but also the conduct itself, corresponds to a moral norm. In moral judgement the motive cannot be separated from the conduct motivated. For this reason also, the concept of morality cannot be restricted to the normative injunction: Repress your inclinations, refrain from realising your egoistic interests. But only if it is so restricted can morality be distinguished from law by maintaining that the former relates only to internal behaviour, whereas the latter also prescribes external behaviour.[4]

3. Morality as a primitive order without coercive character

In respect neither of the creation nor the application of their norms can law and morality be essentially distinguished. Like those of law, the norms of morality are also created through custom and conscious injunction (on the part, say, of a prophet or founder of a religion, such as Jesus). In this sense morality is positive, no less than law, and only a positive morality comes into consideration for a scientific ethics, just as only a positive law does for a scientific theory of law. It is true, indeed, that – unlike law in the modern state – a moral order envisages no functionally specialised, i.e., central organs for the application of its norms. This application consists in moral judgement of the behaviour by others who are governed by this order. But a primitive legal order is likewise wholly decentralised, and cannot in this respect be distinguished from a moral order. It is very characteristic that at times people wish to acknowledge the wholly decentralised general law of nations only as a morality of nations.

A distinction between law and morality can be recognised, not in what the two social orders enjoin or forbid, but only in how they enjoin or forbid a particular piece of human behaviour. Law can be essentially distinguished from morality only if we conceive of law as a coercive order, i.e., as a normative order, which seeks to bring about a particular piece of human behaviour by attaching to the opposite behaviour a socially organised act of coercion; whereas morality is a social order which lays down no such sanctions – an order whose sanctions consist only in approval of conduct conforming to the norm and disapproval of that which goes against it.

4. Law as a part of morality

If law and morality are recognised as different kinds of normative system, the question arises as to how the two are related. This question has a dual meaning. One can mean by it, what the actual relation is between law and morality, but also, what the relation between them ought to be. The two questions get confused with each other, which leads to misunderstandings. The first question is sometimes answered by saying that law is in essence moral, i.e., that behaviour enjoined or forbidden by legal norms is also enjoined or forbidden by the norms of morality. That if a social order enjoins a course of conduct which morality forbids, or forbids one which morality enjoins, this order is not one of law, because it is not just. But the question is also answered to the effect that law can be moral – in the sense just defined, i.e., just – but does not have to be; that a social order which is not moral – and that means just – can nevertheless be an order of law; even if it would be admitted that the law ought to be moral, which is to say, just.

If the question as to the relation of law and morality be understood as a question about the content of law, and not one about its form, if it is maintained that law essentially has a moral content or constitutes a moral value, it is thereby claimed that law has validity within the moral sphere, that the legal order is a constituent of the moral order, that law is moral value, it is thereby claimed that law has validity within the moral justification of law – and that is its real meaning – it has to presuppose that there is only *one* uniquely valid morality, an absolute morality, therefore, an absolute moral value; and that only norms in accordance with this absolute morality, and therefore constituting the absolute moral value, can be regarded as "law". That is to say, we start from a definition of law which designates the latter as a part of morality and identifies law and justice.

5. Relativity of Moral Value

Supposing, however, that from the standpoint of scientific knowledge we reject the assumption of absolute values in general, and of an absolute moral value in particular, since an absolute value can be assumed only on the basis of religious belief in the absolute and transcendent authority of a deity, and it therefore has to be admitted that from the aforesaid standpoint there is no such thing as an absolute morality, i.e., a uniquely valid morality, ruling out the possibility that any other might be valid.

Supposing we deny that what is evil according to this moral order is evil in all circumstances. Supposing we admit that at different times, among different peoples, and even within the same people among different ranks, classes and professions, very diverse and mutually contradictory moral systems obtain; that under varying circumstances different things can be accounted good and evil, just and unjust, and that nothing has to be accounted good or evil, just or unjust, under all possible circumstances – that only relative moral values exist: In that case, the claim that social norms must have a moral content, that they must be just in order to be regarded as law, can only mean that these norms must contain something which is common to all possible systems of morality and for justice. But in view of the extraordinary diversity of what men have actually held good and bad, just and unjust, at different times and places, it is impossible to establish any element common to the contents of the various moral orders. It has been claimed that one requirement common to all moral systems is: To keep peace and do violence to no one. But Heraclitus himself taught that war is not only "father", i.e., cause, of all, but also "king", i.e., supreme norm-giving authority, the highest value, and thus good; and that law is strife, and therefore just.[5] And does not Jesus say: "Suppose ye that I am come to give peace on earth? I tell you, Nay; but rather division:"[6] – thereby proclaiming peace to be by no means the highest value, at least for the moral order of this world. Can it be denied that in the conviction of many, even today, war has an ethical value, because it allows virtues to be exercised and ideals realised which are higher than the values of peace; is the morality of pacifism nowhere in dispute? Is the life-philosophy of liberalism, viz., that emulation and the competitive struggle guarantee the best possible state of society, in accordance with the ideal of peace? The latter by no means represents the highest value in all systems of morality, and in many it is no value at all. And even if we could establish a common element in all moral systems hitherto obtaining, there would be no sufficient reason for considering a coercive order which does not contain this element, which enjoins a form of behaviour which has never yet been held good or just in any society, and forbids one which has never yet been held evil or unjust, to be not "moral" or "just", and therefore not law. For if we presuppose no moral value to be given a priori, and thus to be absolute, we have no means of defining what must be deemed good and evil, just and unjust, under all circumstances. And then it cannot be denied that even what is enjoined in the coercive order under discussion can be held to be good or just, and what is forbidden there, evil or unjust; and that hence even this order is – relatively – moral or just. That which is necessarily common to all possible moral systems is simply that they are social norms, i.e., norms which – directly or indirectly – lay down a specific form of behaviour for man vis-à-vis other men, i.e., posit this as obligatory. What all possible moral systems have in common is their *form*, their obligating or *normative character*. The morally good is that which accords with a social norm laying down a specific type of human behaviour; the morally bad, that which is contrary to such a norm. Relative moral value is constituted by a social norm which posits as obligatory a specific form of human behaviour. Norm and value are correlative concepts.

On these presuppositions, the claim that law is essentially moral means, not that it has a particular content, but that it is a norm, and a social norm indeed, which posits as obligatory a specific form of human behaviour. In this relative sense, then, all law is moral, all law constitutes a – relative – moral value. But this means that the question of the relation between law and morality is a question, not about the content of law, but about its form. It cannot then be said, as is sometimes done, that law is not only a norm (or command), but also constitutes or incorporates a value (such a claim makes sense only on the presupposition of an absolute and divine value). For law constitutes a value precisely through the fact that it is a norm: it constitutes *legal value*, which is at the same time a – relative – moral value; which says no more, however, than that law is a norm.

In so saying, therefore, we by no means accept the theory that law essentially represents a "moral minimum", that for a coercive order to be able to figure as law, it must fulfil a minimum requirement of morality. For this requirement presupposes an absolute morality of determinate content, or at least a content common to all positive moral systems, and for the most part, indeed, it postulates the ideal of peace as the requirement of an absolute morality, or as a content common to all positive moral systems. It emerges from the foregoing that what is here described as legal value is no moral minimum in this sense, and in particular that the value of peace represents no essential element of the concept of law.

6. Separation of Law and Morality

If it is assumed that law *is* essentially moral, then it makes no sense, on the presupposition of an absolute moral value, to insist that law *ought* to be moral. Such a demand is only intelligible, and the morality presupposed here only represents a standard of value for law, if we grant the possibility of an immoral, morally bad law, and thus if the element of moral content is not incorporated in the definition of law. If a theory of positive law insists upon distinguishing law and morality in general, and law and justice in particular, and on not confusing them with one another, it sets itself against the traditional view, by most jurists held to be self-evident, which presupposes that there is only *one, uniquely valid, and thus absolute* morality, and hence an absolute justice. The demand for a separation of law and morality, law and justice, signifies that the validity of a positive legal order is independent of the validity of this one, uniquely valid, absolute morality, "the" morality, morality *par excellence*. If only relative moral values are presupposed, then the demand that law should be moral, and hence just, can only mean that the framework of positive law should be in accordance with some one among the many possible systems of morality; which does not, however, exclude the possibility of demanding that the framework of positive law should accord with some other moral system, and maybe actually does so, while it contradicts another one. If, again on the assumption of merely relative values, it is insisted that law should be separated from morality in general and justice in particular, this demand does not in fact mean that law has nothing to do with morality or justice, that the concept of law does not fall under that of goodness. For the concept of "goodness" can only be defined as that which "ought to be", as that which accords with a norm; and if law is defined as a norm, this implies that what is lawful is a good. To insist, on the presupposition of a relativistic value-theory, upon separating law from morality, and thus justice, means only that if a legal order is evaluated as moral or immoral, just or unjust, this expresses its relation to one of many possible moral systems and not to "the" morality, so that only a relative value-judgement is passed, and not an absolute one; and that the validity of a positive legal order is independent of its conformity or lack of it to any particular system of morality.

A relativistic theory of value does not mean – as it is often misunderstood to do – that there are no values, and in particular no justice, but that there are no absolute, only relative values, no absolute, only relative justice; that the values we constitute by our norm-positing acts and found our value-judgements upon, cannot advance any claim to exclude the possibility of opposing values.

It is self-evident that a purely relative morality cannot – either consciously or unconsciously – perform the required function of furnishing an absolute standard for the evaluation of a positive legal order. Such a standard is not in fact to be had by way of scientific knowledge. This does not mean, however, that there is no standard at all. Every moral system can serve as such a standard. But if the framework of a positive legal order is to be judged "morally", it is necessary to bear in mind that the standard is a relative one, that another evaluation on the basis of another moral system is not excluded; that if a legal order is reckoned unjust by the standard of one moral system, it can be reckoned just by the standard of another.

7. Justification of Law by Morality

If a moral order, such as that proclaimed by St. Paul in his epistle to the Romans, prescribes observance under all circumstances of the norms laid down by the legal authority (because this authority comes from God), and thus rules out in advance any contradiction between itself and positive law, it is essentially directed towards legitimising positive law by lending it moral value. The demand that law should be distinguished from morality, and legal science from ethics, signifies that, from the standpoint of a scientific knowledge of positive law, its legitimisation by a moral order distinct from the legal order is irrelevant, since the task of legal science is neither to approve nor disapprove of its subject-matter, but only to study and describe it. Even if the *legal norms* constitute values, in that they prescribe obligations, the function of legal science is still in no sense a valuing or evaluating, but rather a value-free description of its subject-matter. The scientific jurist identifies himself with no legal value, not even with that which he describes.

If the moral order does not prescribe obedience to the positive legal order under all circumstances, and if it is thus possible for the moral and legal orders to contradict, the demand for a separation of law from morality, and of legal science from ethics, signifies that the validity of positive legal norms does not depend upon their accordance with the moral order; that from the standpoint of a study of positive law, a legal norm can be regarded as valid, even when it contradicts the moral order.

What it all comes to, essentially, is the insight that there is not just one single morality, "the" morality, but rather that there are many moral systems, exceedingly different from one another and often mutually contradictory; that a positive legal order can very well correspond – by and large – to the moral intuitions of a particular group or level within the population subject to it, especially those of the ruling group – and actually does so correspond as a rule – but at the same time contradicts the moral intuitions of another group or level. Above all it must be seen that intuitions about what is ethically good and evil, ethically justifiable and unjustifiable, are subject – just as law is – to constant change; and that a legal order, or certain of its norms, which may have corresponded to the moral claims current at the time of its validity, may nowadays be judged highly immoral. The thesis rejected by the pure theory of law, though widely disseminated in traditional jurisprudence, that law must in essence be moral, that an immoral social order is not law, presupposes, however, an absolute morality, i.e., one which holds good at all times and places. Otherwise it could not achieve its purpose, of applying to the social order a fixed standard, independent of temporal and spatial circumstances, for what is law and what is not.

The thesis that law is essentially moral, i.e., that only a moral social order is an order of law, is rejected by the pure theory of law, not only because this thesis presupposes an absolute morality, but also because in its actual application, through the jurisprudence prevailing in a particular legal community, it tends towards an uncritical legitimisation of the political coercive order constituting that community. For it is presupposed as self-evident that one's own political coercive order is an order of law. The problematic standard of absolute morality is only applied to the coercive orders of foreign states; it is only these which are disqualified as immoral and therefore non-legal, if they fail to comply with certain requirements, adequately met by one's own state, e.g., if they recognise or do not recognise private property, or are democratic or non-democratic in character. But since one's own coercive order is an order of law, it must also, according to the thesis, be moral. Such a legitimisation of positive law may do good service politically, despite its logical inadequacy. For legal science it is inadmissible. For the latter does not have to legitimise law, or in any way to justify – either by an absolute or a relative morality – the normative order which its task is simply to study and describe.

NOTES

* *Estudios Juridico-Sociales. Homenaje al Profesor Luiz Legaz y Lacambra*, 1960, pp. 153–164.

[1] Moritz Schlick, *Problems of Ethics*, Vienna 1930; English translation by D. Rynin, New York 1939, maintains (pp. 21 f.) that ethics is a factual science and that even if it "were a normative science", it would not cease "to be a science of *facts*. Ethics has to do entirely with the *actual*". He bases this view on the claim that "the ultimate valuations are facts existing in human consciousness ...". It is true that "valuations", i.e., the acts whereby a piece of behaviour is judged to conform or otherwise with a norm, are facts of existence, no less than the acts whereby value-constituting norms are laid down. But the norms laid down by these acts, and applied in acts of valuation, are not facts of existence, but meanings, and the meaning, indeed, of the acts laying down the norms. This meaning is an ought. Ethics, like legal science, is a normative science, because it has as its subject-matter norms of obligation as meanings, but not the real acts existing in the causal nexus whose meanings the norms are. That certainly does not mean that the norms, as in Kant's ethics (Schlick, *op. cit.* pp. 10 f), are commands without a commander, demands without a demander, i.e., norms without norm-stating acts. It means that ethics – like legal science – is concerned with norms, but only has to do with norm-stating acts insofar as they are the content of norms, i.e., are governed by norms. The misinterpretation of ethics as a factual science, the view that it is merely a branch of psychology and sociology (cf. A. J. Ayer, *Language, Truth and Logic*, London 1936, p. 168: "It appears, then, that ethics, as a branch of knowledge, is nothing more than a department of psychology and sociology."), rests upon a failure to distinguish between the norm-stating act and the norm laid down as the meaning of this act.

Schlick's attempt to present ethics as an empirical factual science obviously rests upon the perfectly legitimate aim of removing it from the field of metaphysical speculation. But this aim is sufficiently accomplished if the norms which form the subject-matter of ethics are recognised as the meanings of empirical facts brought about by men in the world of sense, and not as the commands of transcendent entities. If the norms of morality, like those of positive law, are the meanings of empirical facts, ethics, no less than legal science, can be described – in contrast to metaphysical speculation – as an empirical science, even though its subject-matter does not consist of facts, but of norms.

[2] This is notoriously the ethical doctrine of Kant. Cf. *Fundamental Principles of the Metaphysics of Ethics*, Transl. by T. K. Abbott, p. 19 [20].

[3] Kant, *op. cit.*, p. 16 [17]: "But I maintain that in such a case an action of this kind [if done from inclination], however proper, however amiable it may be, has nevertheless no true moral worth ...."

[4] For Kant also, if an action is to have moral worth, i.e., be morally good, it must not only be done "from duty", but also "in accordance with duty", i.e., must conform to the moral law. The moral norm: Act not from inclination, but "from duty", therefore presupposes other moral norms which obligate to particular actions. One of the most essential points

in his ethics is that the concept of good and evil "must not be determined before the moral law..., but only after it and by means of it." (*Critique of Practical Reason*, transl. by Abbott, p. 154 [183]).

For Kant, a person acts "from inclination" who "finds an [inner] pleasure" in acting as he does (*Fundamental Principles*, p. 16 [17]). But even a person who acts "from duty", i.e., "from respect for the law", acts from inclination; for he acts in this way because he finds an inner pleasure in obeying the law, because the consciousness of acting lawfully or dutifully gives him "inner pleasure"; he acts, therefore, from an inclination to act dutifully. From a psychological standpoint there is no disputing this; and the question of what motives a man acts from is a psychological question.

Kant distinguishes law as a regulation of outward behaviour, from morality as a regulation of inward behaviour, namely of the motive of this behaviour, and accordingly contrasts "legality" with "morality". He says (*Metaphysic of Morals*, Introduction, transl. by J. Ellington: *The Metaphysical Principles of Virtue*, New York 1964, pp. 12–13 [214]): "In contradistinction to natural laws, these laws of freedom are called moral laws. Insofar as they are directed to mere external actions and the lawfulness of such actions, they are called juridical; but when they also demand that these laws themselves are to be the determining grounds of actions, then they are ethical. Accordingly, we say that agreement with juridical laws constitutes the legality of action, while agreement with ethical ones constitutes its morality". This means that "legality", too, is agreement with moral laws. Legal norms are moral norms; and so moral norms also refer to external actions; there is, however, a moral norm prescribing that one should act, not from inclination, but from respect for the law. When Kant says that only an action in accordance with this norm has moral value, he is distinguishing moral value in the specifically narrower sense, i.e., conformity to this special moral norm, from moral value in the wider sense, i.e., conformity to the other moral norms. Legality, too, is a moral value; for it is conformity with regard to "moral" norms.

[5] That is the meaning of fragments 53, 80, 112 (Diels). "War is father of all and king of all, and some he reveals as gods, others as men, some he makes slaves, others free" (transl. by W. K. C. Guthrie: *A History of Greek Philosophy*, I. p. 446). That in war the victors become gods or free men, the vanquished men or slaves, is just. For "one must know that war is common, and justice strife, and that all things come about by way of strife and necessity" (*ibid.* p. 447; Kelsen misquotes the second occurrence of "strife" as "law (justice)"). Heraclitus' ethics is a sort of natural law theory: "... wisdom is to speak the truth and to act according to nature, paying heed thereto", (transl. by K. Freeman: *Ancilla to the Pre-Socratic Philosophers*, p. 32). From the fact that the reality of nature exhibits war and strife as a general phenomenon, it follows that war and strife are just.

[6] Luke XII, 51; "For from henceforth there shall be five in one house divided, three against two, and two against three. The father shall be divided against the son, and the son against the father; the mother against the daughter, and the daughter against the mother; the mother in law against her daughter in law, and the daughter in law against her mother in law." Luke XII, 52–3. Admittedly Jesus also said "Blessed are the peacemakers: for they shall be called the children of God" (Matthew, V, 9); but other statements attributed to him in the gospels are also in contradiction to one another.

CHAPTER V

STATE-FORM AND WORLD-OUTLOOK*

1. From the time of the great French Revolution, democracy came to be the political ideal of the 19th century. To be sure, there were also not inconsiderable forces in the Western world which were working to uphold the principle of monarchy. But they were reckoned to be reactionary. The idea of the popular state was the thing of the future. It drew the hearts of all who believed in progress and wished to see a higher development of social life. And it was above all the young, rising bourgeoisie who fought for this idea.

In the 20th century – since the Great War – things have been different. At first, indeed, the war gave a quite extraordinary impulse towards a realising of the democratic principle. The newly created states adopted democratic constitutions, and Germany, one of the last powerful bastions of monarchy, became a republic. But at the same time, with the establishment of the Soviet Union in Russia and the fascist state in Italy, a new political and spiritual movement is setting in, which is directly and vehemently opposed to democracy. The ideal of the latter is fading; and on the dark horizon of our age there rises a new star, to which the hopes, not only of the bourgeoisie, but also of a part of the proletarian masses, are turning all the more trustingly, the more bloodily its radiance gleams upon them: it is dictatorship.

Since it is not the passionate outcry of politics which ought to be heard here, but only the cool tones of science, it cannot be the purpose of the following enquiry to make a voluntary decision between two such opposing ideals; our object is only to distinguish them from an epistemic point of view. It is not a matter of defending or attacking one or other of the two basic types of political and social structure as such; the point is to understand them both, to apprehend their nature, which is, however, to lay hold of each by its own roots. Yet it is not enough for this purpose to describe the outward circumstances in which the two opposing principles of organisation, democracy and autocracy, are typically manifested. For we only need to see how the whole history of mankind, regarded as a history of human organisation, is merely an eternal struggle between the ambition of some one man to subdue the others, the many, to his will, and the striving of these many to liberate themselves from an alien rule and to determine their own destiny. We only need to see how, in the history of the spirit which accompanies the real movement of history, and in fact as well, the ideas and ideologies of men contend (in the air, so to speak) above the parties fighting for power on the ground beneath. We only need to see how, in that spiritual history likewise, the battle over the value of democracy and autocracy is no less undecided; how here too it is always having to be started anew, is always having to be lost or won, now for the one side and now for the other. And once all this is recognised, we shall be inclined to think that – for the contending parties at least – the question at issue is not just a problem of social technique, that something more is involved than just two different methods of organisation. The parallels existing between the political and the philosophical issues are too striking for that.

2. That political or social theory and ethics are most intimately interrelated, is nothing to be surprised at. For at bottom both are quite inseparable from each other, the one being merely a component part of the other. More important, however, is the wide-ranging analogy which holds between points of view in political or social theory and those in the theory of knowledge. The core of all ethico-political reasoning is the relation of ruling subject and ruled object, whereas the concern of all epistemological speculation is the relation of knowing subject to the object known. And the manner in which here – in the field of knowledge – the subject takes possession of the object, or the object seizes the subject, has, for a profounder analysis, a very considerable resemblance to the relation of dominance as the subject-matter of politics. Hence, in both cases, an a priori limited number of ways of stating and solving the problem, and the inability to reconcile the opposition in which both are involved. Hence, in both cases, the eternal recurrence, the well-nigh monotonous alternation of the same theorems, the impression as if in politics and philosophy – quite unlike the fields of science and technology – the human mind were obliged to move perpetually in a circle.

Between politics and philosophy there is, however, not only an outward parallel, but also an inner connection. Since it is a subject-object relation which stands at the centre of both of them, the character of the politicising and philosophising subject, his original endowment, is bound to be of decisive importance for the shaping of the intuition which this subject develops concerning his relation to the object – whether of dominance or of knowledge. The common root of political belief, as of philosophical conviction, remains always the psychic structure, the character of the politician or philosopher, the type of self he has, i.e., the manner in which this self experiences itself in relation to the object, the "thou" or "it". Only if we recognise here, in the peculiarities of men themselves, the ultimate determining grounds for the shaping of their political and philosophical systems, can we account for the unbridgeability of the oppositions, the impossibility of complete mutual understanding, the embittered violence with which these antitheses collide – already also in the intellectual sphere, as differences of opinion, and not primarily as conflicts of power. A typology of political and philosophical doctrines must ultimately terminate in a characterology, or at least seek to combine with one. Since it is the same man who has ideas about his relation to his neighbour and the ordering of this relation, just as he does about his relation to the world in general and the possibility of knowing it, we may assume that a particular view of life, especially a particular political attitude, is correlated with a particular world-outlook corresponding to it. But precisely because it is man – *not a well-thought-out book*, but *man with all his contradictions* – in whom the will to practical life-shaping is combined with a world-view, we must be prepared for the fact that a particular political ideal will not always and invariably be associated with the philosophical standpoint adequate to it. It would be a misapprehension to suppose that anyone inclined to a particular philosophical, and especially epistemological viewpoint, must necessarily also possess the political convictions that go with it. Yet as a matter of intellectual history, a connection of this sort can be made out; and I shall also exhibit its presence in a few particularly representative minds. One must beware, however, of neglecting the very powerful forces which again destroy this connection, which prevent the political outlook from matching its philosophical counterpart, or vice versa. In trying to discover the relations between state-form and world-outlook, we must remember above all things, that the nature of man is at bottom non-rational, and therefore non-logical, and that man's will has the power of giving a turn to the judgement which runs counter, not only to the original inclinations, but also to the postulates of consistency. We must take into account the external circumstances, which, if they set no bounds already to philosophical speculation, may yet abolish or endanger the freedom of political opinion. We must take quite particular note of the fact that political value judgements, and especially the decision between democracy and autocracy, are very often founded neither on a thorough investigation of the facts nor on scrupulous self-examination, but are products of a momentary situation and even a passing mood. Nor should we underestimate a well-nigh regular oscillation, arising from the fact that every political régime unavoidably calls forth an opposition to itself. It is obvious enough that in a democracy the discontented will be in favour of autocracy, and vice versa. But besides these there are the discontented – and justifiably so, perhaps – who are always against the currently realised political ideal and in favour of that which at the moment is not yet existent, or exists no longer. Many who from deepest conviction today see in democracy the root of all evil, and therefore call for dictatorship, would probably be liberal democrats in a police state, would have fought on the barricades in 1848 for the black, red and gold of the German republic, and will probably stand again on the same side of the barricades in 1948. Yet these are only the lesser minds, who will not be much loss if they are dropped from the picture. Among the greater, however, the looked-for connection between political and philosophical viewpoint is at times not in evidence, because the philosophers have evolved no political system, while the practical and theoretical politicians have simply not arrived at a consciously philosophical statement of the problem.

Subject only to these limitations is it possible, therefore, to maintain that a connection exists between a political attitude and a philosophical one.

In order to display it, we must begin by setting forth the essential nature of the two archetypal forms of social structure, and that in such a way as to depict their ideal types, the Ideas of democracy and autocracy, as they have never yet been perfectly realised anywhere, but as we have to presuppose them in order to understand political reality, as it approximates more closely now to the one Idea and now to the other. This reality always presents an admixture of elements belonging to both; a mixture in which sometimes elements of the one ideal type are uppermost, and sometimes those of the other.

3. The Idea of democracy is the Idea of freedom as political self-determination. It is found expressed in its relatively purest form where the state order is directly created by those who are themselves subject to it, where a people, in an assembly of the whole population, agrees upon the norms for its conduct. It already constitutes a weakening of this principle of autonomy, only scantily disguised by the fiction of representation, when the popular assembly is replaced by a parliament elected by the people – even if chosen on the principle of universal and equal franchise – which thus restricts self-determination to a creation of the organ which sets up the governmental order. The essential nature of democracy cannot, however, be wholly understood through the Idea of freedom alone. In itself the Idea of freedom is quite incapable of forming the basis of any social order whose essential nature is obligation, and which only constitutes the social bond, the community, as a normative obligation. The ultimate meaning of the democratic principle is that the political subject should will the freedom that is aimed at, not only for himself, but also for others; that the 'I' wills freedom also for the 'thou', because it feels that 'thou' to be of the same nature as itself. Hence the Idea of freedom must be supplemented, and restricted, by the Idea of equality, if the notion of a democratic form of society is to come about. And only in virtue of this peculiar combination of freedom and equality is it possible to justify the majority principle, so characteristic of democracy. The principle of unanimity, which is perfectly in keeping with the Idea of freedom alone, would render impossible any formation of a communal will, and hence any community, although, precisely because of the intrinsic equality of I and thou, community remains enjoined as the goal; and thus the demand that all should be free must be replaced by the requirement that only so many should be free as is possible, i.e., that in regard to self-determination, the will of as many as possible should be in harmony with the communal will, the will of as few as possible in opposition to it. But since all are equal, and it is therefore not a question whether just this one or that should be free, but only that as many as possible should be, the required maxi-

mum of freedom, and minimum of subjection, is attained if the communal will is determined by the wills of the majority of members of the community.

If we ask what type of character it is which corresponds to such a political attitude, in which the longing for freedom is modified by the sense of equality, it is obviously that person in whom the experience of his own self is not so elemental, not so utterly different from all other experiences, the experiencing of all others, the experiencing of the not-self, that this self would be incapable of honouring in fellow-feeling the claim of the thou to be also a self, to be also acknowledged as such. It is the type of personality whose basic experience is the *Tat twam asi*, the man who, when he looks across at another, hears a voice within him saying: That is you. This kind of personality recognises himself again in the other, experiences the other a priori, not as something essentially alien, not as an enemy, but as an equal and therefore a friend, and does not feel himself to be something unique, altogether incomparable and beyond repetition. It is the type whose ego-feeling is relatively subdued, the type of the sympathising, peace-loving, non-aggressive man, the man whose primitive aggressive instincts are turned, not outward so much as inward, and are expressed here as an inclination to self-criticism and an enhanced tendency to feel guilt and a sense of responsibility. Nor is it by any means so paradoxical as might at first sight appear, that precisely the type of a relatively subdued self-consciousness should be matched to a political form characterised by a minimisation of dominance. For the subject's attitude to the problem of authority, the basic problem of politics, is essentially determined by the intensity with which the will to dominate is active in the particular individual whose attitude it is. But the individual tends to identify with a form of state which encourages him, even as a subject under authority, to identify with the ruling power.

The stronger this will to dominance, the smaller the value attached to freedom. The total negation of this value, the maximisation of dominance, is the Idea of autocracy. Here the governmental order is created by a single individual, to whom all others are subordinated – having no part whatever in forming the communal will – and who stands over against all others as one completely different, because unique, as their lord and leader. The radical inequality between ruler and ruled is the a priori presupposition of this form of state, which corresponds, in the characterological sense, to the type having an enhanced consciousness of self. The incapacity or refusal to acknowledge the thou, as a being similar to his originally experienced self, no more permits equality to appear as an ideal to this type of man, than freedom or peace can rank as political values to him, given his vigorous drive to aggression and intensive urge to power. It is one of the characteristic ways of enhancing self-consciousness that the subject should identify with his superego or ideal self, and that the dictator clothed with unrestricted power should represent for him the ideal self. It is by no means a contradiction, and – psychologically speaking – only logical, that precisely this type should be avid for the strictest discipline and blind obedience even, and should also really find his happiness in obeying no less than in issuing commands. The identification with authority: that is the secret of obedience.

4. Democracy, with its limitation of authority, also implies a relaxation of discipline, since where there is in principle no absolute dominance, there is also no absolute dominance of the majority. For the rule of the majority differs from any other kind of rule, in that it not only conceptually presupposes an opposition – since there has to be a minority – but also recognises it politically and even protects it, insofar as democracy develops institutions whereby a minimal potential of existence and function is guaranteed to religious, national and economic groups, even though only a minority belongs to them, and indeed precisely because they are only minority groups. From the permanent tension, inherent in democracy, between majority and minority, government and opposition, there arises the dialectical procedure, so characteristic of decision-making in this form of state. Democracy – it has truly been said – is discussion. And for that very reason, the outcome of the process in which the state's will is formed here is – compromise. Since this guarantees internal peace, the peace-loving character prefers it to an – eventually possible – subjugation of the opponent by force. The life-principle of every democracy is therefore – not, indeed, as has sometimes been supposed, the economic freedom of liberalism, for there can just as well be a socialist democracy as a liberal one – but rather spiritual freedom, freedom to express opinions, freedom of belief and conscience,

the principle of toleration, and more especially, the freedom of science, in conjunction with the belief in its possible objectivity. The constitutions of all democracies bear witness to this spirit. And this attitude, especially towards science, corresponds throughout to the type of character which has here been described as the specifically democratic one. In the great dilemma between willing and knowing, between the drive to mastery of the world and the urge towards understanding it, the pendulum swings more in the direction of knowing than of willing, more towards the side of understanding than of domination; precisely because here the wish for power, the intensity of self-experience therein expressed, the value put on the subject, is relatively subdued, while rational criticism, and hence also self-criticism, are relatively strong and the value of the object therefore relatively enhanced, so that belief in a critical and thus objective science is furnished along with this.

In autocracy, no opposition can be tolerated; here there is no discussion and no compromise, but only decree. And so here also there can be no talk of any freedom of opinion, belief or conscience. The primacy of willing over knowing has as its consequence, that only what is good can be accounted true; but what is good is decided by no-one except the state authority, to whom not only the will, but also the opinion and belief of its subjects must be subjugated, so that anyone resisting this authority is reckoned not only as a wrong-doer, but also as having fallen into error. It is therefore self-evident that in this political system even the freedom of science must also – directly or indirectly – be abolished. So far as science with its findings in any way affects the interests of the ruling power, it can be tolerated only as a serviceable tool of the latter. And nothing is more typical of the turn to an autocratically inclined state of mind, than when belief in the possibility of a science independent of political interests, and therefore worthy of freedom, begins to disappear – than when the ideal of the objectivity of knowledge is abandoned in favour of other ideals. Such a movement normally goes hand in hand with a preference for the irrational over the rational. In the ineradicable conflict between science and religion, the latter claims priority over the former.

5. The rationalism of democracy shows itself particularly clearly, however, in the endeavour to set up the governmental order as a system

of preferably written and deliberately enacted general norms, whereby individual judicial and administrative acts are determined as extensively as possible, and thereby rendered accountable. Democracy has an inherent tendency to shift the centre of gravity of governmental functions into legislation – to become a government of laws. The ideal of legality plays a decisive part here, and hence the idea that individual acts of state can be justified rationally, through their conformity to law. Legal security takes precedence here over justice, which is regarded as problematic; there is more inclination to legal positivism than to a theory of natural law. Autocracy disdains such rationalisations of the communal order. It avoids where possible the binding of the ruler and his aides, who – nominated by him function only as his deputies and personal servants, not, as in democracy, as organs of the state. The concrete act of state is seen, not as the antecedently calculable execution of a law which has essentially provided for it already, but as the free, intuitive creation of the ruler or his agencies. It is one of the basic maxims of autocracy to ensure to the governmental apparatus, which is identified with the ruler, the most extensive freedom of discretion for its operation. If laws are enacted at all, the ruler has the unlimited prerogative of making any exceptions he pleases to them in the concrete case. And every utterance of authority carries with it the claim to be a realisation of justice; a justice which does not express itself rationally in universally valid laws, but is manifested only from case to case, in perfect adaptation to the particularities of each. To have sole possession of this justice, as a virtue, a divine gift and favour, is what constitutes the inalienable quality of the leader, the legitimising source of his dictatorial power. Hence every autocratic system rejects the proposal that it should develop a programme, as the democratic rational systems do. And if, contrary to its nature, it is nonetheless compelled to produce a programme, the latter is either wholly devoid of content or full of contradictions. In answer to criticism, however, it is argued that the programme does not and could not contain what really matters. For the pulse of life can neither be grasped nor regulated by means of general principles. Everything lies in the concrete act, in the mystery of the creative *kairós*.

Since democracy is concerned with legal security, and thus with lawfulness and accountability in the workings of government, there is a strong inclination here to control-mechanisms, as a guarantee for the legality required. And the principle of publicity is therefore paramount, as the most effective guarantee. The tendency to disclosure is typically democratic, and tempts a superficial or ill-disposed judgement of this form of state to assume prematurely that certain political abuses, especially corruption, are commoner here than under autocracy, where in fact they merely remain invisible because the opposite system of government prevails. An absence of control-measures, which could only hamper the working of the state; no publicity, but an intensive effort, in the interests of state authority, to maintain it in awe, to reinforce official discipline and the obedience of the subject; in a word, concealment. Again, in democracy generally, the rationalistic and critical undertone is bound up with a certain hostility to, or no great liking for, ideology, whereas autocracy actually goes about with the greatest energy to surround itself with particular mystico-religious ideologies, and proceeds with much greater severity against attempts to meddle with these power-supporting ideas than it does against injury to its real and immediate ruling interests. The struggle in which democracy prevails over autocracy is in large part conducted by appeal to critical reason as the supreme tribunal, against ideologies which address themselves to the irrational forces of the human soul. But since no régime can wholly dispense with the ideologies which vindicate and glorify it, even the democracies, or more accurately those who hold power in them, make use of such ideologies. Except that these ideologies are more rational, closer to reality and therefore weaker than those of autocracy, which, because its rule is more intensive, is also in need of a heavier veil to conceal its true nature. To be sure, the attempt is sometimes made under democracy to employ the very same ideologies to which autocracies owe, or think they owe, the success of their régime. As for instance, that the will of the rulers is an immediate manifestation of the will of God. But the claim that the voice of the people is the voice of God has never met with true belief. What can be suggested to the masses as the charisma of a single leader is not readily transferable to the many, to the all-too-many, to Everyman: it is the autocrat who evinces the most highly personal relation to the absolute, the divine, as its messenger, instrument or successor. If democracy, with its inmost kernel of rationalism, were to try to legitimise itself in that fashion, it would come dangerously close to the fable of the ass in the lion's skin.

6. This difference between democracy and autocracy also comes out in the different patterning of the problem of leadership. On the autocratic ideology, the leader represents an absolute value. Since he is of divine descent, or else seems endowed with magical, supernatural or rationally inexplicable powers, he does not rank as an agency created by the community, or even as capable of creation thereby. He is pictured, rather, as a force standing outside the community, through whom the latter is first constituted and held together. Hence the origin, vocation or creation of the leader in no way represents a question to be posed or settled by methods of rational cognition. The reality, namely the inevitable usurpation of the position of leader by way of force, is deliberately shrouded in the leadership-myth. In the democratic system, however, the problem of leader-creation is exposed to the glaring light of reasonable consideration. Here leadership represents, not an absolute value, but only a relative one. The leader ranks as *leader* only for a certain time and in certain respects. In other things he is the equal of his fellows, and subject to criticism. From the fact that the leader in an autocracy transcends the community, while in a democracy he is immanent within it, it follows for the former that the man who exercises the function of rulership is conceived as standing above the social order, and is therefore not answerable or – in ideological terms – is answerable only to himself or only to God; whereas under democracy the leader is subject to the social order and is thus essentially answerable, i.e., is actually answerable to the community. Since leadership here is not a supernatural quality, since under democracy one is made leader in a highly rational way, by a publicly controllable method, namely by vote, it is also not possible for leadership to be the permanent monopoly of a single person. Publicity, criticism, answerability, make it impossible for a leader to become irremoveable. Democracy is marked out by the fact of a more or less rapid turnover in the leadership. In this decisive respect it is thoroughly dynamic in character. A steady upstreaming occurs from the community of the led into the position of leadership. Autocracy, however, displays here a markedly static characteristic: the tendency to rigidity in the relation between leader and community.

Democracy, on the whole, is a soil unfavourable to the ideal of a leader, because it does not favour the principle of authority as such. And so far as the archetype of all authority is the father, since that is the original experience of authority, democracy – in Idea, that is – is a fatherless society. It seeks, so far as possible, to be a leaderless association of equals. Its principle is coordination, its most primitive form, the matriarchal fraternity-relation. And thus, in a deeper sense than was ever intended, democracy dwells under the triple star of the French Revolution: liberty, equality, fraternity. Autocracy, however, in its inmost nature is a paternal community. Its appropriate category is the relation of father and child. Its structure is not an order of equals, but an order of higher and lower, a hierarchical division. It is easy to credit it, for that very reason, with a greater vitality. And one really gets the impression that, from a historical viewpoint, autocratic forms occupy a much larger compass than democratic ones, which present themselves only as interludes, so to speak, in the drama of history. Its aversion to ideology makes democracy appear less capable of resistance than autocracy, which ruthlessly destroys every opponent within it, whereas democracy, with its principles of legality, tolerance, freedom of opinion and protection of minorities, virtually nurtures its own foes. That a state-form, by its very own methods of decision-making, should legally, therefore, be able to abolish itself, is the paradoxical privilege which democracy has over autocracy. But the very fact that autocracy, in forming the directing will of the state, provides no opportunity of compensating for the opposing tendencies which even here have some sort of existence, constitutes a serious element of danger. As a matter of psycho-political technique, the mechanisms of democratic institutions aim, in effect, to raise the political affect of the masses, and especially that of opposition groups, above the threshold of social consciousness, in order by this to allow abreaction to take place. In autocracy, however, the social equilibrium rests, conversely, upon the repression of political affect into a sphere which may be compared with the unconscious of individual psychology. It may be left undecided, which technique is the better calculated to insure the state-form against revolutionary upheaval.

7. To the style of domestic politics thus far depicted, there also corresponds a specific attitude in foreign policy. The democratic type has a definite inclination towards an ideal of pacifism, the autocratic, towards one of imperialism. Not indeed, that even democracies have not carried on wars of conquest. But the disposition to do so is much

smaller in this case, and the domestic obstacles to be overcome are much greater, than in the case of autocracy. And hence also there is a particular propensity to justify action in foreign affairs by means of a rational and pacifist ideology: you must never forget to represent the war you are carrying on as a defensive war – a mask which is simply not required for the heroic stance of autocracy. Or the aim of the war is declared to be a final establishment of peace through a world organisation which bears all the marks of a democracy: a community of states having equal rights under a mutually agreed tribunal for the settlement of disputes, if possible a world court, as a first step in the evolution towards a world state; a notion which is not only of no political value to an autocratic and imperialist outlook, but which, owing to the dreary levelling and weakening of national differences involved, implies, in effect, the downfall of culture.

8. The idea of the state's foreign relations gives particularly clear evidence of the differences of outlook on the nature of the state which develop within the democratic and autocratic types of character. The latter, i.e., the man of heightened ego-feeling who identifies himself with the powerful autocrat, finds his perfect counterpart in the doctrine that the state is a supra-individual, in some way collective, reality, essentially distinct from the mass or sum of individuals, a mystical organism, and as such a supreme being, the realisation of an absolute value. It is the concept of sovereignty which here brings about the absolutisation and even deification of the state, which is totally represented in the sovereign ruler. This theory of the state finds altogether typical expression in the familiar statement *"l'état, c'est moi"*. Just as, in this type, the knowledge of the world proceeds outward from the sovereign self, so his political speculation takes its starting-point from his own sovereign state. It therefore founds the existence of other states, and the validity of the order governing behaviour towards them, on the will of this person's own sovereign state, it being the supreme will as such in the social sphere. It is the doctrine, firstly that international law holds for one's own state only so far as the latter acknowledges this in its own regard, and secondly that another state comes into consideration as subject to this law only insofar as it is recognised in that capacity by one's own state. International law accordingly does not figure as a legal

order above particular states, for this would be incompatible with the notion of sovereignty; instead, assuming it is law at all, it is so as a voluntarily accepted component of one's own governmental order, which thus extends also over the legal communities of other states – not, indeed, in terms of its material and territorial jurisdiction, but as a formal ground of validity: the entire legal world, so to speak, as will and idea of the absolute state-self!

This outlook stands in diametrical contrast to that which views the state, not as a supra-empirical entity, distinct from the sum of its members, and thus quite beyond rational apprehension, but as a merely ideal order of the reciprocal behaviour of individuals. This latter does not conceive the state as something existing over and above its subjects, as an entity dominating men and therefore essentially different from those dominated: it proceeds, rather, from the assumption that men make up the state, that as a specific order of human behaviour the state does not exist outside or above men, but in and through them. The political theory of this type of person can be summed up in the words: "*l'état, c'est nous*". The tendency of this view is directed, not to an absolutising, but rather to a relativising of the state. It dismisses the concept of sovereignty as the ideology of particular claims to governmental power, and thereby disposes of the chief obstacle in the way of seeing that above individual states there holds, or can hold, an international law, marking them off from each other legally in their territorial and personal jurisdictions, and in this way first establishing coordination among states. The state is recognised as a legal entity, yet not as an absolutely supreme one, but rather as an intermediate stage in the legal order. From the universal community of international law there runs, by way of the state, to the legal communities incorporated under it, a continuous sequence of legal structures gradually shading off into one another.

In thus tending away from ideology, towards objective, value-free knowledge and a relativising of all allegedly absolute antitheses, the legal, political and social doctrines of the democratic man present themselves simply as the scientific theory of society, while to the autocratic type there corresponds a politico-religious, essentially theological treatment of the problem of society as an object of knowledge. Only the democratic type has the capacity, and what is still more important, the inclination, to pass an objective judgement on the form of state appropriated to him. His scientific strength is his political weakness. So far as the contrast of state-forms can be reduced to a contrast in the mental attitudes of men, the antithesis between a purely scientific mentality, oriented solely to knowledge as a value, and a political outlook which rates other values, such as the social, above that of knowledge, will also have to be connected with the antagonism between democracy and autocracy. And then it is by no means so paradoxical that on the soil of democracy, a true science of the state should flourish better than in an autocracy, where only an ideology of the state can develop; and that a person more inwardly inclined to democracy than autocracy will be more strongly disposed to a purely scientific view of law, state and society than one whose character impels him to autocracy, and thus to what is already from the outset an ideological point of view.

9. In these two antagonistic theories of the state we already find emerging in full clarity the contrast of world-outlooks in which the conflict of political convictions ultimately has its root. And this contrast results from their attitude to the absolute. For that is the decisive question: whether one believes in an absolute value, and thus in an absolute truth and reality, or whether one assumes that only relative values, and hence only relative truth and reality, are accessible to human knowledge. A belief in the absolute, profoundly rooted in feeling, creates the presupposition for a metaphysical view of the world. The denial of this presupposition on the part of the understanding, the view that there are only relative values and thus only relative truths, so that every value and every truth, like man who discovers them, must at all times be ready to retire and make room for others, leads to a world-view of criticism, positivism and empiricism; so far, that is, as we understand by these terms that school of philosophy and science which sets out from the positive, i.e., from the given, from what can be apprehended by the senses and the understanding, from changeable and ever-changing experience, and which consequently rejects the assumption of an absolute transcending this experience. This contrast of world-views corresponds to the contrast in basic political attitudes. The metaphysical and absolutist view is affiliated to the autocratic standpoint, the critical and relativist, or scientific view, to the democratic one.

And in actual fact, all the great metaphysicians have declared themselves against democracy and in favour of autocracy; and the philosophers who have stood up for democracy have almost always been inclined to an empiricist and relativist point of view. Thus in antiquity we find the *sophists*, fortified by advances in the empirical sciences, combining a thoroughly relativist outlook in the field of social theory with democratic sympathies. *Protagoras*, the founder of the school, teaches that man is the measure of all things, and *Euripides*, their poet, extols democracy and peace. But *Plato*, in whom the religious metaphysic again rises up against the rationalism of enlightenment, who declares against Protagoras that God is the measure of all things, is the greatest despiser of democracy, and an admirer, nay a champion, of dictatorship.

In the Middle Ages, the metaphysic of Christianity is quite self-evidently associated with the conviction that monarchy, as the image of divine world-government, is the best form of state. *Thomas Aquinas* may be cited as a leading witness here. *Dante* is obviously influenced by him in writing his celebrated *De Monarchia*. *Marsilius of Padua*, who with *John of Jandun* wrote the *Defensor Pacis*, the work which in the Middle Ages first, or at any rate most clearly, develops the democratic idea of popular sovereignty, was by profession a doctor and enquirer into nature, and his collaborator was one of the followers of Averroes, who, with his doctrine of the eternity of the world and of motion, and his thoroughly scientific viewpoint, stands in a direct contrast to the Christian metaphysic. But above all in this connection we should cite the great *Nicholas of Cusa*. Since, as a metaphysical sceptic – also essentially oriented towards natural science – he teaches that the absolute is unknowable, the knowledge of the infinite changes, for him, into infinite knowledge of the finite. He applies himself – *concordantia oppositorum* – to overcoming and composing all the oppositions which fill the world, i.e., he seeks a compromise; and would like above all things to see even Jews and Mohammedans united together in a tolerant religion of reason, transcending the differences of all religious cults. He thereby comes close to the frontiers of an anti-metaphysical pantheism. Can one wonder that he is politically in favour of democracy and an advocate of human freedom and equality? *Spinoza's* thoroughly anti-metaphysical, scientifically oriented pantheism is also bound up with an outspoken preference for the democratic principle; while *Leibniz*, the metaphysician *par ex-*

cellence, is a defender of monarchy. *Kant's* divided attitude on the cardinal question precludes any unambiguous diagnosis of his system, either on the philosophical or the political side. One can only say that, so far as he contends against metaphysics, he also sympathises with the democratic ideal of the French Revolution. The position of *Hegel*, the greatest of German metaphysicians, is all the more unmistakeable. He is not only the philosopher of absolute spirit, but also the philosopher of absolute monarchy.

It was the very spirit of this philosophy which produced the famous saying: "Authority, not majority". And really, if one believes in the existence of the absolute, which means above all, however, in the existence of absolute good, what could be more senseless than to take a vote about it, and let the majority decide? In face of the paramount authority of this absolute good, what else can there be but obedience from those to whom it brings salvation, an unconditional and thankful obedience to anyone who, possessing absolute good, knows this and wills it? Though such obedience, to be sure, can rely on believing that the authoritative person of the leader is in possession of absolute good, only to the extent that a knowledge of the same is denied to most of the led. But if one holds absolute truth and absolute value to be beyond human ken, then one should at least regard as possible, not only one's own opinion, but also the other, opposing view. Hence relativism is the world-outlook presupposed in the democratic idea. Democracy assigns equal value to the political will of everyone, just as it also has equal respect for every political belief and opinion. It therefore gives every political conviction an equal chance to express itself and gain a hearing in free competition for the minds of men. That is the reason why the dialectical procedure, unfolding in the cut and thrust of argument within a popular or parliamentary assembly, is so specifically democratic. That is the reason why the rule of the majority, so characteristic of democracy, is simply not possible without an opposing minority, and why democracy, from the depths of its nature, must protect this minority. Hence the politics of democracy is necessarily a politics of compromise; just as nothing is also more characteristic of the relativist world-outlook than the tendency to seek a settlement midway between two opposing standpoints, neither of which one can make wholly and unreservedly one's own, in total negation of the other. The relativity of the values postulated by a particular profession of political faith, the impossibility of claiming absolute validity for any political programme or ideal – whatever one's degree of subjective dedication or personal conviction – forcibly compels one also to a rejection of political absolutism, whether it be the absolutism of a monarch or dictator, a priestly or warrior caste, a class or a party. But anyone who can appeal, in his political willing and acting, to divine inspiration or illumination from above, may be entitled to shut his ears to the voice of man and enforce his will, as the will of absolute goodness, even against the majority, even against a world of persons who are infidels or victims of delusion, because they will differently. That is the Divine Right standpoint of an autocracy, which in the past century has become a target of attack on the part of all that has been in favour of intellectual freedom, in favour of a dogma-free science based on human understanding and critical doubt, and politically in favour of democracy. For anyone who relies only on earthly wisdom, and allows only human knowledge to ordain social goals, has scarcely any other way of justifying the coercion still inevitably required for their realisation, save by the consent of at least a majority of those whom the coercive order is intended to benefit. And this coercive order must itself be so arranged that even the minority, since it is not absolutely wrong, not absolutely outlawed, can itself become the majority at any time.

That is the true meaning of the political system which we call democracy, and which we may set against autocracy, or political absolutism, only because it is the expression of a political relativism.

10. In the 18th chapter of St. John's gospel, an incident from the life of Jesus is depicted. This homely account, in all its lapidary simplicity, is among the most wonderful things in literature; and without being so intended, it has become a tragic symbol of the antithesis between a metaphysically autocratic and a relativistically democratic world-view. It is at the time of passover, when Jesus is brought before Pilate, the Roman governor, accused of proclaiming himself the son of God and King of the Jews. And Pilate, in whose eyes, as a Roman, this man can only be a poor fool, asks him ironically: "Art thou the king of the Jews?". And Jesus, in deepest seriousness, and wholly filled with the ardour of his divine mission, answers: "Thou sayest that I am a king. To this end was I born, and for this cause came I into the world, that I should bear

witness unto the truth. Everyone that is of the truth heareth my voice." And Pilate, sceptic that he is, asks: "What is truth?" – And because he does not know what truth is, and because here in his province he is concerned to preserve democratic forms, he appeals to the people and takes – a vote. "He went out again unto the Jews," says the gospel, "and saith unto them, I find in him no fault at all. But ye have a custom, that I should release unto you one at the passover: Will ye therefore that I release unto you the king of the Jews?" – The popular vote is against Jesus. "Then cried they all again, saying, Not this man, but Barabbas." – But the evangelist adds, "Now Barabbas was a robber".

For believers, for political believers, this popular vote must certainly be a powerful argument against democracy. And one has to admit its validity. But only, indeed, on one condition: that given a political truth, which must in the end be imposed by bloody violence, the political believers should be as certain of this truth of theirs, as was the son of God.

NOTE

* *Recht und Staat in Geschichte und Gegenwart*, J. C. B. Mohr (Paul Siebeck), Tübingen 1933.

CHAPTER VI

THE FOUNDATION OF THE THEORY OF NATURAL LAW*

INTRODUCTION

I have accepted your invitation to speak on natural law – in this circle of *supporters* of that doctrine – not with any intention of converting you to my point of view, namely that from a *scientifically* rational standpoint one *cannot accept* the validity of natural law. For I do not consider such a conversion possible, and that for a reason which follows precisely from what I wish to discuss: the foundation of the natural law theory, i.e., the answer to the question, on what presupposition alone can one assume the validity of an eternal, unchangeable law immanent in nature; so that anyone, like myself, who does *not* feel able to accept this presupposition, is also unable to accept its consequence.

This presupposition, as I shall try to show, is the *belief* in a just deity, whose will is not only transcendent to the nature created by Him, but also immanent within it. It is wholly unprofitable to debate about the truth of this belief. Neither he who has this belief, nor he who lacks it, can be persuaded of the opposite by rational arguments. But in taking the view that this belief is the essential and inevitable presupposition for a true doctrine of natural law, I find myself in a strange position vis-à-vis those among you who, despite this belief of yours, are of the widely-held opinion that the validity of natural law is independent of the will of an almighty and all-good deity. I do not step forward here – as you will perhaps expect of me – in the character of an advocatus diaboli, but on the contrary, as an advocatus *dei*. But that, as I hope, will remove from the following discussion any sting that might wound the feelings of either the one party or the other.

1. "Law" – whether we mean by this positive law, actually laid down by men, and distinct from morality, or a correct, just, natural law corresponding to morality, or to a morality – is essentially a norm, a specific sense-content whose verbal expression is an ought-statement. The

import of a norm, or more properly, of the word "norm", is that something ought to be, and especially that living creatures, and particularly men, should behave under certain circumstances in a certain way. Such a meaning we call a prescription, and distinguish it from a description, i.e., a statement whose import is – or more properly, which is the meaning (of the statement) that, something exists, i.e., is present or somehow created, and in particular that things, living creatures or men do actually behave under certain circumstances in a certain way. A norm is not a statement, nor a prescription a description. The distinction is manifest: the norm is the import of an act of will, an act directed to the behaviour of another. The statement is the import of an act of thought. The norm aims at determining the will of another, the statement at determining the thinking or knowing of another; it is intended to let the other know something. To put it figuratively, the norm proceeds from the willing of one to the willing of another, the statement from the thinking or knowing of one to the thinking or knowing of another. Hence a statement is true or false. A norm, however, is neither true nor false, but valid or invalid. And between the truth of a statement and the validity of a norm, no parallel or analogy of any kind exists. I stress this in conscious opposition to a view that is generally accepted, and was also long upheld by myself. If an analogy or parallel were to exist between the truth of a statement and the validity of a norm, the law of non-contradiction, which applies to two statements standing in conflict with one another, would also, or at least *per analogiam*, have to be applicable to two norms standing in conflict with each other. Just as only one of two such conflicting statements can be true, while the other must be false, so of two such conflicting norms, only one could be valid, and the other would have to be invalid. But this is not so. For were it the case that, given two norms, of which one prescribes the performance of something, and the other its nonperformance, only one can be valid, there could then be no conflict of norms. If only one of two norms is valid, there is not a pair of norms, but only one, and hence no conflict. For the validity of a norm is its specific, though ideal, existence – its presence: and a norm without validity has no existence, and is not a norm. Yet there is no denying the existence of norm-conflicts, i.e., of a situation in which two norms are valid, of which one prescribes a certain performance and the other enjoins against it. We encounter such conflicts only too frequently, especially between the norms of a particular positive legal order and those of a particular moral order. If the norm of a morality enjoins us never to kill a man, while the norm of law enjoins us to kill men in war and in execution of the death penalty, we then have to choose which of the two we shall obey and which we shall violate. But we do not have the power to put out of action the norm we do not choose to obey. It remains valid; otherwise we could not violate it. But conflicts between norms of one and the same normative order, and especially within a single legal order, are also possible, and by no means infrequently occur.

Insofar as a norm lays down a particular action as one that ought to be done, it constitutes a value. If something is as it ought to be, it is "good," and has value. If something is not as it ought to be, it is "bad," and has disvalue. Insofar as a statement has reference to reality, i.e., states *that* something really is or *how* it really is, the distinction between ought-norm and existence-statement is founded on the contrast between 'ought' and 'is,' between value and reality. This contrast is presented to us by our rational thinking, according to the principles of logic, as an irremoveable dualism; in such a way, indeed, that an 'ought' cannot be deduced from an 'is', nor an 'is' from an 'ought', since neither is derivable from the other. From the fact that something exists, it cannot follow that anything ought to be so, and from the fact that something ought to be, it cannot follow that anything is. No value can be deduced from reality, nor any reality from value. Our statements about reality are true when they correspond to it (the real). Their truth does not depend on our will. If true at all, they are objectively true. The statement that if a metallic body is heated, it expands, is true whether anyone wills it or not, and is true for all thinking beings. But since value consists in relation to a norm, which is the import of an act of will, values of extremely different and mutually conflicting kinds can be valid. For the validity of a value is the validity of a norm; and for different men, at different times and places, different norms are valid. The dualism of norm and statement, 'ought' and 'is,' willing and thinking, has as its inevitable consequence that there are only subjective values, not objective ones – no values, that is, whose validity is objective in the way that the truth of statements about reality is objective. But if value is by nature subjective, it is also merely relative; relative to the willing whose import is the norm which constitutes the value, and relative to the men for whom this norm is valid and whose behaviour it regulates. That means, however, that the validity of a norm constituting a value does not rule out the validity of another norm conflicting with the first, nor another value at variance with the previous one, in the way that the objective truth of a factual statement excludes any other factual statement that conflicts with it. This is also particularly the case if we include under value, not only the relation to a norm posited by an act of will, but also that of an object to a wish; if the judgement that something is "good" means that it is desired, and that something is "bad," that it is undesired.

But the subjectivity and relativity of value is a consequence which many people – though not all – find it hard to endure. This is so, in the first place, because the assumption that values are merely subjective and relative is inadequate to satisfy the need for a justification of our behaviour. If the validity of the norm we conform to – often only with great difficulty, since it is against our inclination – turns out in the last resort to be arbitrary, and therefore by no means excludes the validity of an opposing norm, we are then less certain of the value of behaviour which accords with such a norm, than we are of the truth of a statement. We are also, and perhaps primarily, uneasy, however, because we do not regard the authority, and hence the motivating power, of a normative moral or legal order as sufficient, if those who are subject to such orders consider the values constituted by the norms of these orders to be merely subjective and relative. Hence the attempt to demonstrate the validity of norms which are not the import of human acts of will, which do not have to be "posited" or be "positive" in order to be valid, which in virtue of their content are binding immediately and independently of a human will, and which constitute values which are just as objective as the truth of statements about reality. But in order to achieve this, it is necessary to get rid of that dualism imposed on us by our logical and rational thinking, between 'is' and 'ought,' reality and value, statement and norm, willing and thinking. This can be done only by stepping outside the realm of rational and logical thought, and hence the realm of empirical reality, in particular that of empirical acts of will and their import, and by having recourse to a transcendent, metaphysical realm, in which it is possible to have a willing that is also thinking, an 'ought' that is also an 'is,' norms that are also statements, a law that is justice and also truth. It is the ascent of man to God, from science or philosophy to theology. And that is the route which leads from a legal or moral positivism to a doctrine of natural law.

2. The element common to the various definitions of natural law, the essence of what we describe as "natural law," is the validity of norms which are not the import of human acts of will; hence the values which they constitute are in no way arbitrary, subjective or relative. To answer the question how a man ought to behave under given circumstances, there is no need – so natural law theory tells us – to ask about the volitions of a man who figures as a moral or legal law-giver, or to enquire about a custom whereby the desired norm has been posited. For the norm desired emerges from the nature of the case to which it relates. This is either the circumstances under which a man ought to behave in a certain fashion, or the man himself whose behaviour is in question. The circumstances are a part of reality, and inseparably bound up with the whole. The nature of the case is thus nature, as the totality of the real, or the nature of man. The latter consists either of the instincts inherent in man, or of that which distinguishes him from the brutes, namely his reason. In the latter case, natural law figures as the law of reason. In all cases, the doctrine of natural law is marked out by the assumption of norms immanent in nature, and hence by the assumption that the values constituted by these norms are immanent in the reality either of nature in general, or of human nature in particular. It is the immanence of an 'ought' within the 'is.' Nature generally, or the nature of man, especially his reason, prescribes a specific course of conduct to him. Nature in general, or human nature in particular, especially reason, emerges as a norm-positing authority.

Now it can perhaps be granted, that norms do not necessarily have to be the import of human acts of will. But in no case can we allow that there are norms which are not the import of any act of will, even if it be not precisely the act of a human will. In a nature to which norms are immanent, a will must also be immanent, whose import these norms are. But from whence can such a will enter into nature, which, from the standpoint of empirical and rational knowledge, is an aggregate of existent facts, conjoined together as causes and effects? A will in nature is either an animistic superstition, or else it is the will of God in the nature He has created, the immanence of divine value within reality. If norms are immanent in man's nature, especially his reason, this reason cannot be the empirical human reason, which, from a purely psychological point of view, is merely a capacity for knowledge or thought. For the reason which posits norms must be a simultaneous capacity for both knowledge and will. There can be no such thing in the field of empirical reality, so far as the latter can be described without logical contradiction. But the principle of non-contradiction, as a principle of human logic, has no application to a transcendent, suprahuman sphere lying beyond all empirical reality, so far as we may presuppose the existence of such a thing. Of the divine reason we may say – what is a contradiction for human reason – that it is at once an agency of both knowledge and will; of God we can say that, in Him, knowing and willing are one. Thus it is already said in Genesis (II, 16 f; III, 4 f):

And the Lord God commanded the man, saying ... of the tree of the knowledge of good and evil, thou shalt not eat .... And the serpent said unto the woman ... in the day ye eat thereof, then ... ye shall be as gods, knowing good and evil.

In that God knows what is good and evil, He wills that the good be done, and the evil left undone. His willing is implicit in His knowledge. The contradiction inherent in the fact that God wills, in that He knows, is of no more importance, from a religious and theological point of view, than that which is involved in the fact that God in His universal benevolence only wills the good, and yet in His omnipotence also creates the evil. That which simultaneously knows and wills, namely the practical reason of man, is the divine reason in man, whom God has created in His own likeness.

3. The theologico-metaphysical character of the assumption that value is immanent in reality, can be shown by an analysis of that philosophy which gives classical expression to the principle of the doctrine in question: the Aristotelian theory of entelechy.

Entelechy (ἐντελέχεια) is the movement inherent in everything, which tends towards a specific end (τέλος). This end is, to bring the thing to its perfection. It is an objective end, which the thing has by nature, i.e., to be as it ought to be, and thus to be "good." In *Metaphysics* I, 7, Aristotle argues against the Platonic theory of Ideas, that according to the latter the end is a transcendent Idea, the Idea of the Good, whereas entelechy is the good-directed movement immanent in things. The concept of entelechy expresses the teleological interpretation of nature which forms the essence of Aristotle's philosophy. But such an interpretation presupposes, consciously or unconsciously, explicitly or implicitly, a theological view of the world. To the unavoidable question, where does the end in nature come from, there is no answer save the assumption of a transcendent authority which lays down the end for nature. This is also the case in the philosophy of Aristotle, although owing to certain peculiarities in his metaphysics it does not get to be very clearly expressed, and is therefore not always recognised by the traditional interpretation of Aristotle.

The central concept of this metaphysics is that of God as the "unmoved mover." Since everything that comes to be moved must be moved by something, there has to be a first mover (*Physics*, VIII, 4, 5), something that moves without being moved (*Metaphysics*, XII, 7). That is the deity, who is "a living being, eternal, most good"(φαμὲν δὲ τὸν θεὸν εἶναι ζῷον ἀίδιον ἄριστον). He is the absolute good, the supreme, absolute end (*De Caelo*, II, 12). Since all movement proceeds directly or indirectly from God, and all movement is directed towards the good, as to the end immanent in nature, this movement towards the good can only be the end laid down for nature by God, and the good in nature can only be the divine value immanent in reality. Since a value can only be posited by a will, the good in nature must be the divine will in nature. And Aristotle actually says in so many words: "God and nature create nothing that has not its use" (ὁ δὲ θεὸς καὶ ἡ φύσις οὐδὲν μάτην ποιοῦσιν: *De Caelo*, I, 4). In the *Nicomachean Ethics* (VII, 1153b) we find: "for all things have by nature something divine in them" (πάντα γὰρ φύσει ἔχει τι θεῖον). In the *Eudemian Ethics* (VIII, 2, 1248a):

> The object of our search is this – what is the commencement of movement in the soul? The answer is clear: as in the universe, so in the soul, God moves everything. For in a sense the divine element in us moves everything.

And in the treatise *De Generatione et Corruptione* (II, 10, 336b) we read,

> God perfected all that is, in that he made becoming an essential feature, having its end in itself... all things in nature strive towards the eternal and unchanging, and so far as possible present their inner coherence by means of the essential and substantial, in that they constantly recreate themselves.[1]

A consistent theological interpretation of the world is necessarily linked to the assumption that God must not only be transcendent to the world, but also immanent to it: a thought which Goethe has expressed in poetic form:

> What were a God, who worked from outside in,
> Who made the world upon His finger spin!
> 'Tis best He move the cosmos from inside,
> Nature in Him, Himself in nature hide.
> That all who in Him live and breathe and move,
> May never want His power, or lack His love.[2]

God's immanence in the world is by no means peculiar only to pantheism. Even Catholic theology is unable to avoid the presumption of divine immanence. Let me cite a Catholic theologian, the Jesuit Walter Brugger: "The true immanence of the world in God and of God in the world does not do away with God's transcendence."[3] The idea of God's immanence in the world is obscured in Aristotle's metaphysics by the fact that the latter describes the nature of God as pure thought, as mere thinking reason (νοῦς); and that he tries to explain his claim that all motion in reality proceeds from God, as first mover, in the following way: God, as the best and therefore most desirable, "produces motion as being loved" (κινεῖ δὲ ὡς ἐρώμενον: *Metaphysics*, XII, 7). But yet finally Aristotle admits that the end immanent in nature is an end posited for nature by the will of God. He raises the question (*Metaphysics*, XII, 10), in what way "the nature of the universe contains the good, and the highest good ...". But that is to ask, surely, how the end enters into nature. And he answers this question by setting up a parallel between the relationship of God to nature and that of a commander to the order of his army. "For its good is found both in its order and in its leader, and more in the latter; for he does not depend on the order but it depends on him." The ordering of the army is the command of the leader, and therefore posited by the leader's will. It is good, because the leader's will is good. And similarly, the order of nature is posited by the will of God. It is good, because God's will is good. The good in nature is the good will of God. At the end, we are told: "The world refuses to be governed badly." And there follows a quotation from Homer: "The rule of many is not good: one ruler let there be." If the world is good, it is so, because it is ruled by God, because it obeys the command of the divine leader. The thinking reason of God finally reveals itself as also a reason that wills, because it commands as a leader does.[4]

But even human reason, according to Aristotle, is not only a thinking and knowing reason, but also one which wills, because it commands, and from which motion emanates. The internal contradiction inherent in the concept of a reason that both thinks and wills is clearly manifested in the fact that Aristotle divides it into a theoretical and a practical reason (the νοῦς θεωρητικός and the νοῦς πρακτικός). We find this dual concept in his treatise *On the Soul* (*De Anima*, III, 10). It is there said that motion has two causes: appetite (ὄρεξις) and mind (reason: νοῦς). Reason comes into consideration as a cause of movement insofar as it relates to action, as it posits to man a particular action as an end. By that very fact it is practical reason. The essential function of practical reason is to prescribe or command. Yet Aristotle says that it is the thinking mind which bids and commands us to pursue or avoid something (III, 9). But this is not possible, psychologically speaking. An injunction or command can only be the import of a volition. In the *Nicomachean Ethics* (I, 13), where Aristotle distinguishes between a rational and an irrational element in the soul, and within the irrational, between a vegetative and an appetitive element, he says that the vegetative element in no way shares in a rational principle, but that the appetitive does in a sense share in it, in so far as it listens to and obeys it, so that "the irrational element is in some sense persuaded by a rational principle." A reason which commands and is listened to can only be one which both thinks and wills, and that simply means a practical reason. But only a divine reason can be that, or divine reason in man. Yet Aristotle himself did not maintain this. It was Thomas Aquinas, his faithful disciple, who first drew this conclusion from the Aristotelian doctrine of reason.

4. It may well seem obvious that the Aristotelian metaphysics, with its theory of an entelechy, i.e., of the immanence of value in reality, is bound to lead to a theory of natural law; but the commonly-held view that Aristotle's philosophy contains such a theory, or the opinion sometimes advanced, that he was the founder of it, will not withstand critical examination.[5]

Since natural law represents a justice emanating from nature, while justice is a demand of morality, Aristotle's relationship to the natural law theory can be understood only in connection with his theory of justice, and the latter only in connection with his ethics. The first thing to establish in this regard is that the Aristotelian ethics has two sides to it.[6] The subject-matter of his ethics is the "good", "at which all things aim" (1094a), and this is the end of human life. This good is happiness, "the chief good" (1097b), and such happiness Aristotle identifies with virtue (1098b). As he already does in the *Protrepticus*, so Aristotle also declares in the *Nicomachean Ethics* that this highest good is pure knowledge, the contemplative activity in man. In Book X he pronounces it the "best" of virtues (1177a). It involves turning away from earthly things and towards eternal ones, and the contemplative activity is thereupon proclaimed to be the supreme moral value. It is for this reason that Aristotle represents the standpoint of such a political morality, justice is "complete virtue" a political morality, which relates to the behaviour of citizens in the state, and is therefore incompatible with the morality of pure knowing. This political morality is the chief topic of the *Nicomachean Ethics*. From the standpoint of such a political morality, justice is "complete virtue" and "virtue entire" (1129b, 1130a). But after the contemplative activity has been praised in Book X as the "best" and "pleasantest of virtuous activities", it is asserted that "in a secondary degree the life in accordance with the other kind of virtue is happy", and justice is named in first place under this "other kind of virtue" (1178a).

Aristotle endeavours to conceal this contradiction by asserting at the outset of Book II that "Virtue [is] of two kinds, intellectual and moral", thereby qualifying the virtue of pure knowledge as a non-moral virtue. But a non-moral "virtue" is a self-contradiction, inasmuch as "virtue" represents the "good", and thus an ethical value.

The morality which forms the chief topic of the *Nicomachean Ethics* is a political morality, since Aristotle speaks of this ethics as "political science" (πολιτική [ἐπιστήμη]) and expressly refers to just actions as those "which political science investigates" (1094b), emphasising also that he is enquiring into "political justice" (πολιτικὸν δίκαιον.1134a). This good is not Plato's transcendent Idea of the Good, but "the good for man" (1094b);"the good for man" in general, but in particular the good of the state. For Aristotle observes:

For even if the end is the same for a single man and for a state, that of the state seems at all events something greater and more complete whether to attain or to preserve; though it is worth while to attain the end merely for one man, it is finer and more godlike to attain it for a nation or for city-states.

Since the good is happiness and happiness is virtue, Aristotle is confronted with the question, what is virtue (1102a)? His immediate answer is:

The true student of politics ... is thought to have studied virtue above all things; for he wishes to make his fellow citizens good and obedient to the laws. As an example of this we have the lawgivers of the Cretans and the Spartans ....

This means that virtue is something which the statesman as lawgiver desires to bring about, in that he persuades the citizens to obey the laws of the state, and therefore positive law. Justice is a virtue, indeed the "perfect" and "complete" virtue, a virtue of the citizen, and as such it consists in behaving according to positive law. Thus already in Book I of the *Nicomachean Ethics*, Aristotle is excluding in advance any justice distinct from positive law, which might possibly conflict therewith.

Aristotle, as already noted, distinguishes an "intellectual" and a "moral" virtue. Justice is a moral virtue. Of this he says at the beginning of Book II (1103a) that "moral virtue comes about as a result of habit" and

that none of the moral virtues arises in us by nature; for nothing that exists by nature can form a habit contrary to its nature. For instance the stone which by nature moves downwards cannot be habituated to move upwards, not even if one tries to train it by throwing it up ten thousand times; nor can fire be habituated to move downwards, nor can anything else that by nature behaves in one way be trained to behave in another. Neither by nature, then, nor contrary to nature do the virtues arise in us; rather we are adapted by nature to receive them, and are made perfect by habit.

Since none of the moral virtues is given us by nature, while justice is a virtue, justice is not given us by nature. Justice cannot be given us by nature, since by "nature" Aristotle understands here the necessary and unchangeable course of events. By nature the stone falls, and by nature fire leaps upwards. Man is not by nature just, in the way that the stone by nature falls and fire leaps upwards. For man can be just or unjust. The stone, however, cannot fall or rise, nor fire leap either up or down. A man is just who behaves as he ought to, but he can also behave otherwise, i.e., be unjust. Since that is "by nature", which necessarily is as it is and cannot be otherwise, justice as a virtue is "neither by nature nor contrary to nature". But if justice is not given by nature, there can be no natural law. For natural law is the justice given by nature. Man is not virtuous in general by nature, or therefore just in particular, but is so as a result of law: that the moral virtues are not given by nature "is confirmed by what happens in states". For legislators make the citizens virtuous by forming habits in them, and that is the aim of every legislator, not merely – as was said earlier – of the "true" student of politics. The legislator, not nature, makes the citizens virtuous, and therefore also just. He makes them virtuous, and more especially just, by making them obedient to the laws. Every legislator has this aim. Hence it is just to obey all the laws of the state. Aristotle adds, however: "those (legislators) who do not effect it miss their mark, and it is in this that a good constitution differs from a bad one". One might be inclined to suppose that Aristotle is telling us that the good statesman makes the citizens virtuous only by subjecting them to good, i.e., just laws. But that is not what the foregoing passages are intended to convey. Their meaning is: *Every* legislator wishes to make the citizens virtuous, in that he persuades them to obey the laws enacted by him. He does not always succeed. And if he fails, this is not because he is unjust, and therefore issues bad and unjust laws, but because he does not employ the proper means of securing the citizens' obedience to the laws he has enacted. Aristotle is probably thinking here of what he points to at the beginning of Book III (1109b 16 – 1110a 15): the "honours and punishments" which the legislator prescribes as a reaction to conformity or nonconformity with the laws he has promulgated. If Aristotle had thought that a statesman only makes the citizens virtuous by subjecting them to good, i.e., just laws, he would surely have had to put the distinction between good and bad, just and unjust laws, at the apex of his enquiry. The words "it is in this", i.e., the fact that a legislator is effective or ineffective "that a good constitution differs from a bad one", cannot be interpreted to mean that this is what distinguishes a legal order containing good or just laws from one containing bad or unjust laws. The constitution of a state is not identical with the laws propounded by the constitutional legislator.

In connection with these observations, Aristotle emphasises once more that we are not by nature good or bad, and hence not by nature just or unjust. He says that one becomes a good lyre-player by playing the lyre well, a good builder by building well, and a bad one by building badly. The qualities (good and bad) arise out of the corresponding activities.

For if this were not so, there would have been no need of a teacher, but all men would have been born good or bad at their craft. This, then, is the case with the virtues also.

This means – since justice is a virtue – that we are not just by nature, or that what is just does not arise from the nature of man, but from elsewhere. It has to be somehow brought to man from without. From the foregoing it emerges that it must come from the laws of the state. Aristotle says here, however, that a teacher is needed, i.e., man must be taught by political science of the morality which, as he says earlier on, "legislates as to what we are to do and what we are to abstain from." But in so doing, Aristotle confuses political science with politics, the activity of the statesman as legislator. For he also declares immediately afterwards (1103b 27):

Since, then, the present inquiry does not aim at theoretical knowledge like the others (for we are inquiring not in order to know what virtue is, but in order to become good, since otherwise our inquiry would have been of no use), we must examine the nature of actions, namely how we ought to do them.

Here Aristotle falls into a confusion, still to be observed almost everywhere even nowadays, between sciences which describe norms, as ethics and legal science do, and the subject-matter of these sciences, namely prescriptive morality and prescriptive law; a confusion based upon the Aristotelian concept of practical reason (νοῦς πρακτικός). For Aristotle goes on: "That we must act according to the right rule is a common principle and must be assumed." And at 1114b 29, after having characterised the virtues as a mean, Aristotle says: "that they are in our power and voluntary, and act as the right rule prescribes."

In another connection also, Aristotle rejects the idea of a natural justice. In arguing that virtues are not "faculties", he says

we are neither called good nor bad, nor praised nor blamed, for the simple capacity of feeling the passions; again, we have the faculties by nature, but we are not made good or bad [or therefore just or unjust] by nature (1106a).

Thus here, too, there is no justice "by nature".

Book V of the *Nicomachean Ethics* is devoted to the problem of justice. Aristotle distinguishes various concepts of justice. Here we are told: "... both the law-abiding and the fair man will be just. The just, then, is the lawful and the fair, the unjust the unlawful and the unfair" (1129a).[6a] Hence the principle of lawfulness and the principle of fairness appear to be two different kinds of justice standing side by side. Soon afterwards it is said:

Since the lawless man was seen to be unjust and the law-abiding man just, evidently all lawful acts are in a sense just acts; for the acts laid down by the legislative art are lawful, and each of these [i.e., each particular determination of the laws], we say, is just.

This justice is identical with law-abidingness, where by "law" we are to understand positive law, whatever its content may be. Aristotle makes no distinction here between a just and an unjust positive law. Every positive law is just, for "all" lawful acts, i.e., those actually laid down in law by a legislator, are "just acts".

For practically the majority of the acts commanded by the law are those which are prescribed from the point of view of virtue taken as a whole; for the law bids us practise every virtue and forbids us to practise any vice (1130b).

Since justice is a virtue, and positive law bids us live according to each individual virtue, positive law, *every* positive law, must be just. And in a later connection (1134a 28) we read:

For justice exists only between men whose mutual relations are governed by law; and law exists for men between whom there is injustice; for legal justice [positive law, surely] is the discrimination of the just and the unjust.

And in the *Politics* (Bk. I, Ch. 2, 1253a) Aristotle says:

But justice is the bond of men in states, for the administration of justice [i.e. positive law], which is the determination of what is just, is the principle of order in political society.

This means nothing more nor less than that positive law and justice coincide.

If the principle of fairness were a principle of justice distinct from and alongside that of lawfulness, then a conflict between the principles of lawfulness and fairness would have to be possible. A positive legal system which violated the principle of fairness would have to be regarded, from the standpoint of that principle, as unjust. But according to Aristotle, this is not so. For he sets forth the concept of lawfulness, of conformity to positive law, as the wider concept of justice, which includes the idea of fairness as a concept of special justice within it. He says of lawfulness: "This form of justice, then, is complete virtue" (1129b 25); and: "Justice in this sense, then, is not part of virtue but virtue entire, nor is the contrary injustice a part of vice but vice entire." And he goes on:

But at all events what we are investigating is the justice which is a *part* of virtue; for there is a justice of this kind, as we maintain. Similarly it is with injustice in the particular sense that we are concerned .... There is, then, another kind of injustice which is a part of injustice in the wide sense, and a use of the word 'unjust' which answers to a part of what is unjust in the wide sense of 'contrary to law' (1130a 13).

Hence there must be a justice as part of the whole of justice, viz., lawfulness as conformity to positive law. The special justice which forms part of total justice, *qua* conformity to positive law, is fairness. For it is later said:

It is clear, then, that there is more than one kind of justice and that there is one which is distinct from virtue entire [namely conformity to positive law]; we must try to grasp its genus and differentia (1130b 6).

Aristotle informs us only of the outcome of this enquiry. And the outcome is, that this "special justice" is fairness, and that this special fairness is related to justice, which is virtue entire, "as part to whole"; "(for all that is unfair is unlawful, but not all that is unlawful is unfair) ... for injustice in this sense is a part of injustice in the wide sense, and similarly justice in the one sense [i.e., the principle of fairness] of justice in the other", of total justice, which is lawfulness, i.e., conformity to positive law. Between this justice and the justice of fairness there can be no conflict, for the latter is contained in the former. All the norms of positive law are just, but within these norms there are some which are just in a special sense: those which apply the principle of fairness.

Now Aristotle cannot ignore the fact that there are positive legal orders which by no means treat all citizens alike. He says:

Now the laws in their enactments on all subjects aim at the common advantage either of all or of the best or of those who hold power [according to virtue], or something of the sort (1129b 15).

Thus there is also vindication, as just, of a positive legal order directed, not to the advantage of all citizens, but only to that of a preferred group. For this preference is held to be just, in that "virtue" or "something of the sort", i.e., a moral value, is regarded as its criterion. In such preference Aristotle sees no violation of what he calls "fairness". And in order to be able to vindicate, not only a democratic legal order, but also an aristocratic and monarchical one, as conforming to the principle of fairness, he develops his doctrine of proportionality as fairness. For all positive legal orders, he says,

agree that what is just in distribution must be according to merit in some sense, though they do not all specify the same sort of merit, but democrats identify it with the status of freeman, supporters of oligarchy with wealth (or with noble birth), and supporters of aristocracy with excellence. The just, then, is a species of the proportionate.... For proportion is equality of ratios... (1131a 25).

"And justice is that in virtue of which the just man... [will] give what is equal in accordance with proportion" (1134a 1). Proportional justice is distribution on the basis of a value, any value, whether it be freedom, wealth or virtue. But this means, on the basis of what is held to be a value. Thus the concept of fairness is replaced by that of subjective, and therefore relative, value. And hence every legal order which distributes duties and rights according to some subjective and thus relative value – and every positive legal order does this – can be vindicated as conforming to the principle of fairness.

This identification of positive law with justice is incompatible with a genuine doctrine of natural law. For the latter must grant – in principle, at least – the possibility of a contrast between the two, even if it endeavours to restrict this possibility to a minimum.

In his vindication of positive law, Aristotle does not go so far as to declare all positive legal orders to be of equal value. The law, he says, bids us to practise every virtue and forbids us to practise any vice, and "the rightly-framed law does this rightly, and the hastily conceived one (ἀπεσχεδιασμένος)[7] less well" (1129b 25). The difference of value is only a greater or lesser degree of goodness or rightness. And this difference is attributed, not to the law's intention, but to legal technique, i.e., to the fact that one law is carefully drafted, while the other is negligently so.

From the fact that "all lawful acts are just acts" and that the law bids us "practise every virtue", it would follow that a good citizen, i.e., a man whose behaviour conforms to all the norms of positive law, must also be a morally good and just man. But, in less than total agreement with the identification of positive law with justice, Aristotle says: "... perhaps it is not the same to be a good man and a good citizen of any state taken at random" (1130b 28). It would seem that the author of the *Nicomachean Ethics* has become somewhat nervous of the consequences of identifying justice and lawfulness. But there can be no doubt that, according to the text before us, positive law is identified with justice.

This is basically just a possible consequence of the assumption, that a reality to which value is immanent must in principle be good. For positive law is law laid down by real acts, the law as it really and actually exists, and must therefore be regarded as essentially good, which means, however, as just. Here can be seen the internal contradiction of a theory of natural law which seeks to furnish a standard of value for positive law. It can only deduce just norms from nature, and especially from human nature, if this nature is good. But if it is good, there is no need of norms to prescribe how men ought to behave, since they are surely bound to behave in accordance with their nature. Such norms are needed only if man's nature is not good. Law exists, as Thomas Aquinas says, not for the good, but for the wicked.[8] But if the nature of man is wicked, no natural law can be deduced from it. The Aristotelian theory of entelechy presupposes a reality essentially good, and represents an optimistic interpretation of nature. Hence it is only logical that Aristotle's ethics should essentially be concerned to vindicate positive morality and positive law, as the social order that has actually been erected by man.

The distinction between φυσικὸν δίκαιον and νομικὸν δίκαιον, the naturally and the legally just, follows in the statement: "Of political justice part is natural, part legal..." (1134b 18). By the politically just (πολιτικὸν δίκαιον), nothing else can be understood save the positive law of a community consisting of the free and equal. For it was previously said

> that what we are looking for is not only what is just without qualification but also political justice (πολιτικὸν δίκαιον). This is found among men who share their life with a view to self-sufficiency, men who are free and ... equal (1134a 25).

By φυσικὸν and νομικὸν δίκαιον Aristotle means to distinguish two kinds of positive law in the state. This is possible, because τὸ δίκαιον means both justice and positive law. The distinction between φυσικὸν and νομικὸν δίκαιον consists in the fact that the naturally just is

> that which everywhere has the same force and does not exist by people's thinking this or that; [the legally just], that which is originally indifferent, but when it has been laid down is not indifferent (1134b 18).

This is to say that among the norms of positive law there are some which specifically regulate a matter which can only be so regulated and not otherwise, such as the norms forbidding murder and theft; and others which specifically regulate a matter which can nonetheless be regulated also in another fashion, so that these norms have an arbitrary character; as do the norms regulating traffic, in prescribing that on-coming vehicles are to be avoided on the right and not on the left. Since the naturally just is concerned with norms of positive law, Aristotle is bound to reject the view that the naturally just is unchangeable:

Now some think that all justice is of this [legal] sort, because that which is by nature is unchangeable and has everywhere the same force (as fire burns both here and in Persia), while they see change in the things recognised as just. This, however, is not true in this unqualified way, but is true in a sense; or rather, with the gods it is perhaps not true at all, while with us there is something that is just even by nature, yet all of it is changeable (1134b 25).

Changeable, however, only to a certain degree! Even the norms of positive law which, like those against murder, theft, etc., are by no means arbitrary, are not absolutely the same everywhere. They differ at different times and among different peoples. But these changes are confined within definite limits. The difference between the norms of positive law described as "naturally" just, and those that are merely called "legally" just, is simply that the former are changeable to a much smaller degree than the latter. But in so saying, the first definition of the "naturally just", as that "which everywhere has the same force", is considerably modified. For if it is changeable, to however slight a degree, it cannot everywhere have the same force. But this is to reject the assumption of a genuine natural law, i.e., one that holds everywhere, and always with the same content, and for all men alike.[9]

Since positive law – and positive law alone, basically – is just, there can simply be no question of that possible conflict, essential for a genuine natural law theory, between the φυσικὸν δίκαιον and the νομικὸν δίκαιον. Let alone the fact that, in case of such a conflict, the natural law theory maintains that positive law, i.e., the νομικὸν δίκαιον, is invalid. According to the mode and manner in which Aristotle, in his *Nicomachean Ethics*, presents the distinction between φυσικὸν and νομικὸν δίκαιον, such a conflict simply cannot arise. For the φυσικὸν δίκαιον, i.e., natural law, is simply a constituent part of the πολιτικὸν δίκαιον, i.e., the positive law of the state. It consists of those norms which are much the same in all positive legal orders.

In the *Magna Moralia* (1195a 2) we are told:

Do not suppose that, if things change owing to our use, there is not therefore a natural justice; because there is. For that which continues for the most part can plainly be seen to be naturally just (τὸ γὰρ ὡς ἐπὶ τὸ πολὺ διαμένον, τοῦτο φύσει δίκαιον προφανές).

Aristotle thinks it possible to establish that, in the regulation of certain relationships, the positive legal orders are approximately in agreement. The norms of positive law which govern these relationships he describes as natural law.[10] But if by "natural law" we understand nothing else but the prescriptions common to all positive legal orders, then every positive law is natural law, and in that case this so-called natural law cannot exercise the function essential to natural law proper, of operating as a standard of evaluation for positive law. One cannot then distinguish, by appeal to natural law, between a just and an unjust system of law. Aristotle admittedly takes over the distinction current in his time between the just "by nature" (φύσει) and "because of the law" (νόμῳ δίκαιον), but he gives it a meaning which makes it entirely otiose from the standpoint of a genuine theory of natural law.[11] He uses the concept of natural law himself, only to vindicate positive law; as can be seen particularly clearly in his attitude to the question of slavery. Aristotle defends this institution on the ground that there are men who are by nature slaves (φύσει δοῦλοι).[12]

If the "nature" of alleged Aristotelian natural law is the nature of which Aristotle says in the *Politics*, I, 2 (1253a) "that the state is a creation *of nature*, and that man is *by nature* a political animal", then positive law, in the light of this doctrine, must be regarded as a *natural* law. For according to this theory, *every* state, and not merely the Greek polis, is a product of nature. For the natural givenness of the state rests on the fact that man is by nature a political, i.e., a state-forming animal – man in general, that is, and not just Greek man.

> And he who by nature and not by mere accident is without a state, is either a bad man or above humanity; ... he who is unable to live in society, or who has no need because he is sufficient for himself, must be either a beast or a god: he is no part of a state. A social [i.e. political] instinct is implanted in *all men* by nature ....

And *every* state has a legal order, "for the administration of justice ... is the principle of order in political society" [to which reference has hitherto been made, i.e., the order in every state]. And so therefore this law which is essential to the state, namely positive law, must be a product of nature, a natural law. And since – as appears from the passage just cited – it is this law which is the determination of what is just, it follows that every system of positive law must be a φύσει δίκαιον, even if Aristotle does not so term it in the present context.

The belief that Aristotle holds a theory of natural law seems to find some support in his distinction between good and bad, true and "perverted" constitutions. But since, for Aristotle, not only the good constitutions – monarchy, aristocracy and polity – but also the perverted ones – tyranny, oligarchy and democracy – are constitutions of *states*, and since these states – as states – together with the legal orders essential to them, are products of nature, this nature can be no criterion for the value of such constitutions, their goodness or badness, truth or perversion. If Aristotle evaluates a constitution as bad or perverted, this cannot mean that it is contrary to the "nature" he refers to in his doctrine of the state as a product of nature, and of man as by nature a political animal. With a "natural" law in this sense of the word the theory of perverted constitutions has nothing to do.

What makes it difficult to see this is that Aristotle, in his political theory, is operating with two different concepts of the state and – possibly – with two different concepts of nature, without expressly stressing the fact. This is connected with the fact that he mingles a descriptive account of given states, i.e., statements about what and how the state actually *is* among different peoples and at different periods, with a prescriptive and evaluative account, i.e., with judgements about what and how the state *ought* to be. After Aristotle, in Book I of the *Politics*, has characterised the state – and that means *every* state – as a natural community, in which men, meaning *all* men, live as naturally political animals, he goes on in Book III (1275b) to define the state as "a body of citizens sufficing for the purposes of life"; but here, by "citizens," he understands only those who have "the power to take part in the deliberative or judicial administration ...". This is not the state as it *is*, everywhere and at all times, but the state as in Aristotle's view it *ought* to be, and as it has been realised, more or less, in some though not all of the Greek communities. Aristotle concedes: "... our definition is best adapted to the citizen of a democracy; but not necessarily to other [forms of government]" (1275b) – though the latter also constitute states. But even the communities under whose constitution there are no "citizens" in this sense, communities which are not democracies, are "states" in terms of the concept defined in Book I; they have constitutions and a legal order which decides what is just. They too, and hence also the positive law inherent in them, exist by nature. Later again (1279a) Aristotle lays it down that "a state is a community of freemen", which only means, however, that the state ought to be such a community, though it is not so in all cases. For Aristotle distinguishes governments "which have a regard to the common interest" from those "which regard only the interest of the rulers" (1279a). The first, he says, "are constituted in accordance with strict principles of justice", not the principles of the justice which is an essential element of every state, and decides what is just. The others he calls "defective and perverted forms, for they are despotic", i.e., they treat the ruled as if they were slaves. But they are governments of *states*. Aristotle expressly speaks of the three perverted forms – tyranny, oligarchy and democracy – as "governments" constituting states (1289a). Even they – oligarchy and democracy – "cling to justice of some kind" (1280a); and these two perverted constitutions Aristotle actually describes as "principal forms of government" (1301b) which must therefore doubtless come about by nature. But in Book III (1287b) we read that there is no justice "naturally appropriate to tyranny or to any other perverted form of government; for these come into being contrary to nature (παρὰ φύσιν)." This passage not only stands in open contradiction to one of the main theses of Aristotelian political theory, regarding the natural givenness of all states, in which men live as naturally political animals; it also contradicts the immediately preceding statement that "there is by nature both a justice and an advantage appropriate to the rule of a master, another to kingly rule, another to constitutional rule" – and the perverted constitutions are, as was said in the remark quoted above, "despotic", and if men are subjected to them who by nature must live under despotic rule, they are in accordance with nature. But the questionable passage is also in conflict with the considerations of Book III (1286b), where Aristotle shows why and under what conditions the perverted forms of state – tyranny, oligarchy and democracy – are bound to arise. Of democracy he says that, under the conditions he specifies, "no other form of government appears to be any longer even easy to establish", and hence again it cannot be contrary to the "nature" referred to in the fundamental discussions of Book I. It is more than doubtful whether the remark concerning the contrariety to nature of the perverted state-forms is authentic, seeing that it contradicts everything that Aristotle otherwise says about the nature of the state. If it is genuine, then Aristotle is here employing a concept of nature other than that from which his political theory sets out, a concept of an ideal nature, not the real one; a nature, not as it is, but as it ought to be from the standpoint of a specific evaluative scheme. This means, however, that that which the perverted constitutions conflict with is a postulate put forward as "nature". Such a "nature" cannot be that of a theory of natural law. This isolated passage, at variance with the intellectual scheme of the whole Aristotelian political theory, cannot be regarded as evidence for Aristotle's having held a theory of natural law.

The idea of a natural law distinct from positive law and possibly in conflict with it, equivalent to justice in the specific sense of the word, is deliberately shunned by Aristotle in his ethics, but emerges with complete clarity in his *Rhetoric*. Here, for the first time, natural law is contrasted, as "universal law", to positive law as "particular law".

Particular law is that which each community lays down and applies to its own members: this is partly written and partly unwritten. Universal law is the law of nature. For there really is, as every one to some extent divines, a natural justice and injustice that is binding on all men ... (I, 13, 1373b).

But earlier (I, 10) it is said:

'Law' is either special or general. By special law I mean that written law which regulates the life of a particular community; by general law, all those unwritten principles which are supposed to be acknowledged everywhere (1368b).

Here "general law" is not expressly identified with natural law, and positive law is characterised as "written" prescription, whereas in the passage where general law *is* identified with natural law, positive law is described as either written or unwritten. At times (I, 14) it is said that "the written laws depend on force while the unwritten ones do not." Later (I, 15), natural law *qua* unwritten law is again contrasted to positive law as written law. The attempts to bring these mutually contradictory formulations into agreement are fruitless. What it comes to, is that stress is being firmly laid on the possibility of a conflict between the unwritten natural and the written positive law; but simply for the purpose of showing the rhetorical, i.e., forensic advantages to be gained by appealing to one or the other. "If" – we are here told (I, 15) –

the written law tells against our case, clearly we must appeal to the universal law, and insist on its greater equity and justice. We must argue that the jurors oath 'I will give my verdict according to my honest opinion' means that one will not simply follow the letter of the written law. We must urge that the principles of equity are permanent and changeless, and that the universal law does not change either, for it is the law of nature, whereas written laws often do change.

It is obvious that what Aristotle is counselling the courtroom advocate to bring forward is not the Aristotelian theory of natural law. For that natural law, in contrast to positive law, is changeless, stands in direct contradiction to what Aristotle says about it in the *Nicomachean Ethics*. The treatise on rhetoric is not concerned with presenting the Aristotelian philosophy of law, but rather with advising the advocate to make use of what was then a commonly held theory of natural law, if the positive law proves unfavourable to the case which he has to present. This is shown by the following passage, where Aristotle recommends him to take up the opposite theory, if this tells in his favour:

If however the written law supports our case, we must urge that the oath 'to give my verdict according to my honest opinion' is not meant to make the judges give a verdict that is contrary to the law, but to save them from the guilt of perjury if they misunderstand what the law really means (I, 15, 1375b).

The advocate is also advised to take the view that violation of the unwritten law is a greater crime than violation of the written law. But Aristotle promptly adds: "It may however be argued otherwise, that the crime is worse which breaks the written laws" (I, 14, 1375a).[13]

There are, then, two mutually exclusive views about the relation of natural and positive law, of which the teacher of rhetoric declares one to be advantageous under some circumstances, and the other under others; but as to which is held true by the teacher of ethics, Aristotle provides no answer. Yet even his silence is an answer – an answer to the question whether he upholds a genuine doctrine of natural law. And this answer can only be in the negative.

5. Though Aristotle himself did not do so, it was on the basis of the Aristotelian philosophy that Thomas Aquinas evolved a theory of natural law, whose theological character is quite unambiguously apparent.

The Aristotelian entelechy appears unmistakeably in the *Summa contra Gentiles*. It is there said (III, 16):

For everything is directed by its action to some end (ordinatur in finem).... The end of a thing is the term of its appetite (appetitus ejus). Now the appetite of a thing terminates in a good ... the end of a thing is its perfection (perfectio).... Therefore every thing is directed to good as its end.

But this good is God. Thus it is said (III, 17):

For if nothing tends to something as its end, except in so far as this is good, it follows that good, as such (bonum in quantum bonum est), is an end. Consequently that which is the supreme good (summum bonum) is supremely the end of all. Now there is but one supreme good, namely God .... Therefore all things are directed to the highest good, namely God, as their end.

It is then added (III, 18): "God is the end of things as something to be obtained (obtinendum) by each thing in its own way." Perfection is the immanent end of things. That is the Aristotelian entelechy. It is the work of God. For it is God who leads things to perfection. In the *Summa theologica* (I, Quaestio 103, Art. 1) we are told:

... it is not fitting that the supreme goodness of God should produce things without giving them their perfection ... it belongs to the divine goodness, as it brought things into being, so to lead them to their end.[14]

If nature tends toward an end, this is because God bids it to tend towards good as its end, and nature hearkens to His bidding. Hence being is essentially good, i.e., as it should be, according to God's command. In the *Summa theologica* (I, Quaestio 5, Art. 1), St. Thomas says: "Goodness and being are really the same (dicendum quod bonum et ens sunt idem secundum rem)." And at I, Quaestio 48, Art. 1:

Hence it is impossible that evil signifies any being, or any form or nature. Therefore, by the name *evil* there must be signified some absence of good. And this is what is meant by saying that *evil is neither a being nor a good*. For since being, as such, is good, the absence of being involves the absence of good.[15]

What is and what ought to be coincide.[16]

This negation of the dualism of 'is' and 'ought' which rests quite essentially on a metaphysico-theological foundation, emerges with especial clarity in the doctrine of the nature of man. Man's inherent urges, implanted in him by God, present themselves as moral demands, i.e., as norms. In the *Summa theologica* (I II, 94, 2) we read: "... the order of the precepts of the natural law is according to the order of natural inclinations." Natural inclinations are precepts of natural law because and insofar as they are determined by practical reason.[17] Thomas distinguishes as Aristotle does between ratio speculativa and ratio practica (*Summa theologica*, I II, 90, 1). The function of ratio practica is to command, to legislate, to lay down norms prescribing good and just behaviour (I–II, 17, 1; I–II, 90, 1). Law is a rule and a measure for what is to be done and omitted (I–II, 90, 1). But in and for itself (secundum se), human practical reason is not this rule and measure. The principles impressed on it by nature (principia ei naturaliter indita) are rules and measures of this sort (I–II, 91, 3).[18] But these principles "naturally" (naturaliter) implanted in human reason are ultimately derived from God, who has endowed man with reason; and human reason is a practical reason, laying down norms, only insofar as divine reason holds sway within it. But divine reason rules the world according to an eternal law (lex aeterna) which must be thought immanent to this reason. Man, created by God, has reason so far as he partakes in divine reason, from which he receives the impulse to a type of conduct in accordance with eternal law (I–II, 91, 1 and 2). The concept of an eternal law immanent in divine reason is taken over by Thomas from Augustine, who defines the lex aeterna, God's eternal world-plan, as: "Ratio divina vel voluntas Dei ordinem naturalem conservari jubens, perturbari vetans" (*Contra Faustum Manich*, 22, 27).

Of natural law, he says: "But who but God has written the law of nature in the hearts of men?"[19] The divine reason, which is immanent in the lex aeterna, and thus in natural law, is volitional reason: "ratio vel voluntas". Hence Thomas teaches, that that is just which is in agreement with the rule of reason, and the first rule of reason is the law of nature (rationis autem prima regula est lex naturalis; I–II, 95, 2). "And this participation of the eternal law in the rational creature is called the natural law" (lex naturalis nihil aliud est quam participatio legis aeternae in rationali creatura; I–II, 91, 2).[20] The eternal law is the government of the world by divine reason. To be sure, natural law proceeds directly from human reason as a practical reason; but this is possible only because and insofar as this human reason participates in divine reason, and the lex naturalis in the lex aeterna. For in natural law is manifested the lex aeterna of divine reason. The authority of natural law is ultimately the authority of God. In *Summa theologica*, I–II, 97, 3, it is stated: "Dicendum quod lex naturalis et divina procedit a voluntate divina." There is no doubting the theologico-metaphysical basis of St. Thomas' theory of natural law. It is a genuine natural law theory. This is also apparent in its attitude to the relation between natural and positive law. The latter has binding force only insofar as it corresponds to natural law. If it conflicts with natural law, it has no validity, and is no law: "Unde omnis lex humanitus posita intantum habet de ratione legis, inquantum a lege naturae derivatur. Si vero in aliquo a lege naturali discordet, jam non erit lex, sed legis corruptio" (I–II, 95, 2). That is the consequence of the divine authority of natural law.[21]

The divine reason which rules the world through the lex aeterna is identical, *qua* legislative reason, with God's will (I–II, 93, 4).[22] So human practical reason is a reason which simultaneously knows and wills, because it is a legislative reason. And hence the good is simultaneously the true, and justice truth:

Since the will [which lies in reason] is the rational appetite, when the rightness of reason [rectitudo rationis], which is called truth, is imprinted on the will, this imprint, on account of its proximity to reason, retains the name of truth; and hence it is that justice sometimes goes by the name of truth (II–II, 58, 4).[23]

When Jesus says to Pilate: "To this end was I born, and for this cause came I into the world, that I should bear witness unto the truth", he uses the word 'truth' to mean justice.[24]

6. Human practical reason, which both knows and wills, and which legislatively posits the norms of natural law as a law of reason, is the divine reason in man; so much is eventually conceded even by Kant, in his theory of practical reason as legislator of the moral law. That the moral law emerges from the will of man as intelligence, constitutes the autonomy of the will, which Kant proclaims (*Fundamental Principles of the Metaphysic of Morals*, transl. by Abbot, p. 71 [440]) as the supreme principle of morality. It is human practical reason which, in accordance with this principle of autonomy, is the giver of the moral law. In this respect, Kant's practical reason seems to differ from the ratio practica of St. Thomas, who sees in human practical reason only a participation in the practical reason of God, who in the last resort is the moral legislator. But Kant is unable to uphold the principle of man's moral autonomy, since he endeavours – precisely by means of man's practical reason – to prove the existence of God as supreme moral lawgiver. In the *Critique of Judgement* (Pt. II, transl. by J. C. Meredith, p. 110 [444]), he says:

It is, then, only as a moral being that we acknowledge man to be the end of creation.... Now the structure of our reason is such that we necessarily refer natural ends to an intelligent world-cause. Above all, then, we have *one* principle... enabling us to think the nature and attributes of this first cause considered as supreme ground in the kingdom of ends.... With such a definite principle as this, of the causality of the original being, we shall not have to regard it merely as an intelligence and as legislating for nature, but as the Sovereign Head legislating in a moral Kingdom of Ends.

Thus it is not man's intelligence as will, or his will as intelligence, but God's intelligence as will or will as intelligence, which forms the ultimate source of the moral law; it is not man, but God, the original being, who is the moral legislator. In the *Fundamental Principles* (p. 90 [455]), we find:

What he [man] morally 'ought' is then what he necessarily 'would' as a member of the world of the understanding, and is conceived by him as an 'ought' only inasmuch as he likewise considers himself as a member of the world of sense.

For man as an intelligible being there is no 'ought', and hence no imperatives apply, for what he would coincides with what he ought. But such an intelligible being, whose willing is an 'ought' for the empirical being, can only be God. Kant also says (*ibid.*, p. 36 [414]): "Therefore no imperatives hold for the Divine will, or in general for a *holy* will; *ought* is here out of place, because the volition is already of itself necessarily in unison with the law" [i.e., with the 'ought']. In the *Critique of Judgement* (*op. cit.*, p. 111 [444]), we are to think of God, the original being, as "omniscient", as "omnipotent", and "as both all-good and just". If God must be postulated as the supreme moral legislator, then moral duties are not to be characterised – or at least not adequately – as commands proceeding from man's own reason, but must be regarded as commands of God, or at least as this too. Kant does say, indeed, in the *Metaphysic of Morals* (*Metaphysical Principles of Virtue*, tr. Ellington, p. 161 [491]),

that in ethics, taken as the pure practical philosophy of internal legislation, only the moral relations of man to man are conceivable for us. But whatever passes for a relation between God and man completely transcends the bounds of ethics and is for us utterly inconceivable.

But in *Religion within the Limits of Reason Alone* (tr. Greene, Rev. ed., p. 5), he says: "Morality thus leads ineluctably to religion, through which it extends itself to the idea of a powerful moral Lawgiver, outside of mankind..."; and on p. 142: "Religion is (subjectively regarded) the recognition of all duties as divine commands." And in Kant's *Opus Postumum* (ed. and crit. Erich Adickes, 1920, p. 802), we find the statement: "In the morally-practical reason there lies the categorical imperative, to regard all human duties as divine commands."

Thus Kant's ethics ends at exactly the point where Thomas Aquinas left the subject five hundred years before him.

7. The theory of natural law, which was dominant throughout the 17th and 18th centuries, after relapsing during the 19th, has again in the 20th re-entered the foreground of social and legal philosophy, in company with religious and metaphysical speculation. Its revival is a product of two world wars, and of the reaction against nazism, fascism and particularly communism. There can be no question that this theory is of religio-metaphysical origin. It goes back to the philosophy of the Stoa, and indeed, ideas very closely approximating to it can already be found in the fragments of Heraclitus. As in Fragment 112: "Moderation is the greatest virtue, and wisdom is to speak the truth and to act according to nature (κατὰ φύσιν), paying heed [thereto]"; and in Fragment 114, where there is talk of a divine Logos, upon which all our human laws must be nourished. But it is only in the Stoic philosophy that a concept of natural law is first clearly defined, and in so doing, unambiguously said to be of divine origin. A fragment of Cleanthes, one of the heads of the Stoa, contains these words:

Most glorious of the Immortals, many-named, Almighty for ever, / Zeus, ruler of Nature, that governest all things with law, / Hail! for lawful it is that all mortals should address Thee, / For we are Thy offspring, taking the image only of Thy voice . . . / Thus dost thou harmonise into One all good and evil things, / That there should be one everlasting Reason of them all . . . / Since there can be no greater glory for men or Gods than this, / Duly to praise for ever the Universal Law.

(*Hymn to Zeus*, transl. by T. W. Rolleston)

And another fragment runs:

Lead me O Zeus, and thou, Destiny, whithersoever ye have appointed me to go, and may I follow fearlessly. But if in an evil mind I be unwilling, still must I follow.

(From Epictetus, *Ench.* 53, transl. by Rolleston)

Sauter [25] justly observes that "Destiny" is not a special power additional to God, but is itself the divine immanent in everything. Chrysippus the Stoic declares: "For it is not possible to discover any principle or beginning of Justice other than from that of the gods and from the common nature" (Von Arnim, *SVF* III, 326, tr. J. L. Saunders). Following the Stoic philosophy, Cicero teaches that the law of nature, which unlike positive law is eternal and immutable, has its originator, its spokesman and its judge in God. (*De Republica*, XXII, 33). The influence of the Stoa and of Cicero is apparent in the patristic doctrine of natural law, and especially in that of Augustine, who – as already noticed – takes over from the Stoa the concept of the lex aeterna, and who exclaims: "For who but God has written the law of nature in the hearts of men?" (*De serm. Dei in monte*, II, ch. 9, 32; transl. by W. Findlay, in *Nicene and Post-Nicene Fathers*, 1st ser., vol. 6, p. 44).

Within the natural law theory, the attempt was nonetheless made to emancipate the doctrine from its theologico-metaphysical foundations. Grotius declares, in the Prolegomena to his *De Jure Belli et Pacis*, that the natural law he is describing would also hold good, even if there were assumed to be no God; but he adds that this "cannot be conceded without the utmost wickedness" (§ 11). In the very next paragraph (§ 12), however, he says:

> But the law of nature of which we have spoken, comprising alike that which relates to the social life of man and that which is so called in a larger sense, proceeding as it does from the essential traits implanted in man, can nevertheless rightly be attributed to God, because of His having willed that such traits exist in us.

And in his definition of natural law he says:

> The law of nature is a dictate of right reason, which points out that an act, according as it is or is not in conformity with rational nature, has in it a quality of moral baseness or moral necessity; and that, in consequence, such an act is either forbidden or enjoined by the author of nature, God. (Book I, ch. 1, §x, 1; transl. by F. W. Kelsey, *On the Law of War and Peace*, 1925, pp. 13, 14, 38–9).

Natural law is a dictate of rational nature; but nature is a creation of God, and hence the dictates of rational nature are commands of God. Grotius is unable to sustain the attempt to render the validity of natural law independent of belief in the existence of God. For he was a believing Christian, as were all the exponents of the classical theory of natural law, even if many of them, as it seems, were aware that without belief in a nature created by a just God, the supposition of a just law immanent in this nature is not consistently tenable. The claim that the validity of natural law is independent of belief in God's existence may spring from the desire to safeguard this validity against unbelievers. But this claim should not be confused with the doctrine that the validity of natural law is independent of God's will. This is meant to assert that the validity of natural law could not be abolished even by the will of God. This results from the doctrine that God can will nothing against His essence or nature, that His power thus finds a limit in His own nature, and that His omnipotence cannot therefore mean that He can will absolutely everything. Since natural law is justice, God cannot will to abolish its validity, for this would mean that God wills to be unjust. But since God is essentially just, if He willed to be unjust, He would not be God. Anselm of Canterbury, in his *Cur Deus Homo*,[26] expresses this idea as follows:

> But when it is said that what He wills is just, and what He does not will is not just, this must not be taken to mean that if God were to will something unfitting, it would be just because He willed it. For it does not follow that if God wills to lie, it is just to lie, but rather, that He is not God.

In another passage[27] Anselm argues that God does not have the power to change the decision "which He had already willed to be changeless." For this "would be powerlessness rather than power." Since God has willed natural law to be changeless, He cannot will to change or even to abolish it.

8. In order to show you how vain is the attempt to conceive the validity of a true, i.e., eternal and immutable natural law to be independent of God's will, I should like in conclusion to refer to a catholic author, whose authority you certainly will not question. Victor Cathrein, in his *Moralphilosophie* (5th edn. 1911, p. 546), defines "natural law as a sum of... binding norms which hold good for all mankind through nature itself, and not primarily as a result of positive decree". Natural law, he says, can be summed up in the two ordinances "thou shalt give everyone his own", and "thou shalt do wrong to no one". These are wholly empty propositions, which designate no human behaviour of any determinate kind, and first become meaningful when it is determined by positive norms, posited, that is, through acts of will, what everyone's own is, and what wrong is. But that is not the procedure here. Cathrein thinks that from these two ordinances determinate norms can be derived by inference, "and that independently of any supernatural revelation, or of any positive command, divine or human", so that these norms

belong "to natural law in the true sense" (p. 547). Such derived norms, according to Cathrein, include "thou shalt not kill, thou shalt not commit adultery, thou shalt not steal, defraud, or bear false witness, thou shalt obey the lawful authorities and adhere to contracts made". Of these norms he expressly admits: "These precepts occur in the decalogue" (p. 549), i.e., are norms posited by the will of God, and thus by no means norms "which hold independently of any command, divine or human". We may object to Cathrein for supposing that these norms do not hold good as the import of divine acts of will, but independently of such acts; we may impute to him the belief that the delivery of the Ten Commandments, pronounced by God on Mount Sinai amid thunder and lightning, and inscribed by Himself upon two tablets of stone, was of merely declarative and not constitutive significance, that God on Mount Sinai merely proclaimed the validity of norms already eternally valid apart from His will; which at all events is not the meaning of the report which Holy Scripture gives of this affair. But even that is not decisive. A norm – and for Cathrein natural law is a norm – can only be the import of an act of will. And Cathrein himself has to admit this, when he discusses the question whether a natural law is – as many assume – a law of reason. It is certainly true, he says (p. 548) that

> natural law consists of the practical, binding principles to whose knowledge reason spontaneously attains. But it would be wrong to suppose that the binding force of these commands comes from reason itself. The obligation of the law is assuredly a demand which the will of the superior directs to the will of the subordinate. But we cannot be the subordinates of our own will. Reason tells us to some extent after the fashion of a herald the requirements which the rational will of the author of nature imposes on our wills. It is therefore better to speak of the law of nature than of the law of reason.

Natural law consists, therefore, of the requirements which the rational will of the author of nature imposes on our wills. If these norms are valid "through nature itself", this is only because they are imposed on our wills by the rational will of the author of nature.

Cathrein vindicates natural law as the necessary basis of positive law. He asks (p. 566): "Whence does human society or human authority obtain the right to oblige us?" "The answer," he says, "can only be that nature itself, or better, the author of nature, lends it the right." We know from the nature of man that God wills the state of society, and without an authority to lay down positive law, society is impossible. It is therefore God who gives this authority the right to promulgate laws.

This right and the corresponding legal duty are given by the natural moral law, and form an indispensable basis of every positive law. They are rooted, not in the will of man, but in the will of God.[28]

NOTES

* *Österreichische Zeitschrift für öffentliches Recht*, **13** (New Series) (1964), 1–37. Also published in *Das Naturrecht in der politischen Theorie* (ed. by Franz-Martin Schmölz), Vienna 1963, pp. 1–37.

[1] From the [German] translation of Franz Biese: *Die Philosophie des Aristoteles*, Berlin, vol. I, p. 480. [Unless otherwise stated, Aristotelian quotations in this essay are drawn from the Oxford *Works of Aristotle*, 1908–31, ed. by W. D. Ross–Transl.]

[2] *Gedichte: Gott, Gemüt und Welt* (Gedichte 1812–1814). [Translator's rendering].

[3] *Philosophisches Wörterbuch*, ed. by Walter Brugger, S. J., 4th edn., Freiburg 1951, art. 'Immanenz', p. 162.

[4] It was already the view of C. A. Brandis: *Geschichte der Entwicklung der griechischen Philosophie*, vol. I, 1862, p. 484, that the Aristotelian metaphysics can be understood only if it is assumed "that the divine thoughts enter in some way into the world of things." The more recent interpretations of Aristotle, especially that of Werner Jaeger (*Aristotle*, 2nd edn., transl. by R. Robinson, Oxford 1948), who rejects the theory of immanence, are unable to get away from this. He argues (p. 385): "God is one with the world not by penetrating it, nor by maintaining the totality of its forms as an intelligible world within himself, but because the world 'hangs' (ἤρτηται) on him; he *is* its unity, although not in it. As each thing strives to realize its own form, it realizes for its part that infinite perfection which as a whole is God." If every thing realizes for its part what God is, it realizes God in itself, and God is *in* every thing. God cannot be the unity of the world and not be *in* the world; for the world's unity cannot be outside the world. The unity of an object which is outside this object is an impossible notion, which ought not to be attributed to Aristotle because he has for some reason failed to lay particular emphasis on that immanence of God in the world which inevitably results from his theory of entelechy. For the rest, Jaeger himself cites the passage above referred to from the *Eudemian Ethics*, in which God's immanence in the universe and in the human soul is plainly expressed. And in Jaeger's opinion, the *Eudemian Ethics* must be regarded as being by Aristotle himself.

[5] Cf. Walther Eckstein: *Das antike Naturrecht in sozialphilosophischer Beleuchtung*, Vienna 1926, p. 72.

[6] Cf. Olof Gigon's introduction to his translation of the Nicomachean Ethics: *Nikomachische Ethik*, introduced and newly translated by Olof Gigon. Artemis-Verlag, Zürich, 1951, p. 40.

[6a] [The German renders this term "Gleichheit" (= "equality", rather than "fairness"); it should be borne in mind that this is the reading adopted throughout the discussions which follow – Transl.].

[7] σχεδιασμός: Speaking and acting extempore; σχεδιάζω: to be flighty, to do something extempore, to improvise.

[8] *Summa theologica*, I–II, 96, Art. 5.

[9] After saying of such natural justice that "all of it is changeable", Aristotle goes on: "but still some is by nature, some not by nature. It is evident which sort of thing, among things capable of being otherwise, is [just] by nature; and which is not but is legal and conventional, assuming that both are equally changeable." If both kinds of justice are changeable, it is by no means evident how we are to decide of what kind and quality the naturally and the

legally just are. Moreover, the naturally and the legally just are here presented as two kinds of justice "among things capable of being otherwise", whereas earlier, what can be so or otherwise was distinguished, as the legally just, from that which has everywhere the same validity, namely the naturally just. We are further told: "And in all other things the same distinction will apply; by nature the right hand is stronger, yet it is possible that all men should come to be ambidextrous." If this is to say that a natural rule may have exceptions, it is a different thing from the earlier claim, that not only the legally, but also the naturally just is changeable. For the changeability of positive law is not a matter of exceptions to a rule. Nor is the sentence following by any means free from logical objections. "The things which are just by virtue of convention and expediency are like measures; for wine and corn measures are not everywhere equal, but larger in wholesale and smaller in retail markets." Taken literally, this is impossible, for buying and selling are simply two sides of one and the same transaction. If the meaning is that in wholesale dealings a larger quantity of wine and corn is bought and sold for the same price than in retail trading, there is no understanding what this has to do with the changeability of the naturally just. The legal determinations resting upon convention and expediency must be presupposed here as part of the naturally just; for the sequel runs, "Similarly, the things which are just not by nature but by human enactment are not everywhere the same, since constitutions also are not the same...". Hence constitutions are in accordance, not with nature, but with merely human law, i.e., legal norms laid down by men. Yet constitutions are thereupon designated as natural law: "... though there is but one which is everywhere by nature the best." But if everywhere there is only one constitution in accordance with nature, this natural law cannot be changeable. Elsewhere, too, the section contains arguments which are so obviously questionable as to be scarcely attributable to so great a thinker as Aristotle. As when it is claimed that a man who lies with a woman, knowing her to be married, but through passion rather than deliberate choice, and a man who has stolen something, act unjustly but yet are not unjust (ἀδικεῖ μὲν οὖν ἄδικος δ᾽οὐκ ἔστίν). Above all, however, after those acts have been called just (1129b 18, 19) that tend to produce and preserve happiness for the political society (πολιτικὴ κοινωνία); after saying that the laws prescribe all virtues, and hence also the virtue of justice; after claiming that this justice produced by the law is the greatest of virtues; and after declaring in the aforementioned section (1134a 26) that what we are looking for is "political justice" (πολιτικὸν δίκαιον) – it is later said (1134b 13): "Political [justice] is neither just nor unjust" (οὐδ᾽ἄρα ἄδικον οὐδὲ δίκαιον τὸ πολιτικόν), for it is according to law, and between people naturally subject to law. Before this, however, justice was virtually identified with lawfulness, i.e., with what conforms to the laws of the state; and later the politically just (πολιτικὸν δίκαιον) is described as in part naturally and in part legally just. This is a contradiction which no interpretation can dispose of. Not even if, as Gigon does in his otherwise admirable translation, we relate the above cited sentence to that which immediately precedes it (διὸ οὐκ ἔστιν ἀδικία πρὸς αὑτόν), "for which reason there can be no injustice towards oneself" and then translate: "not even the politically unjust or just." But in the Greek text the two sentences are separated, not by a comma, but by a full stop, and the sentence in question has τὸ πολιτικόν [δίκαιον] as its subject and means, as J. H. Kirchmann rightly translates it, "Political justice is neither just nor unjust" (*Des Aristoteles Nikomachische Ethik*, Philosophische Bibliothek, vol. 68. Leipzig 1876, p. 107). [The author's strictures on this passage would seem, unfortunately, to be based on a misreading of the text. Aristotle is referring to the relations between master and slave or parent and child, and points out that *these* relations are not just or unjust in the 'political' sense, since they do not hold under law, and between equals. Ross, supported by other English translators, accordingly renders the passage thus: "Therefore the justice or injustice of citizens is not manifested in these relations: for it was as we saw according to law, and between people naturally subject to law ...."–Transl.].

It is hard to suppose that these passages in Book V of the *Nicomachean Ethics*, so crucial to the alleged natural law theory of Aristotle, are not corrupt. If they permit any conclusion at all as to Aristotle's attitude towards natural law theory, they do not, at all events, allow us to regard him as an exponent of that doctrine. In his comments on the *Nicomachean Ethics*, Kirchmann says of the chapter in Book V where the distinction is drawn between φυσικὸν and νομικὸν δίκαιον, between the naturally and the legally just: "This chapter was either very carelessly written down by Aristotle, or the text has been later disfigured ... It also appears that in Book V we are most probably confronted with the compilation of a mediocre pupil, or with a preliminary sketch of Aristotle's, dating from a much earlier period" (*op. cit*., p. 103).

[10] Walter Eckstein, *op. cit*., p. 78: "For Aristotle, natural law is by no means the only valid law; he wishes, rather, to conceive it as a mere subspecies of law, alongside 'legal' law, and the opposition to nomos, such as we have found among the Sophists – and as we might legitimately have expected in the mouth of anyone appealing to natural law – is entirely alien to him." And Max Salomon (*Der Begriff der Gerechtigkeit bei Aristoteles*, Leiden 1937) remarks on p. 53: "The development of natural law thinking has given these words" – φυσικόν, νομικόν– "a meaning not inherent in the arguments of Aristotle. As he apprehends these concepts, natural law is never an ideal or standard for statute law." And on p. 55: "One should not identify the δίκαιον φυσικόν with the jus naturale. Nor has it anything to do with the 'ewigen Rechten, die droben hangen unveräusserlich' [Schiller]. It is in no way a δίκαιον καθ' ὁμοιότητα, but is equally little exalted in validity, rank or value above that which otherwise figures as law."

[11] Many more recent philosophers of law also denature natural law, just as Aristotle does. They argue somewhat as follows: Since men always and everywhere live in society, and submit to an order which regulates their reciprocal behaviour, the validity of such an order must correspond to the nature of man. All these orders agree in regard to certain prescriptions, such as the ban on killing members of the community, or at least certain of them. From this fact is inferred the existence of a natural law proceeding from the nature of man. This inference is unwarranted. From the fact that men always and everywhere live under an order regulating their reciprocal behaviour, it does not follow that this order proceeds from their nature. Such an order compels them to forego the satisfaction of many drives, in particular the so-called aggressive drives, which are just as natural as those directed to mutual aid. The social orders are as much in accordance as they are in conflict with nature, as the actual constitution of man. If nothing else can be pointed to as natural law beyond the determinations common to all legal orders, the same applies to it as was said in the text of the Aristotelian φύσει δίκαιον: it cannot perform the essential function of a true natural law, distinct from positive law and possibly standing in opposition to the latter. And still less so, if it has to be admitted of this so-called natural law that it is changeable, as happens in the modern theory of a changeable natural law.

[12] In Book I of the *Politics*, Aristotle presents slavery as a relation of lordship, and stresses that such relations exist by nature. "For that some should rule and others be ruled is a thing not only necessary, but expedient; from the hour of their birth, some are marked out for subjection, others for rule. And there are many kinds both of rulers and subjects..." (1254 a). This is so from nature. For "in the first place there must be a union of those who cannot exist without each other; namely, of male and female, that the race may continue (and this is a union which is formed, not of deliberate purpose, but because, in common with other animals and with plants, mankind have a natural desire to leave behind them an

images of themselves), and of natural ruler and subject, that both may be preserved. For that which can foresee by the exercise of mind is by nature intended to be lord and master, and that which can with its body give effect to such foresight is a subject, and by nature a slave ..." (1252a). Aristotle distinguishes in this connection two kinds of ruling relation: a "despotical" and a "constitutional": δεσποτικὴν ἀρχὴν καὶ πολιτικήν (1254b). The two forms of rule can be observed in living creatures. "... the living creature...in the first place, consists of soul and body: and of these two, the one is by nature the ruler, and the other the subject" (1254a). "... the soul rules the body with a despotical rule, whereas the intellect rules the appetites with a constitutional ... rule" (1254b). Both kinds of rule – even the despotical – exist by nature. The rule of the master over the slave is a despotic rule. This rule is natural, for there are men who are by nature slaves. "He who is by nature not his own but another's man, is by nature a slave" (1254a). Now some affirm "that the rule of a master over slaves is contrary to nature (παρὰ φύσιν), and that the distinction between slave and freeman exists by law only, and not by nature; and being an interference with nature (βίαιον) is therefore unjust (οὐδὲ δίκαιον)" (1253b). Aristotle does not share this view. But he admits that "in a certain way" it has right on its side (1255a). For there are cases in which slavery is practised on men who are not by nature slaves. "There is a slave or slavery by law... – ἔστι γάρ τις καὶ κατὰ νόμον δοῦλος καὶ δουλεύων".

Having previously stressed emphatically that the state – *every* state – exists by nature, that every state has a legal order, that this positive law decides what is just, and that justice is a political matter (cf. p. 129 above), Aristotle was also bound to acknowledge slavery based on purely legal grounds, i.e., on positive law, to be "natural", and could not reject it as unjust. But his attitude on this question is not very clear. Of the "law" on which slavery rests, he says: "The law [νόμος] of which I speak is a sort of convention – the law by which whatever is taken in war is supposed to belong to the victors. But this right many jurists impeach, as they would an orator who brought forward an unconstitutional [παρὰ νόμον] measure" (1255a). The first thing to notice here is that the word Aristotle uses to describe the "law" accused of being unconstitutional is not the earlier used "νόμος", but the word "δίκαιον", which means not only law, but also justice. It seems that, in keeping with his previous account of positive law in the state, he assumes it to be a just law which is being objected to. Nor does Aristotle by any means agree with this objection. He interprets it as saying that it would be detestable for the vanquished to have to become the slave and subject of one who can conquer and surpass him in strength. But that is not at all Aristotle's view. For he now goes on: "in some sense virtue [ἀρετή], when furnished with means, has actually the greatest power of exercising force: and as *superior* power is only found where there is *superior excellence of some kind, power seems to imply virtue*, and the dispute to be simply one about justice" [H.K.'s italics]. The literal translation of the last sentence: "ἀλλὰ περὶ τοῦ δίκαιον νόμον εἶναι τὴν ἀμφισβήτησιν" would be: "The dispute is only about law (or the just)". But that makes no sense, since the existence of a positive law is not in contention. Gigon therefore translates: "The dispute is only about the *lawful exercise* of rule". Aristotle's view would then be: the objection under discussion is not concerned with the – just – positive law whereby the vanquished becomes the victor's slave; the validity of this law, and hence the legality and justice of the slavery which solely depends upon it, are not in question; the dispute is only about the mode and manner in which this lawful mastery over one so enslaved is exercised. For Aristotle continues: "for it is due to one party identifying justice with goodwill, while the other identifies it with the mere rule of the stronger. If these views are thus set out separately, the other views have no force or plausibility against the view that the superior in virtue ought to rule, or be master." How the first of these two sentences is related to what immediately precedes is not readily intelligible. But what it comes to is that Aristotle is upholding the claim that the superior in virtue should rule, and is thus *vindicating* the positive law whereby the victor may make the vanquished his slave. In a resumé (1255b), Aristotle says: "We see then that there is some foundation for this difference of opinion, and that all are not either slaves by nature or freemen by nature, and also that there is in some cases a marked distinction between the two classes, rendering it expedient and right for the one to be slaves and the others to be masters: the one practising obedience, the others exercising the authority and lordship which nature intended them to have." We now expect to find it asserted, that in cases where slavery is imposed on men who are not by nature slaves, it is not expedient and *right* for the one to be slaves and the others to be masters. But this we are not told. What follows, is: "The abuse of this authority is *injurious* to both" [H.K.'s italics]. This refers to the *exercise of lordship*, not to its basis – nature or law: "for the interests of part and whole, of body and soul, are the same, and the slave is a part of the master, a living but separated part of his bodily frame. Hence, where the relation of master and slave between them is natural they are friends and have a common interest, but where it rests merely on law and force the reverse is true." This means that if the slavery rests only on law, there is no relation of friendship and common interest between master and slaves: not, however – or at least not expressly – that a slavery based only on law *is contrary to nature and unjust*. Aristotle cannot explicitly claim this without lapsing into open contradiction of his theory of the natural givenness of the state and positive law. He does, however, say earlier (1255a), in criticising those who, while not contesting in general the victor's right to enslave the vanquished, restrict it to a just war, and to one against barbarians: "Yet, in using this language, they really mean the natural slave of whom we spoke at first; for it must be admitted that some are slaves everywhere, others nowhere." But in the subsequent resumé, as shown, he expresses himself more cautiously. The overall effect of Aristotle's discussion of slavery is that he wishes to vindicate as natural and just an institution which already in his own day was censured by many as unnatural and unjust.

13 Walther Eckstein, *op. cit.*, p. 74: "Of the discussions in the *Rhetoric* it must be noted in general, that here we are largely concerned with model arguments for the courtroom lawyer, and in part, even, with downright forensic trickery .... So that it is not certain here how many of the opinions advanced are in accordance with the considered views of Aristotle himself."

14 "Secundo autem apparet idem ex consideratione divinae bonitatis, per quam res in esse productae sunt, est ex supradictis (q. 44a, 4; q. 65a, 2) patet. Cum enim *optimi sit optima producere*, non convenit summae Dei bonitati quod res productas ad perfectum non perducat .... Unde ad divinam bonitatem pertinet ut, sicut produxit res in esse, ita etiam eas ad finem perducat."

15 "Unde non potest esse quod malum significet quoddam esse, aut quondam formam seu naturam. Relinquitur igitur quod nomine mali significetur quaedam absentia boni. – Et pro tanto dicitur, quod malum 'neque est existens, neque est bonum'; quia cum ens, inquantum hujus modi, sit bonum, eadem est remotio utrorumque."

16 F. C. Copleston: *Aquinas* (Pelican, 1955), p. 146, observes: "According to Aquinas every being, considered as such, is good. ... Being and good (when the word is used in this ontological sense) have the same denotation .... " Thomas arrives at this identification of what is and what ought to be, i.e., goodness, because he wishes to avoid the consequence arising from belief in God's omnipotence with regard to evil: that God in His goodness has also created evil. Since Thomas cannot absolutely deny the existence of evil – if there were none, there would be no place for a moral order – he interprets it as something negative, a privation. As such, it must not be thought of as "created". Copleston says (loc. cit.): "If, therefore, every being is 'good', there is no need to postulate an evil deity as creator of evil

(as in Manicheism); for evil is not and cannot be the direct term of creative activity. Nor, indeed, could there be an evil deity, if by this we mean a sheerly evil being. For sheer evil is an impossibility."

[17] "Dicendum quod omnes hujusmodi inclinationes quarumcumque partium naturae humanae, puta concupiscibilis et irascibilis, secundum quod regulantur ratione, pertinent ad legem naturalem, et reducuntur ad unum primum praeceptum ...."

[18] "Dicendum quod ratio humana secundum se non est regula rerum; sed principia ei naturaliter indita, sunt regulae quaedam generales et mensurae omnium eorum quae sunt per hominem agenda, quorum ratio naturalis est regula et mensura, licet non sit mensura eorum quae sunt a natura."

[19] Augustine: *De serm. Dei in monte*, II, ch. 9, n. 32: "Quis enim scripsit in cordibus hominum naturalem legem nisi Deus." Cf. Alois Schubert: *Augustinus, Lex-Aeterna-Lehre nach Inhalt und Quellen. Beiträge zur Geschichte der Philosophie des Mittelalters*, vol. XXIV, Pt. 2, 1924, p. 5, 12. The view that natural law is inscribed in the heart of man obviously goes back to St. Paul, *Epistle to the Romans*, II, 14–16: "For when the Gentiles, which have not the law, do by nature the things contained in the law, these, having not the law, are a law unto themselves: Which shew the work of the law written in their hearts, their conscience also bearing witness, and their thoughts the meanwhile accusing or else excusing one another; In the day when God shall judge the secrets of men by Jesus Christ according to my gospel." It can scarcely be doubted that in Paul's teaching it is God who has written in the hearts of all men, and therefore the Gentiles also, the command of the law. That is Augustine's interpretation of Paul's doctrine.

[20] *Summa Theologica*, I–II, 91, Art. 1: "Nihil est aliud lex, quam quoddam dictamen practicae rationis in principe qui gubernat aliquam communitatem perfectam. Manifestum est autem, supposito quod mundus divina providentia regatur, ut in I. habitum est (qu. 22, Art. 1 & 2), quod tota communitas universi gubernatur ratione divina; et ideo ipsa ratio gubernationis rerum in Deo sicut in principe universitatis existens, legis habet rationem; et quia divina ratio nihil concipit ex tempore, sed habet aeternam conceptum, ut dicitur Proverb. 8, inde est quod hujusmodi legem oportet dicere aeternam."

I–II, 91, Art. 2: "... omnia participant aliqualiter legem aeternam, inquantum scilicet ex impressione ejus habent inclinationes in proprios actus et fines. Inter caetera autem rationalis creatura excellentiori quodam modo divinae providentiae subjacet, in quantum et ipsa fit providentiae particeps, sibi ipsi et aliis providens: unde et in ipsa participatur ratio aeterna, per quam habet naturalem inclinationem ad debitum actum et finem; et talis participatio legis aeternae in rationali creatura lex naturalis dicitur – ... unde patet quod lex naturalis nihil aliud est quam participatio legis aeternae in rationali creatura."

A. P. D'Entrèves, who quotes this passage in his *Natural Law, An Introduction to Legal Philosophy*, London 1955, remarks (p. 39): "St. Thomas' theory of natural law is laid down as an interpretation of man's nature and his relation to God and to the universe. Natural law is unintelligible unless we realise its close link with the eternal divine order on which the whole creation ultimately rests."

In his *History of Philosophy*, vol. II, Westminster, Maryland 1955, Frederick Copleston, S.J. lays stress on the metaphysico-theological basis of St. Thomas' theory of natural law (pp. 408–9). Of the lex aeterna he says: "This eternal law, existing in God, is the origin and fount of the natural law, which is a participation in the eternal law" (p. 409). "It is very important to realise clearly that the foundation of the natural law in the eternal law, the metaphysical foundation of the natural law, does not mean that the natural law is capricious or arbitrary; that it could be otherwise than it is: the eternal law does not depend primarily on the divine will but on the divine reason ...". But the divine reason is at the same time the divine will. Copleston's account eventually points to this, when he goes on to say: "... we must not imagine that God is subject to the moral law, as something apart from Himself. God knows His divine essence as imitable in a multiplicity of finite ways, one of those ways being human nature, and in that human nature He discerns the law of its being and wills it: He wills it because He loves Himself, the supreme Good, and because He cannot be inconsistent with Himself. The moral law is thus ultimately founded on the divine essence itself and so cannot change: God wills it certainly, but it does not depend on any arbitrary act of the divine will... ultimately the moral law is what it is because God is what He is, since human nature, the law of whose being is expressed in the natural law, itself depends on God" (pp. 409–10). In his book *Aquinas*, Copleston says (p. 214): "For Aquinas, therefore, it is human reason which is the proximate or immediate promulgator of the natural moral law." But he continues: "This law is not without a relation to something above itself; for it is, as we have seen, the reflection of or a participation in the eternal law." The eternal law comes from God. Hence the definition of natural law: it is nothing else but the participation of the rational creature in the eternal law. Without the divine eternal law, there can be no natural law.

Harry V. Jaffa, in *Thomism and Aristotelianism*, Univ. of Chicago Press, 1952, asserts that, among others of his own adopted principles, St. Thomas also ascribes to Aristotle "Belief in a divinely implanted natural habit of the moral principles." As Jaffa says, this is a principle "of revealed theology". He therefore agrees that according to St. Thomas the moral principles, and thus natural law, are "divinely implanted" in man, i.e., put there by God, a doctrine not to be found in Aristotle.

[21] It must be stated, however, that, viewed from a historical standpoint, the theory of natural law had a predominantly conservative character and was aimed essentially at the vindication of positive law. This also applies in particular to the scholastic natural law theory, as Professor August Knoll has shown in his book *Katholische Kirche und Scholastisches Naturrecht* (Vienna 1962). The theory, he says, having been evolved "as the handmaid of theology", proceeded to defend first slavery, then serfdom, then colonial forced labour in conjunction with the traffic in human beings, and finally the feudal system, so long as all this formed part of the positive law, as "an order willed by God and nature" (*op. cit.* p. 31). He points out that St. Thomas, with the principle "To each his own", which is presented as natural law, offers a justification of slavery, in that he instances the slave attached to his master as a case of someone's "own". *Summa theologica*, I, qu. 21, ad obj. 3: "Dicitur esse alienis quod ad ipsum ordinatur. Sicut servus est domini, et non e converso: nam liberum est, quod sui causa est" (*op. cit.*, pp. 24, 97).

[22] "Lex aeterna est ratio divinae gubernationis... de voluntate Dei dupliciter possumus loqui. – Uno modo, quantum ad ipsam voluntatem. Et, sic, cum voluntas Dei sit ipsa essentia ejus, non subditur gubernationi divinae, neque legi aeternae, sed idem est quod lex aeterna. – Alio modo possumus loqui de voluntate divina quantum ad ipsa quae Deus vult circa creaturas: quae quidem subjecta sunt legi aeternae, inquantum horum ratio est in divina sapientia. Et, ratione horum voluntas Dei dicitur rationabilis. Alioquin, ratione sui ipsius, magis est dicenda ipsa ratio

[23] "Quia voluntas est appetitus rationalis, ideo rectitudo rationis, quae veritas dicitur, voluntati impressa, propter propinquitatem ad rationem nomen retinet veritatis. Et inde est quod quandoque justitia veritas vocatur."

[24] A. F. Utz, O. P., in his commentary on Questions 75–79 of the *Summa theologica*, I–II (*Die deutsche Thomasausgabe*, vol. 18, 1953, p. 444), lays stress on "the law-creating power of practical reason in man". He says "St. Thomas' theory of natural law sees in the natural utterance of practical reason the proximate law-giver of human rights, which then in turn

points higher, namely to the eternal law-giver above this world." If human practical reason is a law-giver subordinated to a higher law-giver, i.e., to God as the legislator of the universe, the legislation through human practical reason can only be a legislation delegated by God, i.e., ultimately a legislation merely through the divine reason: and thus human reason can be "practical", i.e., legislative, only insofar as it participates in divine reason, as it is the divine reason in man. Utz says (p. 482): "Natural inclination is at the same time mental inclination, a natural demand of our reason, and thus naturally given beforehand in us as a law inscribed upon us by the creator." He also says (p. 403) that according to Thomist theology natural law is not created by God, but emphasises that it is founded in the essence of God Himself. "At bottom the rationality of natural law lies rooted in the divine essence and the divine self-knowledge. Hence it is never a rationality outside God."

In relation to Grotius' claim (cf. above, p. 142), that natural law might exist even without the existence of God, Utz says (p. 403): "this is by no means what St. Thomas teaches"; and on p. 443: "there is indeed to this extent some truth in it, that the natural law norms are founded, not in the will of God, but in the nature of man"; but he adds: "natural law would in fact lose its legal force, if we did not go back to God, or more exactly to God's reason as the previously given authority." A natural law that has no "legal force", i.e., is not binding, is not a law of nature. And if its legal force stems from God's reason, as the "previously given authority", the authority which posits natural law is God's reason and not human reason. The claim that, according to St. Thomas, the norms of natural law are not grounded in the will of God, is scarcely compatible with the passage cited above from *Summa theologica*, I–II, 97, 3: "lex naturalis et divina procedit a voluntate divina." Previous to this we read: "Omnis lex proficiscitur a ratione et voluntate legislatoris; lex quidem divina et naturalis a rationabili Dei voluntate; lex autem humana a voluntate hominis ratione regulata." Thomas (*Summa theologica*, I–II, 91, 4) distinguishes lex naturalis, lex humana and lex divina. The lex humana stems from the will of man, the lex divina directly, and the lex naturalis indirectly, from the will of God. This in no way contradicts the view that natural law is based on God's reason. For God's reason implies God's will.

[25] Johann Sauter: *Die philosophischen Grundlagen des Naturrechts*, Vienna 1932, p. 45.

[26] Anselm of Canterbury: *Cur Deus Homo*, (transl. by E. R. Fairweather, in *A Scholastic Miscellany*, Library of Christian Classics, vol. X., 1956), Bk. I, Ch. 12.

[27] Bk. II, Ch. 17. I owe this reference to Anselm of Canterbury to Dr. René Marcic.

[28] A similar view is to be found in what Johannes Messner has to say of the foundation of natural law in his great work *Das Naturrecht* (3rd edn., Innsbruck 1958). On p. 265 he offers the following definition: "Natural law is the order of individual and social jurisdictions grounded in human nature with its particular accountabilities." Jurisdictions are authorisations to act. They are "warranted by the moral law of reason peculiar to it (nature)." Authorisations to act can only come about through norms. These norms constitute natural law, of which Messner says (p. 266) that it consists of "the principles of law peculiar to human reason", or of "norms". Since an "order" is an aggregate of norms, and natural law is an order, natural law consists of these legal norms "peculiar" to the nature of man. Thus, by way of a – highly unnecessary – detour, and in terms of the utmost artificiality, Messner also arrives at the conclusion that natural law is grounded in human nature.

But of the nature of man he says, on pp. 24–25, that it is conditioned by its *spiritual soul*, and that "God ... by assuming man's nature (in Christ), sets His seal upon the divine likeness inscribed in the soul of man, and thereupon attests that the value of the person is ... exalted above all earthly value." This means that man, in virtue of his nature, has divine value. And that means that human nature – because man is the image of God – is itself divine. And hence – whether this be now expressly stated or not – the natural law grounded in the nature of man must ultimately be grounded in God.

Of the moral law, the "moral law of nature" or "moral law of reason", which warrants the "authorisations laid down" in human nature, Messner says (p. 66) that it would be wrong to suppose that "God, as unbounded legislator, has prescribed the moral law by an arbitrary decision to His creation, man." It would be correct, rather, to say that while God, qua causa prima, "imposes" His will upon nature, He "makes His will effective by means of the forces and tendencies He has lodged in nature; that is, with the aid of causae secundae. There is no ground for assuming that the creator has dealt with man in any other way than with the rest of nature." Whence it follows irrefutably that the will of God is the causa prima of the natural law peculiar to the nature of man.

In his most recent work, *Grundlagen einer Rechtstheologie* (Munich 1962), the Catholic theologian Gottlieb Söhngen defines natural law (on pp. 24–25) as: "the law inscribed in human nature by God"; and explains on p. 39 that "even in natural law, the distinction between 'natural and supernatural' does not just disappear, either historically or factually." But that surely means that the nature of natural law is divine nature.

CHAPTER VII

CAUSALITY AND ACCOUNTING*

It is customary to distinguish the natural and social sciences according to their specific subject-matters: nature and society. But are nature and society actually two essentially different things?[1]

Nature, according to one of the many definitions of it, is a determinate order of things, or a system of elements, related to one another as cause and effect, i.e., according to a principle we refer to as causality. The natural laws by which science describes this subject-matter, e.g., that metals expand when heated, are applications of this principle. The relation between heat and expansion is that of cause and effect.

If there is to be a social science distinct from natural science, it must describe its subject-matter according to a principle distinct from that of causality. Society is an order of human behaviour. But there is no sufficient reason why human behaviour should not be conceived as an element of nature, i.e., as determined by the principle of causality, and explained like the facts of nature as cause and effect. That such explanation is possible – at least to some degree – and actually takes place, is not to be doubted. Insofar as a science of human behaviour describes and explains in this fashion, and, because it deals with the mutual behaviour of men, is called social science, such a social science cannot be regarded as essentially different from the natural sciences.

If, nonetheless, we analyse our statements about human behaviour, it appears that we connect acts of human behaviour with one another, and with other facts, not only according to the principle of causality, but also according to another principle distinct from that of causality, a principle for which there is as yet no generally accepted name in science. Only if it can be shown that such a principle is present in our thought, and is employed by sciences which deal in some sense with human behaviour, are we entitled to distinguish society as an order different from nature, and the sciences which use this other ordering principle in describing their subject-matter, as essentially different from the natural sciences.

Law is a characteristic and significant social phenomenon, and the science of law probably the oldest and certainly the most highly developed of the social sciences. It can be shown by way of an analysis of legal thinking, that in statements of law, i.e., statements in which legal science describes its subject-matter, law, a principle is indeed employed, which although analogous to that of causality, is nevertheless markedly different from it. The analogy consists in this, that the principle in question has a function in statements of law entirely similar to that of the principle of causality in laws of nature. A statement of law is some such statement as this: If a man commits a crime, a punishment is to be inflicted upon him; or: If a man does not pay his debt, a distraint is to be executed upon his property. To put it more generally, If a wrong is done, a consequence of wrong-doing is to follow. A statement of law, i.e., a law in the legal sense, also connects two elements together, just as a law of nature does. But the connection expressed in the statement of law has a meaning wholly different from the causal connection stated in the law of nature. Quite obviously, the crime is not connected with the punishment, the civil wrong with the distraint, as a cause is with its effect. In the statement of law it is not said, as it is in the natural law, that if *A* is, *B* is, but that if *A* is, *B* is (or ought) to be, even though *B* perhaps is not, in fact. That the meaning of the conjunction of elements in the statement of law is different from the meaning of such a conjunction in the law of nature, is due to the fact that the connection of cause and effect described in the law of nature is independent of the act of a human or suprahuman will, whereas the connection between wrong and its consequence, as described in the statement of law, is established by a human act of will, the act of positing a norm or creating law. In the context of a religious and metaphysical world-outlook this difference falls into abeyance. For according to such a view, the connection of cause and effect is established by an analogous act: the nature-begetting act of will of a divine creator. In that case, then, even the laws of nature, as an expression of the divine will, possess the character of norms, which prescribe a certain conduct to nature, and which nature obeys. A metaphysical theory of law believes it possible, therefore, to discover a system of 'natural law' in nature. But in the context of a scientific world-outlook, which has room only for a positivist theory of law, having positive law as its sole subject-matter, the distinction between a law of nature and a law in the legal sense must be most emphatically insisted on.

The act of will whose meaning is a norm can be performed in various ways: by a gesture, by spoken or written words, by a series of acts which constitute a complex process of legislation or a so-called custom. When we say that by such an act or acts a norm is "created" or "posited", this is merely a figurative expression for the fact that the meaning of the act or acts is a norm. A norm posited by a human act or acts is a positive, i.e., simply a posited, norm. Its specific existence we refer to as its validity. In describing the meaning of a norm-positing act we say that by the act in question some piece of human behaviour is prescribed, i.e., ordered, or authorised, or permitted. If we use the phrase "is to" in a sense which covers both meanings, we can express the validity of a norm by saying: Something is or is not to be, men are to behave in a certain manner, or are to refrain from behaving in a certain way.

We may assume that law is essentially a coercive order, i.e., a social order which seeks to bring about a particular kind of human behaviour by ordaining, in the case of contrary behaviour or wrong-doing, an act of coercion as a reaction against it, i.e., as a consequence of wrong-doing, a sanction. The description of the relation between wrong-doing and its consequences established by a legal norm is given in a statement of law. This description is a function of legal science, whereas the positing of the legal norm is a function of the legal authority. Legal science is essentially confined to describing, in the statements of law it formulates, the law, i.e., the legal norms posited by the law-creating acts of the legal authority. In traditional legal science, however, the words "legal *norm*" and "*statement* of law" are employed as synonymous terms, whereby it comes about that *law* and *knowledge of the law* are not kept clearly separated, and functions of legal knowledge are ascribed to law, and *vice versa*.

When the fact of wrong-doing, as condition, is conjoined in the statement of law (or legal ordinance) with the sanction, as consequence of wrong-doing, by means of the words "is to", when the legal ordinance is so formulated that if a wrong is done a consequence of wrong-doing is to ensue, the words "is to" express the specific sense, distinct from causality, in which condition and consequence are conjoined in the ordinance of law. This conjunction of wrong-doing and consequence, expressed in the legal ordinance by the words "is to", I have proposed to call *accounting*. This is by no means to introduce a new word into a discipline which has already long been operating with the concept of accountability. A person is accountable if he can be punished for his behaviour, i.e., can be called to answer for it, whereas a person is unaccountable who cannot be punished, i.e., called to answer for, similar behaviour – because, say, he is a minor or of unsound mind. We say, indeed, that his act or omission is accounted to the one, whereas a similar act or omission is not accounted to the other. But the act or omission in question is legally speaking accounted or not accounted by the fact that in the one case the behaviour is conjoined with a consequence of wrong-doing and thus qualified as a wrong, whereas in the other case this does not happen, and an unaccountable person can therefore do no wrong. This means, however, that accounting consists in nothing else whatever save this conjunction of a particular piece of behaviour with a sanction, i.e., the conjunction of wrongdoing and consequence. The accounting expressed in the concept of accountability is thus not – as the traditional theory assumes – the conjunction of a particular piece of behaviour with the man who so behaves; no conjunction by a legal norm is needed for this, since the behaviour is utterly inseparable from the man so behaving; even the behaviour of an unaccountable person is *his* behaviour, his act or omission, although it is no wrong, i.e., is not behaviour conjoined with a consequence of wrong-doing. The accounting expressed in the concept of accountability is the conjunction of a particular piece of behaviour, namely wrong-doing, with a consequence of this. It can therefore be said that the consequence of wrong-doing is accounted to the wrong, but it is not brought about by the wrong as its cause. It is self-evident, indeed, that legal science in no way aims at a causal explanation of such legal phenomena as wrong-doing and its consequence. In the statements of law with which legal science describes these phenomena it employs, not the principle of causality, but a principle which – as this analysis shows – may be called that of accounting.

An investigation of primitive societies and the peculiar nature of the primitive mind shows that the same principle underlies the primitive's interpretation of nature. It is more than probable that the primitive does not yet explain the phenomena of nature by the principle of causality. This principle, as the basic principle of natural science, is like the latter in being the achievement of a relatively advanced state of civilisation. Early man interprets the facts he perceives with his senses according to the same principles which govern his relations with his fellows, namely according to social norms.

If men live together in a group, the idea enters their minds that a certain kind of behaviour is right or good, another kind wrong or bad, in other words the idea that the members of the group should behave under certain conditions in a certain way. This is to say that men living together in a group judge their mutual behaviour according to certain norms, which in fact arise by way of custom, but are interpreted as the commands of a supra-human authority. The oldest norms of mankind are probably those which aim at a restriction of the sexual and aggressive drives. Incest and murder are doubtless the most ancient crimes; outlawry (i.e., exclusion from the group) and blood-feud the most ancient socially organised sanctions. They are based on a rule which dominates the entire social life of the primitive, the rule of retribution. It embraces both punishment and reward. It can be formulated somewhat as follows: If you behave rightly, you are to be rewarded, i.e., some good is to fall to your lot; if you behave badly, you are to be punished, i.e., some evil is to come your way. In this fundamental rule, condition and consequence are connected, not according to the principle of causality, but according to the accounting-principle. So far as there is any need at all in the primitive mind for an explanation of the phenomena, they are explained by the principle of retribution. If an occurrence is felt to be evil, it is interpreted as punishment for bad behaviour or wrong-doing; if it is felt as a benefit, it is seen as a reward for good behaviour. In other words, misfortunes, i.e., damaging occurrences such as bad harvests, unsuccessful hunting, defeat in battle, sickness and above all death are accounted, as a punishment, to the norm-contravening behaviour of members of the group; beneficial happenings such as good harvests, success in the chase, victory in battle, health and long life are accounted, as a reward, to the norm-observing behaviour of the group-members. If something happens which calls for explanation in the primitive's mind – and that is only something which directly touches his interests – he does not ask, what is the cause of it, but, who is responsible for it? It is not a causal, but a normative interpretation of nature; and since the norm of retribution which governs this interpretation is a specifically social principle, regulating the mutual behaviour of men, one may term this way of construing nature a socio-normative interpretation.

Primitive animism, so-called, is the view that not only men have souls, but that all things, including what we see as inanimate objects, are animate, that invisible but powerful spirits exist in things; which is to say that all things are men, or man-like beings, or persons. This view rests on the belief that things behave towards men exactly as men do among themselves, i.e., according to the principle of retribution, the principle of punishment and reward. In primitive belief it is from these souls or spirits that man's misfortunes come as a punishment, his good luck as a reward. If a connection exists in the belief of primitives, on the one hand between the bad behaviour of men and their ill-fortune as punishment, and on the other between good behaviour and good fortune as its reward, it is because they believe that nature behaves towards men in accordance with the principle of retribution, that in natural phenomena personal forces are active according to this law. The essence of animism is a personalistic, i.e., socio-normative interpretation of nature, an interpretation which operates, not according to the causal law, but by the accounting-principle.

In the primitive mind there can therefore be absolutely no such thing as nature in the sense understood by modern science, an order of elements connected together by the impersonal principle of causality. That which constitutes nature from the standpoint of modern science is, for the primitive, a part of his society, as a normative order whose elements are connected together according to the accounting-principle. The dualism of nature as a causal order, and society as a normative order, the dualism of two different methods of connecting the given elements together, is entirely alien to the primitive mind. The existence of such a dualism in the thought of civilised man is the outcome of a spiritual development, during which a distinction comes to be made between human and other beings, especially between men and things or persons and objects – a distinction unknown to the primitive – and the causal explanation of the relations between things becomes detached from the normative interpretation of the relations between men. Modern natural science is the result of an emancipation from the social interpretation of nature, i.e., from animism. In a somewhat paradoxically pointed formula it might be said that at the outset of this development, during man's animistic period, only society (as a normative order) existed; and that nature as a causal order was first created by science, after the latter had freed itself from animism. The instrument of this emancipation is the principle of causality.

It is more than probable that the law of causality is an outcome of the norm of retribution. It is the result of a transformation of the accounting-principle, whereby under the norm of retribution wrong behaviour is connected with punishment and right behaviour with reward. This process of transformation begins in the nature-philosophy of the Ancient Greeks. It is extremely characteristic that αἰτία, the Greek word for cause, originally means the same as guilt: the cause is guilty of the effect, or bears responsibility for it; the effect is accounted to the cause as punishment is to wrong-doing. One of the first formulations of the causal law is the celebrated fragment of Heraclitus, in which the course of the sun is depicted as governed by natural necessity. It runs: "The sun will not overstep his measures; otherwise the Erinyes, ministers of Justice, will find him out", i.e., put him on the prescribed path. Here the law of nature still appears as a legal ordinance: the sun does not leave the path prescribed for him, for if he did, the organs of justice, the Erinyes, would take steps against him and enforce the law of nature. Natural necessity is still presented as a legal "*thou shalt*". The decisive step in the transition from a normative to a causal interpretation of nature, from the accounting-principle to the principle of causality, consists in man's becoming conscious that the relations between things, unlike those between men as persons, are independent of a human or suprahuman will; or, what comes to the same thing, that the relations between things are not governed by norms – that the behaviour of things is not prescribed or permitted by any sort of authority. The total purification of the causal principle from all elements of animistic, i.e., personalistic thought, the apprehension of causality as a principle distinct from the accounting-principle, could only take place in stages. Thus the idea, for example, that causality represents an absolute necessity immanent in the relation of cause and effect – an idea still dominant at the beginning of the 20th century – is assuredly a consequence of the view that it is the will of an absolute, almighty and thus transcendent authority, existing beyond the realm of human experience, which establishes the connection between cause and effect. Once this view is abandoned, there is nothing to prevent the elimination of the element of necessity from the concept of causality, and its replacement by mere probability; as has actually happened, of course, in modern physics. But if the element of necessity is retained nonetheless, it must undergo a change of meaning, must be transformed from the absolute necessity of the divine will, which finds expression in the relation of cause and effect, into a necessity of human thinking, i.e., the universal validity of a postulate of human knowledge.

The verbal form in which the causal principle, like the accounting principle, is presented, is a hypothetical judgement in which a specific condition is conjoined with a specific consequence. But as we have seen, the meaning of the connection is different in the two cases. The principle of causality says that if *A* is, then *B* is (or will be). The accounting-principle says that if *A* is, *B* is (or ought) to be. For an example of the application of the causal principle in a concrete law of nature, I may refer to the law already mentioned, describing the effect of heat upon metals. The following are instances of employment of the accounting-principle in the field of the normative social sciences: If anyone has done you some good, you are to show him gratitude; if anyone has given his life for his country, his memory is to be honoured; if anyone has transgressed, he is to do penance. These are ethical propositions presenting positive moral norms, laid down, that is, by the commands of a religious leader or by custom. The following are examples of statements of law, or legal ordinances, presenting positive legal norms laid down by a legislator or by custom: If anyone has committed a crime, he is to be punished; if anyone does not pay his debts, a distraint is to be executed on his property.

As already mentioned, the distinction between causality and accounting consists in the fact that the relation between the condition as cause and the consequence as effect, which is stated in the law of nature, is not established – like the relation of condition and consequence presented in a moral or legal law – through the intervention of a human act of will, but is independent of any such intervention. Since the specific meaning of the act establishing the relation of condition and consequence in a moral or legal law is a norm, we may speak of a normative relation, in contrast to a causal one. "Accounting" denotes a normative relation. Only this relation is expressed in the words "is (or ought) to be".

Another difference between causality and accounting consists in this, that every concrete cause must be regarded as the effect of another cause, and every concrete effect as the cause of another effect, so that it is of the essence of causality that the chain of cause and effect is in both directions infinite. In the case of accounting, the situation is entirely different. The condition to which the consequence is accounted in a moral or legal law, such as dying for one's country requiring honour to one's memory, a good deed requiring gratitude, transgression requiring penance, or a crime requiring punishment – none of these conditions are necessarily at the same time consequences requiring to be accounted to other conditions. And the consequences, such as the honour to one's memory required by dying for one's country, the gratitude required by a good deed, the penance required by transgression, and the punishment by crime, do not necessarily have at the same time to be conditions to which further consequences must be accounted. Unlike the causal series, the accounting series does not have an unlimited number of members, but basically only two. When we say that a particular consequence is accounted to a particular condition, such as reward to merit, or punishment to crime, the condition, i.e., the human behaviour represented by the merit or the crime, is the end-point of the accounting. But in the causal series there is no such thing as an endpoint. The postulation of a first cause, a *prima causa*, the analogue of the end-point in accounting, is incompatible with the idea of causality; at least with the idea of causality expressed in the laws of classical physics. The notion of a first cause which, in the form of God's creative will or the free will of man, plays a decisive role in religious metaphysics, is characteristic of a mode of thought in which the principle of causality is not separated on any grounds from the accounting-principle.

It is precisely this fundamental difference between accounting and causality, the fact that the former has an end-point while the latter does not, which underlies the contrast between the necessity prevailing in nature and the freedom existing within society and essential to the normative relations of man. When we say that man as a part of nature is not free, we mean that his behaviour, viewed as a natural fact, must be regarded as caused according to the law of nature by other facts, i.e., as the effect of these facts, and therefore as determined by them. But when a human act is construed under a moral or legal law as a merit, transgression or crime, the consequence decreed by the moral or legal law, namely reward for merit, penance for transgression or punishment for crime, is accounted without the merit, transgression or crime being accounted to anything else. The decisive feature is that the mental process of accounting comes to an end, and does so, indeed, in that human act which figures in a moral or legal law as the condition to which this law adjoins as a consequence the reward, penance or punishment; whereas causal thinking, on the other hand, cannot terminate in any fact regarded as a cause, but must enquire into the cause of this cause.

That is the true meaning of the idea that, as subject of a moral or legal order, as member of a society, or as moral or legal personality, man is free. Freedom is ordinarily understood to be the opposite of causal determinacy. That which is not subject to the law of causality is held to be free. That the human will is free is understood to mean that it is not causally determined. It is customary to say that because man is free or has a free will, he is morally or legally accountable. Only because he is free in this sense, can he be held responsible for his behaviour, can he be rewarded for his merit, expected to do penance for his sins, or be punished for his crime. It is customary to assume that only man's freedom, the fact that his will is not subject to the causal law, makes it possible to hold him to account. But the very opposite is the case. Man is not held to account because he is free; he is free because he is held to account. Accounting and freedom are indeed essentially connected with each other. But this "freedom" cannot exclude causality; and nor, in fact, does it do so in the least. If the claim that, as moral or legal personality, man is free, is to be possible from a scientific point of view, then this moral or legal freedom must be compatible with the determinacy of his behaviour under the causal law. Man is free because and insofar as reward, atonement or punishment are accounted as consequences to a particular piece of human behaviour as condition: not because this behaviour is causally undetermined, but although it is causally determined. Man is free because this behaviour of his is an end-point of accounting. And this it can be, even though it is causally determined.

Every positive moral or legal order in fact presupposes the causal determinability of man's will, i.e., it presupposes that he can be caused to behave according to a norm by the idea he has of the norms of morality or law. If the causal determinability of the human will were not presupposed, a positive moral or legal order would make no sense, since it could have no possible effect.

If it is assumed that freedom means absence of determination by the causal law, it is impossible to uphold the freedom of the will as a matter of scientific knowledge. One has to appeal to the metaphysico-religious dogma that man was created in the image of God, and that his will is therefore no less free than the will of God, who has exempted man's will from the causal law. Such an assumption is not only unacceptable from a scientific standpoint; it is also superfluous. For freedom and causality also become compatible from the standpoint of rational science as soon as it is realised that freedom refers to an end-point of accounting, and that accounting is a principle different, indeed, from causality, but analogous to and perfectly compatible with it. Accounting fulfils in the field of the normative social sciences the function performed by causality in the field of the natural sciences: the conjoining of the elements of the object of knowledge. Except only that the meaning of conjunction in the two cases is different. This may be reckoned a satisfactory solution of an old problem. In truth it is the dissolution of a pseudo-problem: the pseudo-problem of an antinomy between causal *determinacy* in nature and *freedom* in society. Since science is unable to resolve this antinomy, the recourse from science to religion seems unavoidable, and hence there appears to be justification for the *dualism* of science and religion, as two equally warranted kinds of *knowledge*; two kinds of knowledge which *complement* one another in regard to the problem of causality and freedom. But that which leads to this dualism of two fundamentally *opposed* and mutually incompatible world-views – the rational-empirical and the metaphysico-religious – proves to be the parallelism of two different methods of knowledge, which are both of them rational and empirical, which both – albeit in different senses – conjoin the elements of their object of knowledge together, and are thus perfectly compatible with one another. This is the parallelism between causality and accounting.

NOTES

* *Archiv für Rechts- und Sozialphilosophie* **46** (1960) 13. (For other versions of this essay, see *What is Justice?*, pp. 324–49 and *Pure Theory of Law*, pp. 75–95 – Transl.).

[1] Cf. Hans Kelsen, *Kausalität und Vergeltung*, The Hague 1939, and *Society and Nature*, Chicago 1953. The essay reproduces a lecture given by the author in the Great Hall of Mainz University, 5th July 1960.

CHAPTER VIII

THE EMERGENCE OF THE CAUSAL LAW FROM THE PRINCIPLE OF RETRIBUTION*

PREFACE

If we believe the findings of modern physics, and its interpretation by leading exponents of this most exact of all the sciences, we stand in the midst of a most significant change in our picture of the world. The foundation of that picture, the causal law by which all events are determined with absolute necessity, is considered to be shattered, and if it is not to be eliminated altogether from scientific thought, at least requires to be essentially modified in its formulation. In his much-cited article 'What is a Law of Nature?' [1], Erwin Schrödinger, one of the protagonists in this campaign against the causal law, shows that it cannot be reconciled with the findings of quantum mechanics. He then asks: "Now what is the source of the widespread belief in the absolute causal determinacy of the molecular event, and the conviction that the opposite is inconceivable?" And he answers: "It comes simply from the habit inherited over thousands of years, of thinking causally." But then we must go on to ask, what is the source of this habit of thought, where do we get this assumption, already become self-evident to us, that every event, by an inviolable law, must be the necessary effect of a cause? It is not enough either to point out that so far, at least, this assumption has by and large proved reliable, nor to offer the usual psychological explanation, that the causal interpretation of natural happenings has arisen by way of an analogy with the idea of the efficacy of a man's own will. For experience, the actual observation of reality, could never lead to the assumption of rules of occurrence valid without exception; and the idea of the causative function of one's own self obviously presupposes already the concept of causality. The question of the latter's origin can be answered satisfactorily only if it is possible to show how belief in the causal law has arisen in the history of thought, how it has developed and especially from what ideas it has done so.

This presupposes, however, that causality is not, as has been supposed, a form of thought necessarily given to human consciousness, an innate concept of the understanding, but rather that there have been periods in the history of the human mind in which causal thinking had not yet come about, i.e., in which causality was not yet realised to be an absolutely valid law of all events; it presupposes that the causal law – as Cassirer pertinently remarks – "is no self-evident possession of the mind, but one of its latest methodological achievements".[2] And this presupposition proves to be correct. For in the thought of primitive peoples still extant today, the concept of causality is wholly unfamiliar. They interpret nature on a scheme other than the causal, namely in terms of social categories. For the primitive, there is as yet no "nature", in the sense of a causally determined nexus of elements distinct from society. What the civilised man apprehends as nature is, for the primitive, with his animistic, or more correctly his personalistic apperception, a mere part of his society, and therefore governed by the same laws. The so-called natural man – who in truth is in every respect a social man – believes the order of his society, which is a legal order, to hold good also for nature, and thus interprets the latter according to the same principles which determine his relation to the fellow-members of his group. But the basic norm of the primitive order of society is the principle of retribution, which completely dominates the altogether socially oriented consciousness of early man. The interpretation of nature according to the principle of retribution finds expression in his actual behaviour towards animals, plants and inanimate objects, but especially in his religion and his myths.[3]

If we can assume that the condition of contemporary primitives[4] corresponds to an earlier, long since superseded condition of civilised man, and that the latter in his development has passed through a "primitive" stage, whose remains are still preserved in certain customs, legends, religious ideas, etc., we may then be able to conjecture that, along with the rest of civilisation, scientific and especially causal thinking has arisen from primitive beginnings, which we can reconstruct from the ethnographic material available to us. We are fortunately in a position to establish when and where the causal concept of modern science first took shape in the consciousness of mankind. It was in the nature-philosophy of the ancient Greeks. But this concept emerged from mythico-religious ideas which are in extensive agreement with the mentality of primitives as we know it, and in which the idea of retribution plays the decisive part. If we are able to demonstrate that, and how, the idea of a causal law, and hence the modern view of nature, has developed from this mythico-religious idea of retribution, then the quarrel that has lately been raging about the causal concept will appear in a new light; and in view of the social character of the primitive interpretation of nature, very significant connections in the history of thought will then become evident between social and natural science.

1. That the Greek philosophy of nature is an outgrowth from the mythico-religious thinking of an earlier period is shown by the way that its speculation is closely bound up with normative elements. This first and grandiose attempt, as we are bound to call it, to take a *scientific* grip upon reality, is still imbued with the idea of values stemming from the social sphere. To the extent that this ethico-social sphere, dominated by religious and conservative ideas, must be accepted as a fixed datum, the enquiring mind, the pure striving for knowledge – which in higher and relatively stabilised social conditions flourishes more vigorously alongside the emotional components of consciousness – turns towards the reality perceptible to the senses; and all the more so in that the Greek popular religion presented few obstacles in this direction. Nature becomes the object of a rational thinking which emancipates itself from the emotional, not because society has already or not yet become emancipated, but because its problem has already been solved from the non-scientific or mythico-religious side, or is at least regarded as solved for the time being, and resists other treatment. So unproblematic are the social categories, so confidently are they still viewed as a heritage by the more youthful philosophy of nature, that the latter actually takes them as its starting-point, as a firm base of operations for its first attempt at a scientific apprehension of reality. Just as in the mythical thought of the primitive, so also in the philosophy of the Ionians and Eleatics, nature is construed by analogy with society, but this analogy is steadily broken down as observation progresses. For this first *science* of nature, as already for the primitive view of nature, the authoritative community, the state, provides the primary schema for the order which is attemptedly read into the cosmos; because it is precisely the state which is customarily accepted as order *per se*, and in virtue of much older theological speculation is commonly regarded as an absolute value. But the notion of a law

for the world, i.e., nature, which is initially no more than a projection of state law into the cosmos, manifestly detaches itself from its archetype to take on a wholly independent meaning. It is not truly the case, as Joel supposes, that science begins with a "politicising of the world-picture".[5] For this "politicising" – or better socialising – of nature has already been achieved by myth. The new science of nature only begins at the point where myth leaves off; but it begins with the tendency, visible from the very outset, towards separating φύσις from νόμος, nature from society, and towards creating an opposition between them, and hence between science and politics, or at least towards establishing a dualism of both, which was still wholly alien to the primitive mind.[6]

If Thales of Miletus, with whom Greek philosophy begins, and with him and after him Anaximander and Anaximenes, are looking for an ultimate ground or basic principle from which the world can be unitarily explained, they also think of it as something which rules the world as a monarch does. And if Thales – still in just the same way as the Homeric myth, which declares the god Okeanos to be the origin of everything[7] – believes that he has found this something in water, while Anaximander finds it in the Unlimited (ἄπειρον) and Anaximenes in air, they have all three thereby set up the universe as a monarchy. The law of ἀρχή institutes a μοναρχία here; and as Heraclitus says: "To obey the will of one man is also law (νομός)"[8]. It is certainly no accident that this philosophy of nature flowers at a period when the influence of oriental despotisms was growing increasingly powerful in Greece.[9] The basic principle employed by the Milesian school in the construction of their world-picture is expressly described by Anaximander as ἀρχή; and the term here means not only "beginning", but also, at the same time, "rule". Of this principle, the ἄπειρον, he says that it seems "to surround all things and steer (κυβερνᾶν) all".[10] And a fragment of Anaximenes says "As our soul, being air, holds us together and *controls* (συγκρατεῖ) us, so does wind [or breath] and air enclose the whole world".[11] When Anaximenes takes the soul to be an air-like thing,[12] it should be noted that he holds that "air is a god"[13], i.e., endowed, no doubt, with reason and will. In this sense air "controls" the world as a basic principle. Joel believes that in air as world-principle Anaximenes "actually saw the world-soul"; in the old nature-philosophers, the question of the world's origin does not mean looking for "a principle of substantiality, but a principle of mobility".[14] Aristotle[15] says of Thales, that he seems "to have supposed that the soul was something kinetic, if he said that the (Magnesian) stone possesses soul because it moves iron". The cause, as mover, is still conceived wholly animistically, or better, in a personal way: it puts something deliberately in motion, it rules something, it attracts something – as a magnet does iron; a view that is still not wholly alien to the popular idea of causality in our own day. In regard to the tendency to conceive the "soul" as cause of motion – and thus as cause absolutely – it should not be overlooked that the concept of the soul arose from that of the dead man's soul, and that the latter's original function, its primary "effect", so to speak, is revenge.

This idea of the nature of causation is in general strongly reminiscent of the primitive view of the nature of retribution; the cause brings on the effect, just as guilt, or more exactly, the individual with his evil deed, brings punishment on himself. But that the notion of retribution plays a decisive part in the idea of ἀρχή, as basic principle, is to be seen in the most diverse aspects of this primary concept of the ancient Ionian nature-philosophy.

Its deeper meaning is revealed to us in a fragment from Diogenes of Apollonia, of whom Aristotle[16] relays to us the statement that "unless all things were derived from one, reciprocal action and passion could not have occurred". The fragment in question[17] runs as follows:

> My opinion, in sum, is that all existing things are differentiated from the same thing, and *are* the same thing. And this is manifest: for if the things that exist at present in this world-order – earth and water and air and fire and all the other things apparent in this world-order – if any of these were different from the other (different, that is, in its own proper nature), and did not retain an essential identity while undergoing many changes and differentiations, it would be in no way possible for them to mix with each other, or for one to help or harm the other, or for a growing plant to grow out of the earth or for a living creature or anything else to come into being, unless they were so composed as to be the same thing. But all these things, being differentiated from the same thing, become of different kinds at different times and return into the same thing.

In these observations of Diogenes of Apollonia, the crucial thing for an understanding of the idea of the basic substance is the notion he here takes to be self-evidently presupposed: that only *like can act upon like*; a notion which constantly recurs in a multitude of variations in the Greek philosophy of nature: as it does in Empedocles, when he teaches that *like is attracted only by like*: "Thus sweet seized on sweet, bitter rushed towards bitter, sour moved towards sour, and hot settled upon hot."[18] Or "these the fire sent forth, desiring to reach its like".[19] And especially in his famous doctrine, taken over by Plato and even by Goethe, that *like can only be known by like*: "For with earth do we see earth, with water water, with air bright air, with fire consuming fire; with love do we see love, strife with dread strife".[20] This idea, that like can only act upon like, is still found among the atomists, who went furthest in detaching the causal principle from its mythological origins. The thesis that like can act only on like, that the cause must be "similar" to the effect – in which form it survived even into 19th century physics – obviously has its source in the principle of retribution. Here it has its proper meaning, here only a genuinely tenable significance, namely, that "likeness" exists between punishment and guilt, between reward and merit, and initially, indeed, a *qualitative* likeness, in that evil is assigned to evil, good to good, the evil of guilt linked with the evil of punishment, the goodness of merit with the goodness of reward. And here already in the context of the retribution ideology we find the idea that evil engenders or "gives birth to" evil, that the likeness between guilt and punishment is of the kind whereby children are like the parents who produce them. Thus Aeschylus proclaims, in opposition to the view that it is excess of fortune which brings about misfortune:

> Alone, alone, I deem far otherwise;
> Not bliss or wealth it is, but impious deed,
> From which that after-growth of ill doth rise!
> Woe springs from wrong, *the plant is like the seed* –
> While Right, in honour's house, doth *its own likeness breed*.
> Some past impiety, some grey old crime,
> *Breeds the young curse*, that wantons in our ill,
> Early or late, when haps th'appointed time –
> And out of light brings power of darkness still,
> A master-fiend, a foe, unseen, invincible;
> A pride accursed, that broods upon the race
> And home in which dark Atè holds her sway –
> Sin's child and Woe's, that *wears its parents' face* ...[21]

The idea of "likeness" between guilt and punishment extends to the identity of both: punishment consists simply in new guilt. – But the likeness is not merely qualitative, it is also *quantitative*, in that the greater the guilt, the greater the punishment, the greater the merit, the greater the reward must be. A fragment of Heraclitus runs "The greater the fate (*death*), the greater the reward".[22] If things are to stand to each other in the relation of cause and effect, they must be "alike" in their nature, as like as guilt and punishment, merit and reward; and for that very reason, they must ultimately spring from one and the same primary substance – water or air. It is no mere image when, in Diogenes of Apollonia's statement, the fact that one thing operates on another is expressed by saying that one of them "helps" or "harms" the other. For "help" is merit and reward, "harm", guilt and punishment.

In another application, the notion of likeness concealed in the concept of ἀρχή appears as that of *balance*, which – so far as it means *justice* – is the specific function of retribution, which weighs out punishment for guilt, reward for merit, as if in the scales, and holds the balance between them. Thales had taught that water was the original substance of everything. Since the change of this material into other things than water was not easily explicable, Anaximander starts from the ἄπειρον, i.e., from an infinite substance engendering from itself the opposites moist and dry, cold and hot. Finite things are at war with each other, e.g., the hot fire with the cold air, the dry earth with the wet sea. The predominance of one over the other is unjust, their *equilibrium* just. Heat commits injustice in summer, cold in winter. To restore the balance – as Burnet[23] states the doctrine of Anaximander, after a careful examination of the sources – they must pass away once more into their common ground, into their ἀρχή as cause. If fire gradually dries up water, that is an injustice which must eventually lead to the destruction of the world. But fire mixed with water has lost its special nature and become the original substance. The function of the latter is thus to restore the balance as a kind of retributive justice.[24] Only in this role as a universal adjustment does it also serve as a universal explanation of the world. If we take this to be Anaximander's basic idea, we then first are able to understand the only one of his fragments that has come down almost in his own words: "And the source of coming-to-be for existing things is that into which destruction, too, happens, 'according to necessity; for they pay penalty and retribution to each other for their injustice according to the assessment of time'" [25] Here, in Capelle's view,[26] we find "for the first time in the thought of mankind, an apprehension of the concept of a legality immanent in and governing all that happens, i.e., the entire world-process; in short, the idea of a world-law". It is the first apprehension of the *causal law*. Yet though generalised, since it relates to all events whatever, this law is still essentially the law of retribution:[27] the cause is still guilt, the effect still punishment. As guilt precedes punishment, so the cause must precede the effect, the effect, as punishment, must follow guilt as the cause "according to the assessment of time" (κατὰ τήν τοῦ χρόνου τάξιν). Just as necessity (τὸ χρεών) is the coercion of the law of retribution, so the temporal ordering of earlier and later is the sequence of guilt and punishment. Through this dynamic of retribution, scientific thought first becomes aware of the category of time (τοῦ χρόνου τάξις).[28] If modern science still marks out the cause-effect relation as asymmetrical, if we still insist even nowadays that the cause must precede the effect in time, this is because the cause was originally guilt, and the effect punishment.

Heraclitus also, no less than Anaximander, sees a tension of opposites in nature; and like his predecessor, he conceives the play of forces in nature under a thoroughly social category, that of πόλεμος, or war. Diogenes Laertius tells us he teaches that "everything is produced by contrariety"[29], and that "existing things are harmonised, and made to agree together by opposite tendencies".[30] A famous and much-quoted saying is as follows: "War is the father of all and king of all ...."[31] But while Anaximander sees an injustice in the contention of things, Heraclitus teaches that: "It is necessary to know that war is common and right is strife and that all things happen by strife and necessity".[32] In this war which the elements wage on one another, he sees a law of all life, and this world-law, the "central concept of his whole philosophy" is "the idea of the Logos, which is equivalent to the eternal, super-sensory world reason guiding everything".[33] "Of the Logos which is as I describe it men always prove to be uncomprehending, both before they have heard it and when once they have heard it. For although *all things happen according to this Logos*, men are like people of no experience ...."[34] It is plainly the *causal law* that is intended by this Logos whereby all things happen. And hence the law is identified with destiny, εἱμαρμένη: "Everything happens according to destiny", so Heraclitus teaches, according to Diogenes Laertius[35], and according to Aetius:[36] "Destiny is the world-law (Logos) which shapes things in consequence of the opposing back and forth". "Everything takes place according to destiny and this is just the same as necessity". "Heraclitus declares the nature of destiny to be the world-reason (Logos) which permeates the whole universe...." The necessity of events, this essential function of causality, is for Heraclitus the inviolable will of a deity which is presented as the personification of reason. It is an expression of the absolute validity of the order in which the will of God is expressed, and inviolability can appear as an absolute only as the quality of a transcendent entity presupposed beyond all experience. This necessity, destiny, is expressed by the word εἱμαρμένη. The verb μείρομαι means to receive as a share. Etymology: from σμερίομαι, root: *smer*=to allot, lat. *mereo*= to deserve.[37] Thus the word expressing causal necessity means originally, the (deserved) allotment. A person's fate is that which is alloted to him – whether as reward or punishment. It is presumably the idea of retribution which leads to the concept of fate, to the concept of destiny as that which is allotted to a person, in virtue of merit or guilt, through the inexorable will of a rewarding and punishing deity. And in fact it is precisely in Heraclitus that εἱμαρμένη represents the inviolability of the law, and the law assuredly the law of retribution. The thoroughly normative character of the Heraclitean world-law, which is a norm that *ought* to be obeyed, and yet at times – from folly – is not, is apparent from the following fragments: "Therefore it is necessary to follow the common; but although the Logos is common the many live as though they had a private understanding"[38]. And

> those who speak with sense must rely on what is common to all, as a city must rely on its law (νόμος), and with much greater reliance. For all the laws of men are nourished by [i.e. draw their validity from] one law, the divine law; for it has as much power as it wishes and is sufficient for all and more than sufficient.[39]

If human laws can draw their validity from the divine world-law, this is because this divine world-law, the inviolable causal law, is only the projection of human 'legal' law into the cosmos. And this legal ordinance projected into the cosmos is inviolable, because it is regarded as the absolute will of a deity. It is the basic idea of all natural law that is formulated in this passage. But that this legal ordinance is the law of retribution is most unmistakeably evidenced in the famous fragment, which might be described as the counterpart to that of Anaximander: "The sun will not overstep his measures; otherwise the Erinyes, ministers of Justice [Dike] will find him out".[40] The Erinyes are the famed avenging spirits of Greek religion; and Dike is the goddess of retribution, as she appears, for example, in the fragment which runs: "The most esteemed of them knows but fancies, and holds fast to them, yet of a truth justice [Dike] shall overtake the artificers of lies and the false witnesses".[41] Dike, whom the Orphic writers describe as the "inescapable",[42] is "the punisher of those who fall short of the divine law".[43] The significance of Heraclitus' saying for the history of scientific knowledge is that the inviolability of the causal law whereby the sun keeps his path is the coercion of Dike, the binding force of the legal norm, a normative necessity.[44] And that the inviolability of the world-law does not lie in the fact that it is always observed – the case of the sun overstepping his measures is not absolutely ruled out! It lies, rather, in the fact that a breach of it is always and invariably avenged, because the world-law, as legal ordinance, is a norm prescribing sanctions, a law whose tenor is one of retribution, and as such the unshakeable will of a deity. This Logos is Dike, the goddess of inescapable vengeance.[45] The inviolability of the causal law, so hotly contested in modern science, the absolute validity ascribed to it, are ultimately derived from the inviolability ascribed by myth, and by the nature philosophy which only gradually detaches itself therefrom, to the principle of retribution, as the content of a divine and thus absolutely binding will. From this principle of retribution, the first science fashioned its law of nature.[46]

That the principle of retribution underlies the world-law of Heraclitus is also shown in his doctrine of world-fire. This doctrine is often construed to mean that the ultimate ground of the world is fire, from which all things originate, and into which they again return.[47] A fragment runs: "All things are an equal exchange for fire and fire for all things, as goods are for gold and gold for goods."[48] The world-process, as a transformation of fire into things and of things again into fire, is presented as an exchange-process, and exchange is only a special case of retribution. The effect follows upon the cause, just as gold is given for goods. The causal nexus is not just simply compared with the bond which the retribution principle institutes between its two elements, but is an application of this principle. Hence the Christian bishop Hippolytus is not too seriously distorting the Heraclitean doctrine of *ecpyrosis* when he presents it as saying

that a judgement upon the world and all things in it will take place by fire, as the following words show. "Thunderbolt steers all things", that is, it governs them. By "thunderbolt" he means here the eternal fire. He also says this fire is rational and responsible for the government of the whole world. And he calls it "want" and "satiety". "Want" is in his view the ordering of the cosmos, and the universal conflagration is "satiety", for he says that "fire will come and judge and convict everything".[49]

No less clearly than in Heraclitus does it emerge in his great adversary, Parmenides, that the law-like necessity which holds the cosmos together is the absolute binding-power of a divine legal norm, and that this norm – the law of nature, as the law of eternal being – is retribution. To attain to knowledge of this law, and to arrive at truth, he takes the fictitious journey described in his didactic poem; and this journey leads him to Δίκη πολύποινος, "avenging Justice".[50] She has the key to the gates, through which runs the way to light, which is to say, true knowledge. Dike, the goddess of law, is at the same time goddess of truth, for in this still entirely ethico-juristic world-view, truth is identical with justice, whose inexorable quality appears here as "the unshaken heart of well-rounded truth (ἀτρεμὲς ἦτορ)".[51]

The basic truth of the Parmenidean ontology, that all coming into being and perishing is only illusion, that – owing to necessity – there is only eternal, unchanging being, is expressed by the Eleatic in these words: "Wherefore Justice (Dike) looseth not her fetters to allow it [what is] to come into being or perish, but holdeth it fast".[52] This is Δίκη πολύποινος, the goddess of vengance: The same thought recurs again later in the following form:

But, motionless within the limits of mighty bonds, it [what is] is without beginning or end, since coming into being and perishing have been driven far away ... for strong Necessity ('Ανάγκη) holds it firm within the bonds of the limit that keeps it back on every side ....[53]

And further on it is said that "Fate (Μοῖρα) fettered it to be entire and immovable".[54] "Strong Necessity" and "Fate" are identical with Dike, the goddess of vengeance. Determination by natural law, the inviolable rule of being, is the 'ought' of an absolute legal norm. The inviolability of the world-law, the unshaken heart of truth, is the iron will of the deity of law, the impossibility of escaping retribution. It is basically the same idea as that expressed by the poet Aeschylus in his "Prometheus Bound", when he there refers to necessity, Ananke, as the highest "all-ordaining" power, superior even to Zeus. "Who then holds the helm of Necessity?", asks the leader of the chorus. And Prometheus answers: "The Fates triform and the unforgetting Furies".[55]

Retribution is also one basic concept, if not the only one, in the philosophy of Empedocles – influenced as it was by Orphic and Pythagorean elements. At its heart lies the idea of the transmigration of souls [56], whereby the thinker from Acragas – more prophet than trained philosopher – interprets his own fate. Here, as everywhere where it occurs, the doctrine of transmigration represents a specific ideology of retribution.

There is an oracle of Necessity (Ananke), ancient decree of the gods, eternal and sealed with broad oaths: Whenever one of those demigods, whose lot is long-lasting life, has sinfully defiled his dear limbs with bloodshed, or following strife has sworn a false oath, thrice ten thousand seasons does he wander far from the blessed, being born throughout that time in the forms of all manner of mortal things and changing one baleful path of life for another. The might of the air pursues him into the sea, the sea spews him forth on to the dry land, the earth casts him into the rays of the burning sun, and the sun into the eddies of air. One takes him from the other, but all alike abhor him. Of these I too am now one, a fugitive from the gods and a wanderer, who put my trust in raving strife. [57]

It is nature itself, the four elements – earth, air, fire and water – of which, on Empedocles' theory, it is composed, which punishes the evil-doer; it is nature itself whose function is seen here as retribution. And the wrong to which this vengeance responds is by no means merely a social evil, a harm that one man does to another. The idea that the human soul can also be embodied in other beings, in animals or plants, leads here – as it also does elsewhere, e.g., in the systems of totemism – to the assumption of a community embracing not only men, but also all other beings; a community constituted by an order which places all beings under the same law, and in particular grants to all beings the same right to life. The basic norm of this order is the prohibition against killing. In this way nature quite obviously becomes a part of society, and the law of retribution quite self-evidently a law of nature. Diogenes Laertius [58] reports of Empedocles: "He asserts ... that the soul inhabits every kind of form of animals and plants". Aristotle [59] says:

For there really is, as every one to some extent divines, a natural justice and injustice that is binding on all men, even on those who have no association or covenant with each other .... And so Empedocles, when he bids us kill no living creature, says that doing this is not just for some people while unjust for others ....

In Cicero [60] we are told:

It is ... Pythagoras and Empedocles who declare that the same principles of justice apply to all living creatures (unam omnium animantium condicionem juris), and insist that inevitable penalties threaten those who injure an animal.

A saying of Empedocles that has come down verbatim to us runs: "Will ye not cease from ill-sounding bloodshed? See ye not that in careless folly ye are consuming one another?" [61] And another:

Father lifts up his own dear son, his form changed, and, praying, slays him – witless fool; and the people are distracted as they sacrifice the imploring victim; and he [the father], deaf to its cries, slays it and makes ready in his halls an evil feast. And likewise son seizes father, and children their mother, and tearing out the life, eat the flesh of their dear ones. [62]

It seems that Empedocles held this law of the life embracing man, animal and plant, guaranteed as it was by retribution, since sanctioned by "inevitable penalties", to be only a special case of a still more general law governing the entire cosmos, which he describes in these words: "But this, the law for all, extends unendingly through the wide-ruling air and through the immense light of heaven". [63] And this world-law also is for him a law of retribution. [64]

In the philosophy of Empedocles, this world-law is exhibited in the eternal and necessary interplay of two basic forces: one principle which combines and mingles the elements, and another which separates and isolates them. He calls them Love (φιλία 'Αφροδίτη) and Strife (νεῖκος), and by no means employs these concepts merely as metaphors, but undoubtedly has in mind here the social categories of association and dissociation; though still, to be sure, in a mythico-sociological sense. For Love and Strife appear here not only as states or processes within the elements, but also as personal beings, as gods or demons who are themselves at war with one another, so that now the one and now the other emerges victorious.

A double tale will I tell: at one time it grew to be one only from many, at another it divided again to be many from one. There is a double coming into being of mortal things and a double passing away. One is brought about, and again destroyed, by the coming together of all things, the other grows up and is scattered as things [the elements] are again divided. And these things never cease from continual shifting, at one time all coming together, through Love, into one, at another each borne apart from the others through Strife. (So, in so far as they have learnt to grow into one from many) and again, when the one is sundered, are once more many, thus far they come into being and they have no lasting life; but in so far as they never cease from continual interchange of places, thus far are they ever changeless in the cycle. [65]

That "Love" and "Strife" have to do, not with a purely mechanical attraction and repulsion, but with social value and disvalue so described, is already evident from the fact that, even in his speculations directed purely to the interpretation of nature, Empedocles speaks of the "gentle immortal stream of blameless Love",[66] and of the "evil spirits of discord".[67] A fragment runs:

For all of these [elements] – the shining sun, earth, sky and sea – are one with their own parts which are scattered far from them in mortal things; and in the same way all that are fitted rather for mixture are assimilated by Aphrodite and hold one another dear. But enemies are those that are farthest from each other in origin, composition and moulded form, in every way unaccustomed to unite and very grim ....[68]

The eternal cycle of the world-process, dominated now by Love and now by Strife, begins with a period in which Love is sole mistress and which is clearly designated as a state of harmony, i.e., of happiness and peace. All things are formed into a single whole, the rounded "Sphairos", of which Empedocles says: "but rather, equal (to himself) from every side and quite without end, ... a rounded sphere rejoicing in his circular solitude".[69] Through the fact that Strife then supervenes, and hence that division and separation ensue, there takes place a sort of "abandonment of the original state of blessedness" (to use Zeller's words). This is a social evaluation, whereby the initial state of the cosmos exhibits a quite striking parallel to the original condition of society, which Empedocles depicts[70] as a sort of golden age of peace and general happiness, whose end is brought about – so we may complete the fragment – by the outbreak of strife. The thought can therefore by no means be dismissed, that in his cosmology Empedocles has merely transferred the basic outlook of his social philosophy to the universe at large.[71]

That φιλία and νεῖκος in the cosmos are merely a projection of human love and enmity is also evident from the saying already cited, to the effect that like can be known only by like. For if this means that it is only with our love (i.e., the love in us) that we can know the love (in the cosmos), and only with our strife the "dread strife" (in the world-process), it is certainly not to be understood only in a biological sense; as saying, that is, that it is by means of the elements of love and hatred contained in our blood, that we are acquainted with cosmic love and cosmic hatred.[72] For we are at least also and primarily to understand it as saying that these cosmic processes are similar to the social phenomena we experience as love and hatred, and are therefore knowable to us by means of them. Because it was customary in myth to regard these forces as gods, they also appear as such in the cosmology of Empedocles: "But as one divine element mingled further with another [i.e., Love with Strife] ..." [73] it says in one fragment; and in another: "But when Strife waxed great in the limbs, and sprang to his prerogatives as the time was fulfilled which is fixed for them in turn by a broad oath ...". [74] Aristotle remarks:

[It] would seem to be the view of Empedocles ... that the constitution of the world is of necessity such that Love and Strife alternately predominate and cause motion, while in the intermediate period of time there is a state of rest. [75]

And he is surely on the right track in viewing the struggle between Empedocles' two hostile and alternately triumphant principles as the opposition between good and evil. [76] The widespread interpretation of the world-process as a struggle of good against evil always presupposes the idea of retribution. For it is essentially the reaction against evil, the ill-doer, which evokes the idea of a "struggle" against evil. And in fact, on closer examination of the surviving fragments, we get the impression that the law of eternal and necessary alternation between Love and Strife in Empedocles is a matter of retribution. Strife is the evil element, the guilt of those who have lapsed into strife. But it is simultaneously their punishment (just as Strife in Empedocles – as Aristotle already points out – is by no means merely a separating, i.e., evil principle, but also a uniting and therefore good one). [77] In Greek mythology itself, it is not infrequently the same divinity which seduces into evil and then punishes it. "Whenever anyone" we are told in that fragment already cited, which gives expression both to the retributory character of transmigration, and to the shattering confession of Empedocles himself – "whenever anyone ... following strife" has done what is forbidden, that is, committed perjury or murder, he is guilty of strife; and "I too . . . a fugitive from the gods [am] a wanderer, who put my trust in raving strife". Hippolytus [78] interprets these lines as follows:

By 'baleful paths of life' he means the soul's ever-changing entry into different bodies .... For souls change from one body to another, being transplanted by strife, and punished, and not left in the peace of their original unity. Rather, the souls are chastised by strife with every kind of punishment, who must exchange one body for another.

And then, with reference to the words "The might of the air pursues him [the evildoer] into the sea, and the sea spews him forth." etc.: "... That is the punishment the demiurge (of strife) visits upon them, as a smith transforms the iron and plunges it from the fire into water". Strife, which leads men astray, so that trusting it they fall into strife and then into guilt, punishes the guilty. And such retribution is practised, not only on sinful men who have fallen into strife, but also on the fragmenting elements. The passage already cited, which speaks of affinities and enmities in nature, and first of those "that are fitted rather for mixture" because they are "assimilated by Aphrodite and hold one another dear" ends with the words: "But enemies are those that are farthest from each other ... in every way unaccustomed to unite and very grim by the bidding of Strife, because it has brought about their birth".[79] It is the obviously punishing and retributory bidding of Strife which makes the fragmenting things "grim" on account of their cleavage. Hippolytus' interpretation is fully confirmed at this point. As things pass out of the condition of love and goodness, which is a state of peace and happiness, into the condition of strife and evil, they fall at once into misfortune, which is to say, punishment. The eternal law of alternation between love and strife is the law of retribution. Its inviolability therefore has a specifically normative character: the oracle of Necessity which proclaims this law is an "ancient decree of the gods, eternal and sealed with broad oaths". This norm has the fixity of a covenant sealed with an oath. So also the time which Love and Strife have for fulfilment is "fixed for them in turn by a broad oath".[80] The oath is a specific guarantee of law. In Empedocles, too, Ananke is identical with Dike, the inviolability of nature's law has the absoluteness of a normative bond.

With the atomists – Leucippus and Democritus – we arrive essentially at the modern notion of causality. The well-nigh complete detachment of the causal law from the principle of retribution is achieved by the two founders of pure science by means of a thoroughgoing exclusion of all teleological aspects from their view of nature, by a strict rejection of so-called final causes. So long as the world-order is construed on the analogy of the social order, as the expression of a more or less personally conceived, rational, and thus purposively functioning will, the law of all that happens must have the character of a norm, which, on the analogy of the legal ordinance, the basic social norm, guarantees the normal order of things by means of sanctions; in short, the world-law must be a law of retribution. Any departure of events from this law, which experience, deepened by observation, recognises to be not ruled out in advance, is seen as the condition for a reaction proceeding from the divine will and again restoring equilibrium in nature; so that the law's inviolability, the absolute necessity that it shall hold, relates not so much to the norm of "correct" happening, but rather to its sanctions. Assuredly the sun must keep to his appointed path; but if, on occasion, he were not to do so, the goddess of vengeance would unhesitatingly set him right again, through her ministers of punishment. That is how Heraclitus still views the law of nature. But with the atomists, it has ceased to be a norm, i.e., the expression of a will. "Democritus", says Aristotle,[81] "ignoring the final cause, refers all the operations of nature to necessity". The atomists, indeed, assign no cause to the original movement of matter. They regard it as a primary property of the atoms[82], and start out by assuming atoms in motion as a basic hypothesis, precisely because they renounce the further assumption of a divine will engendering this motion. But all change within the world process, interpreted on the basis of this hypothesis, as the starting-point for scientific consideration, proceeds according to the law of cause and effect. Democritus seems – so Simplicius tells us[83] "... to have made use of chance in forming the world, whereas he does not regard chance as a cause in any individual detail [of natural processes], but refers them to other causes". And in Pseudo-Plutarch[84] we read:

> Democritus ... supposed that the sum of things is infinite because it certainly has not been fashioned by anyone .... He says that the causes of present events have no beginning and that absolutely everything that was, is, and shall be is completely determined previously by necessity from infinite time past.

Nothing is more characteristic of this truly scientific spirit of atomism, founded entirely on the basis of a mechanistic picture of the world, than the statement ascribed to Democritus, that he would 'rather discover one cause [i.e., establish the cause of a phenomenon] than gain the kingdom of Persia".[85]

The detachment, among the atomists, of the interpretation of nature from the principle of retribution, is a complete parallel to the analogous emancipation of social theory among the sophists. It was Protagoras, the contemporary of Leucippus, who taught that the specific technique of the governmental order, whereby it reacts to a deed held to be socially damaging by means of an act of coercion against the doer, was to be accounted for, not by the religious idea of retribution, but by the rational aim of prevention. Punishment follows, not from an obscure reason, but for a clear purpose.

No one punishes the evil-doer under the notion, or for the reason, that he has done wrong.... [The punisher] does not retaliate for a past wrong which cannot be undone; he has regard to the future, and is desirous that the man who is punished, and he who sees him punished, may be deterred from doing wrong again. He punishes for the sake of prevention....[86]

The social law, like the natural law, strikes off the fetters of the myth of retribution.

Yet even in the purified form that it takes in the atomists, the causal law cannot wholly disavow its origin. As in Leucippus' version of it, transmitted by Aetius[87], who tells us:

Leucippus says that everything happens by a necessity (ἀνάγκη) which is identical with fate (εἱμαρμένη). For he says in his book *On Mind* (περὶ νοῦ)[88]: 'Nothing occurs at random, but everything for a reason and by necessity (ἐκ λόγου τε καὶ ὑπ' ἀνάγκης)'.

The concept of cause is expressed here by λόγος. That is the λόγος of Heraclitus, whose teaching had a decisive influence on the atomists.[89] The λόγος, the world-reason, whereby "all things happen (γιγνομένων γὰρ πάντων κατὰ τὸν λογόν)"[90] is transformed in Leucippus into a mechanical cause. If the latter operates here with the absolute compulsion of ἀνάγκη, it has taken on this quality from the irrefragable nature of the divine will, which is how the λόγος appears in Heraclitus. And the provenance of the idea of strict causality is more evident still in Democritus. For by "necessity", so Aetius tells us,[91] the great Abderite understands "the resistance [of the colliding atoms] and movement and blows of matter [atoms]". In order to understand this formulation of physical causality,[92] one has to be aware that according to Leucippus and Democritus – so Alexander of Aphrodisias reports[93] – "the atoms move by mutual collisions and blows"; according to Aetius[94] "Democritus says that the primary bodies, or solids [atoms], have no weight but move according as they strike one another in the infinite [void]"; and "Democritus said there was only one kind of motion [of atoms], that due to vibration (παλμός)".[95] Simplicius[96] presents the theory of the atomists as follows:

... these atoms move in the infinite void, separate one from the other and differing in shapes, sizes, position and arrangement; overtaking each other they collide, and some are shaken away in any chance direction, while others, becoming intertwined one with another according to the congruity of their shapes, sizes, positions and arrangements, stay together and so effect the coming into being of compound bodies.

In Diogenes Laertius[97] we read – as the view of Leucippus –

that the worlds were produced by bodies [= atoms] falling into the void and becoming entangled with one another .... The worlds come into being as follows: many bodies of all sorts of shapes move 'by abscission from the infinite' into a great void; they come together there and produce a single whirl, in which, colliding with one another and revolving in all manner of ways, they begin to separate apart, like to like.

Simplicius [98] says of Democritus that

the nature of the eternal [bodies] consists of innumerable small substances .... He thinks that they are so small as to elude our senses, but they have all sorts of forms and shapes and differences in size. So he is already enabled from them, as from elements, to create by aggregation bulks that are perceptible to sight and the other senses. They struggle and move in the void because of the dissimilarities between them and the other differences already mentioned; and as they move they collide and become entangled in such a way as to cling in close contact to one another ....

If Democritus, therefore, as Aetius has it, conceives necessity to be "the resistance and movement of blows of matter", this means that he sees causality in a process that is essentially viewed as the clash and recoil of mutually colliding atoms. But this is construed entirely on the analogy of the retribution principle, that an action is linked with its specific reaction, guilt with punishment, and merit with reward. It points in the same direction, that the mutually rebounding atoms "struggle", just as in Heraclitus things are "at war" with one another and "made to agree together by opposite tendencies" [99] in the same manner as guilt and punishment. And just as the elements conjoined together by the retribution principle, though opposed in the direction of their action, are yet by nature alike, in that like is requited with like, so also under the causal law of Democritus it is only like that can act upon like among the "struggling" atoms. Simplicius [100] reports it as the teaching of Leucippus and Democritus that:

they take atoms as the material for things and make everything else come about from their differences. These, however, are three in number: shape, position and arrangement [grouping]. For it is in the nature of the like to be set in motion by the like, as things related hasten to one another ....

In the Hibeh Papyri [101] we find the following passage: "... he [Democritus] says that in a wet substance like is (drawn) to like as in the whole creation, and thus the sea was created and all else that is ... through the combination of homogeneous atoms". A fragment of Democritus that has come down to us runs:

Living creatures consort with their kind, as doves with doves, and cranes with cranes, and similarly with the rest of the animal world. So it is with inanimate things, as one can see with the sieving of seeds and with the pebbles on beaches. In the former, through the circulation of the sieve, beans are separated and ranged with beans, barley-grains with barley, and wheat with wheat; in the latter, with the motion of the wave, oval pebbles are driven to the same place as oval, and round to round, as if *the similarity in these things had a sort of power over them which had brought them together.*[102]

And Aristotle[103] says of Democritus:

He held that agent and patient are the same or similar: it is impossible for disparate things to act on each other, but if, though different, they should nevertheless have some mutual effect, this occurs not because they are different but insofar as they have some common characteristic.

If the magnet attracts iron, it is because "like is drawn to like". "Having made these hypotheses" says Alexander of Aphrodisias,[104] "he [Democritus] supposes that the lodestone and iron consist of similar atoms". As guilt attracts a like punishment, as murder brings on murder (by blood revenge or death penalty), as merit induces a comparable reward, so the magnet attracts iron, because the latter is "like" the former. And when Democritus construes "being acted upon" as the suffering of a "patient", the idea lying behind this is the "suffering" of a punishment. It is therefore entirely credible when Pliny[105] asserts that Democritus recognized only two divinities, "poenam et beneficium", punishment and reward. And when Aristotle[106] states the causal law of the atomists in these words: "They say that nothing happens by chance, but that everything which we ascribe to chance or spontaneity has some definite cause (τι αἴτιον)"; and when in Democritus himself,[107] and elsewhere also in the ancient philosophy of nature, a cause is referred to as "αἰτία", we should not forget that this word originally meant much the same as "guilt".[108] Just as even nowadays in German "etwas verschulden" (to be guilty of something) is often equivalent to "etwas verursachen" (to cause something).[109] The cause is "guilty of" (or "responsible for") the effect. That is the internal connection between the two elements of the causal law, and it has not yet wholly vanished from the scientific thinking of the modern age.

2. The principle of an absolutely valid causality, as a law immanent in nature, and admitting of no exceptions, had thus already been developed in the teaching of the atomists, and was then taken over by Epicurus and his successors; but after the triumph of Christianity it was again in danger of being lost in the theological world-outlook of the Middle Ages.

It was only the new science of nature founded by Bacon, Galileo and Kepler, which again revived it, and since then it has remained the paramount schema for the interpretation of nature, until, quite recently, in certain areas of modern physics, it has come to be questioned, if not actually denied. If – rightly or wrongly – there is talk nowadays of a crisis over the causal principle, it should not be overlooked that in essence this crisis had already begun with Hume's celebrated critique of our belief in causality. Hume's objections were directed in the main against the belief still prevailing in his own day, that between cause and effect there existed an objective connection residing in the things themselves; an inner bond, such that the cause somehow brings about, or draws after it, the effect; that the cause does something in bringing about the effect, and hence is conceived as an agency, or substance which in some way emits force. Such a belief appears to find confirmation in the experience of personal efficacy of will in man, who regards his self or "soul" (a concept analogous to that of force) as the "cause" of his acts. The decisive turn given by Hume to the problem of causality consists in transferring the linkage of cause and effect from the objective into the subjective realm. He thereby transforms the ontological problem into an epistemological one, or more properly splits up the problem of causality into an ontological and an epistemological problem, arguing that in nature there exists no causality, in the sense of a necessary linkage, but only a regular sequence of events. The idea of a universal causal law, whereby like causes must necessarily be followed by like effects, is a mere habit of thought, which, having once arisen through observation of regular sequences, becomes a firm conviction. From thence, by an extension of Hume's argument, Kant arrives at his doctrine, that a mere observation of reality is incapable of justifying the necessity of the connection of two facts as cause and effect, and that causality, as the necessity of this connection, is an innate concept of the understanding, an a priori category of our knowledge, by means of which we order the material of sense-perception empirically given to us. But then whence do we derive this idea, that the necessary connection of cause and effect is objectively grounded and thus immanent in the causal process, that the cause brings about or draws after it the effect, that between the two there is not only a "post hoc", but a "propter hoc"? Quite obviously – as the development of Ancient Greek nature philosophy has shown us – we get it from the retribution principle. The latter is an expression of the transcendent will of a specific objective authority, independent of the men subject to it, who links guilt with punishment and merit with reward, by assigning punishment "on account of" guilt and reward "on account of" merit. So long as the idea persists, of a transcendent authority endowed with reason and will, there can be no difference – so far as the two pairs of concepts are kept separate at all – between the linkage of guilt and punishment or merit and reward on the one hand, and cause and effect on the other. For in both cases this link must be established by the will of the authority, so that there can be no differentiating between the moral law and the law of nature, so long as both are regarded as the divine will. This is the objective bond which still holds cause and effect together, even when the causal law has parted company from the principle of retribution, and when the will of the transcendent element – so far as it is eliminated from the interpretation of nature – has been incorporated into the concrete cause itself, or when the cause-effect relation is construed on the analogy of the god located within man, his causative "soul"; just as primitive thought already locates in the guilt that is thought of as perfectly substantial the primitive will of the deity (who also, indeed wills the guilt); blood, once shed, cries out for revenge, for in it lies the vengeful soul of the murdered man. From the blood of Uranus, criminally castrated by his son Chronos, the Hesiodic myth derives the Erinnyes. When the critique of Hume and Kant transformed the principle of causality from an objectively necessary linkage of cause and effect inherent in nature into a subjective principle of human knowledge, the principle was freed only from one element which it carried with it as heir to the principle of retribution.

Another feature of the causal notion to which modern physics takes exception is the thesis that the effect must be like the cause. Mach had already denounced the complete "emptiness" of this principle, still much employed by Robert Mayer, who discovered the law of the conservation of energy.[110] Philipp Frank observes:

It is a major feature of the popular conception of causality, that cause and effect must be somehow similar to one another, or at least in proportion. The more powerful the cause, the more powerful the effect. But for a long time there was no suitable measure for all possible causes and effects, in order to be able to establish when some portion of the cause was equal to the corresponding portion of the effect. Yet people still believed themselves to have a certain feeling for this. In the physical proposition, that a system of bodies can only acquire so much energy as is withdrawn from the surrounding bodies, there was at last perceived the concrete numerical formulation of the fact that the effect must be equal to the cause. Driesch explicitly says that 'energy is the measure for causality'.[111]

Frank himself, however – after stressing the problematic character of the energy-concept as such[112] – declares most emphatically that it is impossible, from the physical point of view, "just to consider energy in general as the measure of causality".[113]

But even if we take the intrinsically meaningless assertion that the cause must be equal to the effect to have led to the physically correct principle of the conservation of energy, it certainly will not do – as is sometimes done – to pronounce the causal principle to be identical with the principle of energy, or the former to be "logically equivalent" to the latter.[114] The statement that when a certain amount of one kind of energy appears to vanish, a certain amount of another kind comes into existence, differs entirely in meaning from the statement that the cause must be equal to the effect.[115] Only through a most radical change of meaning could the latter turn into (or more accurately, lead to) the principle of the equivalence of energies. As a component of causal theory – now eliminated from modern physics, or replaced by the equivalence-principle – it has its origin in the doctrine of retribution, namely the latter's basic principle, that like will be repaid with like; this, and the significance of that principle, have already been pointed out in our account of the ancient philosophy of nature.[116] Here it may be added that the idea that both factors conjoined in the retribution-law are objectively measureable, and the resultant insistence that the greater the guilt or merit, the greater the punishment or reward must be, are an outcome of the substantialising tendency of primitive thought. For the latter transforms all qualities, states, forces, etc., and "good" and "bad" in particular, into quantitatively determinable substances; so that guilt, wrong or sin, as a substance sticking to the evil-doer, can be literally washed off him by rites of purification, or as a thing lodged inside him can be spat out, thrown up or verbally expelled by confession. Only if the badness of guilt and the badness of punishment are alike in being quantitatively determinable substances, can they be weighed against each other in retribution; that is why the scales are a symbol of justice, regarded as a retributory procedure. Once the ideology of retribution, and with it the associated notion of guilt and punishment as substances, is abandoned in criminal law, and once prevention replaces retribution as the aim of punishment, the equivalence of guilt and punishment loses its meaning. For punishment then no longer follows "on account of" past evil-doing, but to prevent it in the future, and neither wrong nor punishment are objectively measureable quantities. And yet something like an equivalence of guilt and punishment appears to remain. The more the social harm described as wrong-doing is felt as an evil, the more the evil threatened to prevent it must be feared, the more "severe" the punishment must be. But how problematic this proportion is, can already be seen from the fact that the measurements of the two terms of this proportion have no objective character, but are merely subjective evaluations. Within the framework of the prevention-theory, the equivalence of guilt and punishment – so far as it can be sustained at all – has in any case a meaning quite different from that which it possesses within the theory of retribution; just as the principle of energy-equivalence, as a quantitative proportionality of cause and effect,[117] possesses – if such an interpretation is possible at all – a meaning quite different from that of the principle of cause-and-effect likeness, on the old causal theory. The theory of energy represents, in physics, an advance akin to that of the prevention-theory in legal science: both imply a conquest of the principle of retribution.

The dubious nature of the equation between cause and effect is also evident in the fact that the two-term picture of causality, typical of the popular conception, is rooted in the idea that *one* cause has only *one* effect, and that a *single* effect can be traceable only to a *single* cause. But since every cause must itself be regarded in turn as the effect of another cause, and every effect as the cause of further effects, every point to be causally determined is located in an infinite causal series, having the character of a continuum. The phenomena designated as cause and effect stand "in a direct, though often not immediately perceiveable, concatenation of events". The so-called cause passes imperceptibly into the so-called effect.[118] "Cause and effect", as Goethe put it, "are a single indivisible phenomenon". That we nevertheless separate, and even oppose them, that from all the continuing series of infinitely many elements we arbitrarily select just two, as "the" cause, and "the" effect assigned to it and it alone, depends on the age-old habit of interpreting nature according to the retribution-principle, which conjoins just one quite specific process, namely that called wrong-doing, with another, no less specific, and clearly separated in time from the first, namely punishment, and "accounts" the one to the other. The possibility of isolating these facts from the continuing stream of events, rests here on the fact that both are actually determined and conjoined together "voluntarily", i.e., through the *will* – of men or gods – which finds expression in the *norm* of retribution. That the method of isolating sub-sections of what happens has its origin in normative thinking, does not prevent the attainment thereby of both theoretically and practically useful results in the field of natural knowledge as well; once granted that it is corrected by the realisation that every effect has infinitely many causes, and every cause infinitely many effects. And this too because an analysis of reality shows that every effect is not only the – provisional – endpoint of a causal series, but also, as it were, the point of intersection of infinitely many such. No process is dependent on one cause alone. Starting from this viewpoint, attempts have been made to dispense with the concept of cause as such, as useless, and to replace it by that of "conditions" or "components" of events, while eliminating the notion of effect in favour of "that which results".[119] It was thought, however, that among the conditions or components of an event it was necessary to designate *one* in particular as the "decisive" one, so that – in Fritz Mauthner, for example – a distinction is made between the cause as the collective concept of *all* conditions of an effect taken together, and the cause in the narrower sense of the "immediate" or "decisive change in one of the conditioning factors",[120] so that the concept of cause is not really dispensed with, but merely modified. What is dispensed with is simply a component of the idea of causality, which again can stem only from the sphere of the idea of retribution: namely its bipartite character. Here, and here only, it is in fact incontestable in its proper sphere. One delict, one punishment. The postulate that one should not be punished more than once for the same crime, that the law of retribution vents itself in a single reaction to one and the same circumstance, and is thus literally divided into only two parts, finds expression in the old saying: *ne bis in idem*. Even the critique of the causal law, which proceeds from so-called conditionism,[121] aims at nothing else beyond a dissolution of the principle of retribution.

The latter quite essentially conjoins its two factors, inasmuch as the one must precede the other in time. First the delict, and then the punishment; first the merit, and then the reward. The two factors conjoined together by the law of retribution are not reversible. And simultaneity of the two factors is no more conceivable than their reversal. Precisely on the analogy of the retribution-principle, conjoining its two elements in uniform sequence, the causal law is, or was originally, conceived, and in this form regarded as the basic pattern of natural regularity as such. But this idea could no longer be sustained, once it had become necessary to abandon as unjustifiable the assumption of an immanent connection between cause and effect, and to replace it by the idea of a merely functional dependency. In this conception, the temporal sequence of phenomena is no longer retained as an essential element. Functional dependence can also obtain between simultaneous occurrences. But if simultaneous occurrences are in functional dependency, they are also reversible. And modern science is in fact able to point out a multitude of connections, in which no temporal distinction of before and after appears.[122] Hence there are natural laws which do not correspond to the original schema of causality. Yet these relations are still often presented as "causal", i.e., as the relationship of a temporally antecedent cause to a temporally subsequent effect. But in truth, i.e., from the standpoint of physical cognition, there is a functional relation between simultaneous phenomena. Thus the fact that a mass projected upwards describes, under the influence of gravity, a parabolic path, is explained by saying that gravity is the cause which brings it about that the path of a projected mass takes on a parabolic form. The decisive relation, however, subsists between position and acceleration, which are simultaneously existing quantities.[123] The Boyle-Mariotte law asserts a relation between the pressure and volume of a gas, which are likewise simultaneous quantities,[124] although it is customary to say that the greater or lesser pressure is the cause of the increase or diminution of volume. According to Kepler's Third Law, a particular planetary distance from the sun is associated with a certain period of rotation; but it can equally well be said, conversely, that the period of rotation is associated with a particular distance from the sun.[125] In Kirchhoff's law, absorption and emission are functionally conjoined together. Both always describe a piece of matter at the same time,[126] and hence one of the two coefficients can equally well be designated as the "cause" or the "effect" of the other. Which is to say that here causality – in its original sense – has lost its meaning. We shall here say no more of the fact that in the field of quantum-mechanics there are certain microprocesses which appear to be "caused", not by the past, but by the future, since the interpretation and formulation of the phenomena in question is very doubtful. What it amounts to is that the modern concept of natural law, as the concept of functional dependency, has emancipated itself from the old idea of causality, as the concept of a relation between two processes immanently conjoined in uniform temporal sequence. We now have the choice of no longer identifying this extended concept of law with that of the causal law, because we do not wish to speak of causality in connection with simultaneously existing occurrences;[127] and therefore of postulating natural laws which are not causal laws. Or else – as is doubtless in accordance with the historical development – we may see in the modern natural law, which also apprehends the functional dependency of simultaneous occurrences as a connection governed by law, a modification of the causal law, and formulate the latter somewhat as follows: that a particular process – the effect – generally occurs if a particular other process, the cause, has either previously occurred, *or is simultaneously* occurring,[128] so that the causal law remains, as before, the basic form of all natural regularity, albeit in an altered sense. But in this change of meaning we are concerned with nothing else but the emancipation of causality from the intrinsically one-way process of retribution.[129]

The chief blow to the causal law – so it is often assumed – was struck by the very recently founded science of quantum mechanics, the mechanics of sub-atomic particles. The assumption resting on the causal law, that from knowledge of an initial state, mechanical processes can be determined in advance in their inevitable course, proved to be unuseable here, since in the field of atomic physics an initial state can never be univocally determined. Of the two quantities which constitute it, such as position and momentum, or time and energy, it is always *one* only that can be measured as accurately as we wish, in such a way that the greater the accuracy in measuring one quantity, the more the inaccuracy of the other increases in proportion. If the one is determined with absolute exactness, the other remains absolutely undetermined. This is the uncertainty relation discovered and formulated by Heisenberg.[130] If, then – as is done in the modern philosophy of nature – we assume the criterion of causality to be predictability,[131] and declare an event to be causally determined if it can be predicted with certainty, there is then – so the matter is usually interpreted – no causality in the field of quantum mechanics, or at least no causality can be established, and never could be established, even if it were "objectively" given. However – so it is said – the causal determinacy of molecular events is unnecessary, and perhaps not even probable – as the physicist Exner was already stressing in 1918 – in order to arrive at physical laws. At laws, anyway, which express no absolute necessity, but merely a statistical probability. In the essay we have already cited, 'What is a Law of Nature', Schrödinger [132] argues as follows against the traditional view of natural law as the statement of a necessary regularity in the course of phenomena:

In the last four to five decades, physical science has plainly and clearly demonstrated that, at least for the overwhelming majority of phenomenal processes whose regularity and permanence have led to the setting-up of the postulate of universal causality, the common root of the strict regularities we observe is *chance*. – In every physical phenomenon where regularity is observed, untold thousands, and generally billions, of individual atoms or molecules are taking part .... At least in a very large number of cases, of the most varied kind, we have now succeeded in giving a full and complete account of the particular regularity by reference to the immensely large number of individual molecular processes involved. The individual molecular process may or may not possess a strict regularity of its own, but in the observed regularity of the mass-phenomenon there is no need to take it into account; on the contrary, it is wholly blotted out in the mean values covering millions of individual processes, to which alone we have access. These mean values display their own purely statistical regularity, which would equally be present if the course of each single molecular process were to be determined by dice, the roulette-wheel, or the drawing of lots.

This gives rise to the "statistical conception of laws". We now know with certainty, says Schrödinger, that the natural regularities we have observed for thousands of years, and which have led to the belief in causality, "are not in any immediate sense causal, but are at bottom statistical regularities".

The change in our view of nature brought about by modern physics, and particularly quantum mechanics, is interpreted by Reichenbach,[133] not as a replacement of causal by statistical regularities, but more pertinently, as a modification of the causal concept. Here we are witnessing "a change in the concept of law" corresponding to the transition from strict certainty to probability, a development, however, which had already begun in classical physics. "Every causal statement, applied to the prediction of a natural event, has the form of a probability statement". And the concept of probability employed here is that of statistics. But this concept of probability proves to be "not a disturbing intruder, but a necessary constituent of every statement about reality, through which the principle of causality first acquires its intelligible meaning". Following Schlick, Bergmann formulates the outcome of the critique of modern physics as follows: Instead of presupposing, with the old causal law, "wholly unambiguous *necessity* of the individual event", we must be content to accept as our highest, most fundamental postulate "that whatever possesses the greater mathematical probability also occurs proportionately more often in nature". "All we have to postulate is the applicability of the probability calculus to reality. This postulate makes fewer assumptions than the causal law, and to that extent has the advantage over it."[134] The "strict regularity of the causal order" has been somewhat relaxed; but the assumption of a regularity in events still stands, save only that the "necessity" in the old formulation of the causal law is replaced by mere "probability"; the assumption, that is, that a necessary connection obtains between cause and effect, is replaced by the assumption that this connection is merely a "probable" one.[135]

From the philosophical side, however, it is often disputed that the findings of quantum mechanics compel us to abandon the assumption of a thorough-going causality, in the sense of an absolute necessity of connection between cause and effect, in favour of a weaker presupposition concerning natural regularity, namely the assumption of mere laws of probability.[136] This view is essentially dependent on the claim that quantum mechanics itself presupposes the strict principle of causality. Thus May,[137] for example, says:

> that quantum mechanics by no means demonstrates – as has so often been maintained – the invalidity of the causal law, but rather presupposes as a postulate the validity of thoroughgoing causal connection, and even requires the schema of mechanical causality, in order to secure any footing at all for its argument....

Even if it be true that quantum mechanics presupposes strict causality "as a postulate" – which must remain undecided here – this would still leave Reichenbach's above-mentioned formula unaffected. For the latter is obviously concerned with causality as a law of reality, as a natural law describing what is actually real, whereas the defenders of strict causality regard it as an epistemological postulate. As such it could continue to have the form of an inviolable *norm* directed to our thinking, bidding us invariably to *seek* a cause for every event. (May says: "Causality means that thought feels itself obligated to seek in all that happens, or has happened, a ground of becoming")[138]; though this does nothing to tell us, to what degree our experience actually allows of conformity to this norm. If quantum mechanics has shown that and why the empirical data can be apprehended statistically only – and even May[139] concedes this – that constitutes proof that natural laws, as statements about the actual behaviour of reality, and hence also the causal law, so far as it is construed as such a statement, can only be formulated as statistical laws. Reichenbach[140] says:

If we describe an event by a finite number of parameters, the future development can be predicted with a certain probability; this probability approaches 1, the more parameters are taken into account.

May[141] misses the corollary, that even when all parameters are included, the statement still remains only a statement of probability, and the 1 will never be completely reached. Only such a formulation would bring out that we are no longer presupposing the validity of the causal principle, but rather that the law of probability discloses an "objective feature of the course of nature". But he admits that experience teaches us "that we seldom or never arrive at the absolute 1 which leads from probability to true causality, even when we think we have all the parameters assembled". This is sufficient, however, to lead us to the conclusion that, if the causal law is to be a description of what actually happens, it can only be formulated as a law of probability. What May has to offer against this is merely an appeal to strict causality as a postulate of knowledge.[142]

Whether the replacement of absolute necessity by statistical probability in the concept of natural law can be traced back solely to quantum mechanics, with the uncertainty-relations established in that field, there is no need to decide. If the causal law is used for predicting the future, then even prior to Heisenberg's discovery, it would have been possible to employ only a probability-calculus. Thus Reichenbach also states that even the description of reality in classical physics cannot be formulated without making use of the concept of probability.[143]

There is no difference of principle between Heisenberg's uncertainty relation and the Laplacean intelligence. The one merely demonstrates of a single concrete problem what the other maintains quite generally: the insufficiency of human knowledge. "An intelligence", says Laplace in his *Essai philosophique sur les probabilités*, which at a given moment knows all the forces that are effective in nature and the respective situation of the beings who compose it – an intelligence sufficiently vast to submit these data to analysis – would embrace in the same formula the movements of the greatest bodies of the universe and those of the lightest atoms. Nothing would be uncertain for it, the future, like the past, would be open to it. The human mind in the perfection which it has achieved in astronomy is a weak model of this intelligence.... All its efforts in the quest for truth have the tendency incessantly to draw the human mind closer to the intelligence which we have just mentioned but from which it will always remain infinitely remote.[144]

Since it is therefore quite impossible for the human mind, in its always infinite remoteness from the Laplacean intelligence, to know all the forces at a given moment, it can only predict the future in terms of probability; but it can likewise explain the present from the past with probability only, since this too it is only imperfectly acquainted with. It is said, indeed, that when Laplace was asked what role God played in his system, he replied that he had no need of that hypothesis. But his omniscient intelligence is only a euphemistic definition of the notion of God, clothed in the form of an artificial epistemological limiting case.

In the infinite distance between God and man, theology has from time immemorial given utterance to the finitude of human nature, in contrast to the infinity of the divine. God alone can foresee the future with absolute certainty, since He alone is completely acquainted with the present; and God alone can grasp the present completely, since He alone is completely acquainted with the past. The strict Idea of causality, the absolute necessity of what happens, is realised only in the unlimited knowledge of God, not in the limited knowledge of man;[145] it makes no difference whether it is a matter of determining the future through the present, or the present through the past. This is at bottom the age-old idea – transferred merely from the emotional to the rational, to the sphere of knowledge – that the world-process and the law which rules it is the will of God, and that this law is a norm. But the meaning of the norm points to the future. It determines what is to happen in time to come. Not so the law of nature, which explains the real by seeking the cause for an event, and so describes the given reality in the most general and simple fashion.[146] Predictability is a criterion of causality, not the thing itself,[147] and by no means the sole criterion. The presence of a causal nexus is not only demonstrated by the fact that – as in an experiment – a predicted effect actually follows, but also by the fact that something assumed to be the cause of a given phenomenon turns out actually to have occurred in the past. The application of the causal law to future happenings, an application springing from the needs of practice, is a secondary function, as appears from the fact that knowledge independent of willing and acting is invoked in the service of this willing and acting. Prophecy is no longer pure knowledge, but knowledge employed for a technical purpose. The future can be known from the present only on the presupposition that the past, whereby we explain the present, is repeated in the future. What we seize, with our knowledge, in the future, is at bottom always simply the past again. If we see the essence of the causal law in the fact that it determines the future – though only a Laplacean intelligence could know of this – then we thereby exhibit, albeit quite unconsciously, its normative provenance. Hence it is no accident, but betrays an inner connection, when T. H. Huxley [148] construes rules of law as laws of nature, or at least as similar thereto, since they state how men *will* behave: If anyone steals, the magistrate will punish him. This is a misunderstanding. The norms of law, like all norms, are functions of the will, whereas the laws of nature are functions of knowledge.[149] And norms, even legal norms, are not, like natural laws (when conceived as prophecies), statements about what is going to happen; they are not statements about reality at all, and hence also cannot be true or false; they are demands, rather, which lay down what ought to happen, and can thus only be good or bad, useful or harmful. But norms are in fact related to future happenings, and in God's mind – but there only, and not in a human one – the fact that a thing ought to happen is identical with the fact that it will. If rules of law are so easily confused with laws of nature, the reason is that the law of nature was originally a rule of law, expressing the will of God.

If we follow attentively the history of the causal concept, we arrive at the astonishing discovery that – at least until Hume's time – the law of causality was regarded as nothing more nor less than a norm, being seen as the expression of a will, namely the divine will. That Galileo should still regard the regularity of nature as a revelation of the divine essence, that Gassendi, in taking over the atomism of Epicurus, should have taught that the first cause of everything was God, who first pushed the atoms into motion, that Descartes should have appealed to the causal law as a proof of God's existence, and derived the laws of nature from the "free will" of the deity,[150] – all this one might still have attempted to attribute to a merely external influence on the part of Christian theology. But this will no longer do in face of Malebranche's doctrine, when the latter argues that on the basis of our experience we are unacquainted with any necessary connection between phenomena, or any truly causative forces, but can observe only regular successions. On asking what the cause is, that a moving ball, on colliding with another at rest, puts the latter in motion, he replies:

Les hommes ne doivent pas juger qu une boule agitée soit la principale et la véritable cause du mouvement de la boule qu'elle trouve dans son chemin; puisque la première n'a point elle-même la puissance de se mouvoir. Ils peuvent seulement juger que cette rencontre des deux boules est occasion à l'auteur du mouvement de la matière d'exécuter le décret de sa volonté qui est la cause universelle de toutes choses.[151]

The regularity in the behaviour of things is interpreted as the execution of a divine command. As Wentscher very rightly says, Malebranche transfers the causal connection he fails to discover in the finite to the transcendent sphere, to God, or more precisely, "to the will of God".[152] This means, however, that he regards the causal law as a norm, and also directly refers to it as a "décret". On this point Spinoza does not differ from Malebranche, when he traces all finite causality back to the infinite causality of God, which is to say, to the latter's omnipotence. Nor does Leibniz, when he argues that the causality of events can be grasped neither through reason nor experience, and that it is necessary to go back to the first cause of all being, namely God, in whose mind the source of all regularity lies.[153] Locke, too, declared that the human understanding could not know how an effect comes about, the true causes remain hidden from us, because human knowledge is by nature limited, and even this empiricist therefore appeals to God's omnipotence, to explain the connection of cause and effect.[154]

The same line is taken by Berkeley, for whom all causality lies solely and exclusively in the will of God.[155] And Thomas Reid, a contemporary of Hume's, lays it down that the assumption which forms the presupposition for all empirical inferences, namely that the future will resemble the past, does not itself rest upon experience, since this can only inform us about the past, but rather upon an instinct implanted in man by God; the latter rules nature, however, by fixed laws.[156] In other words, the laws of nature, in whose absence there would certainly be no experience, are – as in Malebranche – a sort of ruling ordinances, in which the will of God is expressed. Hume's achievement does not really consist in recognising that no necessary connection of cause and effect can be assumed on the basis of experience; that had already been established before him. What he did, rather, was to give up looking for the necessity of the causal nexus in the will of God, and so to abandon this necessity, and with it the previous concept of causality as such. He conceives himself obliged to make do merely with the *belief* in necessity; and this belief he attributes to a habit of thought. But his argument exhibits a gap which is of special interest in the present connection. He points out that in experience we observe only regular sequences of events, e.g., that flame is succeeded by heat and snow by cold. The understanding does not permit us to assume that the two elements which regularly follow one another are necessarily, i.e., always and without exception, conjoined together. Hence there must be another principle which impels us to this assumption.[157] And now he maintains: "This principle is *custom* or *habit*". But the fact that we are accustomed to observe that a particular event *a* is followed by another event *b*, has in itself no effect upon us beyond that of leading us always to *expect* that whenever *a* occurs, *b will* follow; it does not lead us to assume that it is impossible for *b* not to follow *a*, that *b must* follow *a*, that the two are *necessarily* connected together. And Hume, in fact, simply tells us:

having found, in many instances, that any two kinds of objects – flame and heat, snow and cold – have always been conjoined together; if flame or snow be presented anew to the senses, the mind is carried by custom to expect heat or cold, and to *believe* that such a quality does exist, and will discover itself upon a nearer approach.[158]

The question of whence comes the idea of the absolute necessity of the conjunction, of the inviolability of the causal nexus, is not answered by an appeal to the psychological function of custom. That Hume failed to sense this gap is probably due to the fact that he presupposes as self-evident a notion which can perhaps be reconstructed from the mode and manner in which he poses the problem of causality. His argument runs: From observation of the fact that *b* has hitherto regularly followed *a*, it cannot be rationally inferred that *b must* follow *a*. But on what principle – not given a priori to the understanding – must *b* follow *a*, if *b* has hitherto regularly followed *a*? To an Englishman [sic!] in particular, this principle is perfectly self-evident; for it is one of the foundations of English law, the basic principle, not of custom, but of customary or common law, which states that one *ought* so to behave as one's fellows have commonly or customarily been wont to behave as a rule. "Custom, then, is the great guide of human life", says Hume at this point; and it is more than probable that here he was thinking above all of Customary Law. If, from the observation that *a* is customarily followed by *b*, we conclude that *b must* follow *a*, we are presupposing the validity of a norm which institutes this necessary connection, in that it posits as obligatory the behaviour which accords with custom. This necessity is a normative one; the "must" whereby the conjunction of *a* and *b* is represented is an "ought". But that was the very character attributed to causal necessity in Hume's day.

If we see the decisive turning-point in the development of the causal concept in the fact that this latter no longer expresses an absolute necessity, but a merely statistical probability, then this turning-point had already in essence been reached, or at least adequately prepared for, in Hume's critique. If causality is no objective bond between cause and effect, but a mere habit of thought evoked by the observation of regular sequences, we have done away with that element to which alone an absolute necessity or inviolability can attach: the transcendent will which institutes this objective conjunction. Kant, indeed, endeavoured to salvage something of this inviolability by explaining causality as an innate concept of the understanding, an a priori category, without which knowledge of any kind would be impossible. But in this we should see a retreat rather than an advance over Hume. For the assumption that causality is an absolute necessary condition of knowledge has no foundation in the facts. As already noted, the primitive interprets the world, i.e., "knows" it, entirely without benefit of the causal principle, at least in the form envisaged by Kant. He is content to explain what immediately touches his interests, and is helpful or hurtful to him; and explains it as reward or punishment on the part of the transcendent authority ruling over behaviour that accords with, or runs counter to, the norm. Though it is sometimes maintained that he orientates his actual behaviour according to the causal law, and can act only by relying upon causality, this is no argument for the necessity of the category of cause. For in regard to his actual behaviour, the primitive is no different from the animal, who certainly cannot be supposed to possess causality as an innate concept of the understanding. But if this is not so, causality would have to be given objectively as an inviolable law in nature itself, and nature would have to be ruled by it, i.e., by a transcendent will whose inviolability finds expression in the causal law. Since Hume, however, such an idea is no longer tenable. What man trusts to in his actual behaviour is not the inviolable causal law, but a certain regularity in events, which he by no means knows to operate without exception,[159] and which he can interpret in the most diverse ways: according to the principle of retribution, as the primitive does, or according to the causal law evolved from it by gradual modification, as does the civilised man. That this law has so long been regarded as an objective law, prevailing without exception in nature, and expressing an absolute necessity, is – as we have shown here – explicable only in that the causal law has developed from the norm of retribution, which was inviolable because it derived from the divine will. Only a norm can lay claim to inviolability, for it is not a statement about reality, and can therefore never come into contradiction with the latter. But this reality – as it is actually given to human knowledge – does not admit of interpretation as a system of inviolable law.

If we see in this modification of the concept of law, whose final stage is the replacement of absolute necessity by merely statistical probability, a "revolution" in scientific thought, this is true only in the sense that it represents a stripping-off of the cardinal element whereby the causal concept had still been burdened with that Idea from which it has gradually emerged: the ἀνάγκη with which Δίκη, the goddess of retribution, both punishes the wicked and holds nature upon her appointed course.

3. In the metamorphosis of the retribution principle into the causal law, two tendencies are of decisive importance: the first is generalisation. The primitive need for explanation is still confined to those circumstances which directly touch the interests of the individual, which are felt by him as hurtful or helpful, and again, given the altogether collective orientation of his consciousness, which are felt to be hurtful or helpful to his group. It is only these circumstances that he is impelled to interpret, and these alone which strike him as problematic. In conceiving of some as punishments and others as rewards, whereby the inviolable will of a superhuman authority reacts to the human behaviour it approves or condemns, he believes that events are strictly subordinated to law:

no punishment without guilt, no reward without merit. As the rational components of his consciousness come to prevail over the emotional, the range of circumstances to be interpreted extends beyond those objects which immediately arouse his feelings of pleasure or aversion. He seeks to interpret all circumstances whatsoever, including those which are indifferent from the standpoint of individual, or more properly, group interest. Hence they can no longer be regarded as punishments or rewards in the original and narrower sense. Punishments and rewards become effects, and hence can no longer be conjoined with guilt and merit. Whereas the original principle was: No punishment without guilt, it now becomes: No occurrence of any kind without "guilt"; and here the guilt has become the cause. The Greek αἰτία, as already noted, still has two meanings; and the effect is still conjoined with this cause exactly as punishment is conjoined with guilt, and reward with merit. Because the effect, as a sort of punishment or reward, is connected with the cause regarded as a sort of guilt or merit, this conjunction retains the character of an absolute necessity, namely Ananke.

Hand in hand with the generalising of the concept of law there goes a certain increase in objectivity, consisting in an abandonment of the egocentric, or more properly, the sociocentric standpoint, in the observation of nature. If this latter takes place according to the retribution principle, the processes of nature – so far as they call for any explanation at all – are related to the individual or his group, because they bear upon the collectively-sustained guilt of the group, or the merit of its members. Once the principle of retribution has been generalised into that of causality, circumstances are conjoined as effects with other circumstances as causes, which are in no way merely acts of individuals conforming or running counter to norms. Unlike the retribution principle, the causal law no longer connects natural happenings with the individual as member of society, but conjoins them, as it were, solely within nature itself. An abstraction is thereby made from the knowing subject. Causality connects matters, so to speak, on the periphery, and not to a centre, as the retribution principle does. The final residue of the anthropo- or sociocentric view of nature, associated with the retribution principle as scheme of interpretation, namely the Ptolemaic world-picture, with man's earth at the centre, is overcome with the reinstatement of causal thinking, in the Copernican and Keplerian astronomy.

Along with the dissociation of the causal law from the retribution principle, there goes a separation of the concepts of nature and society. When nature is interpreted according to the retribution principle, it appears as a part of society. Once the retribution principle has been extended into the still normatively conceived world-law, which is viewed as the archetype of all social laws, nature appears as the ideal society, since it constitutes an absolutely just order of which actual human society presents only a highly imperfect copy. Here the dualism of nature and society begins. But it is still a dualism of nature-*law* and society, i.e., *positive* law. The idea of natural law is essentially bound up with the notion that nature is a work of God, and the laws of its behaviour the will of God; that natural laws are norms, and therefore akin to social or juridical laws, whose true content is evinced in the order of nature. With the emancipation of causality from retribution, of the law of nature from the norm, nature and society present themselves as two regions entirely distinct, because they are governed by essentially different kinds of law. The idea of natural law, i.e., the notion of a natural society whose order corresponds to that of nature, now becomes impossible, an absurdity, because it cannot be reconciled with the presupposed dualism of nature and society. As we have seen, the Idea of natural law presupposes a dualism within nature conceived as a universal society: the ideal society of the cosmos stands contrasted with the real, inadequate society of man. It is the dualism of God and man, of transcendence and the empirical. With the emancipation of the causal from the normative interpretation of nature, i.e., of nature as a creation under the authority of the divine will, the dualism of transcendence and the empirical disappears, at least from the realm of natural science; and hence it also becomes shaken in the realm of social theory as well. In this sense it can be said that the dualism of nature and society spells the overthrow of metaphysical dualism.

But the dualism of nature and society is by no means the last word in the advance of knowledge. It too is overcome, and that by means of a dissolution of the concept of norm. The claim of the "ought", as something entirely different from what is, the claim of normativity to rank as a social order of law, independent of causality and distinct from the orderliness of nature, is seen through as mere "ideology", behind which there lies concealed the reality of highly concrete interests on the part of individuals and groups; interests which, on achieving power, present themselves as norms. The dualism of nature and society is superseded by that of reality and ideology. As a portion of reality, the social process appears to modern sociology to be capable of apprehension under the same laws as the natural one. The impossibility of recognising in social processes laws as inviolable as those in nature, disappears as soon as the laws of nature have themselves abandoned the claim to absolute necessity, and are content to be statements about statistical probability. There is in principle no obstacle to arriving at social laws of this type. If nature, at the outset of human speculation, was a part of society, society is now a part of nature, thanks to the total emancipation of causality from retribution in the modern concept of law.

NOTES

* *The Journal of Unified Science (Erkenntnis)* **8** (1939) 69–130. [For a – slightly differing – English version, cf. *Society and Nature*, Chicago, 1943, Chapters V and VII; an abridgement also appears in 'Causality and Retribution', *Philosophy of Science* **8** (1941), reprinted in *What is Justice?* pp. 303–323 – Transl.]

[1] *Die Naturwissenschaften* **17** (1929) 9ff.

[2] Ernst Cassirer, *Die Begriffsform im mythischen Denken*, 1922, p. 31.

[3] The depiction of this state of affairs is the subject of my work *Die Idee der Vergeltung und das Gesetz der Kausalität: eine ethno-soziologische Untersuchung*, which is shortly due to appear in the *Library of Unified Science* series (Van Stockum & Zoon). [It eventually appeared under the title *Vergeltung und Kausalität. Eine soziologische Studie*, The Hague 1964 (copyright 1941) – Transl.].

[4] A discussion of the much-debated concept of the "primitive" seems unnecessary here. The word is taken in the sense customary among modern ethnologists.

[5] Karl Joel, *Geschichte der antiken Philosophie*, 1921, I, p. 258.

[6] The elements of social interpretation in the Greek philosophy of nature may also be connected with the fact that the earliest nature-philosophers and schools of nature-philosophy, those of Thales of Miletus, Parmenides, Empedocles and Zeno, were also involved in political activity. Cf. John Burnet, *Early Greek Philosophy*, 4th edn., 1930, pp. 46, 171, 198f., 311.

[7] Karl Joel: *Der Ursprung der Naturphilosophie aus dem Geiste der Mystik*, 1906, writes on p. 6: "No modern commentator will so compress this innocent poetic phrase (of Homer) ... as to squeeze the water-principle of Thales out of it. It is a long way from the personally conceived and locally defined Okeanos to all water as such, and further still from all water to all being". True, but the way is there, and it is no longer than that from myth (or even mysticism) to nature-philosophy!

[8] H. Diels, *Die Fragmente der Vorsokratiker*, 5th edn., I, 1934, Fr. 33 (English translation from Kathleen Freeman: *Ancilla to the Pre-Socratic Philosophers*, 1948, p. 27. Cited hereafter as Freeman).

[9] Joel, *Geschichte*, *op. cit.*, p. 269.

[10] From Aristotle, *Physics* III, 4, 203b, 6ff. (English translation from G. S. Kirk and J. E. Raven, *The Presocratic Philosophers*, 1971, Fr. 110. Cited hereafter as Kirk & Raven; references are to the fragment-numbers which run consecutively throughout this work).

[11] Diels, Fr. 2 (Kirk & Raven, 163).
[12] Cf. Wilhelm Capelle, *Die Vorsokratiker*, 2nd edn., 1938, No. 25, p. 97.
[13] Cicero, *De natura deorum*, 1, 10, 26; (Kirk & Raven, 147): "Anaximenes determined that air is a god". Diogenes of Apollonia writes, under the influence of Anaximenes: "And it seems to me that that which has intelligence is what men call air, and that all men are steered by this and that it has power over all things. For this very thing seems to me to be a god and to have reached everywhere and to dispose all things and to be in everything". (Kirk & Raven, 606).
[14] Joel, *Der Ursprung ..., op. cit.*, pp. 66f.
[15] Aristotle, *De Anima*, I, 2, 405a 19 (Kirk & Raven, 91). According to Aristotle's interpretation (*De An.*, I, 2, 405a 5ff; I, 3, 406b 15ff.; I, 5, 409a 32ff.), the soul is also found as principle or cause of motion in Democritus.
[16] Aristotle, *De Generatione et Corruptione*, I, 6, 322b 12ff. (Oxford translation).
[17] Diels, Fr. 2 (Kirk & Raven, 602).
[18] Diels, Fr. 90 (Freeman, p. 61).
[19] Diels, Fr. 62, 6 (Kirk & Raven, 448).
[20] Diels, Fr. 109 (Kirk & Raven, 454).
[21] Aeschylus, *Agamemnon* 757ff. (E. D. R. Morshead's translation).
[22] Diels, Fr. 25 (Freeman, p. 25).
[23] Burnet, *op. cit.*, p. 54.
[24] In medicine, health corresponds to justice; it is in this sense that it must be understood when, under Pythagorean influence, the physician Alcmaeon of Croton teaches "... the bond of health is the 'equal balance' of the powers, moist and dry, cold and hot, bitter and sweet, and the rest, while the 'supremacy' of one of them is the cause of disease ..." (Diels, Fr. 4; Kirk & Raven, 286).
[25] Diels, 12 A 9, Fr. 1 (Kirk & Raven, 112).
[26] Capelle, *op. cit.*, p. 75.
[27] Werner Jaeger, *Paideia: the Ideals of Greek Culture* (transl. by Gilbert Highet, Oxford, 1939), takes the view (pp. 157ff.) that the idea of legality which finds expression in this fragment of Anaximander has as its model the Greek city-state's legal idea of the 'polis', which was binding on each individual.
[28] Ernst Cassirer, *Philosophy of Symbolic Forms*, II (Transl. by Ralph Manheim, Yale, 1955), observes on p. 114 that in mythical thinking there is a relation "between the universal temporal order, which governs all events, and the eternal order of justice, which likewise presides over [them]". Thus in the Babylonian-Assyrian religion, for example, Marduk, the god of justice, i.e., of retribution, having gained his victory over the monster Tiamat, fixes the stars as the abode of the gods and determines their courses. In the Egyptian religion the moon-god Thoth, who as surveyor is the divider of time and lord of just measurement, functions both as scribe of the gods and at the same time as *judge* of the heavens. It is he who has bestowed language and writing on mankind and who, through the arts of counting and reckoning, has given gods and men to know *what is their due*. (Cassirer, *op. cit.*, p. 114; Kelsen's italics). There are similar relations between temporal and legal order in Chinese religion. Here, as Cassirer puts it, "the ethical bonds governing men's acts merge with the temporal, in fact with the calendarial regulation of these acts ..." Cassirer also points out the connection of legal and temporal order in the religion of the Indo-Germanic peoples. Cf. *op. cit.*, p. 115.
[29] Diogenes Laertius, IX, 6 (Transl. by C. D. Yonge).
[30] *Ibid.*
[31] Diels, Fr. 53 (Kirk & Raven, 215).
[32] Diels, Fr. 80 (Kirk & Raven, 214).

[33] Capelle, *op. cit.*, p. 127.
[34] Diels, Fr. 1 (Kirk & Raven, 197).
[35] Diogenes Laertius, IX, 6.
[36] Aetius I, 7, 22 (H. Diels, *Doxographi Graeci*, 1929, p. 303); *ibid.*, I, 27, 1 (Diels, p. 322); *ibid.*, I, 28, 1 (Diels, p. 323).
[37] Cf. Prellwitz, *Etymologisches Wörterbuch der Griechischen Sprache*, 2nd edn., 1905, p. 286; Emile Boisacq: *Dictionnaire étymologique de la langue grecque*, 1916, p. 621.
[38] Diels, Fr. 2 (Kirk & Raven, 198).
[39] Diels, Fr. 114 (Kirk & Raven, 253).
[40] Diels, Fr. 94 (Kirk & Raven, 229).
[41] Diels, Fr. 28 (Burnet, *op. cit.*, p. 141 [Fr. 118]).
[42] Pseudo-Demosthenes against Aristogeiton, I, 11 (Freeman, p. 3 [Fr. 14]): "Implacable and reverend Justice (Dike), which Orpheus, who revealed to us the most holy rites, says is seated beside the throne of Zeus and looks upon all mortal happenings".
[43] Plato, *Laws*, IV, 715e (Jowett): "God, as the old tradition declares, holding in His hand the beginning, middle and end of all that is, travels according to His nature in a straight line towards the accomplishment of His end. Justice (Dike) always accompanies Him, and is the punisher of those who fall short of the divine law". The idea of the inviolability of the world-law – conceived as the divine will – appears among the Orphics in mythical guise. According to Damascius, *de principiis*, 123 bis (Diels-Kranz 1, B, 13; Freeman, p. 3 [Fr. 13]), the Orphic theory "... gives the first two elements as Water and Earth. The third Element was begotten of these two, and was a serpent having the heads of a bull and a lion with the face of a god in between; it had wings, and was called Ageless Time [Chronos] or Unchanging Heracles. With him was united Necessity or Adrasteia, an element having no body (ἀσώματος – a corrupt term, and most likely δισώματος = bi-sexual), and *spread over the whole universe, fastening it together* (H. K.'s italics). This, I believe, is considered the third principle ... only that it is depicted as both male and female, to indicate the cause generating everything". *Adrasteia* means the *inescapable*. It is obviously the personification of the inviolability of the world-law, which among the Orphics, whose doctrine of the soul is completely dominated by the notion of reward and punishment, can be no other than the law of retribution. It is punishment that one cannot "escape". It is very significant that the "inviolability" of the world-law, the inescapable character of retribution, is essentially linked with Chronos, or time. At the end of this account of the Orphic theology we are told: "This theogony sings of Protogonos (First-born [God]), and calls him Zeus the *Marshaller of All Things and of the Whole Universe* (H. K.'s italics). Hence he is also called Pan (i.e., universal God)".
[44] Thus in Euripides' *Medea*, 410f., the law of gravity appears as a legal norm. On perceiving the heroine's criminal intentions, the poet has the Chorus say (Loeb translation):

> "Upward and back to their fountains the sacred rivers are stealing;
> Justice is turned to injustice, the order of old to confusion."

[45] The inviolability of the world-law as the unshakeable will of a god of justice, whose specific function is retribution, is also found in Babylonian religion. In the Creation Epic (Tablet V), it is said of Marduk:

> "He constructed stations for the great gods,
> Fixing their astral likenesses as constellations.
> He determined the year by designating the zones:
> He set up three constellations for each of the twelve months.

After defining the days of the year by heavenly figures,
He founded the station of Nebiru [Jupiter] to mark their bounds,
That none [of the days] might transgress or fall short.
Alongside it he set up the stations of Enlil and Ea". (1–8).

This god, who establishes the order of the cosmos and thus the ordering of time, is the god of justice. His name is also (Tablet VII):

"Shazu, who knows the heart of the gods, who examines the inside:
From whom the evildoer cannot escape; (35–36)
...
Who subdues the insubmissive...
Who directs justice... (38–9)
....
Who blots out all the wicked ones... (45)
...
Firm in his order, his command unalterable,
The utterance of his mouth no god shall change". (151–2)

In the Creation myth, Marduk figures as an "avenger". His battle against Tiamat and her horde, together with their destruction, is presented as an act of retribution. Thus in Tablet III, for example:

"Tiamat, She who bore us, detests us.
She has set up the [Assembly] and is furious with rage.
All the Gods have rallied to her;
Even those whom you brought forth march at her side.
They throng and march at the side of Tiamat.
Enraged, they plot without cease night and day.
They are set for combat, growling, raging,
They have formed a council to prepare for the fight". (15–22)

Before going out to do battle against Tiamat, Marduk says:

"If I indeed, as your avenger,
Am to vanquish Tiamat and save your lives,
Set up the Assembly, proclaim supreme my destiny!
When jointly in Ubshukinna you have sat down rejoicing,
Let my word, instead of you, determine the fates,
Unalterable shall be what I may bring into being;
Neither recalled nor changed shall be the command of my lips!" (58–64)

And in Tablet IV we read:

"Thou, Marduk, art the most honoured of the great gods,
Thy decree is unrivalled, thy word is Anu.
From this day unchangeable shall be thy pronouncement.
To raise or bring low – these shall be in thy hand.
Thy utterance shall be true, thy command shall be unimpeachable.
No one among the gods shall transgress thy bounds! . . . (5–10)
O Marduk, thou art indeed our avenger.
We have granted thee kingship over the universe entire. (13–14)

O lord, spare the life of him who trusts thee,
But pour out the life of the god who seized evil." (17–18)

Before the battle, Marduk says to Tiamat:

"... thou seekest evil;
[Against] the gods, my fathers, thou hast confirmed thy wickedness.
[Though] drawn up be thy forces, girded on thy weapons,
Stand thou up, that I and thou meet in single combat!" (83–6)

After Marduk has defeated the followers of Tiamat and fettered them in bonds "they could not escape", the epic says of them that

"Bearing his wrath, they were held imprisoned". (114)

[Quotations are from the translation by E. A. Speiser, in James B. Pritchard, *Ancient Near Eastern Texts*, Princeton 1950, pp. 60–72]. Cf. also Cassirer, *op. cit.*, pp. 113–14.

[46] Joel, *Der Ursprung* ..., *op. cit.*, p. 87, says in regard to Heraclitus' fragment 94: "that the concept of nature's law is an anthropomorphism." It would be truer still to say that it is a 'sociomorphism'.

[47] Simplicius, *in Phys. Aristot.*, 23, 33ff.

[48] Diels, Fr. 90 (Kirk & Raven, 222).

[49] Hippolytus, *Refutatio* ... IX, 10 (Diels, Frs. 63–66; quoted in part from W. K. C. Guthrie – *History of Greek Philosophy*, II, 1965, pp. 432, 474). This account of the Heraclitean doctrine of world-conflagration is strongly reminiscent of the ethico-juristic view of the world-process typical of the Judaeo-Christian belief – influenced as it is by ancient Persian ideas – in a Last Judgement. There is much to be said, therefore, for seeing in this account of Hippolytus a Christian reinterpretation of the Heraclitean doctrine. But there is no denying that the unquestionably genuine fragments of Heraclitus display such a strongly normative tone – "He does not see, he evaluates", says Joel (*Geschichte* ... I, p. 286) – that his teachings offered plentiful inducements for Christian authors to reinterpret them; and his pessimistic attitude may also have contributed largely to this. His utterances concerning the incomprehension and wickedness of men are in fact reminiscent of the wrathful tirades of some of the Jewish prophets. Justin called him a Christian before Christ. So why should one understand his doctrine of the primal fire by reference to the ἐκπύρωσις believed in only, after all, by the Stoics, and not as the prophesying of a day of judgement upon the sinful world? The altogether normative, i.e., ethico-juristical character of the Heraclitean world-picture, has been emphasised by Nietzsche ('Philosophy in the Tragic Age of the Greeks', *Early Greek Philosophy*, Transl. by M. A. Mügge, 1924, p. 97). His account of the Ephesian's doctrine can in this respect be termed a sympathetic re-creation: "I contemplate the Becoming, he exclaimed, and nobody has so attentively watched this eternal wave-surging and rhythm of things. And what do I behold? Lawfulness, infallible certainty, ever equal paths of Justice, condemning Erinnyes behind all transgressions of the laws, the whole world a spectacle of a governing justice and of demoniacally omnipresent natural forces subject to justice's sway. I do not behold the punishment of that which has become, but the justification of becoming. When has sacrilege, when has apostasy manifested itself in inviolable forms, in laws esteemed sacred? Where injustice sways, there is caprice, disorder, irregularity, contradiction; where, however, Law and Zeus's daughter, Dike, rule alone, as in this world, how could the sphere of guilt, of expiation, of judgement, and as it were the place of execution of all condemned ones, be there?" But Dike rules – as Nietzsche fails to notice – by punishing injustice, which is therefore far from being excluded. Hence it is entirely in the spirit of the pessimistic Heraclitus to suppose that "*this* world is a sphere of guilt".

[50] Diels, Fr. 1 (Kirk & Raven, 342).
[51] *Ibid.*
[52] Diels, Fr. 8 (Kirk & Raven, 347).
[53] Diels, Fr. 8 (Kirk & Raven, 350).
[54] Diels, Fr. 8 (Kirk & Raven, 352).
[55] Aeschylus, *Prometheus Bound*, 514f. (P. E. More's translation).
[56] Joel, *Der Ursprung* ..., *op. cit.*, p. 142, observes that the early nature-philosophers as such were not merely subject to Orphic influence, but were actually "far too much of one mind with the Orphics to have need of their influence." The central tenet of Orphism is the doctrine of transmigration. And Joel maintains, on p. 151, that he recognises, in fact, "in the doctrine of transmigration a necessary basis for the ancient philosophy of nature". But that doctrine is simply an ideology of the principle of retribution.
[57] Diels, Fr. 115 (Kirk & Raven, 471).
[58] Diogenes Laertius, VIII, 77 (Yonge, p. 368).
[59] Aristotle, *Rhetoric*, I, 13, 1373b 6ff. (Oxford translation).
[60] Cicero, *De Republica*, III, 11, 19 (Loeb).
[61] Diels, Fr. 136 (Kirk & Raven, 468).
[62] Diels, Fr. 137 (Kirk & Raven, 469).
[63] Diels, Fr. 135 (Guthrie, *op. cit.*, II, p. 249).
[64] Joel, *op. cit.*, p. 156, remarks: "The world-process, in Anaximander as in Heraclitus, in the Pythagoreans as in Empedocles, is everywhere a moral one".
[65] Diels, Fr. 17 (Kirk & Raven, 423).
[66] Diels, Fr. 35 (Kirk & Raven, 464).
[67] Diels, Fr. 20 (Guthrie, *op. cit.*, II, p. 202).
[68] Diels, Fr. 22 (Guthrie, II, p. 158).
[69] Diels, Fr. 28 (Kirk & Raven, 421).
[70] Among them (the people of the Golden Age) "they had no god Ares [strife] nor Kudoimos [noise of battle], nor king Zeus nor Kronos nor Poseidon, but Kupris [love] as queen. Her did they propitiate with holy images, with paintings of living creatures [not real sacrifices], with perfumes of varied fragrance and with sacrifice of pure myrrh and sweet-scented frankincense, casting to the ground libations of golden honey. Their altar was not steeped in the pure blood of bulls, but rather was this the greatest abomination among men, to tear out the life from the goodly limbs and eat them." (Diels, Fr. 128 [Kirk & Raven, 466]). In those days, "all things were tame and kindly to man, and loving kindness was kindled abroad". (Diels, Fr. 130 [Guthrie, II, p. 249]).
[71] Cf. F. Dümmler, *Akademika*, 1889, p. 221.
[72] Cf. Capelle, *op. cit.*, p. 236, n. 1.
[73] Diels, Fr. 59 (Kirk & Raven, 444).
[74] Diels, Fr. 30 (Kirk & Raven, 429).
[75] Aristotle, *Physics* VIII, 1, 252a 7ff. (Oxford).
[76] Aristotle, *Metaphysics* I, 4, 984b 32ff.
[77] *Ibid.*, I, 4, 985a 21ff: "And Empedocles, though he uses the causes to a greater extent than [Anaxagoras], neither does so sufficiently nor attains consistency in their use. At least, in many cases he makes love segregate things, and strife aggregate them. For whenever the universe is dissolved into its [four] elements by strife, fire is aggregated into one, and so is each of the other elements [separated to itself]; but whenever again under the influence of love they come together into one, the parts must again be segregated out of each element". (Oxford).
[78] Hippolytus, *Refutatio*, VII, 17 (Capelle, *op. cit.*, 182, p. 243 [from the German]).
[79] Diels, Fr. 22 (Guthrie, II, p. 158).

80 Diels, Fr. 30 (Kirk & Raven, 429).
81 Aristotle, *De Gen. Anim*, V, 8, 789b 2 (Cf. Guthrie, II, p. 415).
82 Capelle, *op. cit.*, pp. 287f.
83 Simplicius, *in Physica* 37, 24, commenting on Aristotle, *Physics*, 196a 14 (Capelle, 48, p. 415 [from the German; but cf. Kirk & Raven, 570]).
84 Pseudoplutarch, *Stromateis*, 7 (Plutarch's *Moralia* XV [Loeb], pp. 333–35).
85 Dionysius Alex. in Eusebius, XIV, 27, 4; Diels, Fr. 8 (Freeman, p. 104).
86 Plato, *Protagoras* 324 (Jowett). That the reference here is to a specifically sophistic doctrine, is chiefly attested by the fact that Plato himself adheres to the theory of retribution; especially in his doctrine of the soul, which culminates, of course, in the idea of retribution in the next world.
87 Aetius I, 25, 4 (Diels, Fr. 2 [Kirk & Raven, 568]).
88 The title of this work – so Capelle observes, *op. cit.*, p. 303 – is quite uncertain (as a work of Leucippus).
89 Cf. Capelle, *op. cit.*, p. 281.
90 Diels, Fr. 1 (Kirk & Raven, 197).
91 Aetius I, 26, 2 (Kirk & Raven, 566).
92 Capelle remarks on this passage: "By necessity Democritus obviously understands the world-law, or more exactly, the *causal law*, which has always operated in an ineluctable chain of consequences. According to 68 A 66 (Aristotle, *De Gen. Anim.* V, 8, 789b 2) he simply means by this the law of nature, physical causality, i.e., more precisely, that which acts by pressure or impact".
93 Alexander Aphrodisiensis, *in Metaph.*, 36, 21 H (Kirk & Raven, 579).
94 Aetius, I, 12, 6 (Guthrie, II, p. 402) and I, 23, 3 (Guthrie, p. 404; Kirk & Raven, 580).
95 παλμός here can also mean "impact". Capelle, *op. cit.*, p. 403.
96 Simplicius, *in Arist. de coelo*, 242, 21 H (Kirk & Raven, 582).
97 Diogenes Laertius, IX, 30ff. (Kirk & Raven, 562).
98 Simplicius, *in Arist. de coelo*, p. 294, 33ff. Heiberg (Kirk & Raven, 555, 577, 581).
99 Capelle, *op. cit.*, 23, p. 134 (Diogenes Laertius, IX, 6 [Yonge]; cf. Heraclitus Fr. 10 [Diels]).
100 Simplicius, *op. cit.*, 23 15ff. (from Theophrastus). (Capelle, 4, p. 398 [From the German]).
101 *The Hibeh Papyrus* (ed. by B. P. Grenfell and A. S. Hunt) 1906, Pt. I, 16, pp. 62ff.
102 Diels, Fr. 164 (Freeman, p. 107).
103 Aristotle, *De gen. et cor.* I, 7, 323b 10ff. (Guthrie, II, p. 409). It is characteristic that, among the categories he lays down, Aristotle does not include those of cause and effect. The only two bearing in that direction are *actio* and *passio* (doing and suffering). Attention is drawn to this by Leopold Ziegler: *Überlieferung*, 1936, p. 212.
104 Alexander Aphrodisiensis, *Quaestiones*, II, 23 (Guthrie, p. 426).
105 Pliny, *Natural History*, II, 14: "Innumeros quidem credere (i.e., deos) ... aut, ut Democrito placuit, duos omnino, Poenam et Beneficium" (Diels, 55 A 76). "Beneficium" not only means "merit", but also – as here – "reward". Here language itself shows the "likeness" of the two factors linked by the principle of retribution. M. Wellmann (cited from Diels, *op. cit.*, II, p. ix) observes that "I ascribe this fragment to the Mendesian who, as a Pythagorean, knew the doctrine of retribution". That Bolos of Mendes was a Pythagorean, and as such was acquainted with the doctrine of retribution, is certainly not reason enough to presume an error on Pliny's part. The doctrine of retribution, or more properly the retribution principle as the basic norm of all ethics, was common property in Greek thought!
106 Aristotle, *Physics*, II, 4, 195b 36ff. (Oxford).
107 E.g., Diels, Fr. 83 (Freeman, p. 102).

[108] The word αἰτία, which first appears in Pindar and Aeschylus, here means "guilt". But already in Herodotus' prologue to his history it is found with the meaning of "cause". In Homer the substantive αἰτία does not occur, but we do find the adjective αἴτιος and the verb αἰτιάομαι. The former has the exclusive meaning of "guilty" here, and the latter means exclusively "to accuse" or "to charge". – The word αἰτία is etymologically connected with the Sanscrit *áinas*, which signifies "sacrilege", "sin" or "guilt". Cf. Leo Meyer, *Handbuch der Griechischen Etymologie*, 1901, vol. II, pp. 80–81.
[109] Cf. Leopold Ziegler, *op. cit.*, pp. 212f. The Latin *causa* also has the double meaning of "cause" and "guilt"; the latter, for example, in the phrase *causam alicujus rei sustinere*: to bear the blame for something. Above all, however, *causa* has the meaning of a legal case (or issue in dispute), and is thus also a juristic concept.
[110] Ernst Mach, *Die Mechanik in ihrer Entwicklung*, 3rd edn., 1897, pp. 493, 496.
[111] Philipp Frank, *Das Kausalgesetz und seine Grenzen. Schriften zur Wissenschaftlichen Weltauffassung* (ed. by P. Frank and M. Schlick). vol. 6, 1932, p. 136.
[112] Frank, *op. cit.*, pp. 137ff. On p. 139 he remarks: "The reverence in which energy is held by philosophers is doubtless largely due to its name, in which they may possibly also detect something soul-like or 'psychoid' in nature".
[113] *Ibid.*, p. 140.
[114] Cf., for example, *Philosophisches Wörterbuch*, by Heinrich Schmidt (Kröners Taschenausgabe, vol. 13), 9th edn., 1934, art. 'Energie'.
[115] For the rest, Fritz Mauthner, *Wörterbuch der Philosophie*, 1910, vol. I, p. 275, pertinently remarks; "The old scholastic principle, *causa aequat effectum*, has lost its validity. Since Carnot and Clausius we have known that when heat is transformed into work, a considerable portion of the heat is uselessly expended and not transformed into the particular effect we desired as such. If this law can be generalised, the theoretical principle of the conservation of energy remains intact, indeed, but the cause is no longer equal to the effect (the one we are interested in); it divides into two forces, of which the one produces an effect, while the other disappears to no purpose".
[116] This source for the principle of energy-equivalence in a sphere of normative thinking is also indicated by the fact that from this principle a reverse tendency in the same direction occurs. The view that the effect is equal in energy to the cause leads – according to Frank, *op. cit.*, p. 136 – "to the assumption that changes in which the energy remains unaltered require no physical causes at all. Many have hoped thereby to find a way of understanding the intervention of supernatural, spiritual factors in the world of our physical experience, and bringing them into accord with the findings of exact science. – Such an intervention is often needed, for example, in order to salvage the so-called freedom of the will.... For supporters of 'Freewill', this extra-physical factor is in fact free choice, which is, of course, a special case of an entelechy in Driesch's sense". It is solely from the standpoint of normative speculation about values that the assumption of freewill has meaning, since it is thought to be required only in order to justify the ethico-juristic responsibility of the individual.
[117] *Philosophisches Wörterbuch*, art. 'äquivalent': "The quantitative determinations of natural processes, expressed in common measures, always yield equal amounts in respect of both cause and effect".
[118] *Ibid.*, art. 'Kausalität'.
[119] *Ibid.*, art. 'Ursache'.
[120] Mauthner, *op. cit.*, vol. I, p. 96. "It would thus be a perfectly adequate usage, to include also under the notion of cause the totality of all conditions of an effect, and to describe as the immediate cause, say, only those changes whose occurrence sets off the effect; just as for centuries the totality of mental experiences has been called the soul, the totality of all things the universe, without there being a universe additional to the things, a soul additional to the

experiences, or a cause additional to the changes".

[121] Cf. Max Verworn, *Die Frage nach den Grenzen der Erkenntnis*, 1908, pp. 15f., 44: "Careful observation shows that in no case does an event come about through one single factor .... If we abandon the idea that an event is brought about by a single cause, and grant that there are two or more causes occasioning it, the concept of cause loses its meaning and becomes identical with that of a condition .... Things condition one another, and all science, if it wishes to be exact, can consist only in establishing their regular relations of interdependency. If one must have an 'ism' at all, then, it should be, not causalism, but conditionism". Cf. also Mauthner, *op. cit.*, arts. 'Bedingung' and 'Konditionismus'.

[122] Cf. Edgar Zilsel, Über die Asymmetrie der Kausalität und die Einsinnigkeit der Zeit', *Die Naturwissenschaften* **15** (1927) 280ff.

[123] Cf. Frank, *op. cit.*, p. 142.

[124] *Ibid.*

[125] Cf. Zilsel, *op. cit.*, p. 280.

[126] *Ibid.*, pp. 284f.

[127] Thus Moritz Schlick, for example, observes in his 'Die Kausalität in der gegenwärtigen Physik', *Die Naturwissenschaften* **19** (1931) 145ff.: "Where events exist at the same time, we obviously do not speak of causality".

[128] Cf. the definition of the concept of causality in *Philosophisches Wörterbuch*, art. 'Kausalität'.

[129] Eduard May, in *Die Bedeutung der modernen Physik fur die Theorie der Erkenntnis*, 1937, pp. 80ff., points out how in physical thinking both the "post hoc" and the "propter hoc" are eliminated from the concept of causality. "If physical time is reversible, so too is the physical causal nexus. A mathematical dependency-relation can be read both from right to left and from left to right; cause and effect are interchangeable". He considers that the attempts which have been made to obviate the reversibility of the mathematico-physical causal nexus must be regarded as failures.

[130] Cf. Max Planck, *Der Kausalbegriff in der Physik*, 1932, p. 13.

[131] E.g., Schlick, *op. cit.*, p. 146; Planck, *op. cit.*, p. 4: "An event is causally conditioned if it can be predicted with certainty".

[132] Schrödinger, *op. cit.*, pp. 9ff.

[133] Hans Reichenbach, 'Das Kausalproblem in der Physik', *Die Naturwissenschaften* **19** (1931) 713ff.

[134] H. Bergmann, *Der Kampf um das Kausalgesetz in der jüngsten Physik*. Sammlung Viehweg, no. 98, 1929, p. 49; M. Schlick, *Naturphilosophie*, 1925, p. 457.

[135] H. Reichenbach, 'Die Kausalstruktur der Welt', *Sitzungsberichte der Bayr. Akad., Math.-Naturw. Abt.* (1925) 138. Here we read: "Let us then imagine a world in which all dependencies are of the same kind as the turn-up of one face of a die in connection with the throw; every step in the course of events is thus a dice-game, and only the high probability of certain sequences has tempted us to see an established regularity concealed in them. On such a view we shall then in any case have arrived at a uniform assumption about the character of events, except for having let go of the causal assumption. In all its elements, such a world possesses only a probability-connection. It is the demand for a minimum of presuppositions which forces us into a renunciation of strict causality".

[136] Grete Hermann in *Die Bedeutung der modernen Physik für die Theorie der Erkenntnis*, 1937, p. 43.

[137] May, *op. cit.*, p. 124.

[138] *Ibid.*, p. 80.

[139] *Ibid.*, pp. 125–26.

[140] Reichenbach, 'Das Kausalproblem in der Physik', p. 716.

[141] May, *op. cit.*, p. 130.
[142] *Ibid.*, "Now the causal principle cannot in fact be either confirmed or refuted by experience. We must, however, hold fast to it as a postulate, if we do not wish to renounce knowledge altogether." Yet May denies the a priori character of this postulate. It is not a true axiom, since its validity is not immediately perceived; no unconditioned necessity of thought attaches to it. "Thought is aware that it is not absolutely necessarily compelled to think causality, but it knows at the same time that it abandons itself, if it does not postulate this absolute necessity of thought". Yet he admits "that one can think of an uncaused event". That is a contradiction.
[143] Cf. on this point Schrödinger, *Über Indeterminismus in der Physik*, 1932, p. 16. Planck, too, *op. cit.*, pp. 5ff., also affirms, without any reference to Heisenberg's uncertainty relation: "In no single case is it possible to predict a physical event exactly". In observing the reality given to our senses, however fine the measuring instruments we use, there remains "always a certain residue of uncertainty behind. No strict causality can be established in the world of the senses; this is an assumption that holds only for the physical picture of the world, which to some extent represents an arbitrary construction of thought." A clear distinction between the world of sense and the physical world-picture is indispensable, according to Planck.
[144] Pierre Simon de Laplace, *Essai philosophique sur les probabilités*, 4th edn. 1819, pp. 3–4; English translation, by F. W. Truscott and F. L. Emory, *A Philosophical Essay on Probabilities*, 1951, p. 4.
[145] Otto Rank, *Seelenglaube und Psychologie*, 1930, p. 182, pertinently remarks: "The teaching of Jesus, that not a sparrow falls to the ground without God's will, and Newton's discovery, that no apple could fall without a cosmic law, are products of one and the same voluntarist ideology. It was logical, therefore, that, especially in neo-Scholasticism, the causal principle should also have been employed as a basis for the cosmological proof of God's existence. The interminable dispute about it, which reflects the conflict of science and religion, was bound to have such an unfruitful outcome, since the causal principle and the principle of will are at bottom identical."

The attempt to uphold strict causality by invoking belief in God, or a divine supra-human spirit, seems not to be disclaimed even by Planck. He writes, *op. cit.*, p. 22: "... we must adhere to our initial principle that an event is causally conditioned if it can be predicted with certainty; for otherwise we should lose the only firm ground under our feet. And we should equally feel committed to the second principle, that it is impossible in any one case to predict an event exactly. From this it then follows, that in order to be able to talk of causality in nature at all, we must introduce some modification into the first principle". This modification will have to relate "to the predicting subject". In order for an event to be causally conditioned, it will not have to be predictable with certainty by an actual human mind, for that is impossible. Even a scientifically trained meteorologist, equipped with the very best instruments, cannot predict tomorrow's weather today with absolute certainty. Yet it is "natural to assume that an ideal intelligence, who perceived all physical events everywhere at the present moment, down to the last detail, would be in a position to predict tomorrow's weather in every respect with complete certainty, and the same holds for all other predictions of physical events". "The actual impossibility of predicting an event exactly, even in only one case" seems "from the standpoints of classical and quantum physics alike, to be a natural consequence of the fact that man, with his sense-organs and measuring instruments, is himself a part of the nature to whose laws he is subject, and from which he can never escape; whereas no such limitations are imposed on the ideal intelligence". As to the nature of this Planckean intelligence – who is merely that of Laplace – there can really be no doubt, when Planck insists "We must beware of attempting to make the ideal intelligence an object of scientific criticism". For it is an intelligence beyond the reach of human comprehension. The objection that the idea of such an intelligence is "vacuous and unnecessary" is met by Planck with the claim "that not all propositions devoid of logical foundation are scientifically worthless", and that such "short-sighted formalism" blocks up those very sources "at which men like Galileo, Kepler and Newton, and many other great physicists, have nourished their urge to scientific research. For all these men, the devotion to science was, consciously or otherwise, a matter of faith, of imperturbable faith in a rational world-order." A "rational" world-order is above all a *just* world-order, and can only be the work of a suprahuman being endowed with reason and will. "Faith" in it is faith in God. Here it emerges with perfect clarity, how intimate the connection is between the idea of strict, absolute causality and that of the absolute reason and will of a deity. An inviolable world-law is conceivable only as the expression of such a divine reason and will. Planck, however, concludes his observations with the claim: "The causal law is ... a heuristic principle, a sign-post ...", which is difficult to reconcile with imperturbable faith in a rational world-order as the necessary presupposition for strict causality. For the rest, the Laplace-Planck fiction of an "ideal intelligence" will not serve to vindicate the notion of strict causal determinacy, in the sense of an assured predictability of events. For to an "ideal" intelligence, untrammelled by the bounds of human knowledge, there can be no past, present or future, since the intuitive form of time is an inherent feature only of the humanly-limited mind, and indeed is one of its specific limitations. Theology is right in assuming that God stands outside time.

146 Theodor Vogel, in *Die Bedeuting der modernen Physik für die Theorie der Erkenntnis*, 1937, p. 177: "*In practice*, laws have the task of making prophetic utterances possible, and thus of predicting particular states of affairs. *Ideally* they have the task of presenting the structure of the given reality in the most general, but also the simplest manner" (H. K.'s italics).

147 Hermann, *op. cit.*, pp. 12ff.; May, *op. cit.*, p. 145.

148 T. H. Huxley, *Science Primers. Introductory.* (ed. by T. H. Huxley, H. E. Roscoe and Balfour Stewart), pp. 13ff., starts out from the undoubtedly correct assertion that natural laws are not the causes of the fact that things behave as the laws say they do, are not the "causes of the order of nature", but are rather the mere expression or presentation of "as much as we have made out of that order" in experience. But he goes wrong in maintaining that natural laws are in this respect similar to juridical laws, since these too are not causes of the fact that men are law-abiding, and thus pay their taxes and refrain from murder and theft, being nothing else but a statement of what will happen if someone fails to pay his taxes, or commits murder or theft. This is already wrong, if only because the juridical law connecting some circumstance with a punishment or other act of coercion, so far as it enters a man's consciousness and thus becomes a motive of his action, can actually be the cause of his law-abiding behaviour, and is also so intended by the legislator. It is only to motivate the men whose behaviour is regulated by laws, only to induce law-abiding behaviour causally, as an element in their thoughts, that juridical laws are "enacted", i.e., posited as acts of will; and are indeed employed just like any other means – as causes to achieve an intended effect, i.e., to attain a specific end. No such thing can be said of natural laws, for these are not acts of will, but of knowledge. Hence it is completely irrelevant when Huxley says: "A law of man tells us what we may expect society will do under certain circumstances; and a law of nature tells us what we may expect natural objects will do under certain circumstances. Each contains information addressed to our intelligence". The juridical law is not, like the natural law, a piece of information, addressed to our intelligence, about a future event, but a demand addressed to our will; and this indeed according to whether it is taken in its primary or secondary form: as addressed to the will of the organs which have to institute the act of

coercion (punishment or distraint) laid down in the statute, or to that of the subject who has to display the behaviour which avoids this coercive act. Huxley's error consists in failing to recognise that the juridical law – unlike the law of nature – is not a statement about reality, and therefore cannot be true or false, but only beneficial or harmful, in accordance with or contrary to an end. But his mistake is explicable in that the logico-linguistic form of the juridical law is the same as that of the natural law, namely a conditional proposition, and especially in that the juridical law does indeed relate, like the prophetically intended natural law, to a future event. It does so, however, in an entirely different sense, for it does not state what will happen, but what should happen – or, if we want to leave the problematic concept of "should" out of account – what the legislators, i.e., those having power within the social community, desire to happen.

[149] This has been stressed against Huxley by William A. Robson: *Civilisation and the Growth of Law*, 1935, pp. 338ff. He says: "Juridical laws ... presuppose a voluntary element in the activities to which they relate and are to some extent designed for the express purpose of producing in the real world relations which would not otherwise exist". If – as Robson here admits – the juridical law is an expression of will, it is then a "command" and aims at "obedience", regardless of whether it is formulated as a norm decreeing the behaviour of the subject which the legislator intends, or that of the communal organs who have to react with sanctions to contrary behaviour on the part of the subject. Robson's polemic (p. 336f.) against the view that juridical law is a "command", and the subject's relation to it that of "obedience", stands in direct contradiction to his insight into the voluntary character of juridical law. For the rest, Huxley, whose reference to the similarity of juridical and natural laws is cited by Robson in passing, expressly says that juridical laws are "commands", while "natural laws, on the contrary, are not commands but assertions".

Robson rejects my account of the contrast between natural laws and norms on the ground that: "men of science no longer claim for natural laws the inexorable and objective validity they were formerly deemed to possess"; but the reply to that is that I did not base my distinction between the two kinds of laws on the fact that the first are inexorably valid, while the second admit of exceptions, but rather on the fact that the first are statements about what is, while the second are decrees about what ought to be. (Cf. my *Hauptprobleme der Staatsrechtslehre*, 1911, p. 27). In what it says, the norm is no less inviolable than the law of nature, regarded as an absolute rule. The so-called "breaches" of the norm are not exceptions to its validity; they are exceptions to the rule asserting the efficacy of the idea of this norm, and hence to a factual rule. My account in the text shows that the inviolability of natural law, in the shape of the causal law, is derived from the field of normative thinking; it can indeed be definitely stated, that only the norm can advance a claim to inviolable validity, since it is not a statement about reality.

[150] Else Wentscher, *Geschichte des Kausalitätsproblems*, 1921, pp. 6ff., 15, 23.

[151] Nicholas Malebranche, *De la recherche de la vérité*, new edn., by M. F. Bouillier, Paris 1897, vol. 1, p. 319.

[152] Wentscher, *op. cit.*, pp. 32f.

[153] *Ibid.*, pp. 41f., 68.

[154] *Ibid.*, pp. 76f.

[155] *Ibid.*, pp. 80ff.

[156] *Ibid.*, pp. 111f.

[157] David Hume, *An Enquiry concerning Human Understanding* (ed. by L. A. Selby-Bigge), Oxford 1894, Sect. V, pp. 40ff.

[158] *Ibid.*, p. 46.

[159] Frank, *op. cit.*, p. 287, conceives a "conflict" to exist "between the fact that in practical life we always rely on the causal law and even found the security of our life upon it, whereas

on the other hand we are not able so to formulate this law that anything certain can be inferred from it concerning our experience". However, he says later, on p. 288, that we do not depend in practical life on the causal law, "but on special laws having the form of the causal law." In "practice", i.e., in naive, pre-scientific theory, we presuppose no more than a certain regularity in events. But this assumption sometime leaves us in the lurch, and our "confidence" is in a sense deluded. It is in fact so-called "practice" which shows us that the regularity we rely upon is not without exceptions. On this point there is no conflict between theory and practice.

CHAPTER IX

ON THE CONCEPT OF NORM*

The word "norm" comes from the Latin *norma*, and has acquired in German the character of a loan-word, designating – primarily if not exclusively – an order, prescription or command. But commanding is not the only function of a norm. Authorising, permitting and derogating are also functions of norms. We refer to norms of morality or law as prescriptions for the mutual behaviour of men, and are thereby concerned to bring out that what we call "morality" or "law" consists of norms, is an aggregate or system of norms. We also speak of "norms" of logic as prescriptions for thinking; but the assumption that such logical principles as the law of non-contradiction or the rules of inference have the character of norms, that logic as a science deals with norms just as ethics or legal science do, is open to dispute. In German, too, there is no name distinct from the word "logic", as the name of a science, for the norms which comprise the subject-matter of the science describing these norms, as the name "morality" exists for the norms comprising the subject-matter of ethics, and the name "law" for the norms comprising the subject-matter of legal science. If we assume that there are norms of thinking, norms of logic, just as there are norms of morality or law, we are using "logic" to designate both a science and also its subject-matter; or else – as is commonly the case – we are assuming that it is the science of logic itself which does not describe the norms of thought – as ethics does moral norms, or legal science legal norms – but posits them, and thus makes prescriptions and ordains a particular kind of thinking; which is hard to reconcile with the essential nature of a science, as the knowledge of its given subject-matter. But there is also a tendency to identify the science of ethics with *its* subject-matter, morality, and legal science with its, namely law, and to speak of both as "normative" sciences, meaning sciences which posit norms or make prescriptions, and do not merely describe norms, as a subject-matter presented to them.

Insofar as the word "norm" figures in the adjective "normal", it is not in fact an 'ought' that is meant there, but an 'is'. A thing is "normal" if it is what actually happens as a rule. So far as any 'ought' is also meant there, we are presupposing the validity of the norm that what tends to happen as a rule is also what ought to happen, and in particular that a man ought so to behave as men do behave as a rule. It is significant in this connection that the words *Pflicht* (duty) and *pflegen* (to be accustomed) are related. To believe that, because a thing regularly happens in fact, it also ought to happen, is a fallacy. An 'ought' cannot logically be derived from an 'is'. Only a validly operative norm can decree that what tends to happen as a rule, also ought to happen. The assumption that those things ought to happen which regularly do happen, is particularly congenial to men of a religious turn of mind. Since everything which happens occurs according to the will of God, that which regularly happens must be regarded as willed by God, and hence as what ought to occur, and thus as "good"; so that if something happens which is not judged good, such as a bad harvest or a crime, this will certainly have to be accepted, in consistency, as also willed by God, but is interpreted as an exception to the rule, or to what is "normal". In many cases, however, the assumption that what regularly happens also ought to happen, does not work out. A positive morality can forbid some piece of behaviour, although it regularly occurs; and a positive legal order can rule out the application of a customary law, whose validity rests on the assumption under discussion. It has to be admitted, however, that a norm loses its validity, i.e., that what the norm prescribes no longer ranks as obligatory, if the norm is in fact no longer followed, or, if not followed, is not actually applied. That is the problem of the relation between a norm's obligatoriness and its efficacy in fact.

Insofar as the word "norm" designates a prescription or command, it means that something ought to be or to happen. The verbal expression of it is an ought-statement. The act whereby something is commanded or prescribed is an act of will. That which is commanded or prescribed is, in the first instance, a particular piece of human behaviour. Anyone who commands or prescribes something *wills* that something should happen. Obligation, the norm, is the meaning of an act of will,[1] i.e., an act directed to the behaviour of another, an act whose meaning is that the other (or others) should behave in a certain way. 'Thou shalt' is the meaning of an 'I will'.[2] The act of will, whose meaning is the norm, is the act of which we say figuratively that the norm is "created" by it; it is the act whereby the norm is posited, the norm-positing act. In order to exist, i.e., to be valid, the norm must be posited by an act of will, or – as the principle is often formulated – no imperative without an *imperator*, no command without a commander.[3] A norm posited by an act of will occurring in the real world is a *positive* norm. From the standpoint of a moral or legal positivism, account is taken only of positive norms, i.e., those posited by real acts of will, and, so far as only men can have a will, of norms posited only by actual human acts of will.

Norms posited by human acts of will possess – in the true meaning of the word – an arbitrary character. Any behaviour we please, that is, can be decreed in them to be obligatory. The assumption that there must be norms which do not spring from "arbitrary choice" leads to the concept of norms which are not the meaning of human acts of will; of norms in no way the meaning of any kind of "acts" or thoughts, or, if they *are* the meaning of acts of will, the meaning not of human but of suprahuman volitions, in particular those of God.

Moral or legal norms, it is claimed, do not have to be posited by acts of any kind in order to be valid; for there are norms valid immediately, or immediately making themselves so, because they are given in reality or "nature", and thus *immanent* in nature. Hence their validity is no more "arbitrary" than that of the causal laws of nature. It is conditioned neither by the will of the subjects whose behaviour is regulated thereby, nor by that of any subject who posits them. Their validity is in this sense no less objective than that of the law that metals expand on heating.

The nature to which these norms are immanent is either nature in general, i.e., the totality of the real, or a special nature, the nature of man. That is the assumption of *natural law theory*, so-called, which stands contrasted to moral and legal positivism.[4] This natural law theory rests, consciously or otherwise, on a metaphysico-theological foundation.[5] Nature is a complex of actual facts and factual processes; and a knowledge directed to this subject-matter can only state that something is, and not that it ought to be. Even if it can be established that under certain conditions certain consequences always or usually occur in fact, and in particular that under certain conditions certain organisms behave in the same way, it cannot be maintained that under certain conditions the observed consequences ought or ought not to occur, that under certain conditions certain organisms ought or ought not to behave as they actually do behave, or at any rate are usually accustomed to behave. From the fact that something is, it does not and cannot follow that something ought or ought not to be. The inference from 'is' to 'ought' is a logical fallacy.

In order to be able to see nature as a source of norms, it has to be assumed that there is a will immanent in nature, directed to a particular sort of behaviour in things, and especially in organisms.[6] Since the norms of natural law decree a particular sort of human behaviour to be obligatory, they must be the meaning of a will directed to human behaviour. This cannot be the will of men. For the latter stands as a motivating force behind all their actions, good and bad alike, and also behind those that are morally indifferent. It can only be a will of nature, the will, directed solely to the "good", of a nature thought of as endowed with will and reason, or what Aristotle calls *entelechy*, i.e., the movement, immanent in nature, towards the good. It can easily be shown that this good will in nature is the will of the good God in the nature He has created, or – as in Aristotle – the movement proceeding from the unmoved mover out towards the good. But the assumption that the movement proceeding from the unmoved mover is in fact directed to the "good", i.e., to something that ought to be, remains wholly unfounded, unless it is also assumed that it is directed to the good, i.e., to what ought to be, because it stems from the unmoved mover, who gives the movement this direction; and that therefore the 'ought' must also proceed from this author of the movement; even though Aristotle cannot admit this, if only because he would thereby have had to concede the origin of his unmoved mover in the Platonic Idea of the Good, which he rejects. This is the metaphysico-theological presupposition, without which a theory of natural law is impossible, and by which this theory stands or falls. The ultimate source of natural law is the will of God. Its norms are the meaning of His acts of will, or – insofar as we think of God as inactive, or like Aristotle, as unmoved – they are immanent to His nature. If this divine nature is construed as reason, i.e., as thought, the norms of natural law are the meaning of His acts of thought, or are contained in His thought. But then they must simultaneously be the meaning of His acts of will, or contained in His will. That is possible insofar as, in God, thinking and willing coincide. In that He knows what is good and bad, He wills that the good ought to be and that the bad ought not to be, as is already made explicit in the myth of the Tree of Knowledge.[7]

If the "nature" to which the norms of natural law are immanent is the nature of man, and if the nature of man is seen – in contrast to the nature of animals – in human reason, natural law makes its appearance as a *law of reason*. Since reason is the capacity for thought and knowledge, the norms of this law of reason figure as the meaning of acts of thought – they are not willed norms, but *thought* norms. Now there are indeed norms merely thought – in contrast to positive norms posited by real acts of will. But these merely thought norms are not the meaning of acts of thought, but of acts of will which do not have a place in reality, but are thought or imagined, as one can think or imagine anything possible which is not existent in the real. I can think to myself a norm which has not been actually posited by any authority and is not the meaning of any real act of will occurring in the world. But I can think of such a norm only as the meaning of an act of will that I *think along with it*. I can think of a norm *as if* it were posited by an authority, although it has not actually been posited, and there is actually no act of will whose meaning it is. The principle of "no norm without a norm-positing authority" remains standing, even though the authoritative act of will which has the merely thought norm as its meaning is a fictitious one. A merely thought norm is the meaning of a fictitious act of will, in contrast to a positive norm, which is the meaning of a real act of will. To put it quite generally: no 'thou shalt' without an 'I will' – even if it be merely a fictitious one.[8]

Since human reason is a capacity for knowledge or thought, the norms of the so-called law of reason cannot be posited by reason. By means of reason one can recognise the norms posited by an authority through acts of will, one can engender concepts, but not norms.[9] Reason as the moral law-giver is the central concept of Kant's ethics. But this reason, according to Kant, is *practical reason*, and this – like the divine reason – is at the same time both thinking and willing, and is, if we look closer, the divine reason in man, the reason of God in which man has a share, having been created by God in His own image. The attempt undertaken in the theory of the law of reason, to construe the norm as the meaning of an act of thought rather than an act of will, is also based on meta-physico-theological speculations, and stands or falls by them.[10]

The norm can have either an individual or a general character. It has an individual character when what is obligated is a particular piece of individually defined behaviour on the part of a particular individually defined man; for example, the judge's sentence that the thief Smith is to be committed to prison for one year, or the father's order to his son Tom: "Shut this window." A norm has a general character if a generally defined piece of behaviour is posited as obligatory upon a specifically qualified class of persons, as in the norm, for example, that all thieves are to be punished by the competent judges with imprisonment. But even a norm imposing obligations on the behaviour of *one* particular person can have a general character, if what is obligated is not merely a particular piece of individually defined behaviour but some generally defined course of behaviour, as in the father's order to his son Tom: "You are to go to church every Sunday", or the command addressed by a competent authority to an individually defined subject: "You, John, are not to lie". If a command is addressed to a number of individually defined subjects, and only one individually defined piece of behaviour is commanded, as when a father orders his three sons, Tom, Dick and Harry, to congratulate their teacher, Mr. Jones, on his 50th birthday, there are as many individual norms as there are addressees. That which is obligated in a norm, or commanded in an imperative, is a particular course of behaviour. This can be a particular piece of individually defined behaviour on the part of one or many individually defined persons, but it can also be an initially undetermined number of acts or omissions on the part of a particular category of persons. That is the essential difference. If a norm is addressed to a category of persons, they are thereby obligated to an initially undetermined number of human acts or omissions. Indeed, the "addressing" of a norm to a person means nothing more than that the *behaviour* of a person, a piece of human behaviour, is obligated. It is not the person as such, in the totality of his existence and behaviour, that the norm relates to, but rather a particular piece of human behaviour. The norm is "addressed to a person", in that it posits as obligatory some piece of behaviour on the part of *one* person, or a determinate or indeterminate number of persons. To be the "addressee" of a norm is only a way of saying that the behaviour decreed in the norm to be obligatory is human behaviour, the behaviour of a person.[11]

If the norm has a general character, it is a normative *rule*.[12] To speak of a "norm" in this case only, i.e., to regard generality as essential to the concept of a norm, is unwarranted.[13] For the essential feature of a norm is that behaviour of some sort is decreed as obligatory. This can be done either in a general way, or in an individual way. In the case of an individual norm we commonly speak of an "order". The view that it is of the essence of a norm to be general is connected with the fact that – as already observed – the word "norm" also figures in common usage as a term for factual regularity, and in this usage does actually have a general character. If a happening is described as "normal", then by this – as already noted – it is for the most part not intended to say that it is as it ought to be, that it conforms to a normative rule, but rather that something is happening which actually does tend to happen as a rule.

The rule of fact may have the character of a causal law, whereby under certain conditions some particular thing must occur. The "must" expresses causal necessity. If it is assumed that the "ought" also expresses necessity, the causal necessity must be kept clearly distinct from the normative necessity. But since in ordinary usage the word "norm" can be used to mean not only a rule of obligation, but also a rule of fact, the two kinds of necessity are often not clearly distinguished, and the words "ought" and "must" are employed synonymously, which is highly misleading.

NOTES

* From *Festschrift für C. Nipperdey*, vol. I, Munich-Berlin 1965, pp. 57–70. This essay forms the first chapter of a larger study, "The General Theory of Norms", which the author hopes he will be able to complete in due course (Author's note).

1 The necessity of distinguishing between an act and the meaning of an act has been shown by Heinrich Rickert: 'Vom Begriff der Philosophie', *Logos* 1 (1910) 19 ff. In so doing, however, he does not set out from the act whose meaning is a norm, the normpositing act, but rather from the act in which an object is valued.

2 Cf. Rudolf Eisler: *Der Zweck, seine Bedeutung für Natur und Geist*, Berlin, 1914, p. 77: "... but the 'ought' originally always leads back to a will; the obligatory always appears as a positing by a will, and is ultimately justified only by pointing out the possible goal of a will, which is what first makes the demand a truly warranted, rational and legitimate one."

3 Cf. Walter Dubislav: 'Zur Unbegründbarkeit der Forderungssätze', in *Theoria* **3** (1937) 335, where he speaks of the "absurdity of an imperative without an *imperator*".

4 Karl Georg Wurzel, in *Das juristische Denken*, Vienna 1904, maintains it to be certain (p. 32), that in reality "(at least to a high degree) the rules of law are no less immanent to the facts they relate to than the laws of motion are to bodies, say, and are not a check imposed on them from without." He therefore says on p. 31: "Legal norms are to a certain extent natural laws of social development". That is the theory of natural law. But Wurzel rejects the natural law theory. It has failed because it "could not stand up to the test of reality; reality showed it to be fallacious, in that it did not continue to coincide with the findings of *this* juristic thinking". But there are very different theories of natural law. One can reject one of them, while embracing another.

[5] *Cf. supra*, Ch. VI, pp. 114ff.

[6] The specifically natural law assumption – conscious or otherwise – that particular norms of human behaviour are immanent to particular actual situations, governs the customary usage whereby a particular situation is said to "demand" a particular form of behaviour, or to give rise to particular duties, or to be the ground thereof. This usage is misleading. For it is not the actual situation which demands any particular behaviour or is the ground of obligation to it. The situation is merely the condition under which a norm, presupposed as valid, posits a particular piece of behaviour as obligatory or required. If we allow ourselves to be guided by linguistic usage, we arrive at the view that ethics – like science – has no other basis beyond a knowledge of facts. For an example of this, see E. F. Carritt, *Ethical and Political Thinking*, Oxford 1950, who says on p. 6: "...moral philosophy...like other sciences... has no other basis than our apprehension of the facts...." In the chapter entitled 'The Ground of Obligation' he goes on (p. 14): "The general question is whether our obligations, and consequently our duties (meaning by 'duty', 'the strongest present obligation', p. 3) depend upon our actual situation, including our capacities for affecting it and the consequences of what we may immediately bring about, or upon our beliefs about that situation, or about our moral estimate of what the supposed situation demands". On p. 77 Carritt claims "that obligations and duties arise out of some actual or believed situation, that on the objective view they arise from the actual, on the subjective from the believed situation, and on the putative from the belief about what is morally *required* by the believed situation" (my italics). Without referring at all to the validity of norms, Carritt proceeds from the assumption that a particular situation "demands" a particular duty, that a particular duty is "required" by a particular situation. But the fact that it is "morally" required is possible only if a moral norm constitutes this duty. This moral norm is not immanent to the situation. But Carritt speaks on p. 21 of "the situation and its *moral implications*" (my italics). That is a specifically natural law view of the problems of ethics.

[7] *Genesis*, 3.

[8] Edmund Husserl, in *Logical Investigations*, 2nd edn., Transl. by J. N. Findlay, London & New York 1970, p. 82, thinks it possible to establish a meaning of "shall" or "should" having no relation to willing. He says: "The original sense of 'shall' or 'should', which relates to a certain wish or will, a certain demand or command, is plainly too narrow, e.g., You shall listen to me, X shall come to me. As we speak in a wider sense of a demand, where there is no one who demands, and perhaps no one on whom demand is made, so we frequently speak of a 'shall' or a 'should' which is independent of anyone's wishing or willing. If we say 'A soldier should be brave', this does not mean that we or anyone else are wishing or willing, commanding or requiring this.... 'A soldier should be brave' rather means that only a brave soldier is a 'good' soldier...." That is a value-judgement, and indeed – as emerges from what follows – an *objective* value-judgement, which holds good not only for the subject making this value-judgement, but for everyone. For Husserl says: "*Since* this value-judgement holds, everyone is entitled to demand of a soldier that he should be brave...." Here Husserl is referring to anyone who really demands; and the value-judgement holds – as an objective value-judgement – only if there is a valid norm prescribing that a soldier should be brave, and as a subjective value-judgement only if he who makes the judgement wills that a soldier should be brave, and hence – according to Husserl – it is not everyone, but only this subject, who can demand that a soldier should be brave. If 'shall' or 'should' can have a sense – or more accurately, be a sense – without having relation to a will, if one can speak of a demand "where there is no one who demands", then one can also speak of a norm where there is no act of will whose sense this norm is. Now we can certainly speak of a demand where there is no one there in reality who demands. But we

then speak of a demand *as if* someone were there who demands, a purely imagined or fictitious demander. The example that Husserl offers, of a 'should' having no relation to a willing, proves the very opposite of what he maintains. It is the should-statement, "A soldier should be brave", which according to Husserl is "identical or at least equivalent" to a value-judgement, namely that "A brave soldier is a good soldier". That a brave soldier is a "good" soldier, or more accurately, that the brave conduct of a soldier is "good" conduct, means, however, if this value-judgement is an objective one, that the brave conduct of a soldier is such as it should be, and that means nothing else but that it is such as to be prescribed as obligatory in a norm presupposed to be valid, that it corresponds to this 'should'-norm. But in order to be valid, this norm must actually be posited by some authority, must be the meaning of a real act of will, or be supposed to be posited by an imaginary authority in a merely fancied or fictitious act of will. Only on such a presupposition is the value-judgement possible, for it merely establishes the relation of certain conduct to a norm. Even if it be merely fictitious, the norm is presupposed by the value-judgement, and not *vice versa*, as Husserl assumes.

The statement "A soldier should be brave" is – so Husserl says on p. 83 – a judgement, and indeed a judgement "of normative form". If it is a judgement, it must be true or false. But when is the judgement "A soldier should be brave" true? It is true only if there is a valid norm, posited by a moral or legal authority, or engendered by way of custom, which prescribes that soldiers should be brave. The judgement "A soldier should be cowardly" is obviously false, because there is no valid norm prescribing this. But a norm is valid only as the meaning of an act of will. If we say, "A soldier should be brave", we make a true statement only if we thereby make a statement about a valid norm, i.e., about the meaning of an act of will.

The word "should" can be used not only in a *pre*scriptive sense, but also in a *de*scriptive one, i.e., not as the immediate expression of an act of will directed to the behaviour of another, but as the expression of an act of thought. But this can be so only insofar as some ethic or legal science thereby maintains the validity of a norm, constituting the meaning of an act of will, and posited by the moral or legal authority. In customary usage the word "should" is employed not only in a *norm*, prescribing or ordering some particular behaviour, and in a *statement* describing the validity of such a norm, but also as the expression of a mere recommendation, e.g., in "You should be more careful in crossing the road". Or as the expression of a hope or wish: "It should rain eventually". "Wishing" differs from "willing", in that wishing can be directed to something other than human behaviour. I can only "will" that of which I assume that it can be causally occasioned by the expression of my willing; and this can only be the behaviour of a being who understands the expression of my willing. The assumption that God created the world through the expression of His will, i.e., the belief in *divine omnipotence*: "And God said, Let there be light: and there was light", has a religious and metaphysical character, and does not come into consideration for a scientific ethics or theory of law. The word "should" can also be used, however, in the sense of "allegedly" or "supposedly": "Jones should be a rich man, by all accounts". And sometimes it signifies a "willing", as when one says: "If a metallic body should be [i.e., is to be] expanded, it must be heated", meaning thereby that "If one wills that a metallic body should be expanded . . ."

[9] The norm is not a concept. But a concept is sometimes credited with a normative function, or represented as a norm. This is a characteristic feature of Ideas in Platonist metaphysics. Cf. *Reine Rechtslehre* 2nd edn., pp. 17 f, 51, 363, 398. If the concept is a norm, then the norm – *qua* concept – is a function of thinking, not willing. The metaphysico-theological basis of this view comes out very clearly in a philosophical disciple of Kant, Ernst Reinhold

(1793–1856), to whom Peter Freund has drawn attention in a very valuable Berlin Inaugural Dissertation: *Die Entwicklung des Normbegriffs von Kant bis Windelband*, Berlin 1933. In his *Theorie des menschlichen Erkenntnisvermögens*, Gotha 1832, p. 98 (cited by Freund, *op. cit.*, p. 64), Reinhold says that concepts are "in part the necessary *norms of order* for our thinking, whereby we divide up the manifold material of thought into disciplines and seize hold of what is peculiar to each discipline in a single idea, and in part the necessary *norms of formation*, by whose guidance we must in many cases project for ourselves the ideas of individual objects. More especially, in these norms of formation, do we hold up to ourselves the general rules and *patterns* whereby our active powers in every field of human creative achievement and human willing as such are directed to a purposive efficacy, and whereby everything individual is shaped, which we are in any way able to bring about by dint of our will and capacity." That is pure Platonism. In Reinhold's *System der Metaphysik*, Jena 1842, p. 91, Freund finds, among other things (p. 69) the notion that concepts must be viewed in the likeness of *archetypes*, whereby God, the Absolute, creates individual structures. The ends willed by God are realised by means of them. Concepts also represent the norms of our *activity*, in that we ought to be guided by them. Of the norms represented by the concepts, Reinhold says (*Metaphysik*, p. 324) that "the infinite spirit directs the work of nature by no other or higher laws than that of the purpose he ascribes to the norms contained in his thought." The concepts contained in God's thinking are norms. Norms are functions of the divine thinking, which in any case is also at the same time a willing.

[10] As the meaning of an act of will, the norm has an ideal, rather than a real, existence. This does not mean, however, that norms are thoughts, i.e., thought-contents, like statements are, and that the principles of logic are therefore applicable to them. Julius Moor, in 'Das Logische im Recht', *Internationale Zeitschrift für Theorie des Rechts*, **2** (1927–28) 158 f., says "Law is on the one hand the great system of purely ideally existent norms and rules, but on the other, the great system of human actions associated with these norms." "If we consider the role of logic in the law, we" must "take account only of the first component, the norm-system of law.... If we wish to enquire how far logic holds good within the law, we must therefore attend only to the fact that law, as 'norma agendi', is a system of prescriptions, rules or norms existing purely in thought. This means that every legal system is a system of thoughts. Whence it becomes evident that logic plays an extraordinary part. For if the legal system is a system of thoughts, every legal norm has logical content." Norms do indeed "exist, purely ideally", or more accurately, have ideal existence, for they are merely meanings; but they are not the meanings of acts of thought, nor are they thoughts, therefore, but are rather the meanings of acts of will.

Norms, as the meanings of acts of will, can be the subject-matter of our thinking or knowledge, the subject-matter of such sciences as ethics or legal science. Norms as meanings can be made an object of knowledge, without thereby bringing into consideration the acts of will whose meanings they are. Ernst Mally, in *Die Grundgesetze des Sollens. Elemente der Logik des Willens*, Graz 1926, p. 11, remarks that there are cases of obligation "where we should be somewhat perplexed to state the subject or subjects of the willing involved. A more decisive factor, however, is that in these very cases, which include the most important, namely those of ethical obligation, the ordinary person just does not miss such a subject, since he simply does not think of a willing or a willer at all". That is correct. But all it says is that one can make the obligation or norm, *qua* meaning, into an object of one's knowledge, and make statements about it, while yet abstracting from the willing whose meaning is the obligation. That does not mean, however, that this obligation is not the meaning of a willing, or that there could be a 'thou shalt' without an 'I will' whose meaning it is. If statements that are not norms are should-statements, this 'should' has a descriptive rather than a prescriptive meaning. Mally doubtless has this in mind when he says on p. 12: "For 'A should be' one can always put 'there is (or exists) an *A* that should be', for the one plainly does not hold without the other; and thus the demand has again been replaced by what might be called an ordinary theoretical state-of-affairs, something that, whether in judging or merely assuming, can be *thought*, without willing anything at all." The judgement to which Mally refers can only be a statement about the validity of a norm, not the validity or presence of a norm itself, which is the object of cognition in ethics or legal science.

[11] Manfred Moritz, in 'Der praktische Syllogismus und das juristische Denken', *Theoria* **20** (1954) 88, describes as "general imperatives" those addressed to a number of persons not mentioned by name. But even an imperative directed to a named, i.e., individually defined person can have a general character, if the behaviour ordered is not individually but generally defined, so that the order is to be obeyed by its individually defined addressee in a number of cases not limited in advance.

[12] "Regel" means "rule" in English, and "Rechtsregel", "rule of law." But in English this term does not stand only for a general norm of positive law. It is also used for certain politico-legal postulates. Thus Norman S. Marsh, in an article, 'The Rule of Law as a Supra-National Concept', in *Oxford Essays in Jurisprudence* (ed. by A. G. Guest), Oxford Univ. Press, 1961, p. 223, says that: "More recently there has been a revival of interest in the Rule of Law, although less as a peculiar feature of English constitutional law than as the common basis of legal ideals and practice which unites or might unite what Article 38 (1) (c) of the Statute of the International Court of Justice calls 'civilised nations'; the Rule of Law in this latest reincarnation has in fact much in common with 'the general principles of law recognised by civilised nations' which *inter alia* Article 38 directs the Court to apply". Such ideals or postulates include in the first place the demand that the acts of courts, especially of criminal courts, should be executed in pursuance of laws, i.e., of general norms posited by a specific organ (*nulla poena sine lege*); that this demand for legality should also hold – with certain exceptions – for administrative acts; that the courts should be independent, that certain freedoms protected by law should be reserved to individuals, that the latter should all be "equal before the law", and at times also that the legality of administrative acts should be subject to judicial review. By and large, the usage of the formula "Rule of Law" – so far as this does not mean a general norm of positive law – amounts to an ideal of natural law. A normative order of coercion should rank as "law", only if it accords with the postulates described as the "Rule of Law". Here it is a question of something very similar to what is involved in the concept of the "legal state".

The typically politico-legal character of the "Rule of Law" formula comes out in Ilmar Tammelo's essay, 'The Rule of Law and the Rule of Reason in International Legal Relations', *Logique et Analyse*, New Series, **6** (December 1963), Louvain and Paris 1963, pp. 335–368. The problem of this article is: "Is there a rule of law between nations?" and "Ought there to be a rule of law between nations?" (p. 336). Such a posing of the problem is possible only if "rule of law" is not taken to mean positive law. For there is no question but that a positive law of nations exists in the relationship between different countries. On p. 338, Tammelo says that the formula "rule of law" involves "the invocation of ideas such as 'freedom', 'legality' and 'human dignity'", and on p. 354, "equality". "Freedom", "human dignity" and "equality" are values which can be very differently interpreted, and which can be, but by no means have to be, realised in a positive legal order. On p. 350, Tammelo says of the "rule of law" formula: "In certain contexts this phrase means the same as is denoted by 'legal norm'. This meaning would be, however, obviously inappropriate in the context of our present concern". He therefore proposes to replace the phrase "rule of law" by that of "rule of reason". On p. 363 he says: "It stands to reason that it is our duty to obey the law, even in case of *dura lex*. The moral duty to obey the law can be challenged only in the name of its patent and outrageous absurdity and incompatibility with what we cannot help regarding as indispensable and overriding requirements of common good". The concept of "common good" involves an exceedingly subjective judgement of value. What is viewed as the "common good" from a socialist's standpoint will be judged as the exact opposite from that of a capitalist. Tammelo obviously presupposes that "reason" furnishes the answer as to what the "common good" is, a typical illusion of natural law when it is characterised as a law of reason. Although he has to admit on p. 358 "that the word 'reason' is ambiguous and indeterminate", he still (pp. 362–63) proclaims "reasonableness as a constitutive element of international law". This means that if a positive norm engendered by custom or treaty between states is not "reasonable" in the eyes of the subject who has to obey or apply this norm, it is not to be regarded as binding by this subject. On pp. 365–66 we read: "These are the points at which fundamental justification flows into or overrides legal justification. There are instances in which what can still be shown to be valid as the law can be shown not to be valid by reference to considerations that must be regarded as higher than legality". The reference under consideration here is that towards "reason", i.e., towards what the individual subject to the law considers to be "reasonable". That is the theory, opposed to legal positivism, of natural or rational law, which, if actually applied, is bound to lead to total anarchy.

[13] A typical representative of the view that a norm must necessarily have a general character is Mieczylaw Wallis-Walfisz, in his 'Les énoncés des appréciations et des normes', *Studia Philosophica*, **2** (Leopoli 1937), 434. He says: "Norms and their enunciations, the normative phrases, always have a general character, in contrast to orders, which have an immediate character, and whose validity expires as soon as they are executed. The advice 'Take your umbrella' is not a normative phrase, whereas the Chinese proverb 'Always carry your umbrella, even if the weather is fine' is one. The statement 'Peter should go for a walk' does not constitute a normative phrase, but it is one if we say 'Peter should go for a walk every day'". If – as appears from the above – the reason why norms must have a general character is that an individual order loses its validity if it is carried out, we may reply to this that even a general norm loses its validity if it actually is carried out in all cases in which it could be obeyed, and thus the condition under which it is valid can no longer come about. If Peter dies, and the general norm "Peter should go for a walk every day" can no longer be obeyed in any way, it ceases to be valid just as the individual order "Peter should go for a walk" does, when it is actually carried out.

CHAPTER X

LAW AND LOGIC*

It is a widely-held view among jurists that there is a particularly close relation between law and logic (in the traditional, two-valued, true-or-false sense) – that it is a specific property of law to be "logical"; which is to say, that in their mutual relations the norms of law correspond to the principles of logic. This presupposes that these principles – notably the law of non-contradiction and the rule of inference – are applicable to norms in general and to legal norms in particular.

This is assumed by jurists to be self-evident.[1] A *conflict of norms*, i.e., a situation in which two norms are valid, of which one prescribes a certain course of conduct, and the other a course incompatible with this, is regarded as a *logical contradiction*. And just as, of two mutually contradictory statements, such as that God does, and does not, exist, only one can be true and the other must be false, so, according to this assumption, only one of the two conflicting norms can be valid and the other must be invalid. This finds expression in the principle: "*lex posterior derogat priori*", which is considered an axiom of legal logic. The logical rule of inference always finds application, however, when a concrete case is decided by a court on the basis of a law, i.e., of a valid general norm. This decision, i.e., the validity of an individual norm, such as that "Smith, a thief, is to be committed to prison", follows logically from the validity of the general norm, "All thieves are to be committed to prison", in exactly the same way that the truth of the individual statement, "Socrates is mortal", follows from that of the general statement, "All men are mortal".

However, the application of logical principles, and in particular the principle of non-contradiction and the rule of inference, to norms in general and legal norms in particular, is by no means so self-evident as jurists assume. For the two logical principles are by nature applicable – or at least directly applicable – only to statements, insofar as these are the meaning of acts of thought and can be true or false. It is self-evidently not logic, but factual knowledge, which establishes *whether* a statement is true or false.[2] The two logical principles of non-contradiction and of inference merely establish under what conditions a statement (as the meaning of an act of thought) *can* be true, and under what conditions such a statement *must* be false.[3] Norms, however, decree an 'ought', and since this is a correlate of willing,[4] they are the meaning of acts of will, and as such neither true nor false. It cannot be said of a norm such as "Love your enemies" or "murder is to be punished by the death of the murderer", that it is "true" or "false". For unlike a statement such as "All men are mortal", it does not purport to be true. It purports to be valid. That it is "valid" means that it ought to be obeyed. A norm is valid or invalid. The attempt is made to circumvent this obstacle by assuming that the willing is essentially bound up with an act of thought. Anyone who wills something must know what he is willing. What is willed is thus at the same time a thought, the latter being immanent to the former, and hence the logical principles of non-contradiction and inference are applicable to norms.

The problem in question has been expounded as follows by the Danish philosopher Jörgen Jörgensen in his article "Imperatives and Logic" (*Erkenntnis* 7, pp. 288–291). He begins by merely raising the question, whether the rule of inference is applicable to imperatives – which also means to norms. He characterises the logical process of inference "as a process of thought which, starting from one or more judgements, ends in another judgement whose truth is seen involved [*sic*] in that of the former". He then lays it down that imperative sentences

> can neither be true nor false in any sense in which these words are used in logic, therefore they are not capable of being implied in other sentences and consequently are incapable of being conclusions in logical inferences. Indeed they are even incapable too of being premisses in such inferences because also the premisses must be capable of being either true or false in order to function as premisses.

Finally he says: "Imperative sentences... are unable to function as part of any logical argument at all". But Jörgensen thinks, on the other hand, that he has to concede that:

> It seems... evident that inferences can be formulated in which the one premiss at least and the conclusion are imperative sentences. For instance: Keep your promises. – This is a promise of yours. – Therefore keep this promise.

This is a "puzzle", and he tries to resolve it as follows:

> This puzzle may be dealt with by analyzing the imperative sentences into two factors: an

imperative factor and an indicative factor, the first being merely the expression of the speaker's state of mind, his willing, wishing, commanding, etc., and therefore of no logical consequence, whereas the last may be formulated in an indicative sentence describing the contents of the imperative sentences and therefore being capable of having a meaning and of being governed by the ordinary rules of logic.

Any imperative sentence may therefore be considered as containing two factors which I may call the imperative factor and the indicative factor, the first indicating that something is commanded or wished, and the latter describing what it is, that is commanded or wished.

To this we must object that the imperative or norm cannot contain both an imperative, i.e., prescriptive, *and* an indicative, i.e., descriptive factor. For prescription is the meaning of an act of will, while description is that of an act of thought. Willing and thinking are two essentially different functions, and there can therefore be no thinking immanent in willing. It is true enough that he who wills must know what he is willing. But the act of thought constituting the knowing precedes the act of will whose meaning is the norm, and is not immanent to it. The act of thought preceding the act of will does not make the latter's meaning, the norm, true or false. In spite of the act of thought preceding the act of will, one cannot say of a norm that it is true or false. Hence the logical principles of non-contradiction and inference cannot be applied to norms, directly at least, and if applied at all, can only be so *per analogiam*. And even that would be possible only if there was an analogy between the truth of a statement and the validity of a norm. But such an analogy does not exist.

The primary reason for this is that truth and falsity are properties of a statement, whereas validity is not the property of a norm, but is its existence, its specific ideal existence. That a norm is valid means that it is present. That a norm is not valid means that it is absent. An invalid norm is one that does not exist, and is thus *not* a norm. But a false statement is also a statement: it is present as a statement, even if it is false. A norm takes on validity, i.e., begins to be valid in time, and goes out of validity, i.e., ceases to be valid in time or loses its validity. A statement does not begin or cease to be true. *If* it is true, it always has been and always will be. It cannot lose its truth. Even a statement about something limited in time, e.g., the statement that the earth at a certain time is at a certain distance from the sun, is no less true before this time than after it. Newton's statements about gravitation, if they were true, were true long before Newton made them, and will be true long after his making of them. A statement is the meaning of an act of thought, and its truth is independent of this act, i.e., of the fact that it has been made, i.e., thought and uttered;[5] whereas the validity of a norm, which is the meaning of an act of will, is conditioned by the act which posits it. The norm is the meaning of an act of will directed to the behaviour of another; its meaning is an 'ought'; and this 'ought' – as already noted – is the correlate of a willing. No 'ought' that is a norm without a willing whose meaning is this 'ought'. No norm without a willing that posits norms, i.e., no norm without a norm-positing authority. A norm is valid only if it is posited by an act of will, if it is the meaning of such an act. Herein lies its *positivity*. And only positive norms, *posited* by human acts of will, by legislation or custom or national treaty, are taken into consideration by a scientific ethics or a legal *science*.

1. Contradiction of Natural Law

Natural law appears to contradict this; for that which is common to the various definitions of natural law, the essence of what we speak of as "natural law", is the validity of norms which are not the meaning of human acts of will; the values they constitute are therefore in no sense arbitrary, subjective or relative. In order to decide how a man should behave under certain circumstances, there is no need – so natural law theory tells us – to enquire about the act of will of some man who figures as a moral or legal legislator, or about a custom whereby the desired norm has been posited. For the desired norm emerges from the nature of the case to which the norm relates. This consists either of the circumstances under which a man should behave in a particular way, or the man himself whose behaviour is in question. The circumstances are a piece of reality and inseparably bound up with the whole of reality. The nature of the case is thus nature, as the totality of the real, or the nature of man. The latter consists either of the drives inherent in man, or of that which separates man from the beasts – his reason. In the latter case, natural law figures as a law of reason. A typical feature of natural law theory is in every case the assumption of norms immanent in nature, and hence the assumption that the values constituted by these norms are immanent in the reality of nature in general, or of human nature in particular. It is the immanence of an 'ought' in the 'is'. Nature in general, or the nature of man – particularly his reason – prescribes a certain form of behaviour to him. Nature in general or human nature in particular – especially his reason – figures as a norm-positing authority.

Now it may perhaps be granted that norms do not necessarily have to be the meanings of *human* acts of will. But it cannot be granted under any circumstances that there are norms which are not the meaning of an act of will, even if it is not in fact a human one. A nature to which norms are immanent must also have immanent within it a will whose meaning these norms are. But where can such a will come from in nature, which from the standpoint of empirical and rational knowledge is an aggregate of particulars conjoined together as causes and effects? A will in nature is either an animistic superstition or else it is the will of God in the nature He has created, the immanence of divine value in reality. If norms are immanent to the nature of man, in particular his reason, the latter cannot be the empirical human reason, which from a purely psychological standpoint is merely a capacity for thought or knowledge. For a norm-positing reason must be a capacity for both knowing and willing at once. Such a thing cannot exist in the sphere of empirical reality, insofar as the latter can be described without logical contradiction. But so far as we presuppose the existence of a transcendent, suprahuman sphere lying beyond all empirical reality, the principle of non-contradiction, as a principle of human logic, finds no application there. Of the divine reason one may say, what is a contradictory statement about human reason, that it is a function of both knowledge and will at once; one can say of God that in Him knowing and willing are one. As it says already in *Genesis* (2, 16–17; 3, 5):

> And the Lord God commanded the man, saying, ... of the tree of the knowledge of good and evil, thou shalt not eat .... And the serpent said unto the woman ... in the day ye eat thereof ... ye shall be as gods, knowing good and evil.

In that God knows what is good and evil, He wills that the good should be done and the evil left undone. His willing is inherent in His knowing. The contradiction implicit here, that God wills in that He knows, is no less trivial, from a religious or theological standpoint, than that involved in the fact that God in His benevolence only wills the good, and yet also in His omnipotence creates the evil. That which both knows and wills at once, namely the practical reason of man, is the divine reason in man, whom God has made in His own image.

The above-mentioned assumption, that a thinking is immanent to the willing whose meaning is a norm, and the associated concept of a practical reason which wills as it thinks, are religious and theological in origin.[6]

Since there is no analogy between the truth of a statement, so far as it is the meaning of an act of thought, and the validity of a norm, which is the meaning of an act of will, a conflict of norms cannot be a logical contradiction, or anything analogous to such a thing; and hence it cannot be resolved either according to the logical principle of non-contradiction, or by any principle analogous to this.[7]

2. Morality and law

There can be no denying that there are genuine conflicts of norms, i.e., situations in which two norms are valid, of which one posits as obligatory a particular course of conduct, while the other posits a course incompatible with this. Conflicts between the norms of a morality and those of a system of law are familiar to everyone. For example, a moral norm tells us not to kill. A legal norm tells us to kill men in execution of the death-penalty, and enemies in war. Anyone who obeys the one norm, violates the other. He has the choice of which of the two to follow, and which, therefore, to violate. But he has no power to abrogate the validity of the norm he chooses not to obey. Even within one and the same legal system, moreover, conflicts of norms are possible and by no means rare: conflicts between norms of higher and lower order, such as that between a constitution which forbids all abridgement of religious freedom, and a law forbidding the public practice of a particular religion, i.e., the case of a so-called "unconstitutional" law: conflicts between norms of the same order, such as that between a law saying that a particular act, such as adultery, should be punished, and another saying that it should not be. There can even be conflicts, indeed, between norms of one and the same law. What is essential to all of them is that *both* the conflicting norms are valid, so that if one is obeyed the other must be violated; and it can only be violated if it, too, remains valid.[8]

Now of two statements in logical contradiction to one another, only one can be true, or, as we say in this case, only one can "hold" and the other must be false, i.e., cannot "hold". A conflict of norms can be resolved only insofar as one of the two norms loses its validity, or both of them do so. There are two ways only in which this loss of validity can occur. Either through the fact that one of the conflicting norms loses its validity because it has lost its efficacy; for a minimum of efficacy is a condition of its validity; or through *derogation.*

In addition to ordering, permitting and authorising, derogating is the specific function of a norm. A derogating norm, i.e., one whose function consists in abolishing the validity of another norm, differs from those others which order, permit or authorise some particular course of conduct in that it does not relate, as they do, to a particular course of conduct, but rather to the validity of another norm, namely that whose validity it abolishes. An example of a derogating norm would be this: a norm to the effect that "Adultery is to be punished", posited by the law-giver at some particular time, is valid. Later on the law-giver – another man, perhaps, or an assembly consisting of other men than those who laid down this norm – finds that its validity is undesired. The law-giver therefore lays down the norm: "The validity of the norm, 'Adultery is to be punished' is hereby abolished." This derogating norm relates to the validity of a norm that precedes it – not to any particular course of conduct, for it prescribes none. It is thus a dependent norm, presupposing that another norm is valid.

Here is an example of a conflict of norms: there is a norm to the effect that "Murder is to be punished by the death of the murderer". A later norm prescribes that "Murder is to be punished with life imprisonment". This norm, which is in conflict with the first, relates to a particular course of conduct; it prescribes a particular punishment. It does not relate to the validity of the first norm. It is not a dependent norm, for it can hold good even if the first does not.

Derogation, as these examples show, can occur without a conflict of norms being present, if the law-giver considers the validity of a previously posited norm to be undesired. It can also occur, however – though it does not have to – in the case where norms conflict. Thus derogation cannot be the function of one of the two conflicting norms, but must be that of a third norm distinct from them both. For the two conflicting norms each relate to a course of conduct – the one to some particular course and the other to a course incompatible with this – and neither relates to the validity of the other; whereas the derogating norm must relate, not to any course of conduct, but to the validity of one or both of the conflicting norms.

The situation in the case of a logical contradiction between two statements is entirely different. For in the field of propositional logic there is nothing analogous to the efficacy of a norm, or the derogation of a norm's validity. Of the two contradictory statements, "God exists" and "God does not exist", neither loses its truth because it ceases to be efficacious or ceases to be true in virtue of a statement to that effect. *If* one of the statements is true, the other is false, always has been and always will be. If one of two conflicting norms has lost its validity through loss of efficacy or by derogation, only one remains valid, i.e., only one still exists. But the two contradictory statements both continue to exist as statements; it is just that one is true, the other false. That two mutually contradictory statements should both be true, is impossible; that two mutually conflicting norms should both be valid, is possible. And this conflict cannot, like a logical contradiction, be resolved by way of knowledge, with the aid, say, of legal science. Legal science can only confirm the existence of this conflict, and must leave its resolution to the act of will of the legal authority, or to customary non-observance.[9]

3. The Issue Clouded by Roman Law

A conflict of norms is thus something entirely different from a logical contradiction. If it can be compared with anything at all, it is not with a contradiction in logic, but rather – since a norm's validity is its specific existence – with two forces operating in opposing directions on the same point. Both situations, the conflict of norms and the conflict of forces, can be described without any contradiction. That a conflict of forces represents a logical contradiction, that there are logical contradictions in the reality of nature or society, is the fatefully erroneous doctrine of the Hegelian dialectic.

An insight into the nature of a norm-conflict, and of derogation, has been very considerably clouded by the precept "*lex posterior derogat priori*", taken over from Roman jurisprudence and quite generally acknowledged by traditional legal science. We must begin by noting that this principle is applicable, not to conflicts between the norms of a legal order and other norms, especially those of a morality, but only to conflicts between norms of one and the same legal order; and even in the latter case, only to conflicts between norms of the same level, which have been posited at different times. Where legal norms of higher and lower level are in conflict, as in the clash between a constitution and a law, it is not usually the constitution that loses its validity; but the validity of the unconstitutional law, so-called, can be abolished – though it does not have to be – in a special procedure prescribed by the constitution. In that case it is not the *lex prior* but the *lex posterior* that is derogated. Again, in the case of two conflicting norms which are not in the relation of earlier and later, but have acquired their validity at the same moment – because both are contained, say, in the same law – the principle of *lex posterior derogat priori* cannot be applied; not even *per analogiam*, i.e., on the assumption that each of the two norms abolishes the validity of the other.

The main objection to the formula *lex posterior derogat priori* is that it presents derogation as the function of one of the two conflicting norms, and this according to a specific logic immanent, so to say, in law. But that is impossible, since the two conflicting norms both relate to the same behaviour; thus in "Adultery is to be punished" – "Adultery is not to be punished", they both relate to the "punishing of adultery"; in "Murder is to be punished by death" – "Murder is to be punished with life imprisonment", they relate to the "punishing of murder". A derogating norm, however, a norm abolishing the validity of another, is related, not to a course of behaviour, but to the validity of another norm. That in case of conflict between norms of the same level, one of the two valid norms, and that the older, loses its validity, is not a principle of logic, or of legal logic either, and hence is also not a principle that can be applied by legal *science*; as has already been shown by Adolf Merkl ('Die Rechtseinheit des Österreichischen Staates', *Archiv des öffentlichen Rechts* **37** (1918) no. 1, p. 75), the production of such a result is the function of a positive derogating legal norm, which is posited by the legal authority, or presupposed as valid.

Abolition of the validity of a norm prescribing a particular course of conduct, as in the norm: "The validity of the norm 'Adultery is to be punished' is hereby abolished", and prescription of the opposite course, as in the norm: "Adultery is not to be punished", are two completely different functions. If a norm prescribing a particular course of conduct is valid, and if the law-giver posits a norm prescribing a course incompatible with this, he may well want to be rid of the earlier norm. But the will to do this is not expressed in the later norm, which is directed to a particular course of conduct, and not to the validity of another norm. And this will must be expressed in a norm distinct from that which prescribes a particular course of conduct; just as it must be, when the validity of a norm is abolished by a derogating norm, without there being any new regulation of the matter that was regulated by the norm now abolished. That in making a new rule the derogating norm is not expressly formulated by the legislator, is due to his taking it for granted that, if he posits a norm in conflict with an older one, he abolishes the validity of this older norm. This he does particularly under the influence of the doctrine espoused by the traditional jurisprudence – that the newer norm derogates the older one. But even a norm which the legislator takes for granted, and therefore does not expressly formulate, but tacitly presupposes, is still a posited, positive norm.

4. No imperative without an 'imperator'

The applicability of logical principles to norms is sometimes founded on an analogy which it is thought possible to assume, not indeed between the truth of a statement and the validity of a norm, but between the truth of the one and the observance of the other. As an example I may point to Walter Dubislav's essay, 'Zur Unbegründbarkeit der Forderungssätze' (*Theoria* **3** (1937)), in which he examines the question of inferring from the validity of a general norm to that of an individual norm. Dubislav argues that there can be no imperative without an *imperator*, that the one without the other is an "absurdity", and that a fundamental difference exists between affirmations and demands, in that demands are not subject to the alternative of being true or false. Hence the logical rule of inference is not applicable to demands. But he goes on to say that if we nevertheless infer from a demand, such as "Men should not kill other men", another demand, such as "Cain should not kill Abel" (p. 339), this is possible only insofar as we carry out a "transformation" of the demands (p. 340), and in such a way as to turn them into affirmations, which are subject to the alternative of being true or false. The demand that "Men should not kill other men" is transformed into an affirmation which Dubislav formulates as follows: "The demand-instance calls upon men to realise a situation describable in the following way: If *X* is a man, then there are no men that he kills." – "This 'if-then statement' is said to be the affirmation pertaining to the demand." It can also be formulated, much more simply, as "Men do not kill other men". The affirmation pertaining to the demand: "Cain should not kill Abel" is left unformulated by Dubislav. But from what he says of the transformation, it would have to run: "Cain does not kill Abel". The affirmation "pertaining" to the demand is thus a statement asserting that the demand has been observed. But from the fact that from a statement about the observance of a general norm, there follows logically a statement about the observance of an individual norm corresponding thereto, it does not follow that the validity of the individual norm is logically entailed by the validity of the general norm.[10]

According to Dubislav, then, the application of the logical rule of inference to demands takes place according to the following principle:

> A demand *D* is said to be derivable in the wider sense from a demand *C*, if the affirmation pertaining to *D* is at least derivable from the affirmation pertaining to *C*, in conjunction with true affirmations which are consistent with the first-mentioned affirmation (p. 341).

As applied to the example given, this yields: The demand "Cain should not kill Abel" is derivable from the demand "Men should not kill other men" insofar as the affirmation "Cain does not kill Abel" is derivable from the affirmations "Men do not kill other men" and "Cain and Abel are men".

5. THE ANALOGY IS MISLEADING

An analogy between the truth of a statement and the observance of a norm does in fact seem to exist in regard to the application of the principle of non-contradiction and the rule of inference. Just as, of two contradictory statements, such as "All men are mortal" and "All men are not mortal", only one can be true and the other must be false, so of two conflicting norms, such as "Theft from relatives should be punished" and "Theft from relatives should not be punished", only one can be observed and the other must then be violated, i.e. not observed. And just as, from the truth of the general statement "All men are mortal", it follows logically that the individual statement "Socrates is mortal" is true, so from the observance of the general norm "All thieves should be punished", i.e., from the fact that all thieves *are* punished, it follows logically that the individual norm "Smith, a thief, should be punished" is observed, i.e., that Smith the thief is punished. But if one looks closer, the supposed analogy does not hold, or holds only to a very limited extent; and that which does actually hold has no sort of bearing upon the applicability of logical principles to the norms observed.

We must begin by pointing out that there is an essential difference between the truth and falsity of two contradictory general statements and the observance and non-observance of two conflicting general norms. The norm "Theft from relatives should be punished" can be observed by some judge, and hence the norm "Theft from relatives should not be punished" is not observed by this judge; but the second norm can be observed by another judge, and hence the first norm be left unobserved. One and the same judge, indeed, can observe the first norm on one occasion, and so not observe the second, while on another occasion, conversely, he can follow the second and so not observe the first. Each of the two conflicting norms can therefore be just as well observed as not observed, and both may thus be operative to some degree. The incompatibility between observance of the one norm and observance of the other is restricted to the behaviour of one and the same man, and to the period of observance of one of the two conflicting norms. But of two contradictory statements, one cannot be both true and false, or be true for one man and false for another. If it is true, it is true for everyone, and the other false for everyone. Nor is the incompatibility of the truth of the one statement with that of the other restricted to any period of time. If the one is true, it is always true, and the other always false. No real analogy can therefore be said to exist between the truth of a statement and the observance of a norm.

6. Statement and norm

It should be noted above all, however, that while truth and falsity are properties of a statement, observance and non-observance are properties, not of a norm, but of a piece of behaviour. There is no telling from the norm alone whether it is observed or not. This can be done only if some piece of behaviour occurs in reality, which can be compared with the behaviour posited as obligatory in the norm. The behaviour of the judge who punishes a theft from relatives has the property of being an observance of the norm prescribing such punishment, and of being a non-observance of the norm prescribing non-punishment of such theft. That if anyone observes a norm, he cannot simultaneously observe the norm conflicting with it, i.e., both observe the first norm and not observe it, is indeed an application of the logical principle of non-contradiction. For this principle merely signifies that if it is true that a person behaves in a certain way, it cannot be true that he does not so behave. But this is to apply the principle to two statements about matters of fact, and its application to such statements is not in question. The question is whether it applies to norms, and from an answer on the one point, nothing whatever follows about an answer on the other.

The same applies to the rule of *inference*. Nobody denies that from the truth of the statement: "The general norm 'All thieves are to be punished' is observed", i.e., from the truth of "All thieves are punished", it follows logically that such statements as "The individual norm 'Smith the thief is to be punished' is observed", and "Smith the thief is punished" are true. So far as the applicability of the logical rule of inference to legal norms is concerned, the question is whether, from the validity of a general norm such as "All thieves should be punished", the validity of an individual norm such as "Smith the thief should be punished" follows logically in just the same way as it follows from the truth of the general statement "All men are mortal" that the individual statement "Socrates is mortal" is true. And this question must receive a negative answer, so far as it relates to *positive* norms, which are all that can be dealt with in legal science, as a science of positive law.

7. Law is an act of will

The individual norm whose validity is in question, viz. "Smith the thief should be punished, i.e., sent to prison", can only rank as a positive norm if it is posited through an act of will of the competent judge. No norm without an authority which posits it, i.e., no norm without an act of will, of which this norm is the meaning.[11] Now it is undoubtedly possible for the general norm "All thieves should be punished, i.e., sent to prison" to be valid, since created by way of legislation, and for the statement "Smith is a thief" to be true, and even to be asserted by the competent court, while the individual norm "Smith should be sent to prison" is nevertheless not valid, because the competent court has for some reason failed to posit this individual norm; either because it has simply not decided about the case of a theft committed by Smith, and even established by the court, or because it has for some reason acquitted Smith, i.e., decided, or posited the individual norm, that although Smith has stolen he is not to be punished, i.e., sent to prison, and this decision has acquired the force of law. The individual norm "Smith the thief should be sent to prison" can only be the meaning of an act of will, and such an *act of will* cannot be arrived at by way of a logical inference, i.e., by a *thinking* process. If it is true that all men are mortal, it can only be true that Socrates is mortal and not that he is immortal. But even if the general norm holds, that "All thieves should be sent to prison", it is still possible – as shown – for the individual norm to hold, that "Smith the thief should *not* be sent to prison".

By judicial decision, new law can be conjured into validity, which conflicts with the validity of general norms created by legislation, not only in a single concrete case, but in all cases to which the latter norms apply. This happens when by judicial decisions customary law is created which departs from the statutory law then valid. Nothing analogous can happen in the logic of statements, i.e., of propositions that are true or false. The truth of an individual statement which is the conclusion of a theoretical syllogism cannot contradict the truth of a general statement which forms the major premise of that syllogism.

The truth of the conclusion-statement "Socrates is mortal" is implicit in the truth of the two premise-statements "All men are mortal" and "Socrates is a man". But the validity of the individual norm "Smith should be sent to prison" is not implicit in the validity of the general norm "All thieves should be sent to prison" and the truth of the statement "Smith is a thief". For the individual norm is valid only if it is posited by the act of will of the competent court. Its validity is conditioned by this act of positing it, whereas the truth of the statement "Socrates is mortal" is independent of the fact that it is made, i.e., thought and stated. If it is true that all men are mortal, then it is true that Socrates is mortal, even if nobody has thought or stated this. A thing must be thought and stated, not in order to be true, but in order for it to be judged true or false. Logic relates, not to *acts* of thought, but to their meaning; it is psychology that relates to acts of thought.

8. Statement and truth

What logic has to tell us about the theoretical syllogism is this: if a proposition as major premise and another as minor premise are true, then a proposition implicit in both premises is true as conclusion. It makes no difference whether these propositions figure as such actually occurring acts of thought, i.e., whether some man actually thinks them or not. Since the term "statement" designates, not only the meaning of an act of thought, but also the act of thinking and speaking itself, it would be preferable to speak of the application of logical principles, not to statements, but to propositions that are true or false. The act of statement is neither true nor false; only the proposition it expresses can be this. But in investigating the applicability of logical principles to the positive norms of morality or law, one cannot disregard the *act* of will whose meaning they are. For as said, the validity of a norm is conditioned by the act of will whose meaning it is.

The individual norm "Smith the thief should be sent to prison" could be implicit in the general norm "All thieves should be sent to prison" only if the act of will whose meaning is the individual norm were implicit in the act of will whose meaning is the general norm. But the legislator who wills that all thieves should be sent to prison cannot already will that Smith, who has stolen a horse from the farmer, should be sent to prison, since he cannot know that a person called Smith will exist and steal the farmer's horse. For one cannot will that of which one knows nothing, and the will whose meaning is the norm "Smith should be sent to prison" is the condition for the validity of this norm as a *positive* norm. Only the court, which has established that Smith has stolen a horse from the farmer, can will that he should be sent to prison as a thief. And the judge is a different man from the legislator. His act of will cannot be implicit in the act of will of another man.

9. Legislator and judge

But even if the legislator is at the same time the judge, his concrete decision does not follow with logical necessity from the general norm applied, and also posited, by himself; the validity of this individual norm is not implicit in that of the general one. It is perfectly possible that without altering his law – which can only be done by a new act of will – a legislator as judge should make a concrete judicial decision which does not correspond to the general norm he has decreed into law. This individual decision is valid only if it figures as the meaning of an act of will distinct from that whose meaning is the general norm. And the same holds even when the legislator as judge makes a judicial decision *in accordance* with the general norm he has posited. There can be no question of the individual norm being implied in the general, or of the act of will whose meaning it is being implied in the act whose meaning is the general norm. Hence there can be no normative syllogism having a general norm as its major premise and an individual norm as its conclusion.

What *can* be said of the relation between the general norm "All thieves should be sent to prison", and the individual norm "Smith the thief should be sent to prison", is this: *If* the general norm holds, that all thieves should be sent to prison, *and if* the competent court has established that Smith is a thief, *and if* the said court has posited an act whose subjective meaning is that Smith should be sent to prison, then the meaning of the *court's act* is in accordance with the general norm which it has to apply, and the validity of the individual norm forming the meaning of this act can be *justified* by the validity of the general norm. From this it appears that the general norm to be applied by the court is incorrectly formulated in the words "All thieves should be punished, i.e., sent to prison." Its proper formulation is: "If a competent court has established that a person has committed theft, this court is to posit an act whose subjective meaning is, that this person should be sent to prison."

Under a technically advanced legal order, the procedure of applying law takes place in three stages: firstly, establishment of the fact of wrongdoing; then an order of the court directed to an executive organ, to carry out the act of coercion, or sanction, defined in the general norm. This order is the individual norm which the courts have to posit. Finally, the carrying-out of this individual norm by an executive organ distinct from the court.

The condition laid down in the general norm is not a fact of wrong-doing *as such*, but the *establishment* of such a fact by a competent court; and the consequence posited as obligatory in the general norm is not a specific act of coercion, but an *act of the law-applying organ*, in particular a competent *court*, whose subjective meaning is that a specific act of coercion should be posited. What we have here is thus by no means an immediate relation between the general norm "All thieves should be sent to prison" and the individual norm "Smith the thief should be sent to prison", but rather a relation between the validity of the general norm and an act of the court whose subjective meaning can, but also may not, accord with the general norm. If the individual norm posited by the court accords with the general norm the court has to apply, the validity of the individual norm can be *justified* by that of the general one. But that does not mean that the validity of the individual norm to be posited by the law-applying organ follows logically from the validity of the general norm to be applied. If, in spite of its finding that a given man has committed theft, the court acquits him, i.e., if the subjective meaning of its act is not that he should be sent to prison, but that he should *not* be so sent, the validity of this individual norm can *not* be justified by the validity of the general norm regarding theft. That it *can* be justified by the validity of the general norm regarding the *legal force of judicial decisions*, is not at issue here.

10. ROBBER AND JUDGE

As already noted, the act of court is an act of will directed to the behaviour of another organ, the executive organ, and is thus an *act of command*. The subjective meaning of every act of command is an 'ought'; even the act whereby a highway robber commands somebody to hand over his money to him. But the subjective meaning of an act of command is only its objective meaning as well, and thus a binding norm, if the act is authorised by a norm presupposed as valid. If a person fails to comply with the command of a highway robber, he violates no norm and has no duty to obey, as does one who fails to comply with the lawful command of an administrative or judicial organ. That is the difference between the command of a highway robber and that of a legal organ. That the validity of the individual norm posited by the court can be justified by means of the validity of the general norm posited by the legislator, signifies that the subjective meaning of the court's act is also its objective meaning, i.e., is a valid norm, because the act of court is authorised by a norm presupposed as valid.[12]

This state of affairs can be represented in the following syllogism:

Major premise: The *subjective* meaning of an act of will directed to the behaviour of another, i.e., an act of command, is also its *objective* meaning, i.e., a valid norm, if the act is authorised by a norm presupposed as valid.

Minor premise: (a) There is a valid general norm to the effect that, if a competent court has established that a person has commited theft, it is to posit an act whose subjective meaning is that this person should be put in prison by an executive organ.

(b) A competent court has established that Smith has committed theft, and has posited an act whose subjective meaning is that Smith the thief should be sent to prison.

Conclusion: The subjective meaning of the act of court, that Smith should be sent to prison, is also its objective meaning, i.e., a valid norm.

In the conclusion, the validity of the individual norm posited by the court is *justified* by the validity of the general norm which the court has to apply. This justification takes place, however, not in a normative but in a theoretical syllogism, since neither the major premise nor the conclusion are norms, but rather statements, and *statements*, moreover, *about the validity of norms*. In this syllogism it is stated that if what the major premise says is *true*, and if what the two minor premises say is *true*, then what the conclusion says is *true*. The validity of the individual norm to be posited by the court is not logically inferred; the statement about its validity is *presupposed*, rather, as a premise.

In the example given, major premise, minor premise and conclusion of the syllogism are not norms, but statements *about* norms. Such statements are subject, not only to the rule of inference, but also to the law of non-contradiction. The two statements "In legal order *L* the norm 'Adultery is to be punished' is valid" and "In legal order *L* the norm 'Adultery is to be punished' is *not* valid", are logically contradictory; only one or the other can be true. It is self-evident that the two logical principles are applicable to *statements about norms*, since logic is applicable to all statements.

11. Statute book and textbook

The error of believing that the two principles in question are applicable to legal norms is thus partly due to the fact that legal norms and statements about them are not kept clearly separate. This very common confusion of the norm with a statement about it is to some degree explicable – though not excusable – in that both norm and statement are formulated in a 'should'-sentence, and both can sound alike but yet have different meanings. As decreed by the legislator, the sentence "Thieves should be punished with imprisonment" is a norm. The 'should' here has a *pre*scriptive significance. In a textbook of criminal law, the statement about this norm might be formulated in the sentence "Thieves should be punished with imprisonment", which thus sounds the same as the legislator's decree. And the sentence in the textbook must be a 'should'-sentence and cannot be an indicative one. For if it ran "Thieves are punished with imprisonment", it would be false, since thieves are very often not punished in fact. But in the textbook sentence, which is *about* a legal norm, the 'should' has no *pre*scriptive significance; for the author of the textbook is not competent to prescribe anything; instead, it has a *des*criptive significance. I refer in this context to the passages cited in my *Reine Rechtslehre* (2nd edn. 1960, p. 77) from Sigwart (*Logik*, pp. 17 ff) regarding the dual significance of 'should'.

It emerges from the foregoing that the two most important logical principles, the law of non-contradiction and the rule of inference, are applicable to the relations between norms of a positive legal system neither directly nor indirectly – as I still supposed, however, in my *Reine Rechtslehre* (2nd edn. 1960). But yet this is not to say that no logical relations whatever exist between norms. There is, for example, the relation between two general norms which differ only in the degree of their generality, a relation which must be distinguished from that between a general norm and the individual norm which accords with it. But even in the relationship between a general norm and the corresponding individual norm posited by the law-applying organ, a logical relation exists, insofar as the state-of-affairs established *in concreto* by the court can be subsumed under the state-of-affairs defined *in abstracto* in the general norm.

This subsumption is logically of the same type as the subsumption of a concrete idea under an abstract concept. The judge subsumes the state-of-affairs he has established in a concrete case, viz. that Jones has intentionally brought about the death of Smith by shooting him, under the concept of murder contained in the general norm. If the general norm envisages death by hanging as the punishment for murder, and if the judge condemns Jones to death by hanging, the individual norm accords with the general norm. This relation of accordancy is a subsumption-relation, and insofar as the subsumption occurring here is a logical relation, a logical relation exists between the general norm and the individual norm in which this latter is applied to a concrete state-of-affairs. But that does not mean that the validity of the individual norm follows logically from that of the general one. And that is the decisive issue, when it is a matter of applying the rule of inference in the legal process. Moreover, the judicial determination that a state-of-affairs is given *in concreto* which is defined *in abstracto* (as the concept of a state-of-affairs) in the general norm to be applied by the judge, is not only a subsumption from the logical viewpoint, but also has a legally constitutive character. It creates the presupposition for the judge's positing of the individual norm. It is thus an essential component of the process of creating law, and as such, therefore, a function, not of knowledge merely, but also of will.

12. Natural and legal science

It would be natural enough, in regard to the applicability of logical principles, to set up a parallel between the relationship of science to its subject-matter, the reality of nature, and the relationship of legal science to *its* subject-matter, the norms of positive law; and thus to argue that, just as logic is applicable to science but not to its subject-matter, the reality of nature, so it is also applicable to legal science but not to *its* subject-matter, the norms of law. But this parallel does not exist, or only to a certain degree. The crucial difference lies in this, that legal norms, the subject-matter of legal science, are presented in sentences wherein abstract concepts and concrete ideas can find expression; and hence, in the relationship between norms, relations between more or less abstract concepts, and between abstract concepts and concrete ideas, make their appearance. But these relations are logical in character.

Finally, there is still need to answer the question, whether there is a specifically "juridical" logic. In juristic literature the view is sometimes advanced, that the logic applied in legal science – to legal norms especially – is not the general formal logic, but a specifically "juridical" logic different from this. To demonstrate the existence of a specifically juridical logic, the chief instances put forward are the so-called analogical argument appealed to by jurists, and the *argumentum a majore ad minus* which they constantly employ.

The analogical argument, the *argumentum a simile*, makes its appearance chiefly in judicial decisions, where it is a question of applying a general legal norm to a concrete case. The essence of it is this, that the judge applies a valid general norm of law to a state-of-affairs which is not in fact the same as that defined *in abstracto* in the general legal norm, but which the judge considers to be similar, or which coincides in essentials – as it is sometimes put – with the state-of-affairs defined in the operative legal norm. That such a "similarity" or "essential coincidence" is present is a highly subjective judgement, and what appears to one judge as "similar" or "essentially coincident" may not appear so to another.

13. Of the Spirit of the Laws

Inasmuch as the legal order authorises the law-applying organ to apply valid general norms of law *per analogiam*, it guarantees this organ a wide range of free discretion within which the latter can create new law for the case in hand. Attempts are therefore made in juristic theory to show that this judicial discretion is restricted, by claiming that when the judge assumes the state-of-affairs before him to be similar to or essentially coincident with the state-of-affairs defined in the norm to be applied, he must adhere to the "spirit of the law". What this spirit may be, can naturally be determined only by the judge himself, and this determination can turn out very differently in different cases to be decided by different judges.

The "spirit of the law" is basically a fiction serving to sustain the illusion that even in cases of so-called analogical decision the judge is merely applying existing law, whereas in truth he is creating new law for the concrete case. He has to be authorised to do this by the legal order. This is evident from the fact that in certain cases, namely in criminal decisions, a verdict *per analogiam* is forbidden. But such a ban presupposes that in other cases such decisions are – tacitly if not expressly – permitted. What we actually have, when the traditional jurisprudence speaks of a judicial decision *per analogiam*, is by no means an argument in which the validity of the individual norm of the judge's decision follows logically from that of some positive general norm; it is the positing, authorised by the prevailing legal order, of an individual norm which does not correspond to a general legal norm of any defined material content.

This is very clearly evident in the example of a juristic argument by analogy given by Ulrich Klug (*op. cit.*, p. 125). The provisions of §§433 ff. of the German Civil Code, which regulate only the contractual conveyance of tangible property, have been applied by way of analogy to the contractual conveyance of commercial businesses generally, including the goodwill. The contractual conveyance of a business and its goodwill is obviously not a conveyance of tangible property. The judge who applies to the former the provisions which the law decrees only for the latter is positing an individual norm which accords with no general norm. He is creating new law. And the validity of this individual norm can not only not be arrived at by way of logical inference because there is no general norm functioning as major premise, but also because – as already emphasised in the foregoing – the validity of every positive norm, and therefore also of the individual norm representing the judge's decision, is conditioned by an act of will whose meaning it is; and this act of will cannot be produced by way of a logical operation, i.e., an act of thought.

14. Logic and Psychology

It must be noted, furthermore, that it is a disputed question, whether so-called analogical argument has any place at all in logic. It is a probabilistic argument, i.e., its conclusion does not lay claim to strict truth, but only to a greater or less degree of probability. Ernst Mach, in his *Erkenntnis und Irrtum*, 4th edn., 1920, p. 225, has maintained that analogical arguments are a matter, not for logic, but for psychology. If what is called an analogical argument does not represent a logical process at all, this applies far more forcibly still to so-called juridical arguments by analogy. For the positing of the individual norm by the law-applying organ actually takes place – as shown – in the case where this norm is in accordance with an already valid general norm, which connects a generally defined state-of-affairs with an equally generally defined legal consequence; and so does not create new law by way of a logical thought-process, as happens in so-called juridical argument by analogy.

The *argumentum a majore ad minus* is so applied that – as Klug puts it (p. 137) – "a conclusion is drawn, from the validity of a statement of law for a general class of cases, to its validity for special cases". As an example, he points out that, according to §49b, para. III of the Criminal Code,

> a party to a conspiracy aimed at criminally endangering life, or contemplating this as a means to other ends, goes unpunished, if he gives the authorities or the intended victim such timely information, that it is possible to hinder a crime against life intended in pursuit of the endeavours of the conspiracy.

Inference is made from this to the validity of the norm that actual hindrance is immune from punishment. From the validity, that is, of the positively asserted general norm prescribing that the informer should not be punished, it follows logically that validity attaches to a general norm not positively asserted, and prescribing that anyone who actually hinders the crime should not be punished. Here, says Klug, we have the following schema of classical logic:

All S is P *(propositio subalternans)*.
Some S is P *(propositio subalternata)*.

But we should only have this schema if the inference were to run:

All informers go unpunished.
Some informers go unpunished.

However, Klug remarks later that in the example given

> it was presupposed that the statute has laid down the class of cases it refers to in terms so general, that the initially doubtful-seeming cases fall into the general class as special cases.

What this means is that the general norm of law, prescribing that the informer is not to be punished, is so interpreted as also to prescribe that anyone who actually hinders the crime is not to be punished; it being assumed that if the legislator had thought of the case of actual hindrance he would also have prescribed such immunity there. If so, there is no logical inference here from the validity of the one general norm to that of the other; what happens, rather, is that the validity of the norm not positively asserted is assumed to hold good already, on the strength of teleological considerations. That may be justified from a teleological point of view. But a logical inference does not come into it.

15. 'JURIDICAL LOGIC'

Klug also remarks:

> We should not conceal it from ourselves, however, that the use of the term *argumentum a majore ad minus* in juridical practice is extraordinarily inexact. There is no precise allusion to the logical structure of the inference. One may well suspect that many an author would renounce the use of a term thus borrowed from the theory of classical logic, if the exact structure of this subaltern inference, at least as understood by conventional logic, to say nothing of modern theory, were known to him.

If the structure of the subaltern inference is taken into account, it is quite impossible to regard what the traditional jurisprudence calls an *argumentum a majore ad minus* as a logical inference. What we have is something that Klug describes as "interpretative arguments", of which he says that they exemplify no particular logical operations, but serve the purpose of establishing legal theses. There can be no question, therefore, of any specifically "juridical" logic. It is the common logic which is applied to the descriptive propositions of legal science, just as it also is – so far as logic is applicable here at all – to the prescriptive norms of law.

NOTES

* *Forum* XII/142, 143 (October–November 1965), 421–425, 495–500.

[1] Oliver Wendell Holmes' much-quoted remark: "The life of the law has not been logic; it has been experience" (*The Common Law*, 1881, p. 1) seems to express the view that logic has no application to law. But other utterances of Holmes tell against this. Thus he says in an essay 'The Path of the Law' (*Collected Legal Papers*, 1920, p. 180): "The fallacy to which I refer is the notion that the only force at work in the development of the law is logic". That means that logic is not the *sole* principle which determines the validity of the law. For the rest, there is no opposition between experience and logic.

[2] It does not follow from this that logic has nothing to do with truth or falsity, or as Ulrich Klug says (*Juristische Logik*, 2nd edn., Berlin-Göttingen-Heidelberg 1958, p. 23): "that it does not matter for the rules of logic, whether we speak of true or correct statements", since the rules of logic can also be applied to false propositions. The latter is correct, but logic says of the principles under discussion: Of two mutually contradictory statements, only one can be *true*, and if one is true, the other must be *false*; and again: If the premises are *true*, then the conclusion implied by them is *true*. Thus logic can say: If it is true that all men are immortal, then it is false that Socrates is mortal. Or: If it is true that all men are immortal, then it is true that Socrates is immortal. Only in this way, by prefixing the

words, "If it is true that..." can logic also be applied to propositions of which science tells us that they are false. But one cannot ignore the fact that logic is the servant of science, and that science aims at true knowledge.

[3] Christian Sigwart (*Logik*, 3rd edn., 1904, I, p. 1), points out that our thought pursues the aim of arriving at propositions "which are *certain* and universally valid", and that logic is the art which gives instruction in this. On p. 8 he says that the concept of necessary and universally valid thinking is that which "exhausts the essence of '*truth*'". That is how it must be understood when logic is defined – as it is by Alois Höfler (*Logik*, 2nd edn., 1922, p. 63ff.) – as "the theory of correct thinking", and when he stresses that "correct" and "true" are synonymous (p. 59), that "the highest demand which can and should be imposed upon thinking is that of 'truth'". (p. 57).

[4] Sigwart, *op. cit.*, I, p. 18, says: "Should is the correlate of would".

[5] Höfler, *op. cit.*, p. 86, remarks: "In order to perceive the *correctness* of a thought, the *justification* of a pattern of argument, we need not wait to find out whether this *thought has actually* been entertained by anyone, or whether this *pattern of argument* has ever *actually* been employed, or ever will be...."

[6] Cf. Alf Ross, *Kritik der sogenannten praktischen Erkenntnis*, Copenhagen 1933, especially pp. 433f.

[7] For what follows, cf. my article 'Derogation', on pp. 261–275 below. In regard to the applicability of logical principles in general to legal norms, see Paul Amselek, *Méthode Phénoménologique et Théorie du Droit*, Bibliothèque de Philosophie de Droit, vol. II, Paris 1964. Amselek assails the 'logicisme' of my *Reine Rechtslehre* (1960), but is not aware of the essay just cited, in which I depart from the view still held in the larger work and show that a conflict of norms is not a logical contradiction, and that the logical law of non-contradiction is not applicable to it even *per analogiam*.

[8] Rupert Schreiber, *Logik des Rechts*, Berlin-Göttingen-Heidelberg 1962, maintains on p. 87 – and I myself was still arguing a similar view on p. 211 of my *Reine Rechtslehre* – that: "If contradictions occur between legal norms, all the norms that are in contradiction with each other must be legally invalid. For contradictory norms have no legal validity". This is not so. Conflicting norms can be valid. We then indeed have a conflict of norms, and so far as the norms constitute duties, a conflict of duties. Schreiber goes on: "Were no ruling to be introduced for this case of conflict, considerable areas of the legal order could be put out of action by contradictions". But in case of a conflict of norms, the relevant area of the legal order is not put out of action; instead, we merely have a situation typified by the fact that if the one norm is obeyed, the other is violated. But each of the two can be obeyed, since each of them is valid.

[9] This also marks a difference between statements and legal norms. The question whether a statement is true or false is answered by the appropriate science; the question whether a legal norm is valid or not, is answered by the competent legal authority which has to apply the norm, and in particular by the court.

[10] If, like Ulrich Klug, for example (*op. cit.*, p. 1), one defines logic as the theory of correct inference, the law of non-contradiction has no place in logic. But then where does it belong, if not in logic? Sigwart, assuredly one of the most eminent of German logicians, devotes a comprehensive paragraph (§23 in vol. I of his *Logik*) to the law of non-contradiction.

[11] Cf. Walter Dubislav, *op. cit.*, pp. 330ff., who insists (p. 331) on the principle of "No imperative without an *imperator*".

[12] O. C. Jensen, *The Nature of Legal Argument*, Oxford 1957, says in the Foreword (p. XIII): "The aim of this book is to show that one reason for the law's delays and uncertainties is the inconclusiveness of the arguments which are given in support of legal

decisions, or which are advanced by counsel on behalf of their clients, and that this inconclusiveness is due to the nature of the concepts and modes of thought used." But Jensen does not deny that there is a logic of norms. He says (p. 19): "The logic of norms and kindred utterances such as injunctions, commands, requirements, commendations, etc. is still a very controversial topic. It is therefore inadvisable to become involved in it here". And in a section under the heading 'Formal or Logical Deduction' (p. 21) he says: "Formal deduction occurs rarely in legal cases" (p. 25). Rarely, but it does occur.

H. L. A. Hart, in 'The Ascription of Responsibility and Rights' (*Logic and Language*, ed. by A. G. N. Flew, Oxford 1963, p. 156) says: "But sometimes the law is cited as an example of a deductive system at work. 'Given the existing law', it will be said, 'the statement of facts found by the judge entails the legal conclusion'. Of course, this could only be said in the simplest possible cases where no issue is raised at the trial except what common sense would call one of fact, i.e., where the parties are agreed that if the facts go one way the case falls within some legal rule and if they go another way it does not, and no question is raised about the meaning or interpretation of the legal rule. But even here it would be quite wrong to say that the judge was making a deductive inference; for the timeless conclusion of the law (Smith is guilty of murder) is not entailed by the statements of temporal fact (Smith put arsenic in his wife's coffee on May 1st, 1944) which support it: and rules of law even when embodied in statutes are not linguistic or logical rules, but to a great extent rules for deciding". If Hart means by the last sentence – what he does not, indeed, express very clearly – that the logical rule of inference is not applicable to legal norms, one must agree with him.

The Swedish legal philosopher H. Vilhelm Lundstedt, in *Legal Thinking Revised*, Stockholm 1956, rejects the normative syllogism. But in so doing he follows another Swedish legal philosopher, Axel Hägerström, in starting from the assumption that the subject-matter of legal science is not norms (p. 23) but judgements of value, which can be neither true nor false (p. 45), and takes it that in the inference he regards as logically impossible the premises and conclusion are value judgements (p. 48). Cf. on this the essay of one of his supporters, Karl Olivecrona, 'The Legal Theories of Axel Hägerström and Vilhelm Lundstedt' *Scandinavian Studies in Law* **3** (1959) 136ff.; and Leonard G. Boonin, 'The Logic of Legal Decisions', *Ethics, An International Journal of Social, Political and Legal Philosophy* **75** (1965) 179ff.

Arthur Kaufmann also, in *Analogie und 'Natur der Sache'*, Juristische Studiengesellschaft Karlsruhe, Schriftenreihe, No. 65/66, Karlsruhe 1965, denies on p. 8 that the legal finding is a "purely deductive procedure", and argues on p. 29 that the legal finding, as "subsumption", "is not possible through a simple syllogism".

CHAPTER XI

LAW AND LOGIC AGAIN*

On the Applicability of Logical Principles to Legal Norms

In the previous essay I discussed the question whether the law of non-contradiction and the rule of inference are applicable to legal norms, and answered it in the negative. To supplement this discussion, I should like to refer to an article unfortunately still unknown to me at the time, "Die Norm ist kein Urteil", by Karel Engliš, which appeared in *Archiv für Rechts- und Sozialphilosophie* **50** (1964), No. 3, pp. 305–316.

Engliš says on p. 306

> that norms cannot be negated (denied) as judgements can. What is negated is the cognition contained in the judgement about the relation between the logical subject (contained in the preceding question) and the logical predicate (contained in the subsequent answer). The negation puts the judgement out of action (It is not true, it is not correct, that ...). The logical predicate attributed to the logical subject in the judgement negated is again refused to it by the denial of the judgement.

This will not do if, as Engliš rightly says on p. 307,

> by denial of the judgement two mutually contradictory judgements result, of which one must be true (correct) and the other false (incorrect).... No third possibility exists. That is logical contradiction and the law of excluded middle.

In that case the judgement "God exists" is negated by the judgement "God does not exist", and not by the judgement "It is not true that God exists". The latter is a judgement about the truth of a judgement. There is a logical contradiction only in the first case, not in the second. Between the judgement "God exists" and the judgement "It is not true that God exists", no logical contradiction holds. The judgement "God does not exist" cannot put the negated judgement "God exists" out of action. If it did so, there would be no contradiction between two judgements – there would merely be *one* judgement.

Engliš goes on to say:

> The norm does not recognise an existing relation, it establishes one by means of the duty (imposed on another's will). Thus it cannot be put out of action by a denial. The norm is not (like the judgement) correct or true, because only the judgement cognises the relation to be known correctly or truly .... The norm ... can prove or not prove itself in the eyes of the norm-positing (willing) subject. His postulate, embodied in the norm, is attained or not attained.

This means that the norm can be obeyed or not obeyed. But that is not the crux of the matter. What counts is that the norm is *valid* or *not valid*, where the norm's validity is its existence and not, like the truth of a statement, a property it has. "The norm-positing subject", says Engliš,

can employ another act of will to put his norm out of action, recall, abolish or change it, and either do this himself or by means of someone he has authorised for the purpose. The judgement can be negated by any cognising subject.

This, too, is not quite right. The validity of a norm can be abolished only by a *specific* norm, a derogating norm, i.e., one whose function is the total or partial abolition of the validity of another norm, and not the prescription of any particular course of conduct. Then there is only *one* norm left.

This case must be distinguished from that in which the validity of a norm prescribing some sort of conduct is met by that of another prescribing the opposite; as in "Whoever commits murder is to be punished with death" and "Nobody is to be punished with death". There is then a *conflict* of norms, which is not a logical *contradiction*.

Engliš has perceived this correctly when he says on p. 307 that the norm can "have no logical contradiction", that collisions of norms or duties are "assuredly to be distinguished from logical contradiction", and "that the resolution of these collisions has nothing in common with that of the logical contradictions among judgements" (p. 308).

The negation of the norm

The reason he gives, why there can be no logical contradictions between norms, is that "The norm cannot be negated". But this reason is not sound. "To negate a norm" can mean to negate the validity of a norm. That is the statement that a norm prescribing some sort of conduct *is not valid*. Such a statement is possible, and can be true or false. There can be no logical contradiction between norms, because a contradiction can subsist only between propositions that are true or false, whereas norms are neither. Only if we understand by a "negating" the statement that a proposition is *false*, is it impossible for a norm to be "negated", i.e., for it to be stated that a norm is false; since a norm is neither true nor false.

Engliš also denies the possibility of a normative syllogism, i.e., of a syllogism in which one premise and the conclusion are norms. On p. 316

he advances the thesis that "The cognitive process" – and inference is such a process – "contains only judgements about the norm, never the norms themselves". In proof of this he points to the fact

that the conclusion can and must be tested for its truth or correctness.... If the norm were to make up one of the premises, and if the conclusion were a norm, it would make no sense to test them for truth-value, since they express no truth and cannot be denied. It is not for the norm, but only for the judgement about it, that there is any sense in enquiring about its truth-value and eventually deciding this to be negative.

But from the fact that a norm cannot be true it does not necessarily follow that the *validity* of a norm cannot be arrived at by way of inference. The decisive argument against the possibility of a normative syllogism of the kind described by Engliš is that such a syllogism is an operation of *thought*, whereas the validity of a norm is the meaning of an act of *will*, and the latter cannot be arrived at by way of an operation of thought.

Engliš had already set forth previously the views upheld in the article cited, in a work entitled *Malá logika*, published in Prague in 1947. In his essay 'Die Sollsatzproblematik in der modernen Logik', *Rozpravy. Československé Akademie Věd*, Ročník 68, 1958, Sešit 9, p. 1ff., Ota Weinberger has maintained on the contrary that logical principles, in particular the law of non-contradiction and the rule of inference, do have application, albeit only under the proviso that logic be extended by the addition of a special logic of 'ought'-statements (p. 10). His point is that the denial of logical relations between norms rests essentially on the assumption that the norm is to be regarded as an "act of will", and that this view makes a logical analysis impossible.

Just as no acts of thought (or cognition) make their appearance, in the sciences or in the logic of statements, as the objects of logical relations, so also no normative ('ought'-statement) logic can come about, if we start out from acts of will (p. 92f.).

But this objection does not hold, at least in regard to the *Reine Rechtslehre*, which concurs with Engliš about the relationship between law and logic, since it views the norm, not as an "act of will", but as the *meaning* of such an act, and distinguishes very clearly between the act and its meaning (*Reine Rechtslehre*, 2nd edn. 1960, pp. 4 ff.).

NOTE

* *Neues Forum* XIV/157 (Jan. 1967), pp. 39–40.

CHAPTER XII

ON THE PRACTICAL SYLLOGISM*

A practical syllogism is a logical inference in which – unlike a theoretical syllogism – the major premise, minor premise and conclusion are not statements that can be true or false, as in the syllogism:

> All men are mortal;
> Socrates is a man;
> Therefore, Socrates is mortal.

Instead, the major premise is an imperative, the minor a statement, and the conclusion again an imperative. But imperatives are neither true nor false. A practical syllogism of this sort is found, for example, in the inference where the major premise runs:

> Love your enemies;

the minor:

> Jones is the enemy of Smith;

and the conclusion:

> Smith is to love Jones.

In this syllogism, the validity of the imperative forming the conclusion is no less logically derived or deduced from the two premises than is the truth of the judgement "Socrates is mortal" from the truth of the premises that "All men are mortal" and "Socrates is a man". But, as shown in my essay "Law and Logic" (pp. 228–253 above), such a practical syllogism is not logically possible. The essential reason for this is that logic can say: If it is true that all men are mortal and Socrates is a man, then it is true that Socrates is mortal, whether or not such a statement is actually made, i.e., is the meaning of a *real* act of thought, and can do this even if someone makes the statement that "Socrates is not mortal". But logic cannot say: If the imperative "Love your enemies" is valid as a norm, and if it is true, as a statement, that "Jones is the enemy of Smith", then the imperative "Smith is to love Jones" is valid as a norm. For this imperative is valid as a norm only if it is posited as the meaning of a real act of will. The validity, i.e., the specific existence of a norm, is conditioned by the existence of the act of will whose meaning it is. The truth of a statement is not the existence, but a *property* of that statement, and this property is not conditioned by the existence of the act of thought whose meaning it is. The validity of the individual imperative "Smith is to love Jones" cannot be derived from that of the general imperative "Love your enemies", plus the truth of the statement "Jones is the enemy of Smith"; but *if this imperative is actually posited as the meaning of a real act of will*, then it can be *warranted* by the validity of the general imperative "Love your enemies" plus the truth of the statement "Jones is the enemy of Smith".

As a supplement to my remarks in the essay already cited, I should like to refer in this connection to an essay, "Der praktische Syllogismus", by Manfred Moritz (*Theoria* **20** (1954), pts. 1–3, pp. 78–127). Moritz says (p. 81):

> The logical rules of inference hold for propositions that are true or false. The condition for an inference to be valid is that the conclusion should be true if the premises are true. But this condition is essentially unsatisfied when dealing with premises which are not judgements, but imperatives. For imperative premises are never true, since they are neither true nor false. The same holds accordingly for the conclusion as well. Of this 'derived' imperative it must also be said that it can be neither true nor false. *The presupposition for the application of logical rules of inference to imperatives is not given.* (My italics).

"Syllogisms in which one or both premises are not judgements, but imperatives, are described as 'practical syllogisms'". Thus Moritz assumes that there *cannot be practical syllogisms.* He gives as an example (from Jörgen Jörgensen, "Imperatives and Logic", *Erkenntnis,* (7) 4; p. 288): "Keep your promises; This is a promise of yours; Therefore, keep your promise". Of this example he says (p. 82): "We cannot derive the *imperative* 'Keep your promise' from the imperative 'Keep your promises' and the judgement 'This is a promise of yours'". But Moritz thinks it logically possible that "a judge is able to found his judicial decision on the law." (p. 83). His problem, as he describes it (p. 84), is "how, in fact, judicial decisions can be 'founded' by means of the existing laws". On p. 87 he says in so many words that "Practical syllogisms are impossible", and adds that he seeks to show "that the judicial decision can be 'motivated' with the aid of an imperative". By "motivated" he obviously means "founded", but not logically derived. He therefore sees that the problem in hand is the founding of the judicial decision by means of the law – which means, however, what he does not seem to see – the founding of the validity of the individual norm to be posited by the judge by means of the validity of the general norm he has to apply. For he says on p. 108:

Even without the derivation of such an individual imperative from the general law, it can be decided whether the individual subject enjoined under the norm has *followed* the general imperative or not. The detour by way of an individual imperative is not necessary; and as shown earlier, it is also not possible.

But this "detour" *is* necessary, and is no detour, for it is indeed the founding of the validity of this imperative, i.e., of that individual norm, which is in question. That this validity cannot be logically inferred from that of the general norm does not prevent the validity of the individual norm from being founded on that of the general one. That is, indeed, precisely what Moritz is trying to show. We decide that the judge has "followed" or not followed the general imperative by deciding whether the content of the individual imperative he posits is in accordance with that of the general imperative he has to apply. Moritz himself says (p. 127):

A judicial decision is motivated by the law [and that means 'founded', for him], if there is justification for saying that the judge has followed the law, if he *announces* this decision (i.e., a decision of specific content) and there is therefore justification for saying that this judicial act is a following of the law.

And he adds, in parentheses: "If the judge happens to announce a decision with another content, he has not performed the act enjoined upon him". It is thus quite essentially a matter of the *content* of the judge's decision. It is indeed the founding of this *decision* which is in question – as Moritz correctly lays down at the outset in presenting his theory. The determination of what the general imperative (or general norm) prescribes, is in fact admittedly – as Moritz emphasises – an *act* of the judge; but an act having a quite determinate content, defined in the general norm. What the general norm is aiming at is the validity of an individual norm in accordance with the general norm; the law only prescribes an act of the judge, because this individual norm can be valid only if it figures as the meaning of a judicial act, an act of will on the part of the judge; just as the general norm, of course, is valid only if it is posited by an act of the legislator, whose meaning is this general norm. The problem is the nature of the relation between the validity of two *norms*, one general and the other individual. What is essential is that the individual norm posited by the judge should accord with the general norm posited by the legislator. It is this, indeed, that constitutes the "founding" of the validity of the former by that of the latter. That the judge "follows" the general norm is a secondary matter, i.e., merely the condition under which the individual norm he posits is in accordance with the general norm contained in the law. That the judicial decision must be "motivated" by the law – as Moritz puts it – is a very questionable piece of terminology. For by "motivate" we mean in ordinary usage that the judge posits the individual norm corresponding to the general one because he wishes to conform to the general norm he is aware of. Moritz – in conflict with ordinary usage – holds the expression "the decision is founded" to be synonymous with the expression "the decision is motivated". For he says on p. 110:

> The decision is founded by the law when it falls under the concept of the decision set forth in the law. To put it otherwise, the judicial decision is motivated by the law, when it belongs to the class of decisions set forth in the law.

But the decision is "motivated" by the law only when the will of the judge to conform to the law he is aware of, leads him to make his decision in accordance with the law. The "motives" he has in positing the individual norm which accords with the general one, are irrelevant. He can posit it, not because he wishes – as Moritz says – to "follow" the law, but because, say, he considers the individual norm he posits to be just in the concrete case. Moritz says (pp. 115–16):

> In the juristic context it seems to be enough if the act enjoined is performed. It does not seem to be necessary to perform the enjoined act because it is enjoined. In general the mere coincidence of enjoined and performed act seems to be sufficient;

it is sufficient, that is, if an individual norm in accordance with the general one is posited and comes into effect, whatever be the motives it is done from. Not only does this seem so – it *is* so. And the coincidence in question is that between the general norm to be applied by the judge, and the individual norm posited by him in this application.

NOTE

* *Neues Forum* XV/173 (May 1968), pp. 333–34.

CHAPTER XIII

DEROGATION*

Derogation, besides commanding, permitting, and authorising, is a specific function of the norm. It exists when the validity of another norm is repealed. It plays an important part in the sphere of a positive legal order but can also arise within the sphere of a positive moral order where, however, it will hardly be taken into consideration because of the much greater stability of this normative order. Within a positive moral order, a norm ordinarily does not lose its validity by derogation, but either by the expiration of time for which it is valid according to its own or another norm's stipulation, or by the fact that it no longer is obeyed and applied and thus has lost its efficacy and thereby its validity, efficacy being a condition for validity. These ways of losing the validity must be distinguished from losing it by derogation, since derogation is the repeal of the validity of a valid norm by another norm. Unlike other norms, derogation does not refer to a certain behaviour, but to the validity of another norm. It does not establish an *ought* but a *non-ought*. The derogating norm, that is, the norm that repeals the validity of another norm according to which a certain behaviour ought to take place, should not be confused with a norm according to which the omission of this behaviour ought to take place, and the norm that repeals the validity of another norm according to which the omission of a certain behaviour ought to take place, should not be confused with a norm according to which this behaviour ought to take place. According to a norm whose function is the derogation of another norm, neither a certain behaviour nor the omission of a certain behaviour ought to take place. The derogating norm repeals the *ought*, and that means, the validity of another norm according to which a certain behaviour or the omission of a certain behaviour ought to take place. Consequently, a derogating norm cannot exist by itself but only in relation to the norm whose validity it repeals, and in this sense it is a dependent norm.

Derogation is a problem of the sphere of validity of norms, especially of the temporal sphere of validity.[1] A norm is valid for a certain space and for a certain time. It has a spatial and a temporal validity. The derogating norm terminates the temporal validity of another norm. Derogation affects the validity of a norm and not the act of its creation; only the former can be repealed, not the latter. Since derogating norms do not prescribe a certain behaviour, and since they cannot be obeyed and applied like other norms, they also cannot be violated. If it has fulfilled its function, that is to say, if the norm to which it relates has lost its validity, then also the derogating norm, in regard to the norm whose validity it repeals, will lose its validity. Its validity in respect to the norm, whose validity it has repealed, also cannot be repealed; it is not able to be derogated in relation to this norm. The attempt to repeal the validity of a norm which has derogated the validity of another norm in regard to this norm, by means of a derogating norm, would be without effect. The norm whose validity was terminated by the first derogating norm would not regain its validity by the second derogating norm. If the validity of a norm prohibiting marriage of Catholic priests is repealed by a derogating norm, and if the legislator, in order to revalidate the repealed norm, would issue a norm repealing the validity of the derogating norm, he could not achieve his goal. A norm, whose validity has been repealed by a derogating norm, can only be revalidated by a norm of the same content as the repealed norm. As a matter of fact, it can never be revalidated since the new norm is different from the one which was repealed, even though it has the same contents.

The situation is different, when the effect of the derogating norm does not take place immediately after it has been established, but at a later date. If, e.g., the derogating norm stipulates: the validity of the norm stipulating... terminates after six months; then, the validity of this derogating norm can be repealed in the meantime by another derogating norm. Derogating can occur under two different circumstances: either in case of a conflict between two norms, or without such a conflict. The norm-creating authority may hold that the validity of a norm is unwanted and, therefore, may wish to terminate its validity. It can do so by an act of legislation, whose meaning is derogation. In this case, derogation is the sole function of a positive norm. This is not doubted by anyone. For instance, a valid norm is that all men shall serve in the military who have reached the age of 21 years and who have been found physically fit. The legislator can terminate the validity of this norm by a legislative act whose sole function is the repeal of the validity of the said norm. By this norm, military service of qualified men is not prohibited. No definite behaviour is prohibited or ordered. The legislator, however, can also for some reason or another create a norm whose contents are identical with those of an already-existing norm. In this case, derogation of the validity of the first of the two norms is possible. If so, only the second norm remains valid. If the validity of this second norm is repealed by a derogating norm, the derogation does not have the effect of revalidating the first norm.

Since the derogating norm stipulates neither the *ought to* of a certain behaviour, nor the *ought to* of the forbearance of a certain behaviour, but the *non-ought* of a certain behaviour, it cannot be expressed like other norms in an imperative or ought-sentence. The imperative or ought-sentence can express the idea that a certain action or omission ought to take place, but it cannot express the repeal of the *ought* established in another norm. Suppose the legislature were to formulate the following norm: "Men who have reached the age of 21 years and who have been found physically fit ought *not* to serve in the military." That norm would not repeal the validity of the norm prescribing that qualified men ought to do military service, but would establish a separate norm in conflict with the former. The derogating norm, however, does not conflict with the norm whose validity it repeals. To formulate the derogating norm in a manner which is logically correct: "men who have reached the age of 21 years and who have been found physically fit, non-ought to do military service" is, however, linguistically impossible. Therefore, derogating norms assume the form of assertions such as "the norm according to which men who have reached the age of 21 years ought (etc.)... is hereby repealed."

The function of such an assertion is, however, not a descriptive one, as the sentence seems to indicate grammatically, but the function is a normative one, namely, that of repealing the validity of a norm. Norms sometimes assume the grammatical form of assertions. For instance: a criminal code provision, "persons convicted of larceny are punished by imprisonment" is, according to its grammatical form, an assertion describing a fact; according to its function, however, it is a norm directed to the judge, prescribing punishment by imprisonment of all persons convicted of larceny.[2]

The norm whose validity is repealed by a derogating norm can be a general or an individual norm. A good example of the latter is a court's decision which has the character of an individual norm, repealed by the decision of a higher court which does not substitute its own judgment. The norm whose validity is repealed can be one which is established by an act of will consciously directed at the creation of a norm, or it can be one created by custom. The derogating norm, however, cannot be established by custom.

A norm may lose its efficacy and thus also its validity by custom if it is continuously not obeyed and not applied, whereby no norm prescribing certain behaviour is created.

Custom may also create a norm which prescribes the omission of an act which was prescribed by an up-to-now valid norm: or custom can establish a norm which prescribes a certain action whose omission was prescribed up to now by a valid norm. In such a situation, no conflict of norms results, since the custom which creates the new norm implies the fact that the up-to-now valid norm is continuously not obeyed and not applied, and, therefore, loses its efficacy and thus also its validity. In both cases, therefore, no derogation of the up-to-now valid norm takes place, but the loss of validity is caused by the loss of efficacy.

In contradiction of a wide-spread opinion in the field of jurisprudence,[3] the question whether norms exist which cannot be derogated must be answered in the positive if the question means: whether there are norms whose validity – according to their own meaning – cannot be repealed by a derogating norm, and if the question does not mean whether not every norm may lose its efficacy, and thereby its validity, and be replaced by another norm regulating the same subject matter in a different way.

The latter is without doubt the case but derogation does not enter the picture. A norm can exclude its derogation by another norm, but it cannot prevent the loss of its validity by loss of its efficacy. Without doubt, a norm, especially a legal norm, cannot only relate to specific conduct but it can also affect its own validity. It can, for instance, prescribe to be valid for only a certain length of time, for only a certain space, or for only certain persons. It can prescribe to be valid for an unlimited time, for an unlimited space, and for all persons until another norm formulated by the same authority becomes valid which is in conflict with the first one. It can provide that it may be repealed only in a certain manner prescribed by itself or by a norm of the same order. There is, therefore, no reason to assume that it cannot provide that it should not be repealed by another norm. Norms which, according to the belief of man, are issued by God are said to be incapable of being repealed, that is to say, they cannot be repealed by norms which are established by man. A democratic constitution can provide that it shall not be superseded by a monarchial constitution. If a norm *A* is valid stipulating that its validity cannot be repealed and if nevertheless a norm *B* is established stipulating that the validity of norm *A* is terminated, and a norm *C* regulating the subject matter regulated by norm *A* in another way, norm *A* remains valid. Consequently, there exists a conflict between the provision of norm *A* concerning the unrepealability of its validity and the provision of norm *B* concerning the repeal of its validity, and in addition a conflict between norm *A* with respect to its other provisions and norm *C*. These conflicts can be solved only in the way of norm *A* losing its efficacy and therefore its validity as the result of norm *C* becoming effective.

The principle of the force of law of a judicial decision, too, indicates that there are norms which, according to the meaning of this principle, are not to be derogated; for a judicial decision which has the force of law is an individual norm whose validity cannot be repealed by another norm.

Another question is whether and to what extent the principle of force of law of judicial decisions is actually established within a certain legal order. It does not exist in the strict sense of the term if the legal order does not completely exclude the possibility of a procedure by which the judicial decision can be attacked, if such a procedure is always, but only under specific conditions, possible; or if a judicial decision can be repealed by an act of legislation. Then the principle of the force of law of a judicial decision exists only in a relative and not in an absolute sense, and in practical effect means hardly anything other than that the execution of the judgment is possible. Even an executed judgment, one, for instance, which prescribes a prison term or the death penalty, can be repealed. In other words, the validity of an individual norm which prescribes putting a person in prison for the term of one year, or to kill a person by hanging, can be repealed by another norm, even if the punishment has already been served. This of course will not have the effect to undo what has been done, namely, the served prison term or the execution. The function of the repeal is to strip the actions concerned of their character of punishment, without qualifying them as crimes. It must be kept in mind that the individual norm whose validity has been repealed is still valid up to its repeal; that is to say, that its validity is not affected by its execution.

The Roman jurisprudence made a distinction between "abrogatio" (or obrogatio), meaning a complete repeal and "derogatio" meaning a partial repeal. Regelsberger, speaking of the formula: "*lex posterior derogat priori*" states[4]:

> The new legal norm can repeal the old one in whole or in part. Its content can be limited only to the repeal or it can regulate the same facts. In the latter situation, an expressed repeal is not necessary insofar as both norms cannot be applied together.

That which is repealable is, however, not the legal norm but the validity of the legal norm. By complete repeal is meant the repeal of its validity, i.e., its specific existence; but the sphere of validity can have different dimensions. A norm can be valid for an unlimited period of time or for one year only; it can be valid for the whole State or only for a single province, and it can apply to all persons or only to a certain class. Thus, the sphere of validity can be restricted or expanded. The restriction or expansion of the sphere of validity has the effect of changing the content of the norm. The content of the norm can be changed not only with respect to its personal, temporal, or territorial sphere of validity, but also with respect to its material sphere of validity. The material sphere of validity of a norm is that conduct which the norm prescribes and the conditions under which it ought to take place. A norm which is valid for all forms of larceny can be replaced by one which is valid only for a certain form of larceny. A norm which prohibits murder by prescribing the death penalty for murder can be replaced by one which prescribes only a prison term for life.

By partial repeal of a norm is meant the partial change of the content, i.e., of its sphere of validity. The changed content of a norm does not cause the norm to continue to exist as a partially repealed norm, but the result is that the validity of the norm is repealed by a derogating norm, and that in its place another norm is substituted whose content as compared with the first one is only partially different. According to the traditional view, partial derogation of a norm is defined as the partial change of the content whereby the norm continues to exist. Let us assume the following legal norm: larceny shall be punished by imprisonment for a term of from one to three years. Let us also assume that the punishment is changed from six months to five years; according to the traditional view the first norm continues to be valid except that some of its content was changed. Let us assume another example. A norm is valid:

If two persons who are older than 21 years old enter into a contract and if one of the parties does not fulfill his contractual obligation, upon the action of the other party a civil execution ought to be directed against the property of the first one, for the purpose of repairing the damage.

Later, by another norm, the age is reduced to 20 years. According to the traditional opinion the first norm is still valid, only with changed content. This situation occurring within a legal order is presented in analogy to the partial change of a physical object which, in spite of this change, retains its identity. A house still is the same house even though its front windows are enlarged.

However, this analogy is faulty. A norm, especially a legal norm, cannot be changed like a physical object. If the content of a norm is changed, that is to say, if a legal norm begins to be valid whose content is partially different from the content of another legal norm, two possibilities exist: either the first legal norm remains valid and unchanged so that the two legal norms are in conflict with each other, or the first norm is repealed by a positive, derogating legal norm, a third norm; so that only the second norm is valid whose content is partially different from that of the first one. In no case does the first norm continue to exist with changed content, as the theory of partial repeal states. Even if one assumed, in conformity with the traditional theory, that the second legal norm brings about the change of the first norm by derogation, the first norm does not continue to be valid with changed content but the second one remains the only valid norm. This is also true if the second norm is formulated as follows: "the minimum age of the contracting parties determined in the first norm is reduced from 21 years to 20 years", for this is only a short form for the entire norm partially changed. This follows also from the fact that even according to the traditional theory, if the content of the second norm is not different from the first one, the latter becomes invalid by derogation through the second one; and if the validity of the second norm is repealed, the first one with the same content is not revalidated. Therefore, by partial repeal is meant either no repeal at all, or there is a complete repeal not of a legal norm but of the validity of the norm.

However, it is possible to repeal a single legal norm which is part of a statute composed of several legal norms. This can be done in two ways. One is to repeal the validity of one of the single norms without issuing a new single norm regulating the same subject matter in a different way. The other is to repeal the validity of a single norm of the statute and, at the same time, to issue another single norm regulating the same subject matter in another way. In both cases the single norms of the statute which are not repealed continue to be valid. In both cases it is possible to say: the statute continues to be valid, but with a changed content, because of being without the repealed single norms. Since the validity of a statute which consists of several legal norms is nothing more than the validity of these norms (not a separate validity), this process does not mean a partial repeal of the validity of the statute, but a total repeal of one of the legal norms whose aggregate forms the statute. In the second case, too, the statute does not continue to be valid with the new legal norm which took the place of the repealed one. The new legal norm exists side by side (parallel) with the statute which is reduced by the repealed norm. That is also true if the new legal norm is formulated in the following way: the provision of the statute, Title ..., Section ... (cited) providing ... (text of provision), is hereby repealed; in its place the following provision shall apply ... (text of new provision). This formulation is faulty, because the legislator has been misled by the erroneous theory of partial repeal.

Suppose the civil code establishes a minimum age of 20 years at which a person has capacity to contract (to do business), or the criminal code fixes an age of 16 years at which a person assumes full criminal liability, and this age is changed by a later statute, in a sentence similar to this one: "the minimum age of twenty years at which a person has full capacity to contract as defined in Title ... Section ..., is hereby reduced to 18", or: the age of 16 years at which a person assumes full criminal liability is hereby increased to 18 years of age. In such a case, it is said that both codes continue to be valid with partially changed contents. This is, however, an erroneous conclusion. The provisions changing the age determined in the two codes are actually only a short form for a new civil or criminal code with partially changed contents. This can be better understood if it is assumed that the validity of the statutes, changing the age of capacity to contract, or the age of criminal responsibility, were repealed; for then the old civil code and the old criminal code would not become valid, unless by the repeal of these statutes the codes were intended to be revalidated. If this is intended, an express declaration of this intention is required by a correct legal technique.

The distinction between *abrogare* and *derogare* is based on the well-known section of Cicero's *De Re Publica* (3,22): "*Huic legi nec abrogari fas est, neque derogari in hoc aliquid licet, neque tota abrogari potest.*" Obviously, this section relates to a statute composed of several legal norms. But the rule, *lex posterior derogat priori*, is applicable not only to the relations between statutes but also to the relation between single legal norms, and "*derogare*" means not only partial but also total repeal. This writer, therefore, is using the word "derogation" in the sense of repealing the validity of a norm.

Derogation is required if norms stand in conflict with each other. It can also take place if there is no conflict between norms; thus, if the validity of a legal norm is repealed and no new one takes its place, or if a new legal norm is created which has the identical contents of an already valid norm, derogation may take place.

A conflict between two norms occurs if in obeying or applying one norm, the other one is necessarily or possibly violated. The conflict can be bilateral or unilateral. It is bilateral if in obeying or applying each of the two norms, the other one is (possibly or necessarily) violated. The conflict is unilateral if obedience or application of only one of the two norms violates the other one. The conflict is a total one if one norm prescribes a certain behaviour which the other one forbids (prescribes the omission of the behaviour). The conflict is a partial one if the content of one norm is only partially different from the content of the other one.

Examples of necessary (or unavoidable) conflicts of norms are:

I. Norm (1): Love your enemies.
Norm (2): Don't love but hate your enemies.

To obey norm (1) unavoidably violates norm (2) and vice versa.

II. Norm (1): Bigamy shall be punished.
Norm (2): Bigamy shall not be punished.

The application of norm (1) necessarily violates norm (2); the application of norm (2), the failure to punish for bigamy is necessarily a violation of norm (1).

In both examples I and II the conflict is a total one.

III. Norm (1): Murder shall be punished by death.
Norm (2): Murder shall be punished by imprisonment.

The application of either of the two norms necessarily violates the other; the conflict is only partial, and in all three examples, I, II and III, the conflict is bilateral.

Examples of conflicts of norms which are only possible (not necessary) are:

IV. Norm (1): All persons shall forbear to lie.
Norm (2): Physicians shall lie, if this will help their patients.

In obeying norm (2), norm (1) is necessarily violated; but in obeying norm (1) there is only a possibility of violating norm (2) (if a physician lies). The conflict is bilateral, but only in a partial way. It is a necessary one on one side, the side of norm (2), and a possible conflict on the other side, namely, the side of norm (1).

V. Norm (1): Larceny shall be punished.
Norm (2): Larceny from relatives shall not be punished.

The application of norm (2) (the failure to punish larceny from relatives) is necessarily a violation of norm (1); but the application of norm (1) is only possibly a violation of norm (2) (if larceny from relatives is punished). The conflict is bilateral, but only partial. It is a necessary conflict only on one side, namely, on the side of norm (2), and a possible conflict on the side of norm (1).

VI. Norm (1): In case of a certain behaviour the person who behaves in this way shall be punished.
Norm (2): In case of a certain behaviour the person who

behaves in this way shall only be punished if the judge considers punishment to be just.

The conflict is bilateral, partial and only possible on both sides.

VII. Norm (1): Murder is to be punished by death if the perpetrator is over 20 years of age.
Norm (2): Murder is to be punished by death if the perpetrator is over 18 years of age.

The application of norm (1) is not a violation of norm (2). The application of norm (2) is only possibly a violation of norm (1) (if the murderer who is less than 20 years of age, is punished by death). The conflict is only partial and unilateral, namely, on the side of norm (2).

There is no doubt that such conflicts between norms exist. They play an important part under the name of "conflict of duties" in the field of morality and in the field of law, especially, however, in the relationship between morality and law. The conflict between norms presupposes that both norms are valid. The assertions concerning the validity of both conflicting norms are true. Therefore, a conflict between norms is not a logical contradiction and cannot even be compared to a logical contradiction. Derogation repeals the validity of one of the valid norms. But in case of a logical contradiction between two assertions, one of the two assertions is untrue from the very beginning. Its truth is not repealed for it does not exist at the outset. Since the validity of a norm is its own specific existence, a conflict between norms cannot be compared to a logical contradiction. As far as a comparison can be made at all, it could be compared to two forces exerting their power on the same point from opposite directions. A conflict between two norms is an undesirable but possible situation, and occurs quite often.

The conflict can, but need not be, solved by derogation, and derogation will take place only if it is stipulated by a norm-creating authority. Just as the conflict between norms is not a logical contradiction, derogation solving the conflict is not a logical principle either; but it is the function of a positive norm, especially a positive legal norm, just as in the case where derogation takes place without there being a conflict between norms. Derogation is not the function of one of the two conflicting norms, but that of a third norm, which prescribes in case of a conflict between two norms that one of the two or both shall lose their validity.

A conflict can arise between two norms of the same level or between a norm of a higher level and a norm of a lower level, whereby the acts by which the two conflicting norms are created differ in time, so that one is the earlier one and the other the later one.

The authority which creates norms, especially the legislator, can at some point of time issue a norm which prescribes a certain behaviour, and at a later time it can issue a norm which prescribes the forbearance of precisely that behaviour. The constitution of a state can provide that all men regardless of their race shall be treated equally; later the legislator can pass a statute which grants certain rights or which imposes certain obligations only on persons of a certain race.

In the first case a norm can, but need not be valid, which stipulates that the earlier of the two conflicting norms loses its validity; and in the second case, a norm which stipulates that the latter of the two conflicting norms loses its validity. It should, however, be remembered that of the two conflicting norms in the second case, that is, the case of an unconstitutional statute, the so-called "unconstitutional" statute may, according to positive law, be valid, but its validity may be repealed in a special procedure provided for in the constitution, for instance, by the decision of a special court. Then no conflict of norms exists, for if the statute in question is valid, it must be considered to be constitutional, that is to say, the legislator must be considered to be authorized by the constitution to pass such a law. But a possibility exists of repealing the validity of this statute by a special procedure provided for in the constitution.[5]

It is possible that one and the same statute contains two norms which are in conflict with each other. Unless, according to positive law, the law-applying organ has a choice which of the two conflicting norms to apply, a norm can provide that both norms which became valid shall lose their validity.

So far, only conflicts between norms of the same normative order, especially a legal order, have been discussed. Suppose a conflict exists between norms of two different normative orders, such as conflicts between a norm of a legal order and one of a moral order, then the legal order can provide that the legal norm which conflicts with the moral norm shall lose its validity, but the legal order cannot provide that the moral norm which conflicts with the legal norm shall lose its validity. By the same token, the moral order can prescribe that the moral norm which is in conflict with the legal norm shall become invalid for the sphere of validity of the legal order, but it cannot prescribe that the legal norm which is in conflict with the moral norm shall become invalid. Thus, derogation can only occur within one and the same normative order.

An insight into the nature of derogation has been blurred by the formula adopted from the Roman jurisprudence, "*lex posterior derogat priori*."[6] This sentence is misleading because it creates the impression that derogation is the function of one of the two conflicting norms. This is wrong, because both conflicting norms refer to a certain behaviour but neither of them refers to the validity of the other. A derogating norm, however, essentially does not refer to a certain behaviour but to the validity of another norm, and, therefore, is a dependent norm which presupposes the validity of a norm which relates to a certain behaviour. The two conflicting norms are independent norms which can exist by themselves. Between a derogating norm and a norm which is being derogated no conflict exists, since by reason of the validity of the derogating norm the other norm becomes invalid. If derogation occurs in a case of two conflicting norms, one of the two or both will become invalid and thereby the derogating norm too will lose its validity in respect to the norm (or norms) whose validity has been repealed because it has served its purpose. However, if it is a general norm, it can also apply to other conflicts between norms.

The principle "*lex posterior derogat priori*" is incorrect also for the following reason: since derogation is not a logical principle but the function of a positive legal norm, it does not necessarily apply, but can apply only if it is positively stipulated; and even if stipulated, it does not apply in all cases of conflicts of norms.[7] It has been shown above that in conflict between a norm of a higher and a norm of a lower level, not the earlier one but the later one may lose its validity. If it is assumed that derogation is the function of one of the conflicting norms, one should state by analogy: "*lex prior derogat posteriori*" and not "*lex posterior derogat priori*." Moreover, the fact is ignored that by derogation both conflicting norms may become invalid, or, stated on analogy to the formula "*lex posterior derogat priori*", that each repeals the validity of the other.

An argument could be advanced against the assertion that derogation solving the conflict between norms, and especially the principle formulated in the sentence: *lex posterior derogat priori*, is not a logical but a norm of positive law, as far as legal norms are concerned. The argument is that a norm which regulates derogation, taking place when norms are conflicting with each other, is usually not present as an expressly formulated norm in a positive legal order. However, this can be explained by the fact that the legislator omits formulating expressly much which he silently presupposes and assumes to be self-understood. It is quite possible that the above-enumerated principles of solving conflicts of norms are so often applied by the law-applying organs as principles of interpretation, that their existence is taken for granted by the legislator. Thus, it is possible that the authority establishing the constitution takes it for granted that a statute passed by the legislator, which conflicts with the constitution, will lose its validity; or that the legislator in adopting a norm, presupposes as self-evident that a prior norm issued by him will become invalid if it conflicts with the later one; or that the legislator takes for granted that, in adopting a statute containing two conflicting norms, either both norms become invalid or that the law-applying agency has a choice of which one to apply. If this is the case, the principles of derogation are positive legal norms.

In summary, it should be pointed out that the importance in legal theory is: that principles of derogation are not logical principles, and that conflicts between norms remain unsolved unless derogating norms are expressly stipulated or silently presupposed, and that the science of law is just as incompetent to solve by interpretation existing conflicts between norms, or better, to repeal the validity of positive norms, as it is incompetent to issue legal norms.

NOTES

* Reprinted from *Essays in Jurisprudence in Honour of Roscoe Pound*, copyright 1962, by the Bobb's Merrill Co., Inc. Reprinted by permission. All rights reserved. (This essay and the one following are reprinted without amendment from their original sources in English. – Transl.).

[1] Compare *infra* at pp. 264, 266.

[2] The law often makes the expression of certain words or phrases a condition to legal

consequences. It provides, for example, that a document is a valid will only if it is entitled "last will" or "testament." Another example is that for a marriage to be valid, the minister or member of a legally recognized religion must utter the words: "I hereby pronounce you man and wife". From the grammatical point of view, the words "last will" and "testament" are merely descriptive, and the words spoken by the minister are mere descriptions of a legal consequence. But at law, they are not mere descriptions or assertions, but conditions for legal consequences. J. L. Austin's statement in regard to the utterance of words and phrases as a condition to legal consequences is not quite correct when he states: "Even if some language is now purely descriptive, language was not in origin so, and much of it is still not so. Utterance of obvious ritual phrases in the appropriate circumstances is not describing the action we are doing, but doing it ('I do'); in other cases, it functions like tone and expression, or again like punctuation or mood, as an intimation that we are employing language in some special way ('I warn'; 'I ask'; 'I define'). Such phrases cannot strictly be lies, though they can 'imply' lies, as 'I promise' implies that I fully intend, which may be untrue." Austin, 'Other Minds' in *Logic and Language* (2nd series) Essays: ed. by Anthony Flew, Oxford 1955, pp. 146, 147. The words and phrases are not solely descriptive, but also something more. Description is not their essential legal function. Since they are assertions they can be true or untrue. For instance, the word "testament", which is an abbreviation for "this document is a testament", can be untrue if the objects disposed of in the document are not the property of the testator, because the instrument is not a valid will, or better, it has not the legal consequences of a testament. The minister's words, "I hereby pronounce you man and wife", are untrue if both persons to whom the statement is made are not of different sex, but either two males or two females of whom one is dressed as a woman or as a man respectively. For in such a case, the minister's words do not have the legal consequence which they describe.

[3] Regelsberger, *Pandekten, Systematisches Handbuch der Rechtswissenschaft*, pt. I. vol. 1, sec. 7, 1893, p. 109: "There is no law which cannot be changed. A legislator can make a change or the repeal of a legal norm very difficult by imposing conditions and limitations, but he cannot control the unchangeability of a legal norm, even for a limited period of time." There is no doubt that the legislator can "decree" that a norm shall not be changed, but the question is, what legal effect does it have if in spite of such a provision a norm is adopted which conflicts with it.

[4] *Ibid.* n. 3 at p. 110.

[5] Compare Kelsen, *Reine Rechtslehre*, (2nd edn., 1960), p. 275.

[6] According to Regelsberger, *op. cit.*, p. 110, the sentence is not according to sources but substantially agrees with the sources. "The new legal norm can repeal the hitherto existing one in whole or in part, its content can be limited to the repeal only, or it can regulate in a new way the same facts. In the latter case, no express repeal is necessary because both norms could not be applied together." However, there is no reason to assume that one norm repeals the other, just because two conflicting norms can't be applied together. Since the question, which of the two is the repealing one and which is the repealed one, is not answered, it follows that a positive regulation is necessary.

[7] Merkl, *Allgemeines Verwaltungsrecht* (1927) p. 211, "... the precept *'lex posterior derogat priori'* is valid only as a positive rule of law and not as a logical axiom as it is commonly understood."

CHAPTER XIV

NORM AND VALUE*

If a norm stipulates that a certain behaviour "ought" to take place, in the sense of "commanding" the behaviour, the actual behaviour may or may not conform to the norm. The behaviour conforms to the norm if it is such as it ought to be according to an objectively valid norm; it does not conform to the norm if it is not such as it ought to be according to an objectively valid norm because it is the opposite of the behaviour that conforms to the norm. The judgment that an actual behaviour is such as it ought to be according to an objectively valid norm is a value judgment – a positive value judgment. It means that the actual behaviour is "good." The judgment that an actual behaviour is not such as it ought to be according to an objectively valid norm because it is the opposite of the behaviour that conforms to the norm, is a negative value judgment. It means that the actual conduct is "bad" or "evil". An objectively valid norm according to which a certain behaviour "ought to be", constitutes a positive or negative value. The behaviour that conforms to the norm has a positive value, the behaviour that does not conform, a negative value. The norm that is regarded as objectively valid functions as a standard of value applied to actual behaviour. *Value* judgments affirming that an actual behaviour conforms to an objectively valid norm and is, in this sense, "good", or does not conform and is, in this sense, "bad", must be distinguished from judgments about reality that affirm – without reference to a norm regarded as objectively valid – that something is and how it is.

The actual behaviour to which the value judgment refers – the behaviour that constitutes the object of the valuation and that has a positive or negative value – is a fact existing in time and space, a part of reality. Only such a fact can, when compared with a norm, be judged to be good or bad. Only such a fact can have a positive or negative value. It is reality that is being valued. Inasmuch as the norms that are the basis of the value judgments are enacted by human, not superhuman, will, the values constituted by them are arbitrary. Other human acts of will can create other norms opposite to the former ones; and these other norms, then, constitute values that are opposite to those constituted by the former. That which is "good" according to the one norm may be "bad" according to another. Therefore the norms, enacted by men and not by divine authority, can only constitute relative values. Hence, the validity of a norm according to which a certain behaviour ought to be, as well as the value constituted by this norm, does not exclude the possibility of the validity of a norm, according to which the opposite behaviour ought to be, constituting an opposite value. For example, there can be a valid norm forbidding suicide or lying under all circumstances, and another norm which is also valid permitting or even commanding suicide or lying under certain circumstances. Yet it would be impossible to prove rationally that only one of these two norms, and not the other, is the truly valid one.

If, however, the norm prescribing a certain behaviour and thus constituting a certain value is supposed to emanate from a super-human authority – from God or from a nature created by God – then this norm claims that the possibility of a norm prescribing the opposite behaviour is excluded. The value constituted by such a norm is described as "absolute", in contrast to the value constituted by a norm enacted by human will. The object of a scientific theory of value can only be norms enacted by human will and values constituted by these norms.

If the value is constituted by an objectively valid norm, then the judgment that something real – an actual human behaviour – is "good" or "bad", expresses the idea that this behaviour conforms to an objectively valid norm: that the behaviour ought to be the way it is. The judgment that it does not conform to the objectively valid norm is a judgment that the behaviour ought not to be the way it is. Then the value as an "ought" is placed in juxtaposition to the reality as the "is" – value and reality belonging to two different spheres, just as the "ought" and the "is" do.

If the statement that a behaviour conforms or does not conform to an objectively valid norm is designated as a "value judgment", then this value judgment must be distinguished from the norm that constitutes the value. The value judgment can be true or untrue, because it refers to a norm of a valid order. For example, the judgment that according to Christian morality it is "good" to love one's friends and to hate one's enemies is untrue because a norm of the valid Christian morality commands one to love not only one's friends but also one's enemies. The judgment that it is legal to inflict upon a thief the penalty of death is untrue if the valid law in question commands punishment of a thief by deprivation of freedom but not by deprivation of life. A norm, however, cannot be either true or untrue, but only valid or not valid.

The "judgment" pronounced by a judge, is no more a judgment in the logical sense of the word, than the norm that he applies. That "judgment" is, instead, a norm – an *individual* norm, limited in its validity to a concrete case, as distinguished from a general norm, called a "law".

The value constituted by an objectively valid norm must be distinguished from the value that consists, not in the relation to a norm, but in the relation of an object to the wish or will of an individual directed at this object. If the object is in accordance or not in accordance with the wish or will, it has a positive or negative value: it is "good", or "bad". If the judgment describing the relation of an object to the wish or will of an individual is designated as a value judgment and the object which is in accordance with the wish or will as "good", and the object which is not in accordance with the wish or will as "bad", then this value judgment is not different from a judgment about reality. It describes only a relation between two facts, and not a relation between a fact and objectively valid norm. It is therefore only a special judgment about reality.

If a statement by somebody that something is good or bad is merely the immediate expression of his emotional attitude toward a certain object, or an indication that he wishes something or does not wish it but its contrary, then the statement is not a value "judgment", because it is not a function of cognition, but a function of the emotional component of consciousness. And if this emotional reaction refers to the behaviour of an individual other than the speaker, then it is the expression of emotional approval or disapproval, akin to the exclamation "bravo!" or "phooey!"

The value that consists in the relation of an object – particularly of behaviour – to the wish or will of an individual can be designated as *subjective* value, in contradistinction to the value that consists in the relation of a behaviour to an objectively valid norm which can be designated as *objective* value. If the judgment that a behaviour is good merely means that it is wished by another individual, and if the judgment that a behaviour is bad merely means that the opposite behaviour is wished by an individual, then the values "good" and "bad" exist only for the individual who wishes the behaviour, but not for the individual whose behaviour is wished. If a judgment that a behaviour is "good" means that the behaviour conforms to an objectively valid norm (and if the judgment that a behaviour is "bad" means that it does not conform to an objectively valid norm), then the values "good" and "bad" exist for the individuals whose behaviour is being judged, that is, for all individuals whose behaviour is regulated by the objectively valid norm. Their behaviour, then, has a positive or negative value, not because it is wished or not wished, but because it conforms, or does not conform, to a norm. The act of will, whose objective meaning the norm is, does not come into consideration as far as the value judgment is concerned.

Value in the subjective sense – that is, the value that consists in the relation of an object to the wish or will of an individual – is also distinguishable from value in the objective sense – that is, the value that consists in the relation of a behaviour to an objectively valid norm – because subjective values can have various degrees. The wish or will of an individual is capable of different degrees of intensity. A graduation of an objective value, however, is not possible because a behaviour can only conform or not conform to an objectively valid norm, but cannot do so more or less.

If a norm prescribes a behaviour which is possible in differing degrees, it looks as if the norm could be obeyed in differing degrees, that is, more or less. This is a fallacy, however. If, for example, a norm prescribes that murder ought to be punished by twenty years in prison, and then one court punishes murder by life imprisonment and another court punishes murder by ten years' imprisonment, it is not true that one judgment is "more" in conformity to the norm to be applied and the other "less", because neither is in conformity. And if a norm prescribes only that murder ought to be punished by imprisonment, without determining the length of the term, then a judgment imposing life imprisonment is not "more" in conformity with the norm to be applied, and a judgment imposing twenty or ten years not "less", because all three judgments are equally in conformity with the norm. The "more" and "less" do not refer to the conforming but to the punishment.

Value judgments that state an objective value are designated as objective-value judgments; those that state a subjective value as subjective-value judgments. If thus defined, the adjectives "objective" and "subjective" refer to the stated values, and not to judgment as a function of cognition. As a function of cognition any judgment has to be objective, that is, it must be performed without regard to the wishes of the judging individual. This is possible. It is possible to determine the relationship of a specific human behaviour to a normative order – namely whether the behaviour does or does not conform to the order – without taking an emotional position, either approving or disapproving, toward this order. Take, for example, the question whether according to Christian morality, it is good to love one's enemies. The answer to this question, and therefore the value judgment that goes with it, can and must be given without regard to whether the one who has to give the answer approves or disapproves of loving one's enemy. Or take another example: The answer to the question whether according to a valid law the death penalty ought to be imposed upon a murderer and consequently whether – legally – the death penalty in case of murder is valuable, can and must be given without regard to whether the one who has to give the answer approves or disapproves of the death penalty. Only then is the value judgment objective.

To sum up: If the judgment pronounces the relationship of an object (especially of human behaviour) to the wish or will of an individual (that is, a subjective value), then this value judgment is "objective" if the judging individual pronounces it without regard to whether he himself approves or disapproves of the behaviour, but simply ascertains whether one individual or many individuals wish or will an object (or its opposite), or, more particularly, whether they approve or disapprove of a specific behaviour.

We are distinguishing, then, between value judgments that state an *objective* value describing a relationship between a behaviour and a norm regarded as objectively valid, and are therefore fundamentally different from a judgment about reality; and value judgments that state a *subjective* value by describing a relationship between an object (specifically a behaviour) and the fact that an individual or many individuals wish this object or its opposite (specifically approve or disapprove a definite behaviour), and are therefore merely specific judgments about reality. This distinction has been criticized on the ground that the former value judgments are also judgments about reality, because – it is argued – the norm that is the basis of the value judgment is created by a human command or by custom and therefore by empirical facts. It is further argued that the relation of a fact (specifically of actual behaviour) to a norm is therefore merely the relation between two empirical facts. This objection fails to distinguish between the act of command or the acts constituting the custom and the norm that is created by these acts: the former is a fact, the latter a meaning. Therefore, the relation between an actual behaviour and a norm, and the relation between this behaviour to the fact whose meaning the norm is, are two different relations. It is entirely possible to describe the relation between a behaviour and the norm stipulating that this behaviour ought to be, without taking into consideration the act of command or custom by which the norm was created. This is obvious, for example, when we think of norms that were established a long time ago; of norms created by the acts of men long dead or forgotten; or of norms, especially, created by the custom of earlier generations, so that the men whose conduct is regulated by these norms are aware of them only as meanings. When a specific conduct is judged to be morally good or bad (because conforming or not conforming to a moral norm regarded as valid), one is usually not aware of the custom that created the moral norm on which the judgment is based. Above all, however, the acts by which legal norms are created come into consideration as objects of legal cognition only so far as they are determined by legal norms; and the basic norm, the ultimate reason for the validity of these norms, is not created by a real will at all, but is presupposed in legal thinking.

By "value" we also mean the relation of something, specifically human behaviour, as a means to a certain end or purpose. Suitableness, that is, to be suitable for a certain purpose, is the positive value; unsuitableness, the negative value. The purpose may be objective or subjective. An objective purpose is one that *ought* to be realized. This means a purpose that has been stipulated by a norm regarded as objectively valid – a purpose, in other words, prescribed for nature in general or for man in particular by a supernatural or superhuman authority. A *subjective* purpose is one established by man himself, a purpose that he wishes to achieve. The value, therefore, that consists in the conformity to a purpose, is identical either with the value that consists in conformity to a norm or with the value that consists in conformity to a wish.

Disregarding that a realized purpose is something that conforms to a norm or to a wish, the relation between means and end manifests itself as a relation between cause and effect. Something is suitable for a purpose if it is fit to realize that purpose – to bring about, as cause, the effect that constitutes the purpose. The judgment that something is purposeful can be a subjective or objective value judgment, depending on the subjective or objective character of the purpose. But such a value judgment is possible only on the basis of an insight into the causal relationship between the facts that are regarded as means and those regarded as end. If it is recognized that a relation of cause and effect exists between *a* and *b* (that *a* is the cause and *b* the effect), then, and only then, can we arrive at the (subjective or objective) value judgment: If *b* is wished as a purpose, or "ought to be" according to a norm, then *a* is purposeful, that is, suitable for the purpose. The judgment concerning the relation between *a* and *b* is a subjective or objective value judgment only to the extent that *b* is presupposed as a subjective or objective purpose.

NOTE

* *California Law Review* **54** (October 1966), No. 4. (Transl. by Max Knight. This article is an adaptation of chapter I, 4e of Knight's English translation of the author's *Reine Rechtslehre*, Vienna 1960: *The Pure Theory of Law*, Berkeley 1970).

INDEX OF NAMES

INDEX OF SUBJECTS

SYNTHESE LIBRARY

Monographs on Epistemology, Logic, Methodology,
Philosophy of Science, Sociology of Science and of Knowledge, and on the
Mathematical Methods of Social and Behavioral Sciences

PATRICK SUPPES (ed.), *Space, Time and Geometry*. 1973, XI + 424 pp.

I. NIINILUOTO and R. TUOMELA, *Theoretical Concepts and Hypothetico-Inductive Inference*, 1973, X + 259 pp.

ROLAND FRAÏSSÉ, *Course of Mathematical Logic*. Volume I: *Relation and Logical Formula*. 1973, XVI + 186 pp.

I. NIINILUOTO and R. TUOMELA, *Theoretical Concepts and Hypothetico-Inductive Inference*. 1973, X + 259 pp.

RADU J. BOGDAN and ILLKA NIINILUOTO (eds.), *Logic, Language, and Probability*. 1973, X + 323 pp.

GLENN PEARCE and PATRICK MAYNARD (eds.), *Conceptual Change*. XII + 282 pp.

M. BUNGE (ed.), *Exact Philosophy – Problems, Tools, and Goals*. 1973, X + 214 pp.

ROBERT S. COHEN and MARX W. WARTOFSKY (eds.), *Boston Studies in the Philosophy of Science*. Volume IX: *A. A. Zinov'ev: Foundations of the Logical Theory of Scientific Knowledge (Complex Logic)*. Revised and Enlarged English Edition with an Appendix by G. A. Smirnov, E. A. Sidorenka, A. M. Fedina, and L. A. Bobrova. 1973, XXII + 301 pp. (Also in paperback.)

K. J. J. HINTIKKA, J. M. E. MORAVCSIK, and P. SUPPES (eds.), *Approaches to Natural Language. Proceedings of the 1970 Stanford Workshop on Grammar and Semantics*. 1973, VIII + 526 pp. (Also in paperback.)

WILLARD C. HUMPHREYS: JR. (ed.), *Norwood Russell Hanson: Constellations and Conjectures*. 1973, X + 282 pp.

MARIO BUNGE, *Method, Model and Matter*. 1973, VII + 196 pp.

MARIO BUNGE, *Philosophy of Physics*. 1973, IX + 248 pp.

LADISLAV TONDL, *Boston Studies in the Philosophy of Science*. Volume X: *Scientific Procedures*. 1973, XIII + 268 pp. (Also in paperback.)

SÖREN STENLUND, *Combinators, λ-Terms and Proof Theory*. 1972, 184 pp.

DONALD DAVIDSON and GILBERT HARMAN (eds.), *Semantics of Natural Language*. 1972, X + 769 pp. (Also in paperback.)

MARTIN STRAUSS, *Modern Physics and Its Philosophy. Selected Papers in the Logic, History, and Philosophy of Science*. 1972, X + 297 pp.

‡STEPHEN TOULMIN and HARRY WOOLF (eds.), *Norwood Russell Hanson: What I Do Not Believe, and Other Essays*. 1971, XII + 390 pp.

‡ROBERT S. COHEN and MARX W. WARTOFSKY (eds.), *Boston Studies in the Philosophy of Science*. Volume VIII: *PSA 1970. In Memory of Rudolf Carnap* (ed. by Roger C. Buck and Robert S. Cohen). 1971, LXVI+615 pp. (Also in paperback.)

‡YEHOSUA BAR-HILLEL (ed.), *Pragmatics of Natural Languages*. 1971, VII+231 pp.

‡ROBERT S. COHEN and MARX W. WARTOFSKY (eds.), *Boston Studies in the Philosophy of Science*. Volume VII: *Milič Čapek: Bergson and Modern Physics*. 1971, XV+414 pp.

‡CARL R. KORDIG, *The Justification of Scientific Change*. 1971, XIV+119 pp.

‡JOSEPH D. SNEED, *The Logical Structure of Mathematical Physics*. 1971, XV+311 pp.

‡JEAN-LOUIS KRIVINE, *Introduction to Axiomatic Set Theory*. 1971, VII+98 pp.

‡RISTO HILPINEN (ed.), *Deontic Logic: Introductory and Systematic Readings*. 1971, VII+182 pp.

‡EVERT W. BETH, *Aspects of Modern Logic*. 1970, XI+176 pp.

‡PAUL WEINGARTNER and GERHARD ZECHA (eds.), *Induction, Physics, and Ethics, Proceedings and Discussions of the 1968 Salzburg Colloquium in the Philosophy of Science*. 1970, X+382 pp.

‡ROLF A. EBERLE, *Nominalistic Systems*. 1970, IX+217 pp.

‡JAAKKO HINTIKKA and PATRICK SUPPES, *Information and Inference*. 1970, X+336 pp.

‡KAREL LAMBERT, *Philosophical Problems in Logic. Some recent Developments*. 1970, VII+176 pp.

‡P. V. TAVANEC (ed.), *Problems of the Logic of Scientific Knowledge*. 1969, XII+429 pp.

‡ROBERT S. COHEN and RAYMOND J. SEEGER (eds.), *Boston Studies in the Philosophy of Science*. Volume VI: *Ernst Mach: Physicist and Philosopher*. 1970, VIII+295 pp.

‡MARSHALL SWAIN (ed.), *Induction, Acceptance, and Rational Belief*. 1970, VII+232 pp.

‡NICHOLAS RESCHER *et al.* (eds.), *Essays in Honor of Carl G. Hempel. A Tribute on the Occasion of his Sixty-Fifth Birthday*. 1969, VII+272 pp.

‡PATRICK SUPPES, *Studies in the Methodology and Foundations of Science. Selected Papers from 1911 to 1969*. 1969, XII+473 pp.

‡JAAKKO HINTIKKA, *Models for Modalities. Selected Essays*. 1969, IX+220 pp.

‡D. DAVIDSON and J. HINTIKKA (eds.), *Words and Objections: Essays on the Work of W. V. Quine*. 1969, VIII+366 pp.

‡J. W. DAVIS, D. J. HOCKNEY and W. K. WILSON (eds.), *Philosophical Logic*. 1969, VIII+277 pp.

‡ROBERT S. COHEN and MARX W. WARTOFSKY (eds.), *Boston Studies in the Philosophy of Science*. Volume V: *Proceedings of the Boston Colloquium for the Philosophy of Science 1966/1968*. VIII+482 pp.

‡ROBERT S. COHEN and MARX W. WARTOFSKY (eds.), *Boston Studies in the Philosophy of Science*. Volume IV: *Proceedings of the Boston Colloquium for the Philosophy of Science 1966/1968*. VIII+537 pp.

‡NICHOLAS RESCHER, *Topics in Philosophical Logic*. 1968, XIV+347 pp.

‡GÜNTHER PATZIG, *Aristotle's Theory of the Syllogism. A Logical-Philological Study of Book A of the Prior Analytics*. 1968, XVII+215 pp.

‡C. D. BROAD, *Induction, Probability, and Causation. Selected Papers*. 1968, XI+296 pp.

‡ROBERT S. COHEN and MARX W. WARTOFSKY (eds.), *Boston Studies in the Philosophy of Science*. Volume III: *Proceedings of the Boston Colloquium for the Philosophy of Science 1964/1966*. 1967, XLIX+489 pp.

‡GUIDO KÜNG, *Ontology and the Logistic Analysis of Language. An Enquiry into the Contemporary Views on Universals*. 1967, XI+210 pp.

*EVERT W. BETH and JEAN PIAGET, *Mathematical Epistemology and Psychology*. 1966, XXII+326 pp.

*EVERT W. BETH, *Mathematical Thought. An Introduction to the Philosophy of Mathematics*. 1965, XII + 208 pp.

‡PAUL LORENZEN, *Formal Logic*. 1965, VIII + 123 pp.

‡GEORGES GURVITCH, *The Spectrum of Social Time*. 1964, XXVI + 152 pp.

‡A. A. ZINOV'EV, *Philosophical Problems of Many-Valued Logic*. 1963, XIV + 155 pp.

‡MARX W. WARTOFSKY (ed.), *Boston Studies in the Philosophy of Science*. Volume I: *Proceedings of the Boston Colloquium for the Philosophy of Science 1961/1962*. 1963, VIII + 212 pp.

‡B. H. KAZEMIER and D. VUYSJE (eds.), *Logic and Language. Studies dedicated to Professor Rudolf Carnap on the Occasion of his Seventieth Birthday*. 1962, VI + 256 pp.

*EVERT W. BETH, *Formal Methods. An Introduction to Symbolic Logic and to the Study of Effective Operations in Arithmetic and Logic*. 1962, XIV + 170 pp.

*HANS FREUDENTHAL (ed.), *The Concept and the Role of the Model in Mathematics and Natural and Social Sciences. Proceedings of a Colloquium held at Utrecht, The Netherlands, January 1960*. 1961, VI + 194 pp.

‡P. L. GUIRAUD, *Problèmes et méthodes de la statistique linguistique*. 1960, VI + 146 pp.

*J. M. BOCHENSKI, *A Precis of Mathematical Logic*. 1959, X + 100 pp.

SYNTHESE HISTORICAL LIBRARY

Texts and Studies
in the History of Logic and Philosophy

Editors:

J. M. E. MORAVCSIK (ed.), *Patterns in Plato's Thought.* 1973, VIII + 212 pp.
LEWIS WHITE BECK (ed.), *Proceedings of the Third International Kant Congress.* 1972, XI + 718 pp.
‡KARL WOLF and PAUL WEINGARTNER (eds.), *Ernst Mally: Logische Schriften.* 1971, X + 340 pp.
‡LEROY E. LOEMKER (ed.), *Gottfried Wilhelm Leibnitz: Philosophical Papers and Letters.* A Selection Translated and Edited, with an Introduction. 1969, XII + 736 pp.
‡M. T. BEONIO-BROCCHIERI FUMAGALLI, *The Logic of Abelard.* Translated from the Italian. 1969, IX + 101 pp.

Sole Distributors in the U.S.A. and Canada:
*GORDON & BREACH, INC., 440 Park Avenue South, New York, N.Y. 10016
‡HUMANITIES PRESS, INC., 303 Park Avenue South, New York, N.Y. 10010

GPSR Compliance

The European Union's (EU) General Product Safety Regulation (GPSR) is a set of rules that requires consumer products to be safe and our obligations to ensure this.

If you have any concerns about our products, you can contact us on ProductSafety@springernature.com

In case Publisher is established outside the EU, the EU authorized representative is:

Springer Nature Customer Service Center GmbH
Europaplatz 3
69115 Heidelberg, Germany

Batch number: 10823846

Printed by Printforce, the Netherlands